£13

Physical Resistance

Or, A Hundred Years of
Anti-Fascism

Physical Resistance

Or, A Hundred Years of Anti-Fascism

Dave Hann

Winchester, UK
Washington, USA

First published by Zero Books, 2013
Zero Books is an imprint of John Hunt Publishing Ltd., Laurel House, Station Approach,
Alresford, Hants, SO24 9JH, UK
office1@jhpbooks.net
www.johnhuntpublishing.com
www.zero-books.net

For distributor details and how to order please visit the 'Ordering' section on our website.

Text copyright: Dave Hann 2012

ISBN: 978 1 78099 177 1

A CIP catalogue record for this book is available from the British Library.

Design: Stuart Davies

Printed and bound by CPI Group (UK) Ltd, Croydon, CR0 4YY

We operate a distinctive and ethical publishing philosophy in all
areas of our business, from our global network of authors to
production and worldwide distribution.

CONTENTS

Introduction by Louise Purbrick   1

1. The workers' next step against fascism: 1924 – 1934   12

2. A cause worth fighting for: 1935 – 1940   63

3. Hold Madrid for we are coming: 1936 – 1939   107

4. On Guard: 1940 –1953   147

5. You can't beat fascism with fine carpets on
    the floor: 1953 – 1967   197

6. One, two, three and a bit, the National Front is
    a load of shit: 1966 – 1979   231

7. No Retreat: 1979-1990   302

8. Getting out of bed: 1990-2011   340

Postscript   389

Bibliography   391

In memory of Dave Hann, with respect and in solidarity. Dedicated to all the people whose histories helped create this book and all those who stood alongside them in their fight against fascism.

Introduction

by Louise Purbrick

Doesn't a breath of air that pervaded earlier days caress us as well?
In the voices we hear, isn't there an echo of the now silent ones?
Walter Benjamin

When Dave Hann died on 29 September 2009, he left £30 in the bank and a manuscript of over 100,000 words. He had little money of his own because as a jobbing builder, he would work for the cost of his materials plus a day rate then hand over most of his earnings to me to put into our household budget. Dave's manuscript was, and is, a far more substantial inheritance than any amount of money, large or small. It represents his commitment to the politics of anti-fascism and his desire to tell the stories of people like him. Dave fought fascism and his is an activist's history of the anti-fascist struggle.

He started writing *Physical Resistance*, working under the tentative title *A Cause Worth Fighting For*, in 2005. But, before he made the decision to start typing in his opening sentences, he had, like many anti-fascist activists, acquired a great deal of knowledge about the struggle in which he participated. Reading about collective actions or individual lives in leaflets, pamphlets and books bought and sold at anti-fascist meetings is part of a culture of activism. Anti-fascists have produced their own literature recording its strategies and struggles, which are put to use in discussions and debates. Past struggles inform present ones; they provide a guide. Also, Dave liked books. Our shelves were always full of books about anti-fascism.

Writing his book, this book, was part of the rhythm of our lives. We ran out of space on our shelves for the multifarious materials he bought, usually through second hand bookshops or internet dealers, to help his research. He was always pleased get hold of another pamphlet written by a 1930s trade unionist, more biographies of International Brigaders or a little known International Socialists publication; I did not always hide my dismay about where we might put it all in our tiny terraced house. Books and papers were stacked in piles in the corners of our living room. If Dave had a break between building jobs, he would work on his book. He would write in the hours between dropping and collecting our children from school. When I returned from work, he might start again in order to finish a paragraph, sitting at the same table where I sit now to write this. Dave wrote paragraph by paragraph and produced a linear narrative that wove together life histories and political actions in strict chronological order. Occasionally, he would go back over a paragraph and add more details or amend a date but he did not plan, produce drafts or edit his writing in the ways that academics, like myself, have been schooled, cutting our cloth to suit our means. Dave Hann's practice of writing did not conform to the conventions of the textbook, academic monograph, chapter in an edited collection or journal articles. It is, for example, longer. The length of the manuscript straightforwardly reflected what Dave believed had to be said rather than what it might be possible to include in the race for a deadline or the completion of research within limits of funding.

Physical Resistance was not Dave's first piece of writing. Under two pseudonyms, Saboteur then Will Scarlet, he had been a punk poet and, when I first met him in 1994, he was an editor and writer for *Red Attitude*, the Manchester United Anti-Fascists fanzine. In 2003 he, and his friend Steve Tilzey, put together their biographies as anti-fascists in *No Retreat*. Spanning the late 1970s to the mid-1990s and their experiences of Anti-Nazi League and Anti-Fascist Action, it is both a celebration of fight against fascism and a contemporary tale of comradeship and friendship between people thrown together through the act of political struggle. It was received by most of its readers in something like these terms, but was also caught up in the sectarianism that besets political organisations and the tendency to vilify character rather than acknowledge political differences. There was only one criticism Dave took seriously: he had written about himself. He was only one of many. That he knew. He felt honoured just to stand in line. Most anti-fascists understand that everything they do from writing, distributing or reading anti-fascist texts, defending anti-fascist events, breaking up fascist meetings, halting fascist marches, fighting them whenever necessary is a collective endeavour. This was origin of *Physical Resistance*: to write the collective history of anti-fascism.

Such a history could not be written using books, not even the number piling high on our floor. Dave sought out anti-fascists to interview. He sent letters to International Brigaders. A page from

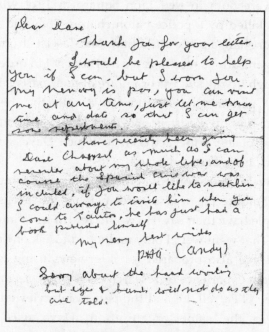

Letter from Howard 'Andy' Andrews

Howard 'Andy' Andrews is typical of the courtesy of their replies and they not only spoke about their experiences in the Spanish Civil War but involvement in anti-fascism before they volunteered and after they returned.

Dave spoke to people he knew, or knew of, from his days of street activism. When unable to locate participants in anti-fascist movements to which he had read references, he advertised. On three successive days in June 2005, the *Morning Star* ran the following request: 'I would be particularly interested in hearing from anyone involved in the V Corps, the 43 and 62 Groups and the Yellow Star Movement.' Of the people whose accounts of anti-fascism are included in *Physical Resistance*, some are already, like Morris Beckman, heroes of its history. Others, such as Betty Davis or Sheila Lahr, are not well known. But all hold the history together. The lives of anti-fascists overlap. For example, student activist Nick Mullen and former 43 Group member Monty Goldman were both in Red Lion Square in 1974 when Kevin Gately was killed by a police baton charge. They did not know each other or share a party affiliation. Anti-fascists from different political organisations were located by Dave not in order to judge them or weigh up the success or failure of their party's line but to ensure that person's contribution to a collective history was recognised. *Physical Resistance* is thus also a response to the sectarianism of left wing activism to which Dave, and far too many others, have been subjected.

Instinctively, he adopted something approaching an oral history technique. He was a quiet person and accustomed to letting people have their say. He would return from interviewing to report: "That went well, I only really had to ask one question." However, Dave also prepared for interviews using knowledge acquired from experience or research even when, as was the case with Mickey O'Farrell, he and the person interviewed had once belonged to the same organisation. Dave used a small unobtrusive Dictaphone then transcribed from its micro cassette tapes. The words of anti-fascists are at the heart of the book. The histories they contained were followed up through his reading of local newspapers reproduced in the microfilm collections of regional archives or reports in pamphlet collections, such as that deposited in London School of Economics. Dave still continued to buy books, often small print run or out of print publications only available through second hand internet or side street markets, many having been de-accessioned from libraries to make way for digital resources. He checked dates and accounts of actions; he tried to get the facts right. Whilst I have a series of degrees to prove that I am historian, Dave only ever asked my advice about practical institutional matters, such as how to get a Reader's Ticket for the British Library. The academic practice of history, which is often based on the assumption that the story has been told and all that is left to do is interpret it, was regarded by Dave as almost irrelevant, interesting, perhaps, but not especially useful. He was a self-taught historian. If I was a romantic, I would be tempted to call Dave Hann one of the last of the autodidacts.

Dave was diagnosed with cancer at the end of February 2009. He only worked on his book two or three times during the short period of illness before his death at the end of September. He conducted one interview in August that he did not have the time to transcribe. He tried to write on a few occasions. Concentration through the haze of chemotherapy and painkillers was never easy. I recall that he asked me to remind him how to double space lines of text. At my reply (go to Format and select Paragraph), he was irritated with himself that such a routine piece of information had escaped him. Dave found his cancer diagnosis and the physical weariness that treatment induces difficult to accept. "My body's strength is everything. It's my work and my politics," he said. We discussed how he wanted to end his book and the interviews required to complete it. I argued that as soon as he was well, rather than worrying about picking up building jobs, he should work on his book until it was done. With some discomfort, I remember joking that he better not die and leave it to me. We write in very different ways. Dave replied with a wry laugh. I wished I had kept my sharp tongue inside my head. Later, when he was dying, the joke was over. I told him I would finish it. I am not certain he heard me, but that's what I said.

The completion of the collective history of anti-fascism that Dave Hann began, upholds a promise I made to my lover and friend. It is also an act of political commitment to an anti-fascist. We met because we were both activists; our lives were shaped by political struggle. We worked together on the stewarding of the1995 Bloody Sunday Commemoration March in Manchester, where we both then lived. The march and its organising body, the Troops Out Movement, of which I was a member, were regular targets of fascist aggression. Anti-Fascist Action defended the Bloody Sunday march and its Manchester activists attended many other Irish solidarity or anti-imperialist events in the city: meetings, stalls, socials. Dave was one of those to whom, as another Troops Out Movement member put it, "we owed our political lives."

However, for many months after Dave's death, I did not even look at the manuscript of his book. I was not quite ready to hear his voice in my head as read his words. I sorted out his building tools. He had many. He liked tools almost as much as he liked books but they were in disarray. In his last weeks of work, Dave became too tired to keep his trowels and brushes, hammers and chisels, drills, screwdrivers, Stanley knives, saws and all in any kind of order. The shed was piled high. Some tools, I passed on to friends who were also builders or who took on building jobs when they had no other work; others I kept in case I needed them in the house or because they reminded me of him. I put every nail and screw, every nut and bolt, into pots according to their size and constituent material. That took weeks. Even less obsessive sorting and tidying is easily analysed as part of a grieving process, although at the time I simply felt that the way to respect the life of a dead person was to give proper consideration to their things. I threw away nothing. The rusting nails and broken bits of metal whose function was impossible to work out were gathered up with some short lengths of copper and lead piping left in the shed and taken to the scrap metal merchant. The increase in the price of base metals at this time of capitalist crisis meant that Dave left more money in the fragments of his building materials than he had in the bank.

Then I read his book. Dave had talked to me, just a little, about the people he interviewed. He did not recount their stories or give up personal details. He spoke of his pleasure in meeting them, his admiration for their longstanding anti-fascism and the dignity with which they had lived the whole of their lives. It was reading their honest and thoughtful, modest and courageous accounts of fighting fascism that gave me the determination to complete this book. They woke me from my slumber. At first, I edited the manuscript only very lightly: checked spellings, added commas, altered capitals. The book's bibliography had to be compiled. Almost as soon as Dave had started writing, he declared that the bibliography would be the means for anyone to check his sources because he did not want to use footnotes. I began working my way down the piles of papers, pamphlets and books, typing in authors, titles and dates of publication. Occasionally, scraps of paper would fall out to reveal Dave's hand-written notes to himself such as 'Fenn arrested in June 1977', a reference to docker and dedicated anti-fascist, Mickey Fenn. Not all his notes related to the book; some were rough building job estimates ('Bedroom – skim - ceiling – wall - 100') that had then been used to mark an important passage in one book or other.

Dave's paragraph by paragraph method of writing meant that the manuscript was in good order for copy-editing and proofing at the moment when he stopped working on it, but the final chapter was unfinished. There were a few activists Dave was still hoping to interview to take the collective anti-fascist history up to the present day and bring his book to a conclusion. I contacted them and conducted interviews in the autumn and winter of 2011. More at ease with a digital recorder than the Dictaphone, I nevertheless followed Dave's way of inviting people to speak about their experiences with an open question: "How did you get involved in anti-fascism?" He undertook further research following interviews. I relied only upon the books, pamphlets, papers and notes he had already gathered without carrying out any new archival work. My priority was to privilege, as he had done, the accounts of activists themselves. His manuscript, which already exceeded the standard length of a published monograph, had got longer. Then followed the hardest task. I cut, with care and a great sense of loss, some of Dave's words. This more substantial editing was based on the principles of his writing: the recorded words of anti-fascists stayed centre stage. It was only the paragraphs that contained material from published sources that were edited and these sources still appear in his bibliography as part of the record of his research.

My attachment to the writing of Dave Hann is balanced, albeit unevenly, with my training as an academic in the interpretation of historical texts. I understand, of course, that there are different ways to read the collective anti-fascist history that he compiled. *Physical Resistance* is pieced together through anti-fascist activists' own accounts of their experiences. It is an oral history. The narrative driven by activists' testimonies collected by Hann is augmented by numerous life histories, memoirs and oral histories often produced by local history groups or Trades Councils. A glance at the book's bibliography reveals how *Physical Resistance* has, quite literally, retrieved the records of lives, organisations and actions that circulate outside mainstream publishing networks. It is a working class history, written by a working class author from working class sources. As such, it is a form of political activism in itself. Thus, it may well be regarded by historians as a historical source that invites debate on, for example, the idea of political activism and how political acts, including writing or fighting, are an everyday matter always entangled in personal lives. Whatever its status as a type of history, *Physical Resistance* is a collective one of anti-fascism that provides a long view, adding to its empirical record by recovering forgotten episodes, short-lived but momentarily effective anti-fascist coalitions and marginalised lives.

The most radical contribution that *Physical Resistance* may make to historical debate is, I suspect, already indicated by the book's title. Large-scale confrontations, damage to property, disruption of meetings and street fighting were all part of the practice of anti-fascism throughout the twentieth century and remain, to a large extent, the means of opposition to new formations of fascism in the opening decades of the twenty-first. Whilst violence is routinely understood as the antithesis of politics, as an angry, emotional outburst that ought to be controlled through reasoned debate, in the history of anti-fascism recorded and written by Dave Hann, it holds a place in everyday political life.

In his book *1848: The British State and the Chartist Movement* (1987), John Saville argued that the significance of physical force has been written out of histories of the nineteenth century working class movement in Britain: revolutionary violence was cast as foreign. The trend that Saville observed has continued. Published histories of the twentieth century socialist and communist parties, for example, have tended to outline their emergence as forces within civil society, illustrating the effort of organisation, the role of local and national leadership figures and the occasion of electoral success. Whilst challenges to the established political relationships of ruling classes over the people or the bosses over the workers are celebrated, dominant ideas of politics itself and what constitutes political action often remain in place. Physical force still seems out of place in British politics. Violence still appears foreign. Indeed, in the late twentieth century and early twenty-first century, it is identified as the work of 'others', labelled criminals or terrorists. Hann's writing of a collective anti-fascist history, however, presents an alternative interpretation of political action that includes physical resistance as part of an everyday pattern of opposition. It was not the policy of one particular party or another, but a shared strategy of activists, affiliated to various anarchist, communist, socialist or Trotskyist groups who worked in alliances, coalitions, committees and campaigns against fascism.

The significance of physical resistance as a political strategy only becomes evident when the lens of single party or organisation is dropped for a wider view of activism. Groups of anarchists, communists, socialists and Trotskyists are not played off against each other as the holders of truth of political struggle but woven by Hann into a narrative that traces the shared strategies of physical resistance. His history offers an alternative way of interpreting the practice of political opposition; it is defined by acts of participation rather than adherence to very precisely defined ideological standpoints. This is the perspective of an activist writer, working independently of the normative ideas about the limits of the political sphere.

Always part of the everyday routines of anti-fascism, physical resistance was also a matter of contention. Or rather, the precise forms of physical resistance were definitively important. Anti-fascist alliances were formed and reformed, created and dissolved, around shared or disputed strategies of physical opposition. Dave Hann was a street-fighting anti-fascist. 'During physical encounters, he would always lead from the front and be one of the first in,' remembers his friend, Liam Heffernan. He stated that Dave was 'one of the most dedicated, determined and courageous anti-fascists' he had ever met. But *Physical Resistance* is not simply a history of fighting. It encompasses more than individual hand-to-hand confrontation. Collective acts of physical opposition are incorporated into every anti-fascist mobilisation, from chalking up the details of meetings on pavements to fly-posting them, from coordinated foot stamping at Oswald Mosley's rallies to the rush of people into a road to stop a National Front or English Defence League march. Physical resistance is shared political commitment to the cause of anti-fascism and an act of personal significance: it makes up the rhythm of lives of activists and has done so, as Dave Hann's writing in the following chapters demonstrates, for almost a hundred years.

I

The workers' next step against fascism: 1924 – 1934

Whenever fascists have attempted to hold meetings, mount election campaigns, march through city centres or local neighbourhoods and attack those whose appearance or beliefs differed from theirs, people have gathered together to oppose them. Anti-fascists have formed groups, committees, fronts, coalitions or alliances. From the first days to most recent times, anti-fascism has involved many thousands of people. It is characterised by collective physical resistance. People have relied upon themselves and depended upon each other as they have stopped fascist meetings, halted fascist marches and prevented fascist control of local areas. This book contains their history.

In Britain, the first anti-fascist organisations were formed in 1924. There were two. One, the People's Defence Force (PDF), was launched by the Communist Party of Great Britain (CPGB or CP) in January at the 1917 Club in Soho, London. The other was started by a woman. Former Lancashire mill worker turned writer and poet, Ethel Carnie Holdsworh, a staunch socialist, was the driving force behind the National Union for Combating Fascism (NUCF). She was its national organiser and alongside her husband, Alfred, edited *The Clear Light*, a monthly anti-fascist journal. The need for such organisations was a sign of the times.

The economic hardship and political disillusionment of the years following the First World War brought about an increase in working class militancy across Europe. Britain was no exception. The 1926 General Strike, the Hunger Marches, the Invergordon Mutiny of 1931 were part of wider working class agitation for political change. The upper echelons of British society saw the frightening spectre of communism behind every red-painted placard calling for social reform, no matter how moderate the demand might be. The formation of a British Communist Party in 1920 and election of the first ever Labour Government in 1924 seemed to suggest that Bolshevism was getting closer to home. Whatever the reality of an imminent revolution in Britain, the fear of one was stimulus enough for some. When Mussolini and his Partito Nazionale Fascista seized power in Italy in 1922 and began an onslaught against communists and anarchists, big bosses and small businessmen of the world saw that fascism provided a bulwark against an organised working class. Most reaffirmed their faith in existing political parties and state structures to safeguard their class privileges and control of the nation, but others sought salvation in fascism.

Small patriotic and anti-Semitic organisations, The Britons and the British Brothers' League, had emerged in the early years of the twentieth century, but the first avowedly fascist organisation to emerge in Britain, was the British Fascisti, later renamed the British Fascists Ltd (BF). Formed in May 1923, the BFs claimed Mussolini as their spiritual inspiration, although they were more closely aligned to ultra-Conservatism than fascism. Their founder was Miss Rotha Lintorn-Orman, who decided to form a fascist party whilst weeding the garden of her dairy farm in Somerset. Alarmed by newspapers' scare stories about the rise of communism, she was convinced that an organised force was needed to combat the 'red threat.' British Fascisti members were mostly right wing, military men, the landed gentry and upper class women. On the bottom rung of the party's hierarchy were a small number of working class toughs, allocated the role of privates in an army full of officers. They stewarded Conservative Party meetings, attacked left-wing and working class organisations and attempted to break strikes.

From the outset, fascists faced opposition. On 7 October 1923 in London, the inaugural meeting of the British Fascisti was disrupted by anti-fascists as were two further meetings in Hammersmith in the following month. Gangs of uniformed fascists targeted gatherings where they assumed revolutionary plots were being hatched. That dedicated opposition to the Fascisti was required became increasingly obvious. From its formation in January 1924, the People's Defence Force (PDF) began monitoring the activities of the Fascisti and organising resistance to fascist disruption of meetings. The PDF was led by members of the Communist Party and the National Unemployed Workers' Committee Movement (NUWCM), which also included many communists. Ethel Carnie Holdsworth's National Union for Combating Fascism (NUFC) was politically independent and co-ordinated the anti-fascist activities of the various left-wing groups rather than allying itself to one organisation. The NUCF declared that it was ready to tackle outbreaks of fascism and would argue the socialist case.

During 1924, there were bitter clashes between fascists and anti-fascists. In July, fighting took place in Hyde Park and in the following month on Clapham Common. William Joyce, the notorious and rabid anti-Semite, led BF stewards into frequent battles with anti-fascists. The meetings of mainstream political parties were often the stage for confrontations, which involved quite astonishing levels of violence. Joyce was slashed from mouth to ear, allegedly by 'Jewish Communists', while stewarding at a Conservative Party meeting at Lambeth Baths on 22 October 1924. Writings about the fascist threat began to appear in the left-wing press. *The New Leader*, the paper of the Independent Labour Party (ILP), carried several articles on its potential danger. The CP also issued warnings in its paper, the *Sunday Worker*. The leadership of the Labour Party judged these calls alarmist. They were wrong. In March 1925, Harry Pollitt, leading CP member, was kidnapped by five British Fascists as he travelled by train to address a meeting in Liverpool. He was later released unharmed and the five were found not guilty after claiming that they were merely taking Pollitt away for a pleasant little weekend in North Wales. The court served notice that the scales of justice would be always weighted in favour of the fascists.

The formation of the PDF and the NUCF heralded the beginning of anti-fascist organisation, although neither grew much beyond the communist and socialist groups already engaged in anti-fascist activities. At its peak, *The Clear Light* had a circulation of about 5,000 but it struggled to retain a regular readership. Nevertheless, the activities of Carnie Holdsworth and her comrades clearly worried the BF, who attempted to infiltrate the NUCF and halt the publication of its journal. They threatened to blow up the NUCF's printer on one occasion and tried to get *The Clear Light* banned by implicating Alfred Holdsworth in a type of treason plot. The NUCF ceased its publishing in 1925. It had withstood sabotage only to swallow most of Carnie Holdsworth's savings. Within a couple of years of their formation, both the NUCF and the PDF had folded.

The National Fascisti, a BF breakaway group, made headlines in October 1925. Formed a year earlier, they claimed they wanted deeds not words. They were smaller in number than the BF, but even more violent. William Joyce joined the new group, as did Arnold Leese, who declared that the BF were too soft on the Jewish question and were merely 'conservatives with knobs on.' Four National Fascisti hijacked at gunpoint a newspaper delivery van containing 8,000 copies of the *Daily Herald*, a pro-Labour paper. The van crashed into the railings of a London church and the four fled. They were eventually arrested and charged not with Larceny but Breach of the Peace and were merely bound over for 12 months. The Labour Party and the Labour Prime Minister, Ramsay MacDonald, denounced the lenient treatment of armed fascists as 'disgraceful and outrageous.' A leaflet headlined *No Justice For Labour* was issued, which condemned the partiality shown to the fascists in court, but failed to address the ideology which had motivated them to carry out the hijack.

The National Fascisti called for the cessation of alien immigration, the deportation of 'undesirable' aliens and the suppression of left-wing activities. In practice, this boiled down to Jew-baiting and raiding meetings at the 1917 Club and other 'centres of internationalism', provoking a number of retaliatory actions. In November 1926, a National Fascisti meeting in Hyde Park was overturned by 70 communists. Banging dustbin lids and kettles drowned out the fascist speakers. Fighting broke out as the two sides vied with each other as they sang the National Anthem and The Red Flag. One of the communists, Walter Coldicott, was arrested after storming the fascist platform. The police failed to restore order and moved in to close down the meeting. A National Fascisti complained that there had been continuous riots at their Sunday meetings and 'yesterday's disturbance was the culminating point.' There were reprisals. On 16 January 1927, a squad of Fascisti circled an International Class War Prisoners' Aid (ICWPA) rally in Trafalgar Square in support of Nicola Sacco and Bartolomeo Vanzetti, two Italian anarchists facing execution in the United States. Twenty or so communists tracked a group of Fascisti leaving the Square. In the fight that followed, a police officer was hit and William Hickey, the Paddington CP branch organiser, was arrested.

The British Fascists (BF) had not entirely left the scene. Hopes that the General Strike would provide their party with a major fillip did not bear fruit. The government declined their offer to help maintain essential industries and sponsored the Organisation for the Maintenance of Supplies (OMS) instead. Several thousand British Fascists helped the OMS on an individual basis. One member, William Fullerton, leader of the infamous Billy Boys sectarian Glasgow street gang and mercenary scab won a medal for his part in the BF's strike-breaking activities.

While the leadership of the Labour Party viewed the OMS (dubbed the Organisation of Mugs and Scabs) as essentially apolitical, for communists it was an inherently anti-working class, fascist-type organisation. In response to its formation, the CP released a statement on 10 January 1926 calling for the creation of 'Workers' Defence Corps.' It was envisaged that these would be 'composed of Trade Unionists and controlled by Trades Councils' and their role was to protect striking workers from harassment by police officers and strike breakers. They would also assist in the 'protection of Trade Union liberties against the Fascisti.' Their main centres of activity were South Wales, London and Fife but Workers' Defence Corps or Workers' Police were also established at Aldershot, Chatham, Colchester, Croydon, Denny and Dunipace, Methil, St. Pancras, Selby, Sowerby Bridge and Willesden. They defended strikers from police and scab violence as well as fascist intimidation. In Croydon, for instance, members of the Corps were tasked with defending the local strike co-ordinating centre, Ruskin House, from possible fascist attack. Corps members also acted as stewards at left-wing rallies. Fascists had taken to parading around the outskirts of meetings then attempting to seize the red flag from the platform. The response of the Home Office to the formation of the Workers' Defence Corps was one of near hysteria. Always in fear of an armed revolution, they saw the makings of Irish Citizens' Army of 1913 in the development of Workers' Defence Corps.

Following the collapse of the General Strike, the Workers' Defence Corps was wound down and the baton passed to the Labour League of Ex-Servicemen (LLX), officially launched in September 1927. The nucleus of the LLX had actually been in existence for about a year, but it had been mothballed for the duration of the strike. A pamphlet entitled *To Hell With War* that was first published in 1926 under the auspices of the National Command of the Labour League of Ex-Servicemen was reprinted in 1927 to coincide with the official re-launch of the group. Its author was Ex-Lieutenant J. S. Snook DCM, a kitchen porter at the Poplar Institution who became one of the LLX's Joint Honorary Secretaries. On 18 September, the *Sunday Worker* reprinted a speech by Snook. He announced:

> Demands for the building of a strong Labour League of Ex-Servicemen have grown more imperative than ever since the epidemic of police and fascist "frightfulness" during the Sacco-Vanzetti agitation.

Dominated by communists and with no official association to the Labour Party, membership of the LLX was 'open to all men and women who have served in the Armed Forces and Auxiliary Forces on payment of a subscription of 6d a month' and who accepted the aims and objects of the LLX Constitution, one of which committed them to 'combat all forms of Fascism and anti-working class action, and to protect the lawful assemblies of the organised working class on all occasions.' In November 1927, this took the form of a hundred-strong armed escort for a Hunger March as it entered London. Government politicians and the Trades Union Congress had condemned the decision of miners from South Wales to embark on the march. Right-wing press coverage along the lines of the reds taking over the town had encouraged groups of fascists to harass the marchers en route. Fearing fascist provocation as the march neared its destination, the LLX was detailed to accompany the march on the final leg of its journey from Chiswick to Trafalgar Square. On this occasion, the fascists failed to make an appearance.

The LLX marched under the banner 'Warriors Against War.' Their opposition to war, which characterised many left groups in this period, was shaped not only by the horrors of the First World War but an analysis of war as capitalist and imperialist adventure. At its height the LLX claimed to have 100 sections throughout the country, the majority of in South Wales, the North-East and London. Manchester, Birmingham and Liverpool had large sections and there were smaller ones across Yorkshire and Scotland. At first, there was no uniform except for a red armband with the initials LLX embroidered in white but, by March 1928, it was decided that all members should wear a full uniform on parade. This consisted of khaki cap, khaki shirt, cord breeches, black leggings, brown belt, red armlet, red tie, and hammer and sickle badge.

The appearance of uniformed bodies of men wearing communist regalia attracted the attention of the Tory press. The *Daily Mail*, ever the mouthpiece of right-wing chauvinism, printed a scaremongering account of a 'Red Police Force in Poplar' in December 1927. The local LLX, numbering 50, had paraded in uniform and provided security at left-wing meetings. The paper also complained in March of the following year that 'Khaki clad figures with red ties and red armlets kept order at a women's demonstration in Trafalgar Square' and were 'armed with heavy sticks.' The LLX also kept Special Branch and their spies busy. Local leader of the League's Liverpool section, John Hedley, who had been jailed three times for sedition and unlawful assembly, was being watched. A police informant reported to his paymasters that Hedley had suggested the LLX should, like the Fascisti, join rifle clubs and learn to shoot. He implied, at least according to the spy, that any opportunities to steal arms and ammunition should be taken.

Towards the end of the decade, the LLX came to a rather confused and abrupt end. On 1 April 1928, the *Sunday Worker* hailed the LLX as the 'Mailed Fist of the Workers' and printed an interview with Joint Honorary Secretary Snook in which he claimed that the League hoped to assemble 1,000 men and 200 women at the May Day parade in London. By 1 February 1929, however, it was announced that the LLX was changing its name to the Workers' Legion and was opening its doors to 'all class-conscious workers.' The Workers' Legion seems to have drifted into obscurity or made no significant impact. Loosely related to it were the Workers' Freedom Groups, which surfaced occasionally in various parts of the country, most notably the South Wales coalfields, throughout the remainder of the 1920s and 1930s. Comprising both Labour and Communist Party members, the Workers' Freedom Groups were initially sponsored by Labour MP Aneurin Bevan and took defensive actions against fascists, the police and bailiffs.

The fate of the LLX corresponded to that of the fascist organisations of the 1920s. The BF and the National Fascisti declined towards the end of the decade. The BF slid into bankruptcy after Lintorn-Orman succumbed to alcoholism and her mother cut her allowance. This signalled years of inactivity and infighting. The misappropriation of funds caused an internal rift in the National Fascisti. Its decline was rapid and terminal. In November 1928, Arnold Leese attempted to step from the ruins of British fascism by setting up the Imperial Fascist League (IFL), which distinguished itself from other fascist parties only in the degree of its poisonous and aggressive anti-Semitism.

Although fascism lacked some organisational coherence, small-scale clashes between gangs of fascists and the National Unemployed Workers' Committee Movement (NUWCM) were commonplace. In 1929, the NUWCM's headquarters was ransacked and daubed with fascist slogans. It was an act of frustration. Fascists had less success recruiting the unemployed than their continental counterparts. They were hampered by the existence of the NUWCM, who campaigned tirelessly on the streets and outside the dole offices on behalf of the jobless.

The Wall Street Crash of 1929 triggered an international financial crisis and opened a decade of economic misery. In Britain, unemployment soared from one million to three million within three years of the Crash. The poorest sections of society were those hardest hit. Betty Davis spent much of her childhood in the East End of London during this period:

There was so much poverty in those days. It was indescribable. You didn't have shoes, you went to school without shoes and when you did have a pair, they were Board of Guardian shoes, or shoes given to you by somebody else. And they would mark them, so you didn't pawn them. You would walk along, clump, clump, clump, in these bloody shoes that were marked all over so you didn't take them down to Uncle's. I didn't realise, along with many other kids I knew, that clothes actually came in different sizes until I was a teenager because everything came from the jumble sale. You just bought what you could afford. It didn't matter about how it fitted. Boys had trousers with bits of string around them to hold them up. Nothing was ever new. The relief man used to come in and if you had more than one chair, which was for the woman of the house, it had to be sold or disposed of. In fact, what people used to do when the relief man came around, was throw all the furniture over the back wall, and in the end you never knew where the hell it ended up, but if you had it in the house it was taken away anyway. I can also remember Petticoat Lane, going around the market late at night and early in the morning, picking up all the scraps that hadn't been sold, all the fruit and that. It was all part of the poverty of the East End because there was no unemployment pay, only relief tickets, and when people did sign on as unemployed, they would send them to places like the hospitals to work the day as porters. This meant that the hospital staff could never organise for higher wages, because the unemployed had to go in there and do the work for next to nothing. If you didn't do that you wouldn't get your relief tickets.

It was in these conditions that fascism gained a foothold in Britain and Oswald Mosley emerged as its key figure. Anti-fascism coalesced around opposition to Mosley. From an old

21

aristocratic family, whose seat was a 3,800 acre estate in Staffordshire, he was first elected a Tory MP in 1918 then became an Independent before eventually joining the Labour Party in 1924. When his call for public spending, protectionism and concentration of power in a small emergency cabinet were rejected by the party, he resigned. Mosley formed the New Party in March 1930 to address what he saw as the paralysis gripping Britain's established political parties. Many detected a strong whiff of fascism about Mosley's new project. As his politics lurched increasingly rightwards, the stench became overpowering. Many of the party's original members, including a number of left-wingers, bailed out when they realised from which direction the wind was blowing but Mosley, even at this early stage, had acquired a core following of loyal followers who would stick with him through thick and thin.

The New Party certainly shared the fascist commitment to violence. NUPA was formed, ostensibly, to protect New Party speakers and ensure orderly conduct at its meetings. Comprised of young, physically fit Oxbridge types trained in judo, fencing and boxing, they were nicknamed the Biff Boys and could easily be mistaken for a private army along the lines of Mussolini's Squadristi. NUPA did not deter the mounting opposition to Mosley. A huge meeting at Birmingham Rag Market developed into a riot as members of the audience fought running battles with the Biff Boys. At one point, Mosley himself jumped down from the platform to assist his beleaguered stewards. They were forced back to the stage under a hail of chairs and bottles and he was advised to leave the building via a side exit by the police. This would not be the last time the police aided Mosley's escape from anti-fascists. More New Party meetings were broken up in Dundee, Hull, Hammersmith and Glasgow. Mosley was loudly heckled during a giant open-air rally at Glasgow Green before being attacked with a life-preserver. He was also hit on the head with a stone after the meeting and his bodyguards attacked with razors and bricks.

Benny Rothman, a young Jewish Communist from the Cheetham area of Manchester attended the first big New Party meeting in his city centre:

I'd been out for a ramble during the day and went straight to the Free Trade Hall in my walking clothes. I felt a little bit out of place because of the way I was dressed but I wanted to see what Mosley had to say for himself. I think he was ill at the time because he wasn't at the meeting. His first wife Cynthia was there, alongside a fellow called John Strachey, who later became a member of the Labour government. We soon realised from the attitudes of the speakers and their supporters that the New Party was very hostile towards the organised working class and was setting itself up to become a fully-fledged fascist movement. It didn't take long before people in the audience began shouting down the speakers and there was a great deal of barracking and heckling. As the meeting was drawing to a close, the police came into the hall to deal with the hecklers, which was something that had never happened before in Manchester. Mosley and the Chief Constable of Manchester were on friendly terms and I'm sure it was all arranged beforehand. Because of the way I was dressed, I stood out like a sore thumb and this one particular officer made a beeline straight for me. Before he could get hold of me, he was tripped up, and fell onto the floor. No sooner had he hit the ground than several people began to kick him and stamp on him, which made me feel very ashamed at the time.

Hostility towards the New Party came from several quarters. The Communist Party understood it as a fascist party in the making, while Labour Party members and trade unionists regarded Mosley as a traitor who split the working class vote. Harry

Johnson was only ten years old when he first encountered the New Party in the Midlands:

> I remember going to Cradley Heath near Dudley. This must have been in the early thirties. There was this bloke holding a meeting in a little side street just off the High Street. He was knocked off his platform and was attacked by these blokes who were heckling him. I only half knew what it was about in those days, but I remember one old bloke saying that Mosley had betrayed the Labour Party, because of course Mosley had been in the Labour party before he formed the New Party. I think a lot of the initial ill feeling towards Mosley came from that.

Following the dismal failure of the New Party at the 1931 General Election, Mosley dumped what remained of his previous allegiance to parliamentary democracy and openly embraced fascism. He visited Mussolini in Rome in January 1932 and met with high-ranking Nazi officials. Upon his return to Britain, he formally disbanded the New Party and set about building the British Union of Fascists (BUF), drawing into its ranks members of the New Party as well as the remnants of fascists groups of the 1920s. The BUF was officially founded on 1 October 1932 at a rally in Great George Street, London. It adopted the Blackshirt uniform of Mussolini's movement.

BUF members were told that they were being prepared for a violent battle against communism that would reach its zenith once the moribund political parties of the 'old gang' were crushed by the impact of the world-wide economic crisis. Mosley recruited a corps of 400 uniformed and armed stewards known as the Fascist Defence Force who were given martial training, lessons in gymnastics, boxing and judo. Within the Defence Force was an elite inner core of jackbooted stewards known as the 'I Squad' who were given *carte blanche* to deal with any disruption of BUF events. They were housed in the Black House in Chelsea, the BUF national headquarters. Defence Force members were given a uniform consisting of black shirts, breeches, and leather boots. Armed with rubber coshes, they were transported to meetings in a fleet of armour plated and wire-grilled vans. Special trains were also chartered to transport hundreds of Defence Force members to meetings all over the country.

Initial BUF public meetings and rallies suffered from isolated interruptions rather than mass attempts at disruption. It was only after hecklers had been violently assaulted that fighting would break out. In Stoke, Mosley stepped down from the platform to fight a heckler at a meeting, provoking a general fracas. Three hecklers also interrupted a speech by Mosley at the Memorial Hall in Farringdon Street, London, on 24 October 1932. His response was to identify them as Jews at which they were abused and assaulted. Scuffles broke out inside the hall and hostilities resumed in the streets outside after the meeting. Mosley was heckled by a group of communists as he led a column of Blackshirts back to the Cenotaph. The police dispersed their march after BUF members had shouted "Down with Gandhi" and "To hell with the Jews."

The rise of Hitler and the Nazi Party meant that comparisons between the Nazis and the Blackshirts were inevitable. The presence of notorious Jew-baiters within their ranks worried the Jewish community. Working class Jews looked to the Communist Party for the lead in combating the BUF. The CP had taken up the challenge thrown down by the fascists but it was fighting with one hand tied behind its back. From 1928 onwards, the CP was curtailed by the sectarian 'Class Against Class' analysis imposed upon it by the Communist International that denounced other left parties as 'social fascists' ruling out any alliances. A divided left opposition can only have helped smooth the Nazi road to power in Germany. Some communists saw political division as a greater problem than political differences. Within days of

Hitler's triumph in March 1933, Harry Pollitt pre-empted the demise of 'Class Against Class' by inviting the leaderships of the labour movement, including the Labour Party, the TUC and the Co-operative Movement, to join forces with the CP in a 'United Front Against Fascism.' He also began to meet frequently with James Maxton and Fenner Brockway of the ILP.

The CP and its various satellite organisations, such as the recently renamed National Unemployed Workers Movement (NUWM), made repeated attempts to persuade the leaders of the labour movement to join forces against fascism but these approaches were rejected time and again. A front was built by communists, the ILP, the NUWM, radical Jewish groups, a number of trades' councils and smaller trade unions beginning to work together on an ad hoc basis in the fight against Mosley. There was some sympathy for the united front proposals from the left-wing of the Labour Party, particularly from the Socialist League, a body formed by socialists who had declined to leave the Labour Party when the ILP disaffiliated in 1932. League members campaigned for greater unity in the face of the fascist threat but the Labour Party leadership withstood pressure from its own ranks and remained resolutely opposed to any united action. Harry Johnson recalls a typical Labour Party reaction to a planned BUF march in the Midlands:

I remember going to Oldbury, where the fascists were holding a march. The Labour Party's attitude in those days was to say "Ignore them. If you ignore them they'll go away." Anyway, I went along to protest against this march. It was a cold winter's night and it was eerie really because it was in the days of gaslights in the streets and it was very quiet and spooky. Then, very silently, these marchers with their flags and banners turned into the street and there was nobody there to watch them except me.

Anti-fascist unity between Communist and Labour Party members did exist at a grassroots level in many parts of the country, however. In the early 1930s, many people put aside ideological differences to fight the fascists as many have done so since. In particular, branches of the Labour League of Youth (LLY) defied the official policy of their parent body to work alongside other youth groups such as the Young Communist League (YCL) and the ILP's Guild of Youth. The determination of anti-fascists to oppose the Blackshirts coupled with the inability of the Labour Party to rein in its errant members rendered its official policy meaningless in some localities.

The need for all workers to take action against fascists is summarised by Howard 'Andy' Andrews, a CP member from Kilburn:

> We could see that Mosley needed to be stopped. He was in cahoots with all the top politicians as well as lots of wealthy businessmen and the police and we knew that when push came to shove they would side with the fascists against the workers. Mosley was not only against the Jews but was also against the freedom to be in a trade union and the freedom to have socialist ideas. We felt that he was a very real danger and that we would soon have to come to terms with him and his thugs.

The first incident to attract public attention occurred at a BUF rally in the Free Trade Hall in Manchester on 12 March 1933. In the days preceding the meeting, local CP members distributed an anti-fascist manifesto calling for all members of the Labour Party, ILP, trade unions and Co-ops to unite against fascism. The meeting itself descended into chaos when someone in the audience asked Mosley if his organisation was anti-Semitic. After a brief argument an I Squad steward, one of a 140 in the hall, hit the questioner over the head with a rubber truncheon. When other members of the audience stood up to object, they were assaulted. They fought back. One man used a row of chairs as a weapon. Running battles between Blackshirts and hecklers took over the central gap between the chairs. The Union Jack was torn down from the platform as the 'Red Flag' versus 'God Save the King' singing contest began. The police entered the hall, ordered the stewards out and led Mosley off the stage in high-dudgeon. Three fascists required hospital treatment. The following day, the *Manchester Guardian* reported that 'a small man whom one had seen desperately fighting with the Fascists a few minutes before... gave the inspector a short piece of rubber hose on a string, saying he had taken it from a steward.' Mosley announced that BUF stewards would be banned from carrying such weapons but only two days later an anti-fascist crowd outside Rochdale Town Hall was attacked by a mob of Blackshirts armed with knuckle-dusters and lead-filled rubber hoses.

Concurrent with the disturbances in Manchester was a siege of a local BUF headquarters in Walworth Road, London, by a crowd of communists. It lasted for over a fortnight and culminated on 28 March in a raid on the building. Office equipment and furniture were smashed up. Tit for tat battles ensued. Blackshirts attacked a NUWM meeting in April 1933 at Carfax Assembly Rooms, Oxford, addressed by veteran trade unionist Tom Mann. The Red Shirts formed in response. Set up by students from Ruskin, the trade union college, they took the first steps in Oxford to 'preserve the standards of the working class against fascism.'

As the citizens of Oxford began to adjust to the sight of men and women in political uniforms, another organisation identified by the colour of its shirts was emerging in London. Anti-fascists became aware of the Green Shirt Movement for Social Credit in April 1933 when 80 uniformed members of the movement attended a 40,000-strong 'united front' anti-fascist rally in Hyde Park. The wider public learnt of the group after several newspapers reported that the police had been called to break up a hostile crowd of Green Shirts demonstrating outside BUF headquarters on 28 June.

The Green Shirts were founded by John Gordon Hargrave on the theories pioneered by Major C. H. Douglas, who argued for the distribution of 'social credit' to every man, woman and child so that the economic depression could be overcome by the mass purchase of goods and services. Some sections of the Social Credit movement allowed themselves to be drawn into conspiracy theories about 'international Jewish finance', but there is no suggestion that the Green Shirts themselves were anti-Semitic. Hargrave declared himself opposed to both fascism and communism, which he compared to 'two rats caught in a trap' but it was the anti-fascism of the Green Shirts that came to the fore during the 1930s. They conducted a vigorous campaign against the BUF throughout this period. At their height, the Green Shirts had 16 branches nationally, produced their own paper, *Attack*, although were never numerous enough to cause the Blackshirts major problems on their own. They did succeed in making such a nuisance of themselves at fascist events that Mosley formally banned uniformed Green Shirts from BUF meetings.

As the year wore on, clashes between fascists and anti-fascist became commonplace. To take just two incidents: communists and Blackshirts fought in Stockton-on-Tees Market Square on 10 September before more than a thousand locals ran the BUF out of town, then, the following month, on 8 October, three men were arrested following a disturbance at an outdoor fascist meeting at Deptford Broadway. Arthur Wright, a 30 year old labourer, was accused of fighting with a Blackshirt student. Sydney Hickman, 49 year old, managed to strike two men before being arrested. He was reported to have repeatedly shouted "Take those dirty black shirts off."

Mosley rarely bothered with street meetings. He preferred

instead to address handpicked audiences of largely sympathetic listeners from the comfort of a flag-bedecked stage in a large hall. These meetings were also prone to disruption. On 16 October 1933, hand-to-hand fighting twice broke out at the back of a BUF meeting at the King's Hall in Belle Vue, Manchester. Hecklers were thrown out and badly beaten. Benny Rothman once more found himself in the thick of things:

We heard on the grapevine that Mosley intended to hold a monster rally at the King's Hall in Belle Vue, so all the anti-fascist groups got together and debated what to do about it. In the end it was decided to hold a rival public meeting in the Free Trade Hall on the same night and ask everyone to go there. I wasn't sure that this was the best course of action and decided to make my own way to Belle Vue and see what was cooking. At the time I was working as a mechanic and I went straight from work to the meeting. I arrived at Belle Vue in my overalls with my spanners still in my pockets. As I stood outside, a chap came over and handed me a ticket and a bundle of anti-Mosley leaflets. "Here you go Benny. Can you hand these out? They know me and they won't let me in." Well I tucked them inside my overalls and walked into the hall. The stewards directed me up the stairs to the balcony and I found a seat near the front. I remember thinking what a lot of Blackshirt stewards there were. There were two or three to each row of seats. I got talking to the steward in my section, a lad from Birmingham. He saw my overalls and told me that he worked in engineering. We had a good-natured disagreement about politics and he warned me to behave myself because the strong-arm boys were looking for any excuse to get tough with the opposition. Shortly afterwards there was a great roll of drums and a blare of trumpets as Mosley marched out onto the stage accompanied by a group of stewards. Some sections of the audience were clapping and cheering hysterically at the appearance of 'the Leader.' It was a quite a disturbing sight. After a while the crowd settled down and Mosley started to speak. He'd not uttered more than a few words before he was interrupted by a barrage of shouts and whistles. A woman called Evelyn Taylor stood up on the balcony opposite and started barracking Mosley. This was perceived to be a great insult to the leader – a woman barracking Mosley. So they sent some women Blackshirt stewards to get her out but she hit out at them and knocked them down. Then they sent the men over to sort her out and it was absolute mayhem. The crowd were shouting at the stewards to leave her alone but they were really hammering her. Anyway, it was time to play my part in the proceedings and I leant over the edge of the balcony and threw my leaflets in a great sweep over the audience below. Well half a dozen stewards came to get me and I curled up in a ball as they set about me with fists and boots. The next thing I knew I was being picked up and thrown over the balcony. As luck would have it, I landed on a couple of Blackshirts stewards, which cushioned my landing. I was winded and a bit stunned but other than a few bruises I was more or less unhurt. Before I'd properly come to my senses, another great lout came after me snarling "Come here yer Yiddisher bastard." He made a grab for me but I was saved by the lad from Birmingham. He pushed the other fella out of the way and escorted me safely out the hall. So I'd have to say that not all the Blackshirts were bad apples, just the majority of them. Thanks to the Birmingham lad, I got out of the hall with only a few bumps and bruises, but some of the other hecklers fared much worse than me. It was like a field hospital outside. People were nursing broken heads and sore faces. A friend of mine, a chap called Wolfie Winnick had been quite badly beaten up in the passageway. That was the gauntlet you had to run in those days. The Blackshirts would line up on either side of the passageway and set about you with lead-filled rubber hoses. They always behaved their worst when they thought nobody was watching them. We decided to go to the Free Trade Hall, where one of the group made a statement to the audience about what had happened at the King's Hall. It was important that instances such as these were widely publicised so that people learnt about the true nature of fascism.

After the Belle Vue meeting had finished, Mosley led a march of four hundred Blackshirts to Longsight Station where a special train was waiting to take them back to London. They had gone no more than a few hundred yards when a group of sixty young men hurled volleys of stones and bricks. A drummer was knocked unconscious and another fascist received medical attention in the station waiting room. Two anti-fascists were injured in the fighting.

At a BUF meeting in Oxford Town Hall the following month, several members of the audience were badly beaten by Blackshirt stewards. The principal of Ruskin College took sworn affidavits from victims who testified that Blackshirts had overpowered hecklers, sometimes four to one, and held them down to be kicked in the face and neck. While one member of audience was down, a Blackshirt rammed his gloved fingers up his nostrils, causing profuse bleeding, another had his head banged repeatedly on the stone floor. It was stated that a man was thrown down a flight of stairs and, in one affidavit, claimed that a fascist's fingernails had pierced a Red Shirt's head to his skull.

The BUF had a strong base of support in Brighton. Mosley was dubbed the town's 'uncrowned king' by the *Observer* newspaper in January 1934. Local Blackshirts were so cocksure that they even invited their enemies to their meetings. When Joyce spoke at the Dome on 1 March, West Sussex BUF organiser, Captain Charles Bentinck-Budd, invited the Labour Party's Walter Faulkner. Faulkner went along with a small group of family and friends. As the evening got underway a journalist from the *Brighton and Hove Herald* described the scene of 'a meeting of that ultra-modern movement, the Fascists' reporting that 'Everywhere, tall young men garbed in dead black stood with folded arms.' The 300 Defence Force stewards had the desired effect of deterring all but the bravest of hecklers. One man in a red shirt shouted "We want bread not bullets." He was a lone voice of opposition. There were no incidents until the National Anthem was sung. Several Blackshirts rushed Faulkner as he bent down to pick up his daughter. He was beaten nearly unconscious with a stick as his arms were held behind his back and was very nearly strangled with his own scarf. His wife, Jessie, was assaulted when she attempted to come to his aid. Three Blackshirts were arrested. One was fined £3 plus court costs, another was given a binding over plus costs, while the third had the charges against him dismissed.

The BUF's travelling circus continued through 1934. Oswald Mosley and William Joyce addressed hundreds of meetings around the country. Many passed without serious incident but others were curtailed by heckling and scuffling. Anti-fascist tactics at BUF meetings had been refined to create maximum disruption as Benny Rothman explains:

One tactic was to get into the meeting in small groups and wait quietly for the main speaker to start his speech. As soon as he opened his mouth or said something controversial one of these groups would start shouting and whistling and causing as much disruption as possible. This would usually result in fascist stewards rushing over to eject them and there would be quite a disturbance as they were bundled out the hall. The speaker would then resume his speech and would immediately be shouted down by another group. This would go on all evening.

If anti-fascists could not gain admittance to meetings, they would demonstrate outside, harassing Blackshirts as they entered and left. When the BUF held open-air meetings, tactics were adapted. Anti-fascists would either push over the platform, bringing the meeting to a premature close, or subject the speaker to verbal interruptions and volleys of missiles. So began a tradition of physical resistance to fascism that would continue for the rest of the century and into the next.

Stafford Cottman, a member of both the YCL and the ILP Guild of Youth recalls in his book *Disciplina Camaradas* a Mosley meeting in Colston Hall, Bristol, in March 1934. 'I was thrown down the steps', he wrote, 'when several of us youngsters had protested against their meeting.' Another protestor, Sydney Kyte, was seriously hurt and was carried away on a stretcher covered in blood with his head swathed in bandages. As he was put into an ambulance, the police had to form a ring around the entrance to the hall to prevent the crowd from surging into the building. Afterwards, as a column of four hundred Blackshirts marched away from the meeting, it came under repeated attack. A series of running battles broke out as the police struggled to contain the situation. Mosley claimed later that he was unaware of any disorder except that two 'Negroes', one armed with a knife, had tried to attack him. His claim was dismissed by Home Secretary, Sir John Gilmour, who said that the police had not reported any knife and that one of the 'Negroes' was, in any case, a 'half-caste Communist' who was merely protesting to the fascists over the treatment of his colleagues. The disorder outside Colston Hall was followed by further fighting at outdoor BUF public meetings in the city leading to one meeting in Bedminster being closed down on the advice of the police and another resulting in 9 arrests after 'hostile elements in the crowd assaulted Fascists as they were marching away.'

On 22 April, Mosley addressed a large meeting at the Albert Hall in London. He spoke for an hour and a half almost without interruption. There was a small anti-fascist presence inside the hall. Anti-fascists from the Surrey Federation of Youth had pulled the wool over the eyes of the BUF stewards. They dressed up in black shirts and distributed 3,000 of their own free programmes undercutting and undermining the 6d official programme sold outside the hall. The BUF's audience were unaware that what they had been given was an anti-fascist pamphlet entitled *British Fascism Explained*. Another anti-fascist group, the New World Fellowship (NWF), also distributed leaflets outside the Albert Hall before they were moved on by the police.

The NWF was founded in 1932 and declared itself to be law-abiding and pacifistic as well as 'non-party and non-sectarian.' NWF members, called Vigilants, were expected 'to assist in every way possible the propagation of the anti-Fascist propaganda of the organisation'. The NWF's sole stated aim was the destruction of fascism. Its strategies included challenging fascist speakers to open debate on shared platforms and occupying popular BUF pitches to point out the contradictions in fascist policy to the assembly. The green loudspeaker vans of the NWF regularly toured the country, appearing, for example, on consecutive months in Worthing, Leeds and Luton. The NWF published a weekly journal entitled *Green Band*. It also produced a number of pamphlets including *The Mailed Fist* by Nathan Birch and *Fascism in England. Is it Inevitable?* by Maurice Isaacs. Birch was the NWF's Director of Propaganda and Isaacs its General Secretary. The NWF's publications indicate that its non-sectarian policy had some limits. It was almost as contemptuous of communists as it was of fascists, reserving special disdain for those communists whose anti-fascism involved physical force. These 'gentlemen' were like warriors 'going out to fight an epidemic of the measles with a suit of armour and a sword.' The pacifism of the NWF did not protect them from brutal assaults by fascists nor did it prevent Isaacs and Birch from being labelled 'extremists' in Special Branch reports.

In the same month as Mosley's Albert Hall meeting, just days later in fact, disturbances between fascists and anti-fascists culminated in a full-scale riot in Plymouth. BUF speaker, John Beckett, attempted to address a meeting at the Corn Exchange on 26 April. A 'free fight' broke out in the hall involving up to a hundred participants who smashed up the chairs and used the broken pieces as weapons. Beckett left the stage to join the fray but was felled by a rugby tackle. His head was being beaten repeatedly on the floor when the police entered the hall in force and restored order. Before he joined the BUF, John Beckett had been a member of the ILP and elected Labour MP for Gateshead in 1924. He lost his parliamentary seat in 1931 and cut his ties to the Labour Party when the ILP disaffiliated. Then, disillusioned with the ILP itself, Beckett resigned in 1933. A developing interest in fascism reached fruition when, after a period of unemployment and a bankruptcy, Mosley offered him full-time employment.

Beckett's short career in the BUF was a turbulent affair but none of his later trials and tribulations proved as memorable as the two consecutive nights he spent on Tyneside during May 1934. Beckett was due to speak alongside Tommy Moran at two big meetings in Newcastle and Gateshead on the weekend of 13 and 14 May. He walked unwittingly into a maelstrom. On 1 May, a group of BUF supporters had attacked an ILP May Day meeting outside Gateshead Labour Exchange. Then, the unemployed workers in the dole queue, numbering nearly a thousand, turned on the fascists and sent them packing. That the fascists had dared to attack a meeting on May Day, a sacred date in the workers' calendar, prompted anti-fascists to adopt a new stance. So far they had merely responded defensively to fascist violence, now they decided to take the bull by the horns and break the BUF on Tyneside. Nine days after the May Day affair, two hundred men and women formed the Anti-Fascist League (AFL), otherwise known as the Greyshirts. The AFL was solidly working class in character and, according to its secretary John Alfred Chater, a former section leader of the Labour League of Ex-Servicemen, contained within its ranks 'all shades of political opinion.' They did not have to wait long for the first opportunity to test their mettle. On the 13 May, members of the AFL formed up in a crowd of several thousand that stormed a BUF meeting at Cowen's Monument on the Town Moor in Newcastle. The platform was smashed to pieces and the injured Blackshirt contingent, including some seriously hurt, escorted back to BUF headquarters in Clayton Street by mounted police. After laying siege to the building, the crowd went off to hear Beckett's former colleague in the ILP, James Maxton, speak at the Palace Theatre. The following evening in Gateshead, a BUF meeting in the Town Hall was surrounded by thousands of belligerent anti-fascists. The tiny band of Blackshirts were smuggled in by the police then escorted out after Beckett's desultory speech was continuously interrupted by cries of 'Traitor.' As the Blackshirts crossed the Tyne Bridge on their way back to Clayton Street, anti-fascists attempted a rush but police stopped them. The bedraggled BUF contingent was then followed back to their headquarters, which was again put under siege.

Over the next few months, the AFL made life almost impossible for fascists. Squads of Greyshirts made regular patrols of the city streets. Market traders and newspaper vendors were recruited as lookouts. Public meetings were organised from an office rented in Smith's Hall, Monk Street. Faced with such determined opposition, fascist activity practically ceased. Moran was packed off to South Wales to try his luck there and Beckett was ordered back to London. Beckett's close friend and cohort, William Joyce, also ran into opposition in Manchester around the same time. He addressed a BUF rally at Hulme Town Hall to be greeted by over 50 members of the Hulme Anti-Fascist Campaign Committee who stormed the platform and broke up the meeting, injuring two Blackshirts as they did so.

The pace of anti-fascist activity was relentless. Just over a week later, on Sunday 13 May, the Relief Committee for the Victims of German Fascism with its eminent speakers and supporters held a packed public meeting at the Free Trade Hall in Manchester. The very same day in Finsbury Park, North London, communists won a series of running battles with Blackshirts, forcing them to flee. The BUF returned with a massive police escort three Sundays later and, despite forceful opposition, held an hour-long meeting. Following the 'Second Battle of Finsbury Park', the *Daily Worker* revealed the level of co-operation between police and fascists. It published a letter from BUF headquarters to local branches retrieved from Finsbury Park after the rally. It read:

As you are doubtless aware, we are holding a Fascist rally at Finsbury Park on Sunday June 3rd, at 11:30 A.M. We have been informed by the local police that we might expect a very serious disturbance in this connection from the Communist Party, who have sent an all London call to their various members. I would greatly appreciate your assistance in the form of sending out as many stewards as is in your power.

In the East End of London, Blackshirt harassment of the Jewish community was a daily problem. Ubby Cowan, a young Jewish textile worker and trade unionist, remembers his first encounter with Mosley's henchmen:

As a result of the situation in the East End, I was asked by the union to help barrack a fascist meeting being held at the gardens of the Tower of London. I went along there with several others and, as we approached, I could see a little crowd of about fifty people with maybe two or three policemen standing nearby, not too close. There was a man stood on the wall of the gardens talking about Cheetham Hill. All of sudden a man in the audience shouted "If you don't shut up about Cheetham Hill, I'll shut you up." I thought "Hello, what's going on here?" The next thing I saw was a hand come up and drag the speaker down. Everyone started stamping on him until the police rushed in and rescued him. That was my first taste of what was happening. I joined the Communist Party as a result of the fact that they were the only ones who were showing any interest in stopping Mosley. Everybody else was ignoring what Mosley was doing to the Jews and, of course, we didn't like it at all.

Lou Kenton was another young working class Jewish East Ender who took part in the fight against fascism. He explains how he became involved:

My memory goes back as a youngster to the East End during the First World War. There was a great deal of anti-Semitism about at the time and after the war even more so. There were areas of Stepney that were no-go areas for Jews and quite often we were attacked, but it really started to come to fruition when Oswald Mosley formed the British Union of Fascists. Up until then there had been the odd fascist group which held meetings and attacked individual Jews, but when Mosley formed the BUF that was the crux. It's interesting that after he formed the BUF, the *Daily Mail* had a full front-page article calling on people to support them. 'Hurrah for the Blackshirts' was the headline. The BUF were quite active around certain areas of the East End, places like Bethnal Green, Wapping, Shoreditch and Dalston. We used to hold meetings there and they did too and quite often we heckled each other and come to blows as well. As time went by, it started to become clear to us that they were a serious, serious threat. Up until then they were just individuals or small groups but under Mosley's leadership they started to become organised. They marched through the streets and into Jewish areas. Parts of the East End became no-go areas for Jews. As time went by, attacks on Jews increased, old people were being attacked as well as men with Jewish beards who were easily identified.

I worked in a place called Iliffes on Fleet Street, which printed magazines like the *Radio Times*. I set up the trade union branch there and became the Father of the Chapel. That's how I became interested in politics and organising. I joined the Communist Party in 1929 and was a member for nearly forty years. Through my trade union work I came into contact with printers from other Chapels. They worked on papers like the *Daily Mail, Daily Express, Daily Telegraph* and *Daily Herald* and they were very powerful Chapels. Through working in the newspapers of course they had a good awareness of what was going on around the world and they decided to form an organisation called the Printers' Anti-Fascist Movement, which became very popular. We had our first meeting in the Kingsway Hall and nearly 500 people signed the enrolment forms. We had our own newspaper, the *Anti-Fascist Printer*. It was a very great success, and regularly sold out. The printers' Chapels in the main all supported us and took copies of the paper. Ours was the biggest of the rank and file papers because, of course, the Chapels took 2-300 copies each and it didn't take long to build up the circulation. At that time people used to stand outside the newspaper offices in Fleet Street selling the *Anti-Fascist Printer* and on one occasion I was there with my wife when a number of fascists came over, about a dozen of them. It was near where the *Daily Mail* office was and they said "We'll be waiting for you when you're through." It was in the middle of the City, which was a pretty desolate place and I thought "We're in trouble here." So I called the Father of the Chapel of the *Daily Mail* branch out and he asked what I wanted. So I told him "You see those blokes on the corner over there, they're waiting for us." "Oh they are, are they?" he said and he went back into work and stopped the process. About thirty or forty blokes came out and said to the Blackshirts "We'll be back in five minutes and if you haven't gone, you're having it." Well, the fascists disappeared straight away. It struck me as a good example of workers supporting each other.

A small point of clarification. The official title of the printer's anti-fascist group was the Printing and Allied Trades Anti-Fascist Movement. Its stated aims, as set out in *Printers and the Fascist Menace* were 'To secure the closing down of fascist barracks. To organise with a view to ensuring full support for all workers who refuse to print and handle fascist propaganda, recognising such as being against working class interests' and 'To co-operate with the Continental workers in every way possible in their heroic struggle against fascist terror.' In its next publication, *The Workers' Next Step Against Fascism*, author J. Cronin issued a call to arms:

The Workers' Next Step Against Fascism, Printing and Allied Trades Anti-Fascist Movement, 1934.

In this present period we are confronted with Fascism. Time is getting short. We face facts, we extend further and deeper our work. We call to you. Fall in! Form with us the United Anti-Fascist Front. Prepare with us to fight and defeat Fascism. Thus will we conquer. That is the next step. Take it now.

The call for unity came against a backdrop of increasing BUF violence. Attacks on the left, including attempts to break up CP meetings in Shepherd's Bush, Uxbridge, Oxford continued. A London rally of the British Anti-War Movement was targetted. There was no let up in the persecution of the Jewish community. But, signs of resistance were starting to show. Organisations, such as the British Cab Drivers Anti-Fascist Committee and the King's Cross Railwayman's Anti-Fascist Group were springing up everywhere. Anti-fascists were gathering together to oppose a BUF rally at Olympia on 7 June. Lou Kenton relates:

As the feeling against the fascists started to grow, anti-fascist clubs and anti-fascist committees were formed in different parts of the country. There were other groups like ours based around different jobs like the railwaymen and busmen but it was the printers who were the best organised. In 1934, Mosley decided to speak at Olympia in Earl's Court, which was a massive place with a capacity of twenty thousand and he planned to bring Blackshirts down from all over the country. Everybody who was anti-fascist wanted to do something about it but nobody was really organised except for the printers. I remember we had a meeting and about 40 or 50 people representing numerous trade unions and working class organisations turned up. We decided to go down to Olympia and heckle them. We were aware that the fascists were very aggressive towards anyone who turned up to oppose them. Their tactics were to hold public meetings with strong-arm guards all around the meetings so that anybody who heckled would be thrown out if it was indoors or beaten up if it was outdoors. This was their first very big meeting, however, and we decided we had to tackle them. We decided that all the anti-fascists would sit themselves around the hall and heckle the speakers. I went in with five or six others and sat near the platform. We were sat three or four seats apart from each other and the plan was that once one was thrown out for heckling another would stand up and replace him. I remember Mosley marching in, lights shining on him, band playing and a gang of lieutenants around him in black shirts, uniforms and boots. We suddenly realised then that we were up against it. The moment he got up to speak, people all over the hall stood up to heckle him and the Blackshirts started to throw them out and very roughly too. The fascists moved to clear one side of the hall and when they came towards our section we all looked at each other as if to say "Here we go." The bloke sitting to my right got up and started heckling, but he didn't get very far. They came in and fetched him out onto the gangway, carrying him out face down, beating him up and kicking him all the way. This went on all over and of course the meeting was disrupted. When it came to my part I was very nervous, as you can imagine. I was thinking "What do I do?" I got up and shouted something. What it was, I don't know, but a couple of Blackshirts dragged me over to the gangway. When I got there I didn't know what to do. It was no use fighting because there were five or six of them. So when they grabbed hold of me I went limp. I could see another bloke in front of me being carried out face down, spread-eagled and being continuously kicked and punched as he was thrown out. He was covered in blood and was pretty well unconscious by the time they got to the foyer. Because I wasn't struggling they just carried me out and when we got to the door the police were standing there just watching, doing nothing. Olympia had steps leading up to it, so when they threw this bloke out he bounced and rolled down the steps and was very badly injured.

A number of journalists were around and up until then people had said we were exaggerating what fascism was. What Hitler was doing in Germany was not yet widely known and when the journalists saw what happened at Olympia they were shocked, genuinely shocked. Afterwards, the journalists managed to interview the bloke who was thrown down the steps and then they came over and interviewed me. They asked me what I had seen and would I verify that I saw the fascists throw the man down the stairs. I said "Yes, I would." So they interviewed me and it appeared the next day in the *News Chronicle*. That was the first time that people became aware of what fascism was. Up until then it was something that happened in another country like Italy or Germany. In the East End we were already very aware of what fascism represented because of the anti-Semitic background but many people around the country were disconnected from it. Olympia did a tremendous amount to stimulate interest in the anti-fascist movement.

Lou was one of the lucky ones. As he noted, witness statements were taken by journalists and published. A number of anti-fascist pamphlets reprinted these statements. One from a R. Rhys, *Daily Herald*, 9 June 1934, began:

The first thing I knew was a squad of Blackshirts rushing in, hitting out indiscriminately, overturning seats and injuring ordinary members of the audience. They battered one man, hitting him over the head and trampling, and kicking him as he lay on the ground. A woman screamed. She was immediately surrounded by Blackshirts and thrown to the women Blackshirts who hit her and clawed at her as she sagged limply to the ground.

Another from J.H. Bently in *News Chronicle* published the same day read:

Leaving the building by the Blythe Road entrance, I saw a man being half carried, half dragged, by eight men in black shirts, to the gates. Here they stopped, stripped him of his trousers, and assaulted him in a way that made him scream with agony. Then they threw him into the road.

After this public display of brutality, some prominent BUF supporters backed off in embarrassment. Lord Rothermere, owner of the *Daily Mail*, withdrew his paper's avid and open support claiming that pressure from Jewish advertisers made him drop Mosley. Mosley himself blamed the hecklers for the violence they suffered in a rapidly produced pamphlet *Red Terror and Blue Lies* containing a photograph an assortment of weapons confiscated from protestors at his Olympia meeting. It was all faked, according to the photographer who took the picture, as was another shot of a Blackshirt swathed in bandages and daubed in red ink.

Some enraged anti-fascists had retaliated against Blackshirts leaving Olympia and were arrested. Amongst them was Marks Barnett (Barney) Becow, a 24 year old communist from Stepney. Becow was sentenced to one month's hard labour for being in possession of an offensive weapon and fined £3 for insulting words, behaviour and obstructing the police. Becow was a staunch anti-fascist and would serve several prison sentences for his commitment to the cause. Ubby Cowan was a member of the same branch of the Communist Party as Becow and remembers him well:

Barney wasn't all that interested in the political side of things. I certainly don't recall him saying anything all that political at meetings but he was very determined to get rid of Mosley and his henchmen. The fascists started sending their storm troopers down to the East End in about '33 or '34. All these strong-arm guys would come down from their barracks in the Kings Road and we would be out mob-handed night after night trying to stop them. Barney and one or two others were always in the thick of things but because Barney was a big, tough guy, the police used to pick on him. They were always looking for an excuse to arrest anti-fascists anyway, but they definitely singled Barney out. He must have been arrested about twenty times in four or five years. It became a common thing in the Stepney branch for someone say "Barney's been arrested again." Some people wouldn't go out with him because of it.

Anti-fascists had certainly taken a beating at Olympia but their growing movement responded in force. In London, on the two days that immediately followed, 9 and 10 June, there were disturbances at BUF meetings in Hackney, Finsbury Park, Regent's Park, Notting Hill, Tottenham, Woolwich and Wood Green. Later in the month, when A.K. Chesterton spoke at the Oriental Hall, Leicester, he was opposed by a large procession of anti-fascists led by a donkey wearing a black shirt. 10,000 demonstrated outside a Mosley meeting at Sheffield's City Hall. They were brought together by the United Action Committee, a local front initiative to 'Fight Fascism and War Now'. In Glasgow, a crowd of two thousand anti-fascists broke up an outdoor meeting addressed by William Joyce. During the same war-torn month, anti-fascists harassed the BUF over an entire week in Plymouth. They began a march on the BUF's headquarters in Lockyer Street that was halted by police. Anti-fascists were arrested. The crowd then besieged the station to demand their release. The police, with a political prejudice identical to the BUF, blamed an 'Alien Communist element.'

Mosley might have expected an easier ride in Brighton where just six months ago the BUF had held a meeting with little opposition. But times had changed. A volatile crowd of several hundred had gathered outside the Dome on 12 July to jeer Mosley when he arrived to make his address. A rumour that Mosley was planning to stand as a parliamentary candidate in

Brighton added to anti-fascist fervour in the wake of Olympia. As the evening wore on, the demonstration outside the Dome was swollen by the arrival of anti-fascists who had cut short a CP-led united front rally on the Level, Brighton's version of Hyde Park's Speakers' Corner. A smaller than expected crowd made those at the Level realise where they should have been all along. When the Blackshirts emerged from their Dome meeting, they found the crowd outside had become more numerous and hostile. Ernie Trory, a local CP organiser, remembered the scene in his book *Between the Wars*:

> After the meeting the Blackshirts attempted a march round the town. As they left the Pavilion Gardens in military formation, the catcalls and jeers from thousands of workers who had assembled to show their hatred rose to a crescendo. The fascists, who had been imported from East London in armoured cars, were obviously riled at this reception in what they had been led to believe was a stronghold of fascism. Breaking their ranks they dashed into the crowd using their knuckledusters and scattering men, women and children. To their astonishment they were met with a determined resistance from workers who fought back strenuously with their fists. In the ensuing struggle, members of the Communist Party and Labour League of Youth were conspicuous. Several Blackshirts took the count and were taken to Victoria Garden for attention.

The following day's *Evening Argus* confirmed reports that several Blackshirts had been 'laid out' during the fighting outside the Dome. It also reported that BUF men had attacked one of the propaganda vans of the New World Fellowship. Maurice Isaacs told the paper that:

> Literature was being distributed when it was attacked by the

Blackshirts. One of them jumped on the footboard and smashed the glass screen with an iron bar; at the same time attempting to pull the driver out of his seat. The driver was taken to hospital suffering a bruised ear and is not now able to drive.

Another enemy of the BUF in Brighton was a man who became known as 'the Guv'nor.' Harry Cowley, a chimney sweep who campaigned for the rights of unemployed workers and the families of homeless ex-servicemen, played a leading role in anti-fascist escapades in the town. He helped disrupt Mosley's meeting at the Dome by wiring a loudspeaker to a gramophone in an adjacent building. Mosley's speech was drowned out by the *Marseillaise* until BUF stewards cut the connection. Harry paid a price for his anti-fascist adventures. He recalled, in an interview with the *Evening Argus*, 16 February 1957, being targeted by Blackshirts:

I was met by some of them in Middle Street one midnight. They were mob-handed and I was alone; they had bottles. They broke my leg and I was eight months in hospital... And then one night they sent a mob down from London in one of them 'armoured' car what they had. They done me house in Grove Street in the middle of the night. They brought bricks with slogans wrapped around them – 'Mind the draught from this one' and 'we're coming to do you in' and things like that. They smashed up the windows with them.

Harry might have been vulnerable when he was alone but had many allies within the working classes of central Brighton:

So next Saturday there was a meeting at the Level. I got some of my boys and mingled 'em in with the crowd and told them beforehand: 'When I put my finger up, away you go.' I put me

finger up and away they went. The ambulances were going to
and fro with broken noses and black eyes and blood spurting
everywhere. Mine wasn't rough boys: they was conscientious.
They stood as one.

After Olympia, anti-fascists fought back but also shouldered the
physical defeat with political development. One of the
pamphlets that documented the violence at Olympia, *Blackshirt
Brutality*, called for the formation of 'anti-fascist groups in every
factory or other place of work, and in every street and district.'
An enrolment form was included which urged interested parties
to contact the secretary of the 'Anti-Fascist and Anti-War
Movement' at 53 Gray's Inn Road, London. The coupling of
campaigns against fascism and war was based on the analysis of
the latter as effect of capitalism and nationalism that always put
workers, whose real interests lay in internationalism, in the
firing line. A YCL pamphlet, *10 Points Against Fascism*, published
around the same time, also urged its readers to affiliate to 'Anti-
Fascist and Anti-War Movement' at the same London address.
This looked like a move to develop a single anti-fascist organisation by adjoining it to the existing organisational structures of
the British Anti-War Movement, another CP satellite whose
chairman was John Strachey, former New Party member turned
communist ally. Large numbers of enrolment forms for the 'Anti-
Fascist and Anti-War Movement' were distributed. However,
some influential anti-fascists had quite different ideas about how
that could be achieved.

On 25 July 1934, a meeting to discuss anti-fascist unity was
held at Conway Hall, Red Lion Square. At the end of the day, a
rather strange creature emerged blinking into the sunlight. The
Co-ordinating Committee for Anti-Fascist Activities was not an
organisation so much as a collection of prominent figures that
offered direction to anti-fascist groups. The Co-ordinating
Committee had one eye on the Labour Party leadership's

stubborn refusal to join an anti-fascist united front as it tried to appeal to sympathetic Labour Party members, trade union groups and Co-operative Guilds. Labour MPs, Ellen Wilkinson and D. N. Pritt KC were Committee members alongside Fenner Brockway and James Maxton of the ILP and CP leaders Harry Pollitt and Willie Gallagher. John Strachey also had a lead role in this group and was elected its secretary.

The British Anti-War Movement made further moves to build an anti-fascist movement on the 4th and 5th of August. Its Youth Section hosted the National Youth Congress Against Fascism and War at Sheffield City Hall attended by 630 delegates. There were the usual suspects, the YCL, ILP Guild of Youth, Labour League of Youth but also Woodcraft Folk, the Co-operative Circle, Rambling and Camping Clubs as well as individual delegates from the Boy Scouts, the Jewish Lad's Brigade and the Clarion Cycling Club. Those present at the Congress agreed:

> To develop the mass movement against fascism and the new Sedition Bill; to turn Fascist meetings into Anti-Fascist actions; to close down the Fascist headquarters; to expose the trickery and phrases of Fascism, and to develop a mass movement for Anti-Fascist defence.

The Youth Front Against Fascism and War was established as a result of the Sheffield Congress. It actively encouraged ordinary members to participate in the running of the organisation. They were required to buy membership cards, sell anti-fascist literature, organise anti-fascist youth rallies and take part in actions against local Blackshirts. Its first *Organisational Bulletin* urged its members to 'seriously consider how to get the comrades from the Labour League of Youth and Co-op Comrades Circles, Woodcraft Groups etc. participating in the Campaign' and promised further advice on how to set up local anti-fascist groups. While other cultural and political youth groups were aligned to the Front, it remained dominated by the YCL.

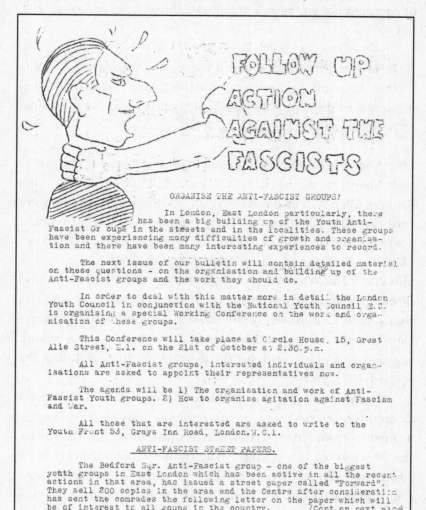

Youth Front Against Fascism and War, *Organisational Bulletin*, No.1, 1934.

The Students' Anti-War Council, another spin-off from the British Anti-War Movement, also had an anti-fascist dimension. Its first issue of its newspaper, *Student Front Against War and*

Fascism in November 1934 included a warning about the dangers of complacency in the face the fascist threat from contributor A. Layne:

In England the exceptionalist theory, the theory which holds that England is somehow different, and because of this supposed difference Fascism will not be able to develop, must be broken down.'

The Women's Committee Against War and Fascism (WCAWF) took shape from the same CP mould. Lilla Brockway, Vera Brittain, Ellen Wilkinson and Sylvia Pankhurst, none of who were card-carrying Communist Party members, held prominent positions but a bloc of CPers, including Charlotte Despard, Marjorie Pollitt and Joan Beauchamp exerted a controlling influence. The WCAWF produced leaflets and pamphlets, held meetings and marches on issues of war, fascism and women's rights. The Committee commemorated International Women's Day. It went on to publish *Woman Today* and to raise money, supplies and public support for the republican side during the Spanish Civil War.

Of the Youth Front, Students' Council and Women's Committee, the first was, by far, the most active in the struggle against fascism. Physical resistance is often, not always but often, the province of the young. Many Youth Front members were concentrated in Jewish enclaves like Cheetham and Stepney and found themselves on the front line in the battle against fascism. Benny Rothman remembers an almost constant level of activity in Cheetham:

We seemed to be involved in anti-fascist activity on an almost daily basis. If we weren't organising our own meetings and events, we were trying to stop the fascists from holding theirs. Whenever we heard about a fascist meeting, we would rush around and alert everybody. It was a very busy time. Many of the most active members of the Youth Front in Cheetham were also in the YCL. We saw it as a way of working with anti-fascists who might not necessarily agree with the Communist Party on other issues. I think it was fairly successful in that respect and there was a great deal of unity amongst the youth. There was a big group where we lived in Cheetham, which was very active in opposing fascism. We had bags of energy and enthusiasm and we were determined to beat the Blackshirts. We felt that it was something we had to do, not only because we were Jewish, but also because we were communists. The Blackshirts in Manchester were very aggressive and Jewish people and communists were frequently attacked. We knew it would only get worse if Mosley came to power.

After a couple of years, the Youth Front just seemed to merge into the YCL. I don't remember if there was any big discussion or fuss about it, it just seemed to happen quite naturally. We had a very strong YCL branch in Cheetham with nearly 200 members. I was branch secretary for a while and helped to keep things ticking over. We had a room above a garage in Hightown, which we used for film shows, political discussions and sporting activities. We held regular Sunday night dances, which were very well attended and used it as a base for rambles and cycle rides. It became known as the Challenge Club, after the YCL paper, and it was the main focus of our lives for a number of years.

Phil Kaiserman was another young YCL member from Cheetham. He also confirms the leading role the Communist Party played in the Youth front:

The YCL and the Labour League of Youth were both involved in the Youth Front. The Party would assign young comrades to the Youth Front and that would be their Party work. The Youth Front was dominated by the YCL but only because we were the only ones, really, who had the political knowledge, because we studied it. A lot of the people in the Labour League of Youth and other groups were only in it because it was a young people's organisation and they'd go to dances and so on. We were in it because of the politics and wanted to push it along. On the cultural side of things, the only thing I remember is going out to Derbyshire on a weekend and singing our bloody heads off. We sang revolutionary songs as we marched across the countryside. I honestly don't remember too many music evenings or anything like that. The only thing I remember was reading Marxism. We had all the various books and we formed study groups and we'd go page, after page, after page, through the books. That was extremely important.

As the summer of 1934 drew to a close, Mosley was forced to relinquish plans for another big fascist show piece in White City when the Chairman of its Board demanded a bond to cover likely damage to the building set so high the BUF leader had to cancel. Without another safe indoor option, the fascists announced a rally on the 9th of September in Hyde Park.

As the Hyde Park rally neared, the Co-ordinating Committee for Anti-Fascist Activities sent out a call for a 'United Front Against Fascism on September 9th' that would 'drown' the fascists in a 'sea of organised working class activity.' The Executive of the Labour Party and the TUC General Council responded by issuing a joint statement urging their supporters and affiliated bodies to have nothing to do with any counter-mobilisation. Both bodies passed a string of resolutions demanding that fascist demonstrations are banned, condemning fascism in general terms, but they baulked at the idea of active opposition to Mosley. Their stance shielded the labour movement from the infection of fascism, hampered BUF recruitment amongst organised workers but did nothing to combat fascist agitation amongst the non-unionised population and singularly failed to prevent fascist aggression towards Jewish communities.

Moderates in the labour movement were hoping to ignore the opposition to Mosley and so were the press. Statements from anti-fascists were greeted with silence. Only the most intense campaigning succeeded in breaking what amounted to a boycott. At CP offices in King Street, former miner Bert Williams gathered a group of party members that went all out to promote the anti-fascist counter-demonstration. Pavements and walls were chalked, Nelson's Column painted in letters 'a yard high' and around a million leaflets distributed. The press still stayed silent. Anti-fascists upped their game. A steam train at King's Cross Station was daubed with 'March Against Fascism on September 9'. Leaflets were dropped at government offices, omnibuses and shops, including the rooftop of Selfridges in Oxford Street. Three live BBC radio broadcasts were interrupted by 'microphone bandits' urging workers to come out against the fascists on the 9th September. Anti-fascist flags were hung from the BBC's Portland Place building and a banner draped around Transport House, the Labour Party and TUC offices, which read 'The United Front from Below is on Top.' With a week to go, John Strachey and Harry Pollitt addressed a meeting. 'Only slaves will agree to stay at home on Sunday', said Pollitt.

On the day, 2,500 Blackshirts were peacefully opposed by an enormous crowd estimated somewhere between 70,000 to150,000 strong. Ubby Cowan was one of many that joined it from the East End:

Thousands of us marched from Stepney Green to Hyde Park to oppose the Mosley rally. It was a twelve-mile march and it was a boiling hot day, so we were all feeling a bit tired by the time we got to central London. Because of the length of the demonstration, the police were stopping it every so often at crossroads to allow the traffic to flow which meant it took even longer than normal. We were absolutely drained when we finally arrived at Hyde Park but standing at the gates was Prince Monolulu, the famous racing tipster. Whenever there was a race meeting he was asked by the press to give his opinion. He was supposed to have been an Ethiopian, but nobody really knew where he came from. He was standing there in a big colourful Jellaba, with Ostrich feathers sticking out of his hat. He greeted us in Yiddish, saying "Come in children." It was such a boost to our spirits after such a long march. It really cheered us up. Three or four different marches from various parts of London all converged on Hyde Park that afternoon, and in the end there were over a hundred thousand people in the park. It was like a carnival with speeches and bands and hundreds of different banners. All gathered together to show their opposition to fascism.

Membership forms for the Anti-War and Anti-Fascist Movement were distributed on the day of the Hyde Park rally. An appeal to

join was repeated in a follow-up pamphlet, *September 9th: Drowned in a Sea of Working Class Activity*, a triumphalist account of the day from a communist perspective. But plans for a national organisation were quashed by John Strachey who argued that such an organisation would distance anti-fascism from the rank and

September 9th: Drowned in a Sea of Working Class Activity, The Communist Party, 1934.

file of the labour movement. His real fears lay not with the anti-fascism of trade unionists but their labour leaders. He doubted they would embrace a national anti-fascist body dominated by communists. For him, the unity achieved by alliances between anti-fascist groups fronted by the Co-ordinating Committee for Anti-Fascist Activities was preferable to tighter organisation and greater division. This diplomacy was never really necessary at local levels. For example, the Labour League of Youth had joined the YCL in the Youth Front. For those outside party bureaucracies and involved in fight against fascism, and these were often younger party members, a united front, if not a single operation, was already in existence.

Mosley's next big outing was in Manchester at the end of September. The BUF had been making inroads in the northwest amongst disaffected textile workers and the unemployed, persuading them that nationalistic protectionism would halt the decline of Lancashire's once booming textile industry. 'Revive Lancashire's Greatness' was their platform and they issued pamphlets with titles such as *Lancashire Betrayed* and *Is Lancashire Doomed?* The CP took up the question of the causes of regional industrial decline and responded to the BUF's offensive by distributing ten thousand leaflets to textile workers. Written by William Rust, *Mosley and Lancashire*, explained that protectionism was not addressed to the long term problem of outdated textile manufacture presided over by negligent factory owners who had not invested in modern machinery. Protectionism also risked loss of trade beyond the British Empire and attendant increases in unemployment, cuts in wages and short time for textile workers. Political debate was accompanied by physical confrontations. Young anti-fascists from the Jewish community and left organisations tackled Blackshirts on the streets. Police reports estimated anti-fascists and fascists clashed in Manchester four or five times a week. Bernard McKenna, a young clerk in a clothing factory, recalls the daily round of anti-fascism in

Manchester and Mosley's 29 September meeting at Belle Vue:

I joined the Labour League of Youth in 1932 when I was 17, but left to join the Young Communist League (YCL) two years later. I felt much happier in the YCL because there was more of a socialist feeling about them. I remember selling the *Daily Worker* in Oldham Street on Saturday evenings while the Blackshirts were trying to sell their papers opposite. There were frequent run-ins between the two groups, which quite often ended in fights. The BUF also held regular meetings in Stevenson Square and, of course, we fought with them there as well. It got quite nasty for a while but in the end we drove them out of that part of the city altogether. There was a large Blackshirt contingent in Manchester at the time and they held several big rallies in the city. At one point during the 1930s, Mosley even tried to make Manchester his national headquarters. I think he wanted to try and capitalise on the decline of the cotton industry but nothing ever came of it. As a member of the Communist Party I took part in protests against all the Blackshirt meetings and joined in with the attempts to disrupt them. The big BUF rallies were usually well marshalled by the police and fascists and sometimes we'd just end up shouting at them.

The meeting that everyone talks about was the big outdoor one at Belle Vue Gardens in September 1934. It wasn't just the Communist Party who opposed it. There was an anti-fascist committee set up, which involved all sorts of different groups. As part of the committee, we did a great deal of work, calling on people to come out and stop Mosley. We handed out leaflets, held street-corner meetings and chalked up pavements and walls all over the place. There were three separate anti-fascist marches on the day of the Mosley rally. Each one set off from a different part of the city and we all met up at Ardwick Green. We then formed up into one big march and set off for Belle Vue. There must have been nearly five thousand marching up Hyde Road. The Chief Constable had supposedly banned all marches that weekend but nobody lifted a finger to stop us. When we finally reached Belle Vue, we met up with another crowd of anti-fascists holding a rally on a plot of waste ground outside the park. A few people stayed outside to listen to the speeches, but most people went inside. Once we got inside, we saw that a microphone and amplifiers had been set up on the gallery and that the area in front of it had been sealed off with wooden barricades. Behind the barricades were hundreds of policemen. At that time there wasn't a Blackshirt to be seen anywhere and we wondered where they all were. After about ten minutes or so, five hundred Blackshirts suddenly marched out of the halls in military formation. I don't know how they got in. They must have hid their shirts under their coats, because we never saw them outside. There was a lot of booing and jeering when they appeared and a few things were thrown but nothing serious because of all the police. I thought that the whole thing was going to be a bit of a wash-out but when Mosley finally came out onto the platform and started speaking thousands of anti-fascists started whistling and booing in an attempt to drown him out. All sorts of things were being sung and shouted. It was a continuous barrage of noise. Mosley had a microphone and powerful amplifiers but I didn't hear a single word he said that day and I don't think anybody else did either. This went on for quite a while and when he finally realised nobody could hear him, he stormed off the platform. I remember seeing him and his Blackshirts marching away from Belle Vue looking very downcast. All the anti-fascists were waving him goodbye and singing "Bye, Bye, Blackshirt" as he left.

On 5 October, a week after the events at Belle Vue, Mosley flew to Plymouth to speak at the Millbank Drill Hall. His words were continuously interrupted by a section of the 3,500 audience who sang the 'Red Flag'. Towards the end of the meeting, fighting broke out at the back of the hall. A journalist and a photographer for a local paper were assaulted by Blackshirt stewards. Fights spread as twenty anti-fascists rushed the platform. Then the lights went out and the police arrived. In the weeks before and after the Mosley rally, there were battles between fascists and anti-fascists at open-air meetings. The NWF had descended on Plymouth with their loudspeaker vans. Three BUF members from London arrived looking for Birch and Isaacs of NWF, found the lodging house in the Octagon where they stayed and, when they learnt both had left, beat up the elderly owner. The Blackshirts were jailed for assault.

Away from the large urban centres where the working class were less organised and Jewish neighbourhoods smaller and more isolated, Mosley was able to speak more or less unopposed. When the Blackshirts rolled in to town with their battlewagons, they did not expect trouble. The seaside resort of Worthing was expected to be one of their safe ports of call. But it was not to be. Opposition started to grow from the announcement that Mosley would address an evening meeting at the Pier Pavilion on 9 October. The NWF turned up in their green propaganda vans and held a series of anti-fascist meetings along Worthing seafront. Issacs and two female members of the NWF were arrested for selling literature on the Parade without the consent of the Corporation. "No More War. Damn Mosley. Fight Fascism" was written in tar on Worthing Town Hall and tar was also spread on the walls of the local fascist headquarters at 27 Marine Parade. On the night, just sixteen members of the Defence Force accompanied Mosley to the Pier Pavilion. He considerably underestimated the depth of local hostility towards him and his movement. As the meeting got underway, a crowd gathered outside that numbered several thousand by the time Blackshirts marched out in military formation. Fireworks were thrown as choruses of "Poor old Mosley's got the wind up" were sung to the tune of John Brown's Body. Mosley was struck, he retaliated and fights started that spread along the Esplanade. Blackshirts were forced to retreat to Barnes Café in the Arcade, a well-known BUF meeting place. The café was stormed, windows were broken, missiles thrown. As midnight neared, the Blackshirts tried to break out of the café but were spotted and attacked. A 'seething, struggling mass of howling people' poured into the road and fought each other in what has become known as the Battle of South Street.

On 28 October 1934, barely two years after the formation of the BUF, Mosley addressed a large meeting at the Albert Hall in London. There were rumours he would declare his, and therefore the BUF's, position on the Jewish question. He did not disappoint the anti-Semites. During his speech, he railed against the 'power of organised Jewry' and declared that the BUF would fight its presence in Britain as 'an unclean, alien influence in our national and imperial life.'

Anti-fascists had mobilised against the Albert Hall meeting but in a rather fragmented fashion indicative of some leadership disagreements about strategies of opposition to the BUF. The Co-ordinating Committee for Anti-Fascist Activities attracted 1,500 people to a demonstration in Hyde Park opposite the Albert Hall. A few hundred anti-fascists got closer. They managed to slip through the police cordon. Plying copies of the *Daily Worker* and *Green Band*, they shouted "Down with Mosley" and "Red United Fighting Front" before being dispersed. The CP was holding a rally in Trafalgar Square against the Sedition Bill. Of the 4,000 that attended, 1,000 left at the end for the Albert Hall. Carrying banners from Spitalfields Market Anti-Fascist Group, the Distributive Workers Anti-Fascist Movement as well as those of Youth Front organisations, the YCL and LLY, the police headed them off before they got near the BUF.

Outside the capital, there was more cohesion in the anti-fascist camp. A Mosley meeting in Gillingham, Kent, just a couple of days later, was opposed by several thousand people. The crowd, mobilised by the Kent County Committee of the United Front, were in militant mood. Blackshirt stewards were pelted with eggs and bottles. Mosley was spat upon and an attempt was made to overturn his sports car. Prominent amongst the protestors were members of the CP, ILP, NUWM and the LLY but the overwhelming majority had no party political affiliation whatsoever.

On 25 November Mosley made another anti-Semitic speech at Manchester's Free Trade Hall. Six anti-fascists were forcibly ejected from the meeting. One was Evelyn Taylor, who had fought Blackshirt stewards at Belle Vue the year before. She was arrested and fined. In her defence, she argued that she had not come to hear Mosley speak and was determined that no one else should either. Disturbances went on until the early hours of the morning.

Membership of the BUF reached 40,000 prior to Olympia and now had fallen to roughly 5,000. That BUF meetings invariably ended in violence deprived the party of political respectability and middle ground or middle class support. It had also suffered considerably from the withdrawal of Lord Rothermere's free publicity. Mosley's open anti-Semitism has been interpreted as an attempt to rally his troops now reduced to its fascist hard core. If it was, it also simply served to sanction both words and deeds of these members over the past two years. Blackshirts got the green light to step up their campaign of intimidation in Jewish quarters. BUF speakers were given carte blanche to vilify the Jewish community.

2

A cause worth fighting for: 1935 – 1940

An ocean of ink has been wasted on the pointless debate over whether Oswald Mosley was genuinely anti-Semitic or whether he used the issue to boost his faltering movement. There is no answer to this question that turns Mosley into a good guy, no matter how hard people have tried in the past. If he was indeed an anti-Semite, and there are numerous reports of Mosley making crude anti-Semitic comments during unguarded moments that support this thesis, then he can be condemned for the bigotry he ambiguously and occasionally denied. If he wasn't, and rivals like Arnold Leese frequently charged him with being soft on the Jewish question, then he can be accused of turning a blind eye towards the lurid and violent anti-Semitism of the men under his command then openly encouraging it to save himself and his party. So either Mosley was an anti-Semite, or an exploiter of anti-Semitism. It is difficult to judge which is the most despicable.

The question would have appeared nonsensical to working class Jews victimised by fascists in the 1930s. Morris Beckman was a young Jewish lad growing up in East London when the BUF were on the prowl:

I was born in Hackney, and attended Hackney Downs School during the Thirties. This, of course, was a part of London that was notorious as a battleground between anti-fascists and Mosley and his Blackshirts during that period. There were times when if I left my house and turned left I had to walk past a fascist meeting at the junction of Downs Park Road and Amhurst Road and if I turned right I had to pass another fascist meeting at the junction between Amhurst Road and

Sandringham Road. Anyway, the fascists were fairly rampant, they were well organised and, of course, their targets were the Jewish population. The Jews in those days were the only ethnic minority of note in this country. Mosley had copied Hitler's political platform and used the Jews as a scapegoat whereby he could blame them for all the ills of the country, the recession and so forth. They made life for the Jewish community in the East End of London very uncomfortable. There was very little that we could do about it really. There were three or four vigilante groups that I was aware of. I belonged to one myself. We called ourselves the Amhurst Road Vigilante Group. We were schoolboys basically and in all honesty we weren't very effective. We did occasionally ambush Blackshirts returning from their meetings after they'd had a few beers inside them and were singing their favourite English version of the Horst Wessel song. We had the odd success and although it didn't make much impact, it did make them more cautious and less arrogant.

Jewish refugees fleeing from vicious anti-Semitic pogroms across Eastern Europe formed the largest ethnic minority in the East End but the area had historically been the first port of call for waves of immigrants from all corners of the world. Huguenot, Chinese and Irish refugees, amongst many others, had settled in the East End in the past and all had, at various times, suffered some form of persecution. Jewish people were the main victims of Blackshirt aggression during the 1930s but they were not the only people to be subjected to racist and fascist hostility. Betty Davis recalls how growing up in a mixed family in the East End had its own perils:

Most of my childhood was spent in the East End. That's where I grew up. There was a lot of poverty in the area but there was also great friendship. The area where I lived was a predominately Jewish area where refugees had settled in the past but people of my age group were mainly first generation who were born here. My mother went missing shortly after I was born and my grandfather looked after us. His name was Ambrose Johnston, although he was known to nearly everyone as Snowy. He wasn't Jewish, he was a Muslim. He was born in Trinidad and came over on the White Star Line. He was stoking from the age of thirteen and then jumped ship in London when he was sixteen. You couldn't say that he was an illegal immigrant because, of course, Trinidad was British at the time. He met my grandmother who had run away from Devon. They got rooms together and they started from there. It was a very happy marriage.

The hatred against the Jews was very widespread at the time. Our family also got a lot of hatred, my grandfather especially but at the time there weren't many black people in England so we weren't as hated as the Jews. My grandfather didn't go out of the East End very often though. He didn't feel very safe out of it. I can remember my grandfather telling us children that there was more of a class difference than a race difference between people. He said that race was used to divide working people so that instead of looking for the real reasons for poverty, hunger, bad housing and evictions, we looked at each other. Therefore it was prejudice that didn't even know where its roots were that kept people fighting amongst themselves. I remember when Oswald Mosley and his Blackshirts used to march through the East End, threatening and attacking the people. Occasionally they added insult to injury by taking their jackets off and turning them inside out to show the pawnbrokers, singing "Abie, Abie, Abie, my boy" and stuff like that. It was quite dangerous there. You were always careful in case the Blackshirts were about. Again, they didn't really know why they hated everybody other than they were told to. Unfortunately, a lot of them were Irish, which always surprised me because I would have thought that they would have remembered the prejudice they had suffered in the past. They had their turn and believe me they still weren't properly accepted but they had this shirt which they wore as a uniform and I suppose they got a kick out of marching around looking tough, pretending they were accepted by society more than the rest of us were.

So that's where I came from and I also came from a strong trade union background where most of my grandfather's friends were dockers who fought very hard for people's rights. It was all mixed up together as part of the struggle.

In the middle years of the decade, the BUF had some difficulty maintaining its national profile. The hectic merry-go-round of big public meetings slowed down as the party was beset by financial problems and personal disputes. The reduction in high-level fascist activity meant the development of anti-fascist unity seemed less urgent. The Co-ordinating Committee for Anti-Fascist Activities lost its focus becoming almost moribund. But the daily grind of local confrontations, as described by Morris Beckman and Betty Davis, continued unabated. Alun Menai Williams, an unemployed miner from South Wales, who was living in London at the time, recalls his share of skirmishes:

During 1935, we were very busy, going on all sorts of activities and getting into confrontations with the police and the Blackshirts. My mate Billy and his band of communists, anarchists and other assorted hopefuls would heckle and disrupt Blackshirt meetings wherever they found them. Anywhere that Mosley or his henchmen went, we would go. Never mind working for a living, we were scrounging off the state and using our free time to enjoy ourselves and fight fascism. There was a crowd of maybe ten or twenty of us. We were a bunch of rabble-rousers and we would have a go at any Blackshirt we came across. Sometimes we'd attack them physically but most of the time we just tried to spoil their meetings.

'Andy' Andrews also clashed with Blackshirts at street corner meetings:

As communists we had quite a lot of scuffles with the Blackshirts. Whenever we heard about a fascist meeting, we made sure that we got enough people down there to stop it. There were only about a dozen of us in Kilburn but we had the support of local people, who joined up with us to stop the Blackshirts from meeting. The BUF tried to hold regular outdoor meetings in Kilburn with the speaker standing on a soapbox or a stall. We disrupted these meetings either by heckling the speaker or throwing stones and, of course, this often led to punch-ups. One occasion that sticks in my mind was on Kilburn High Road in 1935. The police, as usual, were on the side of the Blackshirts and after the first few scuffles, they pushed me into a shop doorway and gave me a good going over with their truncheons. They told me to go home or they would arrest me, but half an hour later I came back and spoke at a street meeting.

Street confrontations were routine and the BUF was able to muster their forces for big rallies, but less regularly. Anti-fascists turned up in large numbers to oppose them. On 14 April 1935, Mosley was constantly interrupted when he addressed a meeting in Granby Halls, Leicester. When he started to speak, a section of the audience stood up and walked out, loudly stamping their feet. One woman continuously barracked him and a chorus of chanting prevented everyone from hearing his answers to questions. Blackshirt stewards bussed in from London,

Birmingham and Nottingham fought the hecklers. Outside, an anti-fascist counter-demonstration was attacked by the police. Out of town Blackshirts were also present at a 3 November meeting at the Palace Cinema, South Shields. Thousands of local anti-fascists, both inside and outside the meeting, made their presence felt. When the Blackshirts stewards got on their buses to return to London, Leeds and Liverpool, they were subjected to barrages of stones and bricks.

But the BUF were not in retreat everywhere. During 1935, their numbers grew in London's East End. Membership in Bow, Shoreditch, Hackney and Bethnal Green began to pick up. Months of street campaigning and Jew-baiting were starting to pay off. In recognition of such success, Mosley made his first public appearance in the East End on 24 July. Two-dozen police were positioned inside Stratford Town Hall to stop the minor disturbances turning into mass disorder. Mounted police held angry crowds at bay outside.

Under the influence of William Joyce, the BUF was renamed The British Union of Fascists and National Socialists in early 1936, although, even in its own publicity, it was now simply referred to as the British Union (BU). Blackshirt propaganda became increasingly anti-Semitic and was targeted at those within both the working and lower middle classes who felt that the immigrant communities were threatening their interests. Leading BU speakers were drafted into the East End to stoke up the tension with hysterical rants against the Jewish community at street corner meetings. Never slow to miss a political opportunity, Arnold Leese and his Imperial Fascist League (IFL) joined in the bun-fight. Jewish cemeteries and synagogues were desecrated, anti-Semitic graffiti was widespread, windows were smashed, Jews and communists assaulted. As the ratchet was cranked up notch after notch, the vocal and physical spoiling of BU street corner meetings also intensified. Ubby Cowan and his comrades from Stepney CP were in the thick of it:

Mosley's men began to hold regular meetings on the fringes of Stepney. There was one at Duckett Street, another at the market on Watney Street, another at Whitehorse Lane and another at Essex Street, which is near Mile End Station. They were doing a lot of mixing and they built up quite a following. In Bethnal Green, they had a lot of support. We were doing a lot of fighting, week in, week out.

Barney Becow was back in police custody for fighting with Blackshirts. He was far from alone. The number of anti-fascists arrested far exceeded those of Blackshirts leading to frequent and not unfounded accusations of police bias.

Then, the BU announced another Albert Hall meeting for 22 March. Briefly reanimated, the Co-ordinating Committee for Anti-Fascist Activities called on all working class organisations to demonstrate outside. The Albert Hall, which had a history of allowing fascists to use it while denying the same facility to anti-fascists, was challenged by leading literary figures, including Aldous Huxley, H. G. Wells and Virginia Woolf. MPs asked questions in Parliament, but the booking went ahead. On the day, a few small groups of protestors snuck through the police cordon and infiltrated the meeting. Andy Andrews was amongst them:

Mosley hired the Albert Hall for one of his big meetings. In the weeks prior to this meeting, all the local groups of the Communist Party were asked to get hold of tickets and get into the hall, which we did. Once inside, we separated into small groups and spread out around the hall. We agreed beforehand that we would only make ourselves known on a given signal. Mosley was part way into his speech when we got the signal and started to throw our leaflets into the crowd. Well, we all had a pretty rough time of it. I was on the second floor balcony and after the leaflets had all fluttered down into the stalls, I was grabbed by a number of Blackshirt stewards and was thrown down two flights of stairs. I was punched and kicked a few times for good measure as well. As I was being manhandled out to the exit by these strong-arm guards, another steward who had just thrown somebody else out gave me a good smack on the jaw. I was then flung out the doorway, down the final few steps and onto the ground. There were a number of policemen on duty and they not only watched us being beaten up but one came over and joined in.

Meanwhile, the police set up a half-mile radius exclusion zone around the Albert Hall enabling them to divert a march of ten thousand anti-fascists. One half was directed towards Hyde Park while the other half made its way to Thurloe Square, which the Co-march organisers believed was just outside the zone. John Strachey stood on the roof of a van, denounced his former friend Mosley and authorities for their refusal to rent the hall to anti-fascists. He was followed by speakers R. McLennan of the NUWM, Ted Willis of the Labour League of Youth and Reverend Leonard Schiff. As Schiff spoke, mounted police charged into the demonstrators now tightly packed in the Square, indiscriminately attacking anti-fascists. Baton charges by foot police followed until the demonstration was cleared. The National Council of Civil Liberties (NCCL) held an inquiry into the events at Thurloe Square, which concluded:

That no warning was given by the police to the crowd to disperse, that the baton charge was carried out with a totally unnecessary degree of brutality and violence, that serious injuries were caused and that fatal injuries might have been caused.

Occasional large meetings and continuous street confrontations were also typical outside London. In Cheetham, Manchester, following two provocative Blackshirt public meetings in the area,

young Jewish anti-fascists ambushed BU members and halted a
tram in the middle of a crossroads to stop them leaving the area
unscathed. Fighting was always part of anti-fascism but never its
only strategy as Phil Kaiserman explained:

> Mosley held a couple of meetings in Cheetham Town Hall. We
> used to counter this by holding public meetings in Marshall
> Croft in Hightown, which was a big open space where you
> could set up a platform. We'd go around the area a couple of
> days beforehand chalking the pavements with "Anti-Fascist
> Meeting. Two o'clock Saturday. Marshall Croft." We'd always
> get a good crowd, especially when the Spanish Civil War was
> going on.

The fascists also tried their luck in Hulme, a tough working class
south Manchester area. Bernard McKenna recalls the strength of
opposition to a visit by Mosley on 28 June:

> I remember Mosley speaking at Hulme Town Hall. He was
> just about to start his meeting when thousands of anti-fascists
> turned up to stop him. The hall was completely surrounded.
> People were throwing bottles and stones and fireworks and
> there was a big fight outside the front of the hall, which went
> on for quite some time. Nearly ten thousand people came out
> to protest against the Blackshirts and Mosley had to be
> smuggled in and out the back door of the hall by the police or
> he would have been killed. As he tried to leave the hall, his
> car was attacked and people threw stones at him. The police
> had to charge into the crowd to rescue him. A section of the
> crowd followed Mosley to his local headquarters in
> Tomlinson Street and surrounded the building. People were
> throwing stones at the windows and the Blackshirt flag was
> torn down and set alight. I could see Mosley and his
> lieutenants scurrying around inside the house like trapped

rats and it looked like he was in very serious trouble, but the police arrived in the nick of time and managed to push everyone away.

In the evening fascists and anti-fascists clashed in the city centre. It took the police until the early hours of morning to restore order. Fearing a street war between the left and the right, Manchester's Council proscribed political uniforms and were the first local authority to do so. Uniform bans would have an important effect, but not yet. A BU meeting at the Albert Croft in Miles Platting was opposed by five thousand anti-fascists. A coalition of communists and socialists jumped the pitch and set up their own platform with loudspeakers. After their five-mile march from the city centre, the fascists were roundly booed as they entered Albert Croft. Missiles were thrown. Shouting down Mosley ended in scuffles. It was rainstorm that ended the fighting as the BU, 600 of them, returned toward the city and, according to *The Manchester Guardian* to towns 'such as Lytham, Leeds and Middlesborough.'

Confrontations between anti-fascists and the police were ever more commonplace. For example, just the Saturday before anti-fascists cooperated to spoil the BU's Miles Platting outing, a demonstration took place at London's Piccadilly Circus to raise awareness of the imprisonment of German communist Ernst Thaelmann with West End theatregoers. The forces of law and order failed to move on demonstrators as they kept separating and re-grouping to hold their ground. Confrontations between anti-fascists and fascists became more violent. In Hull on 12 July, the BU claimed a bullet was fired at Mosley's car. No bullet was found, no complaint made to the police, but a battle did take place at Corporation Fields. A large crowd had gathered and greeted Mosley with jeers and heckles. In the fighting that followed Blackshirts used steel-buckled belts as weapons and eight of them were hit on the head with bricks. The Chief

Constable told Mosley to abandon the meeting or the Riot Act would be read. The BU retreated and another rainstorm sent anti-fascists home or to hospital. Over hundred people required medical treatment.

Fascist activity in South Wales was concentrated in Cardiff, Newport and Swansea. When the BU made incursions into the mining valleys, they met organised resistance. The Rhondda was a communist stronghold. It was both political ideology and collective consciousness that made these communities enemies of fascism. Alun Menai Williams explains:

> I was very anti-fascist and anti-Mosley. I was a politically minded Rhondda boy, so what else could I be? I had been brought up with the belief that working people should stick together. Mosley was against all that. He wanted to be dictator and if the miners or anyone else got in his way he would crush them. I thought that fascism was an evil that had to be stamped out. In my opinion, anti-fascism was a cause worth fighting for.

Minor skirmishes with fascists had already occurred at Aberdare, Mardy and Ebbw Vale. Then at a meeting at Pontypridd Town Hall on 26 April local people decided that should never happen again. A conference attended by representatives from all ten Rhondda miners' lodges, the Communist Party, the NUWM, Pontypridd Trades and Labour Council and the Cambrian Combine Committee agreed to take mass action against fascist meetings.

On 11 June in Tonypandy, a crowd of 2,000 demonstrators were called out to oppose a Blackshirt rally at De Winton Field by anti-fascist haulier Owen Jones, who walked up and down the streets ringing a bell. Once the meeting opened, speaker Tommy Moran was drowned out by catcalls. Anti-fascists threw objects, seized Blackshirt leaflets and tore them up. Punches were thrown. The BU was escorted out of town under police protection never to return. Thirty-six anti-fascists were arrested and charged with offences including riot and incitement to riot. Seven received prison sentences ranging from two to twelve months. Nine were sentenced to twenty days hard labour and the others bound over or found not guilty. One of the defendants told the Pontypridd judge "The Fascists should be standing here on trial, not the workers." When sentenced, he shouted "Down with the Fascists."

The BU did establish one branch in Merthyr Tydfil when two local communists defected. Merthyr had been hit hard by industrial decline exacerbated by economic depression. Unemployment reached 61%. But even in these desperate conditions, the BU did not last long. CPers and NUWM activists took on those regarded as traitors with force. Heckling, missile throwing and fighting wrecked fascist meetings. In one instance, an air gun was fired. After one particularly volatile meeting at Dowlais Top, three fascists and the Chief Constable required hospital treatment. Blackshirts learnt to keep their heads below the parapet in Merthyr.

In September, BU members marched in Leeds. Their chosen route was through a Jewish neighbourhood to Holbeck Moor. The area was plastered with fascist graffiti and gummed labels. Children were handed anti-Semitic literature on their way home from school. The many objections to the march meant that it was redirected but anti-fascists still gathered in huge numbers, some 20,000, to meet Blackshirts on the Moor. They charged. One of the stones chucked at the fascists hit Mosley just under his eye. When the BU formed up to leave, they charged again. Hand-to-hand fighting was broken up by police but the fight wasn't over yet. The BU were ambushed by anti-fascists hiding behind advertising hoardings as they returned along Holbeck Lance. More stones and half-bricks injured forty fascists, one seriously.

Even the orderly displays of disapproval of fascism ended in violence. Mosley's address to the Carfax Assembly Rooms, Oxford, was punctuated by groups in the audience simultaneously opening and closing their newspapers and synchronising foot stamping. The infuriated leader ordered his stewards to start ejecting people. Anti-fascists supported by striking busmen, who were also in the meeting, retaliated by striking BU stewards with metal chairs. Mosley left by the back door and four of his Blackshirts via the hospital.

Anti-fascists had two tasks. One, to prevent the BU from gaining political legitimacy, halting their ability to organise as a political party and, two, to defeat them wherever they had managed to establish a political and organisational presence. Another way of saying this is that there were some sites, halls for rallies and fields or parks for open air meetings, which anti-fascists worked to ensure that fascists could never take over to make their own and there were permanent battlegrounds. In 1936, the most important of these was the East End. Fascist incursions into Jewish districts continued unabated throughout the summer and early autumn. The letters 'PJ' for Perish Judah appeared on walls all over the East End. BU loudspeaker vans made nightly tours of the area, blaring anti-Semitic messages into the homes of Jewish families. Gangs of youths regularly swept through the area chanting "The Yids, the Yids, we've gotta get rid of the Yids" whilst smashing shop windows and attacking individual Jews. Many young Jewish militants responded in kind, as a Metropolitan Police report from that period noted:

A car occupied by five Jews was stopped by City of London police and was found to contain a knuckleduster, seven catapults, part of a horseshoe, three broom handles, a bag of catapult ammunition, a piece of iron grating fixed to a wooden handle, a pair of pliers and three cartridges loaded with pellets.

Labour MP for Hackney, Mr Fred Watkins stated in a parliamentary debate on 10 July that he had "received many letters from Jewish people, young and old, who were being taken in to back streets and beaten." He read out one letter that described how eight or nine men assaulted a young man and his fiancée with iron bars wrapped with paper. Later, Watkins spoke alongside John Strachey and the Reverend Hugh Lister at a meeting at the Old Gravel Pit Hall in Valette Street convened by the Hackney Anti-Fascist Committee. The meeting noted that there were no fewer than five fascist headquarters in the immediate vicinity. An average of 130 political meetings a week were recorded by the police in the East End over August, September and October. They had attended or intervened in many. Fascists attacked anti-fascist meetings and vice versa. In October, 300 extra police a day were drafted in to deal with the high level of political confrontation.

An informal anti-fascist bloc had developed in the East End. It spanned the political spectrum from left to centre and included Jewish anti-fascist bodies. On the left of the bloc stood the CP, the YCL, the ILP, the NUWM, various trade union bodies, and the Labour League of Youth. The LLY continued to organise with the YCL despite the disapproval of its parent body. At its Manchester conference in April 1936 it agreed that 'the possibilities of war and Fascism looming ahead of the workers demand a united front of all working-class youth organisations.' The Green Shirts (renamed the Social Credit Party of Great Britain in 1935) were active in the East End. Anti-fascist demonstrations were seldom without a Green Shirt contingent of uniformed marching columns, flag bearers, and drum corps. Such a highly visible presence marked them out for retribution by fascist gangs. They had, over the previous two years, already experienced attacks. Two Greenshirts, caught chalking slogans on the walls of BUF headquarters in February 1934, were beaten up. A few months later, a vanload of twenty Blackshirts, invaded a Greenshirt meeting at Avenue Road, Lewisham. After a Shoreditch meeting, a female Green Shirt waiting for a bus home was battered by three Blackshirts. Her teeth were broken and she received a black eye. Smaller groups such as the British Union of Democrats, the British Democratic Association and the Legion of Democrats existed on the fringes of the East End anti-fascist bloc and made a more minor contribution. Nigel Copsey, in *Anti-Fascism in Britain*, suggests these groups merged to form the Federation of Democrats but even together they were numerically insignificant compared to the likes of the CP. One of the most curious of these smaller groups was the League of Blue and White Shirts, (also known as the Legion of Blue and White Shirts). Their uniform shirts carried a Union Jack and their publicity claimed that within the 'ranks' were 'all classes of people.' A 1936 pamphlet entitled *The Black Plague* declared:

> We will not tolerate mob rule in England, we will not stand for paid hirelings and thugs attempting to run this country. We will not allow any section of the community, Jew or Gentile, to be attacked by armies of unfortunate fools directed by lunatic-minded egomaniacs with their comic opera childish posturings and lying propaganda.

Two of the largest Jewish anti-fascist organisations active and influential in the East End were the Ex-Servicemen's Movement Against Fascism and the Jewish Peoples' Council Against Fascism and Anti-Semitism (JPC). Both formed in 1936. The Ex-Servicemen's Movement Against Fascism had a strong base of support amongst East End Jews, close relations with communists and was prepared to defend Jewish areas from fascist incursions, claiming to be able to mobilise 1,000 members at short notice. The Jewish Peoples' Council Against Fascism and Anti-Semitism (JPC) was formed at a conference at Asba House on 26 July as a criticism of and alternative to the Board of Deputies, the official leadership of the Jewish community, whom it regarded as being too passive in the face of BU aggression and unresponsive to the needs of working class Jews. The Board of Deputies had issued its public speakers with a series of Speakers' Notes during this period that rebutted specific allegations against Jews but singularly failed to address the issue of fascism. The 87 Jewish working class organisations present at Asba House noted that the Board of Deputies was only interested in fighting anti-Semitism and 'not the movement that propagated it, fascism.' They argued that the two could not be isolated because the fascists were using anti-Semitism to achieve power. In an open letter to the Board of Deputies, the JPC stated that separating anti-Semitism from fascism also separated Jews from potential allies:

> Jewry – itself united against Fascism and thus against anti-Semitism – must seek allies. Who are our possible allies? Only the democratic forces also threatened by Fascism. Can we say to them, "help us in our fight against anti-Semitism, but we will not fight with you against fascism"? Can we expect allies on such terms? Clearly the answer is "No."

On 1 May, at Victoria Park Square, Bethnal Green, Mosley addressed the first in a series of large public events in the East End. His tirade, from on top of a loudspeaker van in front of four or five hundred uniformed fascists, lasted over an hour. Three thousand anti-fascists jeered him throughout and, despite a large police presence, fights broke out. The following month, on 7 June, thousands of Blackshirts marched through the East End to Victoria Park. On the anniversary of Olympia, it was an open challenge to the forces of anti-fascism. Thousands of police from all over London were posted. Any trouble that small numbers of anti-fascists caused them was quickly stamped out.

The next month, on 12 July, a demonstration Against Fascism and War sponsored by the London Trades Council and the

Labour Party took place. Led by three Labour MPs and the Mayor of Poplar, it was a symbolic march rather than a reaction to a fascist event and was intended to steer anti-fascism away from violence and confrontation. Nevertheless, as it passed through Bethnal Green and neared the local BU headquarters in Green Street, Blackshirts on the roof showered the marchers with eggs, bags of flour and soot. Stones were added to the mix of missiles on 30 August when another anti-fascist demonstration, this time comprising ex-servicemen, communists, and Jewish groups, was also attacked. Sylvia Pankhurst and James Hall MP were injured. As the march entered Victoria Park, brawling began. Jeering Blackshirts rampaged up and down Green Street assaulting anyone they thought were Jewish. Two boys aged eight and nine were badly beaten and local YCL offices were broken into and wrecked.

Encouraged by such successes in the East End, Mosley announced a march to celebrate the fourth anniversary of the formation of his fascist movement. But the date, 4 October 1936, would become honoured not by fascists but anti-fascists. Lou Kenton helped gather the forces that fought in the Battle of Cable Street:

I was very well aware of what was going on before Cable Street because I was on the committee that helped organise it. You have to remember, though, that when people talk of the Battle of Cable Street, it was much more than that. Cable Street was just a part of it. When we first heard that Mosley was going to assemble fascists from all over the country in the City of London and march through the East End, there was a strong feeling amongst the people that he had to be stopped. Well the call-to-arms immediately swept the country and hundreds of meetings took place amongst Jewish organisations, political groups and trade union branches, particularly amongst the dockers and garment workers. It was quite amazing and went on for several weeks, although some organisations were opposed to it. The Jewish Board of Deputies took the view that Jews shouldn't mix in with the efforts to stop the fascists, and that they shouldn't make a fuss and should stay indoors. We took the opposite view. We said that we should all mix in and stop Mosley. Debates went on in the synagogues, clubs and, above all, the trade union branches. Fascist posters for the march were torn down or covered in chalk and whitewash. We had people going out every night covering the walls and streets with slogans saying "Bar the Road to Fascism" and "They Shall Not Pass." It was a great effort by all concerned.

A committee was set up by the London Trades Council to organise opposition to the march. I went onto the committee on behalf of the printers' union. I did a great deal of work for the committee during the weeks leading up to the march and, because I had a motorbike, they sent me to places like Dagenham, Hammersmith and Willesden in order to tell people what was going on and ask for their support. I remember two meetings in particular, Hammersmith and Dagenham, where I went along and introduced myself to the chairman of the Trades Council and when he stood up to introduce me, people said "We don't need to hear him speak, we already support them." What many people have forgotten about Cable Street is that during the run-up, the committee was informed by the Communist Party that they were unwilling to cancel a big rally that they had planned for the same day in Trafalgar Square. The civil war in Spain had just started and the rally was organised on behalf of the Spanish workers. There had already been many marches for Spain but this was meant to be an especially big march. We tried to tell the leadership of the Communist Party that you couldn't have the two things on the same day and there was great division for a week or two with lots of debates and arguments until finally the Trafalgar Square rally was called off.

There were also all sorts of discussions going on about how we were going to stop the Blackshirts marching through the East End. We decided that the main thing was to get a crowd of people to Aldgate Station. The committee gave the printers the job of being the first line of defence and all our members were told to go to Aldgate to try and hold up the Blackshirts until we had gathered our forces. We had no idea how many people were going to be there, five thousand, ten thousand, fifty thousand but, as it happened, when we arrived, there were crowds of people from Gardiner's Corner all the way past Aldgate Station and it was so packed that you couldn't move.

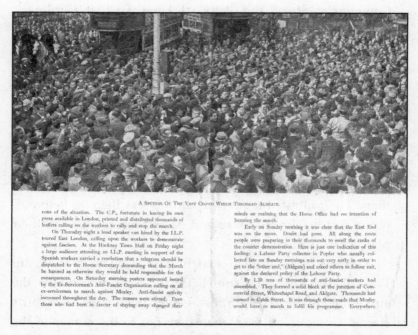

A SECTION OF THE VAST CROWD WHICH THRONGED ALDGATE.

cons of the situation. The C.P., fortunate in having its own press available in London, printed and distributed thousands of leaflets calling on the workers to rally and stop the march.

On Thursday night a loud speaker van hired by the I.L.P. toured East London, calling upon the workers to demonstrate against fascism. At the Hackney Town Hall on Friday night a large audience attending an I.L.P. meeting in support of the Spanish workers carried a resolution that a telegram should be dispatched to the Home Secretary demanding that the March be banned as otherwise they would be held responsible for the consequences. On Saturday morning posters appeared issued by the Ex-Servicemen's Anti-Fascist Organisation calling on all ex-servicemen to march against Mosley. Anti-fascist activity increased throughout the day. The masses were stirred. Even those who had been in favour of staying away changed their

minds on realising that the Home Office had no intention of banning the march.

Early on Sunday morning it was clear that the East End was on the move. Doubt had gone. All along the route people were preparing in their thousands to swell the ranks of the counter demonstration. Here is just one indication of this feeling: a Labour Party collector in Poplar who usually collected late on Sunday mornings was out very early in order to get to the "other end." (Aldgate) and asked others to follow suit, against the declared policy of the Labour Party.

By 1.30 tens of thousands of anti-fascist workers had assembled. They formed a solid block at the junction of Commercial Street, Whitechapel Road, and Aldgate. Thousands had massed in Cable Street. It was through these roads that Mosley would have to march to fulfil his programme. Everywhere

'A section of the vast crowd which thronged Aldgate', *They Did Not Pass*, Independent Labour Party, 1936.

It was impossible to form our line of defence with only

thirty people when there were thousands of people there already doing the same thing. In those days the trams used to finish at Aldgate, just past Gardiner's Corner, where they would turn around and go off again. Several trams got there and the crush was so great that the drivers abandoned them. People crowded around the trams and they became the centre-piece of the defence.

One of my jobs, because I had a motorbike, was to go around the periphery of the crowd and report what was happening to the committee. I went all around the outskirts, Commercial Street, Aldgate, Whitechapel, but even then it was difficult to get through the crowds. They were every-where. People were streaming down Whitechapel Road, Commercial Street and Petticoat Lane, so that Gardiner's Corner became one mass of people. Nobody knows how many people were there that day, maybe up to a quarter of a million. I soon discovered there were other people doing things that day that I shouldn't have really known about. We had one doctor who was member of the Communist Party, Doctor Faulkner, who dressed up smart and went to where the Blackshirts were assembling at the Minories. The Minories was the main thoroughfare between Aldgate and the City and the fascists were all lined up there, about three thousand of them. He infiltrated them and said he was there to help out, but in fact he slipped away and passed information on their plans to the committee.

Mosley's plan was to march past Aldgate Station, up Whitechapel Road and into Bethnal Green, which was the stronghold of the Blackshirt movement. Finally the Blackshirts started to move off, but when they got to the corner of the Minories, the police said "You can't march there, there's too many people, we're not equipped for a battle." In fact, the police had tried to shift the crowds at Gardiner's Corner, but there were so many people there that they had been forced back. So the police informed Mosley that he must find another route, and that was when he turned his attention to Cable Street. Well, Doctor Faulkner very sensibly managed to get word to headquarters of what the fascists were up to and I was immediately told to go around and tell people to go down to Cable Street, not everyone, but enough to help the people already down there.

I still have the vision in my mind of Aldgate as hundreds of people started leaving the area and running down Leman Street towards Cable Street. The area around Cable Street was a very working class area with lots of dockers and tailors and they said "They're not marching down our street." A call went up to the tenements and people were running up and down stairs, knocking on doors telling people "The fascists are coming." Well, when we got to Cable Street, we could see in the distance the fascists marching towards us, so we immediately started putting up the barricades. Anything that could be moved was used. Furniture, handcarts, mattresses, even a lorry was overturned, and quite a barricade was built up. Well, the fascists soon realised that they had no hope of getting through and so the police started trying to clear the way but they were met by fierce resistance and were eventually forced to admit defeat. By this time there were as many people at Cable Street as there was at Aldgate and all the way between the two points there were crowds of people moving backwards and forwards. The police had failed to shift the anti-fascists and it was clear that there was no hope of the Blackshirts reaching Bethnal Green. Eventually the police chief announced to Mosley that "You'll have to call this off, because I can't guarantee your safety" and he ordered them to march away from the East End, past the Tower, and into the City. They couldn't get to Cable Street, Aldgate, Stepney or Bethnal Green and that was a victory. The slogan adopted by the anti-fascists in Spain was "No Pasaran" which meant "They Shall Not Pass" and that was the cry taken up by the crowds at Cable Street. Many had never been out of the East End in their lives but in a lot of people's minds, the whole thing became linked with the war in Spain and the formation of the International Brigades. It was very encouraging.

Ubby Cowan also helped with the preparations for 4 October and played his part on the day:

After studying the situation, we realised that heads were going to be broken, because we'd been baton-charged by the police on demonstrations before. They didn't care who got in their way, they just charged in. So we knew we needed a first-aid area, we needed doctors and nurses and first aid kits. So we went around scrounging and speaking to people and we managed to get about fifteen first aid posts in Church Lane, which was about 150 yards behind Gardiner's Corner. We also got permission from the owners of the premises there to let us use their buildings for that purpose. We also knew from studying the map that there were two possible routes that Mosley could take. The most obvious route would take them past Gardiner's Corner but we were also aware that there was another route along Cable Street, which they could use. We started making preparations to block both routes and finding ways and means of disturbing the police in their efforts to force a way through for Mosley. Don't ask how, but we gathered together a large collection of boxes and bags of missiles, including a tremendous number of marbles. Half filled aerated bottles of Lemonade appeared, which when shook and thrown would explode because of the gas which is in the bottle. That was very good ammunition against the police and the police horses because a horse does not like loud bangs and broken ground. Broken glass cracking under their hooves is not very comfortable for them and quite a few mounted police fell over because of it. We were sorry about that but it was better than our heads being cracked open.

I was delegated to be in charge of the runners at Gardiner's Corner. We had runners all over the place because, of course, there were no mobile phones in those days. The runners were instructed to report back to headquarters in Church Lane every quarter of an hour or twenty minutes to keep them informed of events. I finished work that Sunday morning and walked the short distance from Coat Street to Gardiner's Corner. I arrived at about half past twelve and I was the only one there. Gardiner's was a big merchant navy haberdashery store. They sold everything that a bloke in the merchant navy might need, clothing, underwear, odds and ends. The shop windows were full of dummies wearing uniforms and all the rest of it. Now Gardiner's Corner is a very wide area with three main roads and two side roads all meeting at that spot. There were no traffic lights in those days, so the traffic was directed by policemen with white-half sleeves and gloves. On a Sunday morning there was very little traffic about so there were no policemen there at all that day. By one o'clock a few more people had turned up. My half a dozen runners had turned up and then, as the trams started pulling up, crowds would get off shouting "Down with Mosley." Then more people would get off the buses and slowly but surely the crowd built up. By about half past one, I looked down Whitechapel Road and I was amazed because I could not see the end of the crowd. It has been estimated that two hundred thousand people turned up at Aldgate. I didn't count them, of course, but there were massive numbers of people everywhere you looked.

I went back to my spot and sent back a message to say that everything was under control, when suddenly I heard the clip-clop of horses. I immediately realised what that meant and, when I looked down Aldgate High Street towards

Petticoat Lane, I could see a row of mounted police coming straight towards us. They were about fifty yards away from us, all with their batons drawn. Now a baton is made of a special hard wood and then covered in leather and if you got a wallop with that, you knew that you'd been walloped. So I saw them coming up Aldgate and then in my other ear I heard a similar sound coming from Leman Street. I looked down there and saw another load of mounted police who were galloping up Leman Street. They were wall-to-wall so whoever was in front of them was mown down, no question about it.

In front of me were about six rows of people and, when the police appeared, they all pushed back and I went straight through Gardiner's shop window. Crash. I landed in amongst all these dummies and clothing and all the rest of it. Blood was streaming down my face, blood was on my knuckles where I'd hit the glass. Somehow or another, someone dragged me out the showroom. Don't ask me how. They took me round the corner to one of the first aid posts in Church Lane where they cleaned up my wounds and stuck some plasters and bandages on me. They gave me a cup of tea and I sat there for a little while and watched as more and more people were brought in with injuries because behind the mounted police came the foot police, also with their truncheons drawn. You could hear the screaming and the shouting and the yelling, but the crowd were not withdrawing. They stood where they were and met the police as they came straight at them. People were telling me that the police were falling off their horses and I could hear the bottles exploding and the sound of crashing all over the show.

After about twenty minutes I felt a lot better. The shock had worn off and with a bandaged head, I reported to headquarters. Reports were coming in of all the fighting that was going on and then came a report that Mosley had arrived at the Minories and that the fascists were lined up in their uniforms and he was marching around inspecting his troops like an army general. The next report said that the Blackshirts were ready to march but were waiting for the police to clear a path along Cable Street for them. Now because we'd suspected that the police might try to use this route as a secondary means of getting Mosley to his destination, we went round there the week beforehand to see what was cooking. We found a very convenient builder's yard on the corner of Christian Street and, on several evenings leading up to October 4, the dockers came along and dumped little parcels there. It was agreed beforehand that the dockers would be responsible for preparing barricades in Cable Street should they be required. We sent a team with the dockers so that it was all organised.

When the police started to move towards Cable Street, one runner ran ahead to warn them while another came to tell us. When we heard what was happening, we made a dash for Cable Street and, when we got nearer, we could hear the sound of shouting and smashing and Lemonade bottles exploding. The barricades were up. They were quite high and the police were trying to climb over them but couldn't, because people on the roofs were throwing bricks and water and goodness knows what else at them. We all started throwing whatever rubbish we could find and after about three-quarters of an hour someone on the roof shouted "They're leaving." We said "Who's leaving?" and they said "The coppers." So we climbed up the back of the barricade and the street ahead of us was littered with broken bottles and stones and all the rest of it but we could just see the back of the police horses as they were turning the corner.

About five minutes later, another messenger appeared and told us that the police had withdrawn from Gardiner's Corner and Leman Street and we were all asked to go to Osborn

Street where a mass meeting would be taking place. When we got there it was the end of the meeting but we heard one speaker on top of a loudspeaker van announce "The police have authorised a march today, so we're going to march to Bethnal Green instead of Mosley." There was a lot of cheering and as the march formed up we all joined it. As we marched down Whitechapel Road, everybody was cheering us. Well, in fact, they were cheering themselves because they were all there as well. The van drove in front of everybody and it had a red flag on each side of it and it was playing very loud music. As we reached the corner of Green Street, there was a crowd waiting for Mosley but as soon as they heard the music and saw the red flags, they realised it wasn't their darling and they all disappeared. When we got to Victoria Park Square, a speaker got on the platform and said "The government have officially announced that a public meeting can take place here, and we just want everyone to know that a meeting has taken place here. Not Mosley's, but the people of Stepney's." With that everyone cheered, and the crowd dispersed.

Alun Menai Williams was also at Cable Street. His experience typifies that of thousands of anti-fascists:

We'd heard that Mosley and his Blackshirts were intending to march through the Jewish quarter of the East End the following Sunday and there was a big campaign throughout the week for people to go down there and try and stop them. On Sunday morning, my brother Glyn and I joined up with other groups of anti-fascists outside the Tower of London and, with our flags and banners, we made our way to Gardiner's Corner. I remember that huge numbers had turned up to stop Mosley, thousands upon thousands of people. We spent most of the day as part of a huge crowd being pushed this way and that as it surged backwards and forwards. Not long after we arrived, the pushing and shoving became more violent as policemen used their truncheons to try and force a route through the demonstrators on behalf of the Blackshirts, but the numbers were so great that they couldn't manage it. The police were lashing out at anyone unfortunate enough to find themselves at the front of the demonstration and many people were injured. At one point I found myself at the front with my gang of friends. A few of them had marbles, which they threw on the ground as the police horses charged at the crowd. I was knocked down and injured by a policeman on a horse and was only saved from being more seriously injured by Glyn and my other friends dragging me out of harm's way. Most of the fighting on the day was between the anti-fascists and the police and there were nearly a hundred arrests with an equal number injured. Despite their best efforts however, the police couldn't force a way through for the fascists and it was a serious setback for Mosley and his Blackshirts.

That the Cable Street arrests would include Barney Becow was a safe bet. The police did not miss an opportunity. A spotter reported:

> Marks Barnett Becow, one of the most violent communists in London, was seen at the point where a lorry containing bricks had been placed as a barrier across the road and overturned, the bricks being used as missiles.

Becow was later sentenced to three months imprisonment for assaulting a police officer. The Magistrate who sent him down described him as 'a man trading in violence.'

Betty Davis, just a child at the time, recollects her fears for her family during the physical confrontation on Cable Street and the shared joy when it was over:

I can remember the Battle of Cable Street, because we lived in Cable Street. The fascists said they were going to march through the East End with their insults, like they always did. They always made for areas where they weren't welcome and then, of course, it was you that caused the trouble, not them. However, on this particular occasion, all the people came together and said it wasn't going to happen. Everybody joined together. Gardiner's Corner was blocked off with a tram and there was a barricade in Cable Street. Barrow boys used their barrows to block the way. People were even throwing piddle pots out the windows. The main thing I can remember, because I was only nine at the time, was all the people fighting with the police. Because, of course, the police came in first and tried to clear the way for the Blackshirts. I can remember my grandfather fighting the police and I was very frightened because I thought he would get arrested because being black he would stand out.

In the end of course it was a great victory and everybody was so thrilled. The adults and the kids. We were all so pleased that the fascists didn't get through. The Blackshirt march was turned back and re-routed and actually it was nothing because they hadn't got through the area they had wanted to go through. So if you all stick together you can win.

One week after 4 October, 5,000 anti-fascists celebrated with their own march, which gathered more and more numbers as it wound its way from Tower Hill to Victoria Park. With police attention, as ever, directed towards the anti-fascists, the Mile End Pogrom took place. A hundred youths ran the length of the road assaulting individual Jews and smashing the windows of Jewish-owned businesses. A car was set alight. A man and a seven-year-old girl thrown through a shop window.

A matter of days later, on 14 October, Mosley held forth at a Victoria Park Square meeting, then led 400 Blackshirts to Salmon

Lane, Limehouse, where he spoke again. Ubby Cowan recalls a rumour that went around:

> One story we heard about this march afterwards is that as the Blackshirts were walking along, one of them picked up a stone to throw it through the shop window of a Jewish firm. One of his mates stopped him and said "Don't throw that, I work there, and the guv'nor will be very angry on Monday morning if you do." So that's the sort of person who supported Mosley.

Special Branch reports stated that Mosley was 'enthusiastically received' by a crowd of 12,000 at Victoria Park Square. NCCL representatives Sylvia Scaffardi and Ronald Kidd attended and offered a different interpretation:

> In the meeting that followed at Salmon Lane, Ronald's notes show how disciplined was the 'enthusiasm.' As Mosley was expanding on friendship with Italy and Germany, a man ventured to ask, 'Doesn't Italy want to dominate the Mediterranean?' He was promptly warned by PC N221 to be quiet. He tried again soon after. 'Well Germany wants our colonies...' and was seized by PCs N221 and M507 and ejected from the meeting.

Kidd also records that a mob of Blackshirts stormed the offices of the League of Blue and White Shirts following yet another Mosley meeting in the East End. The secretary had requested police police protection to no avail. Furniture was damaged, windows broken, League members hurt.

Over the years, there have been attempts to downplay the significance of the Battle of Cable Street. Some have identified that BU membership in the East End actually increased after 4 October. Others have pointed to the fact that Mosley marched in the East End without opposition just over a week later and it has been noted that attacks on Jews and Jewish properties increased in intensity and savagery over the following months. All this is true, but what is equally true is that the fascists suffered an immense psychological blow in the one and only area of the country that they could regard as a stronghold. The vast majority of BU resources had been concentrated in the East End over the previous year and more than half its membership lived in the area. It is an undeniable fact that parts of the East End were Blackshirt strongholds, yet they had been prevented from marching through them by thousands upon thousands of ordinary working people proclaiming that they should not pass.

Oswald Mosley could sneak around the edges of the East End at the head of unpublicised marches all he wanted, but everyone now knew that these were not the actions of a man on the verge of taking power. The day-to-day persecution of the Jewish people continued unabated, even heightened for a time, but there was a perceptible feeling in the air that the fascists could not gain the upper hand. Lou Kenton comments:

> Mosley was finished in the East End after Cable Street. You could see the change in the ordinary people going about their day-to-day business. People were no longer scared of the Blackshirts. They were still wary of course, but they weren't terrified anymore. Fear had allowed fascism to grow in the East End but once everyone had seen the Blackshirts beaten and humiliated, the fear disappeared. It was still dangerous to be a Jew on your own in some areas, but there was no longer this awful fear of what the future might bring.

What must have burnt deep into the fascist psyche was the realisation that they had been stopped in their tracks by local people, workers and Jews, acting together and in open defiance of recommendations from the leaders of the labour movement and the

Board of Deputies who told them to stay away. Local people led the struggle. It was East End communists, like Lou Kenton, that compelled the party leadership to alter its plans and fall in to support the alliance against Mosley. Indeed, it was the Ex-Servicemen's Movement and the JPC, in conjunction with the ILP and dissident communists, that carried out most of the early work of building the anti-fascist mobilisation on 4 October. They produced and distributed thousands of leaflets, posters and handbills, whitewashed pavements and walls, organised numerous meetings and rallies. The JPC mounted a petition demanding the banning of the BU march that collected 77,000 signatures in 48 hours. On the eve of the march, at a massive ILP gathering in Hackney Town Hall, Fenner Brockway called for an overwhelming demonstration against Mosley. Thanks to the work of dedicated East End anti-fascists, that's exactly what he got. Above all else, Cable Street was a statement of intent. People would not stand idly by and let the Blackshirts bully their way to power. Mosley and his henchmen must have sensed at that moment that they were not longer pushing at an open door.

The day after Cable Street, Mosley flew to Berlin to get married in secret to Diana Guinness. The wedding was held in the ministerial home of Dr Josef Goebbels, attended by Adolf Hitler. The Nazi leader brought flowers and a present. The following week saw Mosley arrive in Liverpool to scenes of extraordinary violence. The BU were assembling outside the Adelphi Hotel, near Lime Street Station, ready to march to the city's boxing stadium, when they were suddenly surrounded by hundreds of chanting anti-fascists. This bold move was planned by the Liverpool Anti-Fascist Committee, a body of activists from the CP, the ILP, the NUWM and the Trades Council. Mosley, who obviously knew how to show a girl a good time on her honeymoon, was due to take the fascist salute at Lime Street then lead the Blackshirt column to the stadium. The appearance of chanting anti-fascists made this impossible. The police tried, unsuccessfully, to clear them away. Then, mounted officers were sent in. The Blackshirts were able to form up. However, the police neglected to remove an elderly down-and-out slumbering on a bench. When the coast was clear, he suddenly sprang into action and launched at Mosley. The tramp was Jack Coward, a prominent local communist. The police dragged him off but informed Mosley that, for his own safety, he should travel by car. Under heavy police protection, a 300 strong group of Blackshirts, minus their exalted leader, began the long march to the stadium. Immediately, they were faced with an angry crowd of thousands of anti-fascists. The battle began. Mounted police were sent in again and again amidst chaotic and bloody scenes. A constant hail of bricks rained down on the Blackshirts. There were further attempts to break into the march at St John's Lane, Whitechapel and Exchange St. East. Reports also indicate that the march was re-routed to avoid more anti-fascists at Liverpool's Cenotaph.

Anti-fascists, again in large numbers, had gathered at the stadium to await the delayed arrival of Mosley. His car was immediately rushed. The police, with some brutality, forced a passage through the surging crowd. Anti-fascists fought the police but were pushed back. Inside the stadium, some 2,500 BU sympathisers heard Mosley speak to the heckles of a few remaining protestors. Over the day, twelve anti-fascists were arrested. Two were jailed for two months, the others fined.

The new year brought new developments from within and without the anti-fascist movement, which were, one way or another, consequences of Cable Street. In January 1937, the Socialist League offered the Communist Party the prospect of a long awaited breakthrough in its quest for a united front with the labour movement. It was a mark of the success of communist commitment to anti-fascism just as it started to change tack. The CP leadership had only agreed to call out its membership to the East End on 4 October once it realised staying away risked their political credibility in working class London. The Socialist

League initiative had its own logic. The League had become increasingly autonomous under the leadership of Sir Stafford Cripps. In open defiance of Labour Party policy, it produced its own propaganda, including a pamphlet entitled *Fascism! The Socialist Answer*, by J.T. Murphy, that declared 'A Socialist and working-class movement fighting relentlessly for Socialism and in that fight combating the day to day attacks of Capitalism is the *only way* to meet and defeat Fascism and War.' To this end, the League issued a 'Unity Manifesto' in conjunction with the CP and ILP. The Labour Party leadership immediately threatened to disaffiliate those involved. Facing expulsion, the League dissolved itself in May 1937. A communist and left socialist alliance comprised of the CP, ILP and members of the Labour Party would have been interesting, to say the least, and the plots to undermine it probably all too predictable. Anti-fascists would have to look forward to many more years of creating combined organisations, some that worked and others that never left the drawing board, as well as constantly building and re-building alliances between organisations. Their work was set to continue in the face of enhanced police powers to intervene in street confrontations.

The Public Order Act (POA) came into effect in January 1937. It would have a lasting effect upon anti-fascist, and many other, struggles. The POA gave police authority to re-route marches and ban them altogether in a given area for a period of up to three months. It made an offence of the use threatening, abusive or insulting words or behaviour in a public place. It also prohibited the wearing of political uniforms. This, according to Ubby Cowan, brought about the demise of the BU. Cable Street played its part but, for him, it was the reaction of Parliament that was decisive:

Cable Street made a difference, because it shook up the government. They thought they could use the police to push people about and they were shocked when the people stood up for themselves and forced the police to back down. After that, they did the only thing they could do and blamed Mosley for the whole thing. They punished the Blackshirts by banning political uniforms, and that made all the difference to the way the fascists were viewed. Mosley had a big following because he was paying people to be his stooges. He fitted them out in uniforms and you know how the British love a uniform. You only have to look at a traffic warden today. All he's got is a peak cap but he thinks he's the boss. The banning of political uniforms was the start of the downfall of Mosley because without the uniforms they looked like what they were. A scruffy, unemployed rabble, who were unfortunately suffering the same as us.

Legislation banning the wearing of political uniforms had an adverse effect on the BU, but it was far more damaging to groups like the Green Shirts and the League of Blue and White Shirts. Both disappeared from public view. The POA was aimed as much against anti-fascists as fascists, if not more so. It was punishment for the disorder at Cable Street. Its powers have been invoked against the forces of the left far more frequently than those of the right. From government's viewpoint, the Blackshirts were only a danger because of the unifying effect they had on their opponents rather than any threat they posed themselves. They were able to organise pretty much where they pleased, say what they liked, as long as no hornet's nest of angry anti-fascists was stirred up enough to openly defy the forces of the state in order to stop them.

By the summer of 1937, there were signs of the uneven effects of the POA, its use and circumvention. A proposed 4 July BU march from Limehouse through the East End to Trafalgar Square was re-routed. The Home Office invoked the POA's Clause 3 to prohibit parades of a political nature in the area for six weeks. The march would now start at Kentish Town. The Labour Party,

Co-operative Society and trade unions in the St Pancras area registered their opposition and 500 marched on the Town Hall to demand that re-routed march be banned. Their bid failed. This was the Labour Party's cue to withdraw from anti-fascist mobilisation. The CP was left to mount opposition alone. There were tussles at Kentish Town and no one heard Mosley over the cries of 5,000 anti-fascists in Trafalgar Square but, for the fascists, it was a victory that their march had not been physically prevented from reaching its destination. When the rally was over, a few anti-fascists tried to get at Mosley as his car drove away under Charing Cross Bridge.

The absence of major disorder on BU's July march made the POA appear to be working well, but undeterred opposition to another re-routed march of 3 October suggested otherwise. As the BU no doubt anticipated, their initial East End route was prohibited under the POA, and an alternative one from Westminster to Bermondsey accepted. Bermondsey's Mayor, its Labour MPs and religious leaders protested but did not sway the Home Office. It did not want to invoke the POA a second time and insisted a fascist march did not constitute incitement to violence in the Borough because too few Jews lived there. Once a ban was refused, Labour leaders, in line with the policy applied at St Pancras, urged a boycott of any counter-demonstration. Bermondsey was a Labour stronghold with ties between its large Irish-Catholic community, whose livelihood was bound to the docks and its trade unions. Nevertheless, the intended fascist incursion provoked an anger that was not contained by an official party line. Bermondsey and Rotherhithe Trades Council in co-operation with the CP and the ILP made the call for mass opposition to Mosley.

The day before the march, anti-fascists and fascists scrapped on the streets of Bermondsey as BU paper-sellers arrived to ply their wares. One fight is described in *Bermondsey Says No to Fascism,* issued by Bermondsey and Rotherhithe Trades Council:

In the evening an incident reveals the white heat of Bermondsey's rage. Two Fascists stand in St. George's Square selling their paper and shouting provocative slogans. Nearby a dance organised by the Bermondsey Youth is in progress. Word reaches them that the Fascists are outside. As one man they stream out of the hall, surround the Fascists and in a second send them packing.

On the day, as the BU mustered in Westminster, the anti-fascists were standing their ground south of the River Thames. A six year-old Monty Goldman watched the fascists, now in their civvies, cross the water:

In 1937, my father went on another demonstration against Mosley in Bermondsey. I was with my mother and we saw Mosley's fascists march across Westminster Bridge. The thing that sticks in my mind, even though it's seventy years ago, is of my mother saying "Look. There's the lady who lives in the same block as us in Flower and Dean Street." She was marching with the fascists. She was forced to move out a week later because, in the heart of the East End where most of the working class people were anti-fascist, she wasn't welcome. Her name was O'Leary and people were always a bit curious about her. She didn't have any children and, when people asked her where she worked, she always said that she worked in the Civil Service. It turned out she worked for the police, as a cleaner. My father came home from Bermondsey that evening and told us the story of how the fascists had been prevented from marching in Bermondsey. He told us about the vicious fighting in Jamaica Road and Long Lane, and how the police had tried to force a way through for Mosley, but had been stopped by thousands of working class people. Once more the fascists couldn't get through, and they had been forced to turn back. Again it was the Communist Party in

London who called on the working class to resist fascism.

The number that gathered in the area around Borough tube station varies wildly from 12,000 to 150,000. But whatever the true figure, those people put up one of the fiercest fights between anti-fascists and the police. It was at its most intense along Long Lane. Barricades were rapidly erected. Police charged with batons to clear the way. They kept charging, but the anti-fascists refused to yield. Len Shipton, 17 years old, spent the day on the streets:

I come from a solid working class, Labour-voting family in Rotherhithe but when I heard that the Labour Party wanted people to ignore the Mosley march, I thought they were bloody crackers. I wasn't heavily involved in politics like some were but I had an interest and I knew that fascism had to be challenged. Everyone in Rotherhithe was talking about it. You couldn't set foot outside your front door without someone asking whether you were going or not. A lot of the youngsters in my street were very keen on having a go at Mosley. I think it was a case of "We'll sort the bloody fascists out first, and worry about the Labour Party later."

On Sunday morning, a group of us headed over to Bermondsey along with lots of other people all going in the same direction. We'd heard that the anti-fascists were meeting at Borough station but when we got there the roads were completely blocked by thousands upon thousands of people. At first there wasn't much going on and we just sort of hung around waiting to see what would happen but after a while there was a bit of a commotion and the police started trying to clear a way through. There was a bit of resistance from the anti-fascists, and then all hell broke loose as the coppers charged in with their truncheons and horses. We were pushed up Long Lane, which was already full of people, and I noticed that a barricade had been built. It was made up of bits of furniture, barrows and planks of wood, that sort of thing, but what has always stuck in my mind was this bloke standing on top of the barricade waving a red flag. Well, it was like a red rag to a bull. About a hundred coppers charged at the barricade. I don't know what happened to the bloke with the flag but he disappeared pretty sharpish. After a long struggle, the police managed to pull the barricade down and started lashing out at anyone they could reach. It didn't matter if you were guilty of anything or not, if you got in the way you got belted. Another barricade had been built further up the road and the police immediately went for that but no sooner had they pulled it down than another one went up. This seemed to go on for ages and still the police couldn't clear a way through. There were masses of people moving about in all directions. Most were just sort of milling around, making sure the road was never completely cleared. The coppers were trying to push the crowds away but they kept disappearing down side streets and reappearing behind the police lines again. After a few hours of this, people started shouting that we should head for Tooley Street. I'd lost all of my mates by his time except for a lad called Frank Bryce. He reckoned that the police had given up trying to clear Long Lane as a bad job and were diverting Mosley along another route. We decided to follow the crowds and, as we neared Tooley Street, I could hear lots of shouting and screaming and fireworks going off. There was obviously a bit of a tear up with the fascists but I never got near enough to see what happened. I heard afterwards that someone had driven a car into the march and that a few of them had been knocked over but I never actually saw it happen. A big crowd of us got trapped in a narrow street and there was a lot of pushing and shoving. It was starting to get dark by this time and this seemed to be the signal for the police to start lashing out with their truncheons. There was a bit of fighting and I was caught up in the middle of it when I got hit on the head by a truncheon. I was quite badly dazed and remember staggering about in a right old state until a couple of blokes dragged me over to a doorway and tried to look after me. I don't remember much about what happened next but apparently Frank found me and took me home. I was

'All Roads Lead', *Bermondsey Says 'No' to Fascism*, Bermondsey Trades Council, 1937.

in a right old state, blood all over my clothes and as white as a sheet. It frightened my old mum half to death. Thankfully, there was no permanent damage to the old brainbox but it hurt like hell for a few days afterwards.

When the police realised that Long Lane could not be taken for the fascist march, they diverted it and the BU were cordoned off to endure the jeers of a jubilant Bermondsey. Mosley's original rally point in West Lane had already been jumped by Sally Schwartz and Tim Walsh of the Federation of Democrats. Walsh was a former leading light in the New World Fellowship and Schwartz active in the British Union of Democrats. They hosted a local talent show to entertain a crowd. It swelled, as the day wore on, with victorious anti-fascists who listened to local dignitaries. The injured and arrested did not all get to hear the speeches but, by all accounts, were proud of their actions. The magistrate who dealt with the arrested, of which there were 111, whined 'Not one of you has said, "I am sorry to have behaved in this disorderly fashion." You are not sorry. You came for the distinct purpose of creating disorder and you must pay for it.'

A week after the BU in retreat in Bermondsey, Mosley repeated his mistake of the previous year. He tried his hand in Liverpool after defeat in London. The anti-fascists had their tails up. Liverpool League Against Fascism had taken over the BU's pitch, a plot of vacant land near Queens Drive in Walton. By the time the fascists had arrived with their armoured loudspeaker van, 10,000 anti-fascists were there to meet them. The opening BU speaker climbed on top of the van and was hit by a stone. When Mosley followed for the ritual of the fascist salute, he was felled by a brick. He regained his balance to be struck by another and was knocked unconscious. Anti-fascists rushed towards the van and tried to turn it over. The BU ran for cover in the yard of a nearby warehouse. Mounted police were used to restore order. Local communist, Leo McGree, told the victory rally in Islington "they had shown Mosley and his Fascists that the working class of Liverpool would not tolerate him and his organisation in this city."

The BU also faced financial crisis. Mussolini decided he was backing a loser and pulled the plug on secret funding from Italy. Mosley appealed to the Nazis for money and, according to the diary of Dr Goebbels, at least one very large payment was made. It was evidently not enough. Salaried staff were taken off the BU payroll. John Beckett and William Joyce left and set up the short-lived National Socialist League. Although that organisation did not last long, Joyce's career as a Nazi propagandist had barely begun. He is best known for his wartime Germany Calling broadcasts and his nickname, Lord Haw Haw.

By 1937, if not before, the CP's anti-fascist efforts were subsumed by its support for the Aid Spain movement and the International Brigades. The problem of British fascism seemed less pressing and the question of how to fight it was a source of some division. Communists debated the appropriate tactics and effective strategies against fascism and, in particular, the necessity of physical resistance. It was a discussion that would continue within every anti-fascist body over the rest of the twentieth century and beyond. The CP leadership considered that the willingness of communists to use force against Blackshirt aggression had a deleterious effect on their relationship with the wider labour movement. Their reservations hardened into a resolve to curtail the activities of communists committed to the physical fight against fascism. These street fighting communists were often the same people who had helped build local anti-fascist blocs and acted rather autonomously from the party as they did so.

In Stepney, the debate was fiercely contested. Local branch secretary, Joe Jacobs, was one of those who had helped persuade the CP leadership to cancel their 4 October Trafalgar Square rally for Spain and swing behind the East End mobilisation against

Mosley. His commitment had inspired others and helped the anti-fascist movement grow in numbers and confidence. Jacobs insisted that physical confrontations with the BU were a matter of necessity. Fascist incursions into the local community had to be curbed somehow. Phil Piratin made a case against Jacobs and what he regarded as a 'bash the fascists whenever you see them' approach. He argued for door-to-door campaigning that would undercut the fascist base. He urged party members to participate in local housing disputes and support rent strikes against slum landlords. They had real successes. Piratin, who was elected as a councillor and later as an MP, gives an example in his book, *Our Flag Stays Red*. Two families from Paragon Mansions tore up their BU membership cards after the CP intervened over housing on their behalf. Campaigns against landlord exploitation and poor living conditions spread from Stepney and into fascist territory in Bethnal Green. However, according to Albert Meltzer, in *The Anarchists in London 1935 –1955*, the housing struggle in Bethnal Green was initiated by anarchists and supported by ILP. Communists took over, pushed them to the margins, snatched the political success only for themselves. Meltzer makes a convincing case but the greater resources, larger membership and party organisation of the communists certainly sustained the housing campaign. By the summer of 1938, the Jacobs-Piratin debate was over. The CP leadership suspended Jacobs. Piratin's dedicated work against slum conditions in the East End had won him much deserved support. Whether Piratin could have conducted a doorstep campaign had it not been for the likes of Jacobs, who had battled with the BU on the same streets and cleared his way, so to speak, is a moot point.

The CP withdrawal from the fray might have come as something of a relief to the comrades and relatives of Barney Becow, who had somehow contrived to get himself arrested three times for anti-fascist activities in the month of June 1938 alone. The JPC, with the smaller groups such as the Federation of

Democrats, continued the fight but without the numbers the CP could bring out counter demonstrations to large BU set pieces suffered badly. In May 1938, Mosley led a 2,000 strong march through Bermondsey virtually unopposed. On 16 July 1939, he advocated peace with Germany in front of an audience of 11,000 at Earl's Court. There was no organised opposition. In the absence of confrontation, BU membership in and around London began to pick up. It was not the same story outside the capital, especially where a communist presence had been less significant in anti-fascist organising and thus its absence not so badly felt. For example, in Portsmouth in March 1938, as 5,000 protested outside a BU meeting in the Coliseum, some launched themselves at Mosley's car. In September, Aberdeen BU organiser, William Chambers-Hunter, was inside his car when it was overturned by anti-fascists on South Esplanade East in Torry. The next week, on the same spot, he stood on a lorry. It was parked beside a coal yard, which was an oversight. The fascists were showered with lumps of coal. Chambers-Hunter's microphone got stolen and fireworks were thrown into the cab of the lorry. He resigned six months later. However, the effect of the re-orientation of communist anti-fascism upon the poorest of the working class wherever they happened to live was noticed by the NUWM. Wal Hannington warned of BU recruitment amongst the jobless in *Fascist Danger and the Unemployed* and even reported fascist activity in Merthyr, where a BU branch was ousted 1936. But, by the time the pamphlet was published in June 1939, it was nearly all over for those who had been Blackshirts.

The imminence of war with a Nazi power heightened opposition to the BU over the summer of 1939. In August, a platform at the dockyard gates in Portsmouth was smashed up and BU speakers and supporters beaten. Hostility intensified when war was declared in September. BU offices in London were wrecked. In November in Wilmslow, Manchester, two double-decker buses carrying BU members were stoned. On the other side on Manchester in May 1940, Mosley was assaulted when he spoke in support of a Middleton and Prestwich by-election candidate. Several thousand people followed him back to the local BU headquarters and smashed every window in the building. Such opposition was not entirely anti-fascist. Those who had fought against the right-wing reactionary politics, nationalism and anti-Semitism of fascism from the mid-1930s may well have taken part in the wave of war-time protests but many others opposed not the fascism of the BU only its allegiance to Germany.

On 23 May 1940, Mosley was interned under Defence Regulation 18B. His wife was detained a month later. Around a thousand, including most of the BU leadership and membership as well as high profile members of other fascist parties, notably John Beckett and Arnold Leese, were held under the same regulation. It empowered the 'Secretary of State' to detain anyone he had 'reasonable cause to believe' were members of an organisation 'subject to foreign influence or control' or that had 'associations with persons concerned in the government of, or sympathies with the system of government of, any Power with which His Majesty is at war.' State opposition to fascism was based on its political allegiance rather than its political content.

3

Hold Madrid for we are coming:
1936 – 1939

In February 1936, a Popular Front coalition of socialists, left-wing republicans, Catalan nationalists and communists won the Spanish elections, narrowly defeating a right-wing bloc of catholics, monarchists and fascists. The result sent shock waves through the conservative and catholic ruling classes who wasted no time gathering support for a military coup. On July 17 1936, parts of the army and the security forces under the leadership of General Emilio Mola and General Francisco Franco, along with right-wing groups such as the Carlists and the fascist Falange, attempted to seize control of the country. The coup was only partially successful. The navy did not rise against the Republic and militias of workers, armed and unarmed, successfully resisted the uprising in several major cities and provinces. Just over a third of Spain was in anti-republican nationalist hands. General Franco conscripted the 'Army of Africa' stranded in Morocco and recruited elite Foreign Legionaries. He appealed to Mussolini and Hitler for military aid. Within six days, German planes were airlifting troops from Morocco into southern Spain. Arms and ammunition from Germany and Italy began to pour into right-wing nationalist controlled areas.

In August 1936, Britain and France formed the Non-Intervention Committee, which included both Germany and Italy but not Spain. The Committee's purported aim was to ensure that the war in Spain was fought without foreign influence and confined within Spanish borders. In fact, the chief effect of the non-intervention policy was to make it extremely difficult for the Spanish Republic to buy arms and ammunition in order to defend itself, whilst making no impact at all on

German and Italian supplies to the nationalists. Bernard McKenna felt very strongly that non-intervention was designed to appease Hitler and Mussolini at the expense of the Spanish people:

> Non-intervention was a one-sided farce. It allowed the British and French governments to claim they were being impartial, but by turning a blind eye to what the Germans and Italians were doing. They connived in the overthrow of a democratically elected government by fascist gangsters.

As the various strands of the nationalist revolt against the Republic coalesced under the leadership of General Franco, German and Italian support increased dramatically. Italy sent an estimated 75,000 troops to fight on the side of Franco during the course of the Spanish Civil War, supported by 650 aircraft, 150 tanks and over 1,000 artillery pieces, as well as huge quantities of arms and ammunition. Italian warships and submarines also patrolled the seas around Spain for the alleged purpose of implementing the Non-Intervention treaty. The Germans sent their elite Condor Legion to Spain that comprised tanks, aircraft and 5,000 highly trained troops. German aid to Franco throughout the war probably numbered about 20,000 troops, 600 aircraft, 200 tanks and 1,000 artillery pieces. Aid also came from Portugal, which allowed nationalist forces passage back and forth across its long border with Spain as well as the use of its aerodromes, ports and radio stations. An estimated 15,000 Portuguese soldiers also fought on the nationalist side. American motor manufacturers, General Motors, Ford and Studebaker supplied the nationalists with an estimated 12,800 trucks and jeeps during the course of the war. U.S. oil companies, Texaco and Standard Oil, supplied Franco with unlimited petrol on credit without which the German planes, the Italian tanks and the American trucks would have been useless.

The Republic was initially defended by elements of the Civil Guards who had remained loyal to the elected government alongside militias of workers and peasants who fought with whatever weapons they could lay their hands. Untrained and ill equipped, the militias were no match for well-armed and battle-hardened soldiers. Franco's forces advanced on Republican-held positions in Madrid and the Basque region, leaving a trail of death and destruction in their wake. Thousands upon thousands of suspected Republican sympathisers were brutally tortured and executed in captured areas.

Despite the rabid pro-Franco line of the right-wing press and the Catholic Church, the sympathy of the majority of working class peoples of the world was firmly on the side of the Spanish Republic. Within weeks of the nationalist revolt, Aid Spain committees were formed in many countries, including Britain. Lou Kenton recalls:

The support for the people of Spain was immense amongst the ordinary people, there were committees for Spain all over the country, there was hardly a town or city that didn't have a committee. There were posters going up everywhere saying "Aid Spain", "March for Spain", "Support the Spanish People." It was incredible.

More than a thousand Aid Spain committees formed and tens of thousands of people became involved in them. A constant stream of lorries filled with voluntary contributions of food, clothing and medical supplies made the difficult journey across the Pyrenees. Donations were also carried in food ships, the crews of twenty-nine braved mines and sea patrols to deliver their cargos. Many ambulances, staffed by medical volunteers and filled with sorely needed supplies and equipment, were also sent to Spain. Aid Spain committees kept up a constant and varied level of activity for the duration of the civil war, organising marches and rallies, sporting events, film shows, concerts, bazaars, dances, rambles and door to door collections. Speakers addressed trade union meetings, church congregations and political rallies. Millions of pounds were collected in donations, most of it from working class people with little to spare.

The Jewish community in the East End of London was solidly behind the Spanish Republic, needing very little persuasion to put their money in the collecting tins. Ubby Cowan played an active role in his local Aid Spain Committee:

I was heavily involved in the Aid Spain movement. Every Sunday morning, we went around the streets of Stepney, or wherever, with a lorry collecting money, second-hand clothing, blankets and goodness knows what else. There was phenomenal support for the Spanish people. There were lots of meetings all over the place on behalf of the people of Spain. A particularly big Aid for Spain meeting was organised at the Albert Hall. I was a steward on the ground floor when a woman called Isabel Brown spoke. She could squeeze money out of a dead body. When she made an appeal, it got right to your heart. I was responsible for the big bin on the ground floor where all the money was deposited from all the rows and balconies above. When the bin was full I had to take it to the platform, which I did several times. It was a full house, and hundreds of pounds were raised.

Bernard McKenna was also directly involved in his local Aid Spain group in Manchester, and recalls being humbled by the generosity of the ordinary people of the city:

One of the first things we did was to organise food and medical aid for the Spanish people. I can remember collecting food parcels in Manchester, Salford and Bolton, which we sent to Spain. This wasn't unique to Manchester, there were towns and cities all over Britain that did very similar things. At weekends we would hire handcarts for a tanner and push them around the streets shouting, "Aid for Spain" and "Food for Spain." People would come out of their houses and fill up the handcarts with tins of milk, bags of flour or sugar, canned fruit, clothes, all sorts of things. These were people who had very little for themselves. They were unemployed or pensioners, or workers on very low wages, but they would give you whatever they could afford. I'd never experienced anything like it before or since. It made me feel very humble and very proud at the same time. Lots of different people were involved in the Aid for Spain movement. It wasn't just the Communist Party. Labour Party people were involved as well. Not so much at the top end, but at grassroots level they were very active. There were also Liberals and all sorts of religious people and churchgoers. Money was raised to supply and equip ambulances to send over to Spain to help the civilian population. Some people would give a regular amount each week, maybe sixpence or a shilling. It doesn't sound much now, but it was a lot of money in those days. We held big fund-raising events in the Free Trade Hall in Manchester, which collected hundreds of pounds for the Spanish people. I believe the Duchess of Atholl spoke at one rally. She was a Tory, but she was very committed to the cause of Spain. I remember another meeting, which was addressed by Harry Pollitt. He was very popular because he was a Manchester man and was a very forthright and stirring speaker. He urged everyone to re-double their efforts to help the Spanish people in their hour of need. A lot of money was raised for Spain at that meeting. Later on, when the war was nearly over, the people of Manchester sent a food ship over to Spain. The republican people were retreating before the advance of the fascists and they were in desperate need. I was in Spain then, so I wasn't around to play a part in that aspect.

Contributions to the Aid Spain movement demonstrated both personal sympathy and international solidarity with the Spanish people. Spain was at the heart of the struggle against fascism in the 1930s. Not long after the outbreak of hostilities, news began to filter through that a number of foreign volunteers had joined up with the militias and were involved in the fight against Franco. Some of these men and women were already in Spain when the Generals launched their nationalist revolt. Others had made their way to Spain under their own steam and offered themselves to the Republican cause. Felicia Browne, a member of the St. Pancras branch of the Communist Party, was one of early British volunteers and the first to be killed. She was shot through the head as she tried to rescue a wounded comrade on 25 August 1936.

A few British volunteers in Barcelona joined a Spanish militia in an attempt to capture Mallorca. It failed but Nat Cohen, a clothing worker from Stepney, established a reputation for his bravery and he was elected leader of the group that became named the Tom Mann Centuria in honour of the British Trade Unionist. A twist of fate prevented Ubby Cowan from travelling with Nat Cohen to Spain:

I nearly went to Spain, but I didn't quite make it. Nat Cohen, Sam Masters, Alec Sheller and I were going to cycle through France to the Barcelona Olympiad, which was set up in opposition to the Olympic Games being held in Berlin. I was meant to borrow a bicycle from someone but the geezer broke it the night before we were due to leave so they left at six o'clock the following morning without me. Nat Cohen ended up with a Dum-Dum bullet in his knee. I saw him after he came back. He was limping badly. I also met up with Sam Masters when he came home on leave from Spain but he went back and was later killed at Brunete. Alec didn't want to stay in Spain and escaped by swimming a river and climbing up a chain onto a ship. Lots of Stepney lads fought in Spain and quite a few were killed.

The opponents of Franco welcomed the courage of early individual volunteers but it was clear all too quickly that only a co-ordinated and larger scale effort could make a difference to the outcome of the war. Pressure mounted on the international working class organisations to help recruit volunteers to fight fascism in Spain. In September 1936, the Comintern, in collaboration with the Spanish government, called for the formation of brigades of foreign volunteers to fight on behalf of the people of Spain. They become known as the International Brigades. Within a month, the trickle of foreign volunteers became a flood.

When the British members of the Tom Mann Centuria heard that international volunteers were assembling at a newly formed base at Albacete, most left Barcelona and headed south. These British volunteers, few in number, were attached to the German Thaelmann Battalion and sent to help in the defence of Madrid. Unbeknown to them, another group of British volunteers had travelled via Valencia to Albacete and were stationed at a different barracks. They formed into a machine-gun unit attached to the French Commune de Paris Battalion and were also dispatched to Madrid.

The first shipments of Russian arms arrived in Spain on 15 October. The defenders of Madrid met the enemy on something approaching equal terms for the first time. Of the 30 British volunteers in the Thaelmann and Paris Commune Battalions only five were still fit for active duty when the advance on Madrid was halted. The efforts of the International Brigades, Spanish militias and Republican Army in the capital allowed thousands of international volunteers time to be trained and equipped at Albacete. Nearly five hundred recruits from Britain and Ireland arrived during the months of November and December. The foundations of a British Battalion were laid. But before it got off the ground, a unit of 145 British volunteers were sent to the Cordoba front. Known as No. 1 Company and comprised of English, Scottish, Welsh, Irish, Cypriot and Australian volunteers, it took part in fighting around the town of Lopera then moved northwest of Madrid. Alongside the German Thaelmann and the Italian Garibaldi Battalions, No. 1 Company took part in the Guadarrama offensive that helped to capture the towns of Las Rozas and Majadahonda. Only 67 of the 145 returned to Albacete and the nearby Madrigueras village where the British volunteers were based but they brought with them invaluable practical experience to the nascent British Battalion.

At this point, there were 18,000 international volunteers in Spain, just over half the total of 35,000 from 53 countries who joined the International Brigades over the whole period of the Spanish Civil War. There were also 5,000 volunteers who fought with militias belonging to either the anarchists or POUM (Partido Obrero de Unificacion Marxista). In January 1937, the British in the International Brigades numbered 450. Between 2,100 and 2,300 men and women from Britain joined the Brigades. 526 were killed in battle or died of their wounds once they had returned home. 40 served with the POUM militia. The ILP regarded the POUM, an anti-Stalinist Marxist party, as a sister organisation and raised volunteers for them.

So why did so many young men and women leave behind their families and loved ones to risk their lives in a foreign civil war? Some, no doubt, were attracted by the lure of adventure or sought escape from the confines of home, others might have wanted to live out a romantic idealism. The overwhelming majority, however, went to Spain as the result of deeply held political convictions. Many were already active in the fight against fascism and volunteered to fight as an extension of their anti-fascism. Bernard McKenna dismisses the suggestion that the International Brigades were composed of middle class daydreamers:

All this stuff about the International Brigade being composed of poets and writers is nonsense. The vast majority of the lads I met were working class through and through. They were the salt of the earth. They were factory workers, engineers, miners and dockers. I did meet some University students and there were a couple of intellectual types but they were very few and far between. A lot of the lads in the International Brigades were in the Communist Party, a few were in the Labour Party, but I met several who had never been in a political party of any kind. Some of the Irish lads had been in the IRA while some of the British lads had served in the army but the one thing we all had in common was that we were all anti-fascists.

Joining the British Battalion was an extension of a struggle against fascism that had begun at home. The sincere internationalism and class solidarity of the anti-fascist movement produced volunteers motivated to undertake the risky journey to Spain to put themselves in the firing line. Lou Kenton, his wife and his best friend were amongst the first to volunteer their services to the cause of Republican Spain:

I was married to an Austrian girl called Lilian at the time and together with a friend, Ben Glaser, who was a furniture maker, we attended a meeting in Fleet Street which the Printers' Anti-Fascist Movement had organised. One or two people who had been wounded fighting the fascists in Spain had come back and were doing a speaking tour. The leader of the Communist Party, Harry Pollitt, was also there. He was a very powerful speaker. He explained that things were not going well in Spain. The Spanish fascists supported by troops and arms from Germany and Italy were advancing all the way along the front and the Republican army had been dispersed so there was no army just groups of people in factories who formed themselves into militias that fought the fascists. What was significant about this particular meeting was that Harry Pollittt called upon people to form a Brigade to help the people of Spain. Up until that point they had never done that. Individuals had made their own way there but there was no open recruitment.

After the meeting, the three of us went to a café in Fleet Street for a cup of coffee and then decided to go for a walk along the Embankment. In those days they had little coffee stalls all the way along the Embankment and we stopped at every stall along the way and talked about the meeting. We all felt that the fascists had to be stopped but not a word was said about us going. We just talked and talked. When we finally got to Westminster Bridge we stopped at a coffee stall there, looked at each other and said "Yes. We're going." It was just like that. We all embraced and you can imagine the emotion of three young people, who had never dreamt of doing anything like that before. We went to Lyon's Corner House, and by this time it was three or four o'clock in the morning. We had something to eat, embraced each other again and talked about how we would get to Spain. We decided that the next morning we would go to the Communist Party headquarters in King Street and volunteer.

Bernard McKenna immediately grasped the international implications of allowing fascism to go unchecked in Spain and decided to act:

To my mind, it seemed that fascism was sweeping all before it. Mussolini had invaded Abyssinia, Hitler had occupied the Rhine and the League of Nations had just turned a blind eye towards them. It seemed as though there was a policy of appeasement towards fascism from those in power. I was appalled and horrified by the suffering of the Abyssinian people. It was terrible. It really brought it home to me what fascism was all about. I'd also heard all the reports about what the Nazis were doing to the Jews in Germany and felt that something should be done to stop it. When I heard about the formation of the International Brigades, I felt that here at last was an opportunity to actually do something about the spread of fascism rather than just talk about it. I first tried to go to Spain in December 1936 but because I had no military training I was told not to bother by Mick Jenkins, who was the local Communist Party official. In February 1937, I applied again, and this time I was accepted.

Another who followed his political convictions, and those of his friends, was Alun Menai Williams:

My best friend Billy Davies and another friend, John Blackmore, a former member of the Wobblies, the International Workers of the World, had already gone to Spain to fight Franco. I heard later that John had been killed in fighting around Cordoba and that Billy had been slightly injured in the same battle. I thought an awful lot about going to Spain. I was after all an anti-fascist, I had first hand military experience and training, and my best friend Billy was already out there. I thought that it was time to take a stand and after a lot of soul-searching and worrying about whether it would upset my mother, I decided to go. So in January 1937, I went along to the Communist Party headquarters in King Street for an interview to join the International Brigades fighting for freedom in Spain.

Getting into Spain became more difficult as the war progressed, but in the early days volunteers had less trouble. One of the very first to make the journey was 'Andy' Andrews who served as part of the Spanish Medical Aid Committee (SMAC). With official backing from the Labour Party and TUC, it was easier for these medics to cross into Spain than those who went to take up arms:

> I got in touch with the Spanish Medical Aid Committee pretty much as soon as I heard they needed volunteers to go to Spain. This was in August 1936. I attended a huge Aid Spain rally in Trafalgar Square and left pretty much straightaway afterwards. I had a chat with my brother who said I should just disappear and he would tell our mother when I had gone. A group of us travelled in a SMAC ambulance together and made our way through France to Barcelona. We must have been amongst the earliest British volunteers to arrive in Spain. We had no trouble getting across the border as many did later. The French customs were very good to us.

In January 1937, mindful of its obligations under the Non-Intervention pact, the British government forbade the recruitment of volunteers for Spain under the Enlistment in Foreign Services Act of 1870. Bernard McKenna's passage to Spain was illegal and he had to travel in secret but he made it with little bother:

> Three of us travelled in a group from Manchester. We were given our fares from Manchester to London and then travelled to Paris on weekend tickets, which didn't require passports. From Paris we caught a train to Perpignon. We were told not to travel in big groups or look suspicious because the police and the French fascists were on the lookout for International Brigaders. There were groups of volunteers from all over the world in Perpignon. The local Communist Party officials gathered us all together in a large group, put us on coaches, and drove us across the Spanish border. I don't remember experiencing any problems getting across the border although the French government were beginning to clamp down on

volunteers travelling to Spain at that time.

After February 1937, many volunteers were forced to cross the Pyrenees on foot due to the tightening of security on the border. Local guides led them over the mountains using old smugglers' paths to avoid patrols. Former IRA member, Bob Doyle, got in this way:

A group of us were led across the Pyrenees at night by a local trapper. We were told not to smoke or make any noise because there were fascist patrols in the mountains. We walked all night and it was pretty hard going. The mountains were very steep and dangerous and we were all exhausted by the time we reached the Spanish side. We eventually came down by Figueras and found that someone had made coffee and bread for us.

Various means were used to smuggle in volunteers. Alun Menai Williams tried a few:

My first attempt to join the International Brigades ended at Perpignon when I was picked up by the Gendarmes. I was sent back to London but after three or four weeks of twiddling my thumbs I tried again. This time I was sent to Bordeaux, which was close to the Basque region. Franco was launching a major offensive against the Basques and the plan was to smuggle three or four hundred of us into the region to help out in whatever way we could. They tried to smuggle us into Santander on fishing boats but we were forced to turn back when an Italian warship spotted us. Ten days later we made another attempt, but a gunship fired at us and we high-tailed it back to Bordeaux.

We were then sent by train to Marseilles and put on board a cargo ship, the City of Barcelona. We sailed at midnight and about noon the following day I caught my first glimpse of the coast of Spain. I reckoned that we were only a couple of miles offshore. All of a sudden there was one hell of a bang and the ship shook. An Italian submarine had torpedoed us and the ship was sinking fast. I jumped for a lifeboat with a couple of other fellas but the bloody thing turned over and we were all in the water. I was a good swimmer. I felt pretty comfortable in the water and it wasn't cold, so I wasn't too worried for myself but there were lots of fellas who couldn't swim. We were in the sea for about five or six hours before fishing boats came out and picked up the survivors. So that's how I landed in Spain. I swam there!

The clearing station for International Brigaders was a medieval castle near the town of Figueras. Lou Kenton arrived in style on his Douglas Twin motorcycle:

I got to a place called Figueras, which was a meeting place for those volunteers without visas who had been chaperoned on foot across the Pyrenees by Spaniards. At Figueras, I had my first real contact with the war. I was taken to a courtyard in a great big castle. I showed my credentials to two American guards and they told me "Yeah, it's OK. You're allowed in but don't leave your motorbike outside because it'll be requisitioned right away." So I went inside and saw the most wonderful sight, which will always stay in my memory. There were hundreds and hundreds of volunteers, all sat around in small groups, all with their own nationalities, happily singing their own songs. Doctors were tending their feet for blisters but they were all happy. Naturally I found the British group and told them who I was but they were going one way and I was going the other. It's interesting that Laurie Lee, who was going over at the same time, wrote in his book afterwards that he went there and found a group of very depressed people wondering what they had got themselves into. It was the same group of people I saw, but that wasn't how I saw them at all. After I left Figueras, I went down to Barcelona and found the medical aid headquarters. I was sent to Valencia, which was the first stop towards the convalescent home where my wife was working. She was waiting for me to take her to the hospital to which she had been officially allocated. So I finally met her in this little village just past Valencia and we spent the evening together on the beach. In the morning I was given the address of the hospital where we both had to report, which was in a village called Valdeganga. It was a British hospital, which was there to serve British troops and German-speaking troops. We found quite a number of wounded Germans there as well as several English. I remember reporting for duty and they said "Thank goodness you've arrived" and I asked "Why what's happened?" He pointed to the ambulance and said "The driver's been wounded. We haven't got an ambulance driver. You had better get yourself ready because we're sending you to Madrid right away."

I went over to the ambulance and, much to my joy, I realised it was one that had been sent over by my union. I set off immediately for the hospital in Madrid where I had to pick up some casualties and when I got there they filled me up with eight or nine wounded men which I had to drive back to Valdeganga for further treatment. The Medical Aid Committee used to send over a convoy every two or three weeks with drugs and medical equipment on board and this had to be distributed around different parts of Republican Spain. That was my job for quite a long time, driving the ambulance between the hospitals and the frontline and distributing medical supplies on my motorbike to different units on the frontline or to the headquarters of the International Brigades in Albacete.

From Figueras, most International Brigaders were sent to Albacete and, according to nationality, placed in one of the surrounding villages. The British were sent to the village of Madrigueras where they were given a few weeks' rudimentary training before being sent to the front. With his prior medical and military experience, Alun Menai Williams was on the frontline even faster:

> Upon my arrival in Albacete, I was interviewed by a fellow called Peter Kerrigan, who was the British Commissar of the International Brigades. He told me that the Americans were forming another battalion and that I was to join them as a first aid man once it was formed because they were short of medical people. In the meantime, I was sent to the frontline at Jarama with the Thaelmann Battalion, which was mainly comprised of German-speaking volunteers. I stayed the night at Albacete and the next morning I was kitted out with a uniform, a red cross band, and a haversack containing morphine and bandages and the like. I was put in a lorry with some Germans and Spaniards and we were driven all the way to the front at Jarama. I'd been in Spain for three days and I was already in the trenches.

Andy Andrews also had only a matter of days before his enrollment in the 35th International Division Sanitary Corps:

> We spent two or three days in Barcelona, which was the base of the Spanish Medical Aid Committee in Spain and it was here that we got organised to move on. We were sent to a frontline evacuation point with a team of doctors and nurses. The wounded came in to us and we dealt with them before sending them back to the front or off to various hospitals. I had responsibilities for supplies. I sterilised the equipment and helped out in the operating theatre when required. We

managed to stick together as a unit throughout a lot of the offensive and defensive actions of the war. We always had adequate warning whether to move backwards and forwards although enemy planes were a constant problem. We were bombed several times and I'll always remember diving behind a wall to escape being hit by machine-gun fire and hand grenades thrown from the cockpit of a low-flying Italian fighter plane.

Bernard McKenna was luckier than most. He remembers his training as being both thorough and professional:

At Albacete, we were taken into a bullring, divided into our nationalities and asked if we had any particular skills. I had some skill with telegraph and communications equipment because I was a bit of an amateur radio and wireless enthusiast so I was put into a small signals unit whose job was transmission, setting up telephone communications with the various fronts. We were lucky, because the Colonel in charge at the time was a Czech who insisted we all had a sound military training. So as well as training with military radio and telephone systems, laying lines, making connections and repairs, we also learnt how to use rifles, machine guns and grenades. I still remember that training with pride and pleasure to this day. The only problems I remember in the early days were due to the policy of non-intervention, which meant that there were very few weapons available for training purposes and when you did get your hands on one they were usually old pieces from the First World War. Ammunition was also scarce, and rarely fitted the weapon you had been given. Eventually we were all issued with Russian rifles and ammunition, which was a vast improvement. After a few months, I was sent to Madrigueras, where the British were based and I became part of the transmissions unit of the British Battalion.

The British Battalion of 600 men was ready to fight. It was incorporated into the 15th International Brigade alongside the Dimitrov, Franco-Belge and American Battalions. On 6 February, they moved to the front. Franco had failed to take Madrid by direct assault and was mounting a pincer movement from the north and south. The objective of the southern offensive was to cut the Madrid-Valencia road by crossing the River Jarama. On 12 February, in the Jarama Valley, the British Battalion first saw action. They were supposed to be in reserve behind the front line on the east bank of the River Jarama but as they neared their position, they came under heavy rifle and machine-gun fire. The front had broken and the nationalist forces were much further forward than anticipated. The British Battalion was required to check their advance and pulled back to the crest of two hills and took up defensive positions. The Battalion bore the full brunt of the subsequent onslaught and lost nearly half their number defending 'Suicide Hill' and 'Conical Hill.' They fought a numerically superior and better-equipped enemy all through the day before following orders to withdraw to new positions. On the second day of fighting, a dawn attack was successfully repulsed, but the withdrawal of the French 6th of February Battalion left the British right flank exposed and several machine-gun posts were captured. On the third, the whole Republican front was under bombardment and the line abandoned. Tanks and infantry penetrated the British positions. The few survivors retreated back down the hill to the Battalion cookhouse. Irish volunteer Frank Ryan and Jock Cunningham, a Scottish labourer, rallied the disorganised and demoralised men. They led them back to their former positions and recaptured them before nightfall.

Despite losses, the advance on Madrid from the south had been checked. The offensive in the north was also pushed back. The British Battalion, reinforced by more volunteers and an anti-tank battery, dug in for the duration and were to remain in their trenches for several grim months of sniper fire, dysentery and lice. Alun Menai Williams was in these trenches:

My arrival in the trenches was fairly uneventful with just the odd crackle of gunfire every now and then. The first three days were very quiet. No problem at all. On the fourth day, for some unknown reason, Franco decided to bombard this particular section of trenches with mortar bombs and artillery shells. All hell broke loose for about ten minutes and then just as suddenly stopped again. I was bloody terrified. I thought "I didn't come here for this, that's for sure." After the shelling stopped, a cry went out "Sanitario." That's Spanish for medical aid. So I dashed to where people were shouting and sitting on the trench floor, with a few of his comrades around him, was a young German volunteer whose hand had been almost severed at the wrist by shrapnel. It was the first time I'd seen a wound caused by war. I felt slightly panicky. I thought to myself "What the hell do I do now?" Then suddenly my training came back to me and I was able to help him.

Back in Barcelona, the conflict was not that of internationalists against nationalists but between the anti-fascists. On one side were anarchists and the POUM. After the defeat of the nationalist putsch, they had created a process of social revolution. The anarchists had implemented wholesale collectivisation of land, industry and commerce. They were widely supported. On the other, were the Republican government and the communists that controlled between them the majority of Republican-held territory, the Civil Guard, and crucially, the supply of Soviet arms. The anarchists and the POUM believed that only social revolution could halt fascism by eradicating the conditions that created it and only sustaining the revolutionary process would give people sufficient hope to bear the hardships and dangers of war. The Republican government and their communist allies claimed that the revolution was a divisive distraction from the war effort and was only supported in Catalonia not the rest of Republican Spain. For them, a genuinely popular, democratic and anti-fascist government was under attack by the combined might of three fascist armies and in need of defence.

On one level it was a classic case of idealism versus pragmatism, the tantalising promise of social freedom set against the grim necessity of organising a disciplined military force capable of waging war. However, on another level it was a story of sectarian spite, distrust and the battle for power. The Republican government sought to undermine the revolution by disbanding the militias and reversing collectivisation. The communists were suspicious of any revolutionary movement not under their strict control, especially if it was tainted by Trotskyism or anarchism. POUM and the anarchists, for their part, were extremely wary of Soviet-influenced communism in Spain. They also remained unconvinced of the virtues of hierarchical military discipline, leadership and organisation. Mistrust engendered paranoia. Rumours spread that the anarchists were stockpiling weapons in Barcelona that were desperately needed at the front. POUM supporters were initially defamed as Trotskyists (denied by Leon Trotsky himself), then accused of collaboration with fascists and, finally, labelled fascists. The anarchists and POUM reproached the communists for starving them of arms, reinstituting the hated Civil Guard, arresting, torturing and killing their militants and betraying the revolutionary spirit of the people. A Stalinist logic was exported into the middle of the Spanish Civil War. The purges and show trials in the Soviet Union had been criticised in both POUM and anarchist publications. Following the lead from Moscow, Spanish communists concluded they were enemies of Stalin and therefore potential traitors. There was a certain weary inevitability about the following sequence of events.

On 25 April, eight anarchists were killed in a government attack on an anarchist-held frontier post and a leading communist was murdered in Barcelona. A week later, on 3 May, Barcelona's police chief, a communist, ordered the take-over of the anarchist-held central telephone exchange under the pretext of preventing an 'anarcho-Trotskyist putsch' or a 'fascist plot'. Staff Cottman, who had been serving on the Aragon front with the POUM militia, was in Barcelona on leave:

> Word got around from other ILP contingent members that we were to report to the POUM headquarters in Barcelona, the Falcon Hotel. We were in Barcelona at this time as we were on leave from the front. At the Falcon Hotel we were given weapons (our Mausers were at the front being used by other POUM troops). Some of us were given rifles but there were not enough to go around, so I was given a couple of hand grenades…Sporadic fighting lasted for three days before the Communist-controlled police gained control of the Telephone Building. Clashes occurred throughout Barcelona between the Anarchists and POUM on one side, and the Communists and Republicans or Liberals on the other side, who were out to crush the revolution and restore government control in Catalonia.

Ethel MacDonald, an anarchist from Glasgow, was in Barcelona as an English-speaking propagandist for a radio station. She was sitting with her friend and fellow anarchist, Jenny Patrick, when the telephone exchange was stormed:

> News reached Jenny and I as we were having after lunch coffee in a little anarchist restaurant not far from the headquarters in the Via Durruti. The messenger told us that three lorry loads of police had made use of the siesta hour

when shops and offices are closed, to launch their attack. They had no difficulty in seizing the ground floor but our comrades in the building barricaded the stairways and swept them with machine gun fire thus preventing further assault. Immediately, crowds gathered outside the building and the streets were filled with anxious men and women. Suddenly the cry was raised – "To the barricades. To the barricades!" It echoed through the streets and in a very short time firing had broken out all over the city.

After three days of fighting, the anarchists agreed to lay down their arms. Ethel MacDonald recalled the scene:

Altogether 300 of our comrades were killed during those three days and I have no idea how many were wounded. As soon as the fighting stopped, wives and mothers hurried through the streets searching for their loved ones. Some, hearing that they had been wounded, rushed from hospital to hospital. The streets were filled with fear-stricken and frenzied women.

The 'May Days', as they have been called, left dead on both sides but power in Catalonia passed into the hands of the communists and the Republican government. The repression against the POUM and the anarchists began. The POUM was declared an illegal and fascist organisation. Its newspaper *La Batalla* was closed down, its Hotel Falcon headquarters raided. Anarchist radio stations were censored and the collectives dismantled. The left-wing anarchist organisation, the Friends of Durruti, was disbanded.

POUM members and anarchists were arrested, tortured, killed. Staff Cottman, with Britain's most famous volunteer, George Orwell, were forced to flee Spain as fugitives. Other ILP members were imprisoned by Russian secret police, including Bob Smillie, who died in a prison cell.

At the front, the news that anti-fascists were fighting each other in Barcelona was greeted with a mixture of anger and disbelief. Bernard McKenna recalls that his Spanish comrades greeted the propaganda campaign against the anarchists and the POUM with some scepticism:

We used to have a lot of political debate and discussion at the front. We heard all about the May uprising and the suppression of the POUM and the anarchists. We didn't concern ourselves with this too much because we were in the middle of a war but I don't think many of our Spanish comrades really believed the Communist Party when they claimed that the anarchists and Trotskyists were fascists. There were rumours that the anarchists had kept back valuable equipment from the front and I came across one instance of this at Lerida. My friend, Pat Reid, who was an American Wobblie, took me to this big church, which was full of foodstuffs and equipment. It was all under the control of the anarchists and I wouldn't have been allowed within a mile of it if I hadn't been with Pat. It was all stuff that we were crying out for at the front and it was just sitting there unused. It just goes to show the disunity and mistrust that existed on the anti-fascist side. The suppression of the anarchists was underway at this time, so I suppose they had good reason to keep it all hidden away because they knew they would be coming under attack themselves but at the same time people were dying on the front through lack of equipment.

On 17 June 1937, the 15th International Brigade was finally withdrawn from the Jarama front for rest and recuperation. The British Battalion was sent to Mondejar for a short and very welcome break. It was in this small village that Alun Menai Williams met up with his life-long pal, Billy Davies:

I went over to Mondejar where I knew the British Battalion

were stationed, with the intention of finding my old friend Billy. Well you can imagine how shocked he was when he saw me. "Good God, Alun. What the hell are you doing here?" he asked. "The same as you" I replied. It was great to see him again. Later on we had a photograph taken as a souvenir of our days in Spain. Unfortunately, I never saw Billy again as he was killed three days later at Villanueva de la Canada. He has no known grave or marker to say who he was or why he died.

On the 1 July, the British Battalion were moved by truck to the northwest of Madrid in preparation for the Brunete offensive. The Republic's first major offensive of the war, its objective was to relieve the pressure on its besieged territories in the north. Bernard McKenna moved into action with the British Battalion on 6 July:

After assembling at a village called Ambite, we moved by night up into the foothills of the Guadarramas, ready for the offensive at Brunete. At dawn there was a flyover of our aircraft and a heavy artillery barrage. It was all very impressive and we were in good spirits when it was our turn to advance. The transmission unit went into action as infantrymen but we also carried all our signals equipment on our backs. Once a front had been established we immediately started laying lines back to headquarters so that there was always a line of communication. It was a tremendously hot day and I remember that a lot of the men were short of water and very, very thirsty. We were continuously bombarded by enemy artillery and there were all sorts of enemy fire flying around us but we kept advancing towards the fascists. I was with the frontline troops as they advanced towards Villanueva de la Canada and after a heavy exchange of fire, it looked as if the fascists were preparing to surrender. They came out behind a human shield of women and children and when they had drawn our men out into the open they opened up on us knowing we couldn't return fire. George Brown, who was leader of the Communist Party in Manchester, was killed during this incident as well as a number of other British volunteers. I was wounded in the foot and ended up in a hospital in Madrid, which was under enemy bombardment at the time. I remember being kept awake at nights by fascist planes bombing the city.

I returned to the front after a fortnight's convalescence but the battalion was now in retreat and had suffered heavy casualties. The fascists had managed to withstand the assault and were now counter-attacking furiously. Morale was low and we were being continuously shelled and dive-bombed. I was near Colonel George Nathan when he was killed. A bomb fell between us and splinters from the rocks hit him. I was unharmed but we were all shocked as Nathan was a good leader and we all liked and trusted him. Brunete was a real blow to the morale of the Battalion. We had lost so many men we were barely a fighting force at all by this time.

Alun Menai Williams was at Brunete:

Brunete was hell on earth. The heat was indescribable. Men were exhausted and dying from lack of water, their tongues swollen in their mouths. Franco's air superiority gave the fascists an enormous advantage and we were eventually pushed back by a massive fascist counter-offensive. During the retreat, George Nathan was fatally wounded and while I was tending to him I was hit in the leg by a bullet. It wasn't a serious wound but I was taken out of the frontline and sent to Alicante to recuperate. Those three weeks in a hospital bed were the only time I spent between sheets throughout the whole time I was in Spain.

The 15th International Brigade was withdrawn from the frontline. The British Battalion, its number halved, was billeted in Mondejar. On 18 August, it received marching orders for the Aragon front. Its empty ranks were filled with Spanish recruits who had volunteered to fight with the International Brigades. All were held in reserve while the other three battalions of the 15th attacked the fortified town of Quinto near the River Ebro. Bernard McKenna joined Abraham Lincoln Battalion:

I entered the village of Quinto with the Americans, acting as an unpaid infantryman. I shouldn't have done it really but I felt I was missing out on all the action. We went from house to house clearing the fascists out by chucking grenades through the windows and firing off several shots at the retreating fascists. I had a small Mauser carbine, which suited me better than the rifles we had been given. It was a great feeling to see the fascists running for their lives.

Quinto fell and the British were given the job of taking Pulburrel Hill to the east of the village. It was heavily fortified with gun turrets, trench systems and concrete emplacements. Its Achilles heel was its water supply from the River Ebro. The pipe had been cut by an American patrol. The first assault by the British failed but the second supported by the anti-tank battery was successful. Bernard McKenna relates:

A Spanish officer came down from the hill and asked to surrender. They were all pretty much shot up, demoralised and very thirsty. He was told to bring the garrison down and they would be given prisoner of war rights. After a couple of hours he led his men down from the hill and they lined up in front of us and surrendered. The ordinary troops and NCOs were led away and the officers were shot as they were regarded as being traitors who were in open revolt against the government. The fascists routinely killed all their prisoners, especially International Brigaders, so we had no qualms about that. It was only later in the war when the Italians wanted to exchange prisoners that anyone was spared.

His next action was at Fuentes de Ebro in October 1937:

We moved up in the morning to attack the village, but we were strafed by machine gun fire from the church tower, which had good views of the entire area. The fascists were dug in with several lines of trenches and machine gun posts. After coming under constant fire, we were forced to take shelter in a small ditch, no more than 18 inches deep, which was between the road and the River Ebro. We waited here until midday when a tank offensive was launched. Well, I heard the rumbling of these tanks and all of a sudden they came right over the top of our trenches. I thought "I've got a bloody tank on top of me." Fortunately, the little shale ditch withstood the weight of the tank and we were all unharmed. As the tanks advanced we followed them across the open field but they were too fast and we were left behind in the open. The tanks chased the fascists out of the first line of trenches but we were left exposed to machine gun fire and cut down. It was a botched operation that cost many good men their lives. A sheer bloody waste.

The British Battalion was pulled out of the trenches for a period of rest until 10 December. It was then called up to the Aragon front and on again with the 15th Brigade to help halt massive offensive of 80,000 men, 600 artillery pieces and the largest air fleet yet seen against the recently captured town of Tuerel. The British, Canadian Mackenzie-Papineau, Thaelmann and Lincoln Washington Battalions held firm and thwarted Franco's plans to take the city by direct assault. Alun Menai Williams remembers

Teurel for the blizzards and the bitter cold, which reached minus 20 degrees centigrade on some nights:

> I was with the amalgamated Lincoln Washington Battalion at the battle of Teruel, which was on Christmas 1937. It was one hell of a cold winter with blizzards and snowstorms and all I had on my feet was a pair of soft, rope-soled, Spanish alpargatas. It was terribly, bitterly cold. I remember the wind howling through a railway tunnel that we used as a clearing station because it afforded us shelter from the shells and the storms.

In March, Franco's forces broke through the Republican line in half a dozen places. The 15th Brigade rushed in to reinforce the front at Belchite. Bob Doyle, a machine-gunner in the British Battalion, was part of the defence of the town:

> A major fascist offensive forced us to withdraw into Belchite itself, where we made a last stand around the church. The church provided us with cover from the fascist artillery, which bombarded us non-stop. My machine gun had developed a fault and I was given a rifle, which I fired at the enemy until it became too hot to handle. When the fascist tanks finally came into close range, we were ordered to withdraw to the heights outside the town. We tried to dig in but the ground was too stony and you could only make a very shallow trench. We were bombed and machine-gunned by German Stukas, but we held out for two days before withdrawing again. While we were there, I saw an ambulance being attacked by fascist planes. After the fighting at Belchite, we seemed to be in retreat everywhere.

Hospitalised at Teurel, Bernard McKenna hurried back to the fray:

I left hospital for the Aragon front just as a new fascist offensive was launched during the Spring of 1938. Everyone was in retreat. We came under heavy enemy bombardment and during a period of further retreat we became cut off from the rest of the Brigade. We hid by day and moved at night but as time went by progress got slower and slower. Men began to drop their weapons and ammunition through tiredness and hunger. Due to continuous attacks, we found ourselves splitting into smaller and smaller groups, until eventually I was on my own. I was walking down a dirt track at dawn, when two Italian fascists on motorbikes captured me.

Franco hoped to split the Republic in two by pushing through to the Mediterranean. The exhausted remnants of the 15th Brigade slowed the advance at Caspe. A few hundred poorly armed men broke the momentum of the nationalist advance just long enough for reinforcements to form a new line blocking the way to sea. What was left of the British Battalion regrouped at Batea. More recruits arrived and injured volunteers returned to action often against doctor's orders. On 31 March, the British Battalion went to support the front near Lerida. As the Battalion rounded a bend in the road near the small village of Calaceite, they walked into a column of Italian tanks. There was a moment of hesitation. Unaware that the front had been broken and in the half-light of dawn, the Battalion leaders thought they had stumbled into pro-Republican troops. Then the Italians opened fire. The British scattered. Their machine-gun company gave covering fire, enabling many to escape. They knocked out enemy tanks and pinned down the Italian infantry for an hour. They hung on until their encirclement was imminent. More than 150 members of the British Battalion were killed or wounded. A similar number were taken prisoner. Bob Doyle was captured:

We heard a terrific noise of engines, like a motorised column, but we assumed that they were the Listers, who were supposed to be ahead of us. We had no idea that the front had broken and that the fascists were on the advance. I was stood next to Frank Ryan when we were captured. We were surrounded by Italian infantry and surrendered straight away. There was nothing else we could do. The tanks came up the road and opened fire on the men behind us, who began to retreat. Wally Tapsell, who was political commissar of the battalion, still thought they were our own men and shouted at the officer in the lead tank to stop firing, but was shot dead for his troubles.

80 British volunteers regrouped near the town of Gandesa. With the Mackenzie-Papineau Battalion and other assorted Republican troops, they fought a rearguard action which delayed the advance for a whole day and once again allowed Spanish troops time to form a new line behind them. But, on 15 April, Franco's forces reached the sea. Alun Menai Williams recounts the retreat of the Brigades:

Franco launched a massive offensive against Republican lines and broke through in force. Then it was all bloody chaos. Everybody ran for their lives. I was with another first aid man, an American lad called Tiny Holland, and along with a group of about fifty stragglers, we made a stand at a small village called Corbera. German tanks advanced on the village and quite a few of the Americans were killed and wounded. We put the wounded in a hut and tended to them as best we could. Tiny and I could hear the tanks coming nearer but when we looked around all the rest of the Americans had vanished. Tiny and me were on our own. I'll always remember Tiny telling me, and it was the first time I'd heard an American swear, he said "If we don't get away from here quickly, those motherfucking bitches will kill us."

We got away from there as quickly as we could. Never mind the wounded. Never mind the glory. We ran like hell. We were on the run for the next five days, dodging sentries and patrols, hiding by day and travelling by night. We were headed for the River Ebro, hoping that the Republican army had regrouped on the other side. One morning, as we hid in a little hut, we saw a group of four or five men coming towards us through an olive grove. We didn't know what to do, but Tiny whispered that he thought he heard one of them speaking in English. As they came nearer he stood up and said "We're Americans. We're bloody Americans." It turned out that they were stragglers from the British Battalion. They were on the run like us. One of them said that he thought the River Ebro was only a couple of miles away. So we headed for the Ebro. We must have been spotted because we could hear tanks behind us and bullets whizzing over our heads. We were exhausted by the time we reached the river and then we had to decide how we were going to get across. There were no bridges or boats and the only option was to try and swim across. It was obvious that a few of the other men had doubts about their ability to make it over to the other side but bullets were flying all around and after a moment's hesitation everyone waded into the water. I got across, Tiny got across, and two of the others made it across. Two got swept away and drowned and one waded back. I don't know what happened to him.

The remnants of the Republican army assembled on the northern bank of the River Ebro. The British Battalion, just 220 battle-weary men, regrouped there. Under the leadership of Sam Wild, they prepared themselves for the next offensive. It didn't come. Instead, Franco turned his attention south towards Valencia. The Battalion stayed around Marsa, trained and brought its numbers back to its 650 full strength with more Spanish volunteers. Alun

Menai Williams was back in its ranks:

> After making it across the Ebro I rejoined the Americans, but
> after a few days rest and recuperation I decided that I wanted
> to join my fellow countrymen in the British Battalion. There
> was no particular reason, I just decided that I wanted to be
> back amongst my fellow countrymen once more with their
> familiar habits and customs. I saw Sam Wild, the Battalion
> Commander, who agreed to my request and after bidding my
> American friends a fond farewell, I joined up with the British.

As the Brigaders prepared for another fight, the Prime-Minister
of the Spanish Republic, Juan Negrin, opened negotiations with
the Non-Intervention Committee. Negrin vainly hoped that if the
International Brigades were ordered from Spain, the fascists
would respond in kind with the withdrawal of German and
Italian troops. But, it was naive to believe that Hitler and
Mussolini would voluntarily honour such an agreement and no
one in the Non-Intervention Committee was willing to force
them.

One final battle remained to be fought before the Brigaders
returned home. In the early hours of the 25 July and under cover
of darkness, the armies for the Spanish Republic mounted an
audacious attack on Franco's fifty-mile front. Alun Menai
Williams retraced his route of retreat:

> The Battalion re-crossed the Ebro at midnight in a fleet of
> rowing boats. When I last crossed the river it had been in the
> opposite direction and I had been swimming for my life with
> bullets flying all around me. This time I was in a boat
> alongside six other men and a Spanish fisherman who was our
> guide. We were amongst the second wave of troops to cross
> and we emerged on a sandy strip of shore to find the enemy
> in full retreat. The surprise attack caught the fascists

completely off-guard and we advanced rapidly into enemy territory. I don't remember there being too much resistance during this initial phase of the attack, but eventually Franco sent his air force to bomb and machine-gun the advancing columns.

I don't remember all the details of the next three months, which were a nightmare period of advance, defend and retreat but for me this was the worst period of the whole war. The battle for the strategic heights of the Sierra Pandols took a tremendous toll on the Battalion and there were many casualties. Bringing wounded men back down from those bare rocky mountains was a nightmare. We were under almost constant enemy fire and many of the badly wounded men couldn't wait until nightfall for stretcher-bearers to carry them the mile or so to the nearest ambulance so we had to try and bring them down during the day, which was exhausting and dangerous.

For the British Battalion, these last few months, Alun's 'worst', were spent trying to capture hills 481, 666 and 356. When the Republican line held firm, they fell back as reserves. They heard news that the International Brigades were to be withdrawn with mixed emotions. Any hope for home was shot through with sorrow over leaving their Spanish comrades. The day before they were due to go, the 15th International Brigade was called back to the front. The 13th needed support. Bombardment of the Sierra del Lavell de la Torre had caused terrible casualties and it was barely holding out.

On the morning of 23 September, a terrific artillery barrage was unleashed on Republican positions. One shell landed every second on the British sector alone. After five hours of continuous shooting, covered by 250 bomber and fighter planes, the fascist infantry and tanks moved in and overwhelmed the Republican army and their international volunteers. John Power, a Waterford man, managed to escape with a handful of men. Captain George Fletcher gathered the Brigade on a ridge three hundred yards from the battle. This was the last time the line held.

207 men of the British Battalion were killed, missing or taken prisoner on their final day of fighting. Alun was one of the small band that returned:

We crossed back over the Ebro on a small rickety footbridge somewhere near the town of Asco. This was the first stage of our journey home. There were 58 of us in total, the last survivors of the British Battalion. We were sent to Barcelona where we took part in the Farewell Parade of the International Brigades. It was a very moving experience and the reception we received from the people of Barcelona was tremendous. I saw La Pasionaria at the parade. I was aware that she was making a speech but I couldn't hear it because there were no microphones available. It was one of the most famous speeches in history and I never heard a bloody word of it. I was both sad and relieved to be leaving Spain. I had given my all for the cause of anti-fascism but I knew in my heart of hearts that it was a lost cause. The defeat of the Spanish Republic was inevitable. The odds stacked against it were too great. Fascism was going to triumph in Spain and I was just glad to be getting out of it alive.

Alun was right. The Republic managed to continue the unequal struggle for several more months but the writing was on the wall. The fascist war machine cranked up the pressure and crushed it. Andy Andrews' war had also reached its conclusion:

We found ourselves on the Barcelona side of Franco's push to the coast, which split the Republic in two. I had a bout of bad stomach trouble that kept getting in the way of my work and I was put on a plane and sent home, so I wasn't there at the very end. I believe that quite a lot had to find their own way back across the Pyrenees.

For Lou Kenton however, it was far from over:

The Printers' Anti-Fascist Movement decided to send another ambulance to Spain and they asked if I could come back to London and drive it back over. As it was in a quiet period on the front, I was given permission to leave and travelled back with my wife. When we finally arrived back in London, I went to Fleet Street and linked up with the secretary of the union. He told me that things were going very badly in Spain and that Franco was on the verge of entering Madrid. I was told that they didn't need an ambulance any more because they had no use for them and what they needed was a lorry to carry food and equipment to the various hospitals dotted around northern Spain. So they cancelled the order for the ambulance and bought a lorry, which I drove over with two others.

When we got to Perpignon, we heard that Madrid had fallen and that the government was having its last meeting in the city of Gerona. Journalists from the whole world had gathered in Perpignon because this was the end of the civil war and the Spanish Republic. People were being evacuated from Barcelona to the border and they asked us to drive to a small French village called Le Perthus where refugees were already beginning to congregate. Not only refugees, but an army in retreat. It's a sight one can never forget, thousands of people on the road trying to escape being bombed by Franco's forces, the army carrying their wounded, mothers carrying children who were already dead. There was no food or water in the village, so we gave the food in the lorry to the refugees.

We came across two British journalists in Le Perthus, Bill Forrester and Tom Driberg, and offered to give them a lift to

Gerona for the last meeting of the Republican government. It wasn't that far, maybe only 50 miles across the border, but as we drove through the streets that evening it was like a dead city. When they returned to France, these two journalists wrote a blistering report on what the French government was doing, or rather was not doing, to help the thousands of refugees streaming across their border. It was printed in the *Daily Express* and the *News Chronicle* and it created quite a furore. Within a day of the report appearing the French had sent the troops in with food and water. Refugees were still coming out of Spain and we crossed the border again to bring back as many wounded as we could. As we got closer to the front we could hear the guns as the Spanish army covered their retreat. It's not often spoken of but units of the Spanish army acted as suicide troops trying to defend the retreat. Thousands of troops managed to get across the border to France while the suicide troops were killed on sight because Franco wasn't taking any prisoners. We made eight or nine trips and each time we brought more wounded back. The final trip will stick in my mind for the rest of my life. We returned via a mountain route and we had a three-ton lorry that nearly went over the edge several times before we finally made it back. When we got back to France, we found that the refugees were still starving. We each had a bit of money, which the union had given us to get back to England but we spent it on supplies for the refugees, bits of chocolate and loaves of bread, a whole lorry load of loaves. We managed to feed hundreds of people with this little bit of money and then feeling that we had done as much as we could, we found our way home.

Bernard McKenna, captured in Spring of 1938, was in jail:

I was eventually taken to the San Pedro concentration camp at Burgos, which was an old monastery. Conditions there were grim and the guards were brutal. There were more than 600 Brigaders, Cubans, French, Irish, Germans, Americans, British, even a Chinese lad, all crammed together into two rooms. We slept on a stone floor, there was nowhere to wash and we all had lice, dysentery and skin diseases. The food was very poor and watery. Many of the prisoners were suffering from injuries, but there was no attempt to give them medical treatment. We were very brutally treated in San Pedro. We were marched out in the mornings and forced to sing the Spanish fascist anthem and give the fascist salute. If you didn't you were beaten. Beatings were a regular occurrence. We were also interrogated on a weekly basis. I was questioned several times by German Gestapo interrogators who seemed especially keen to know about our way of life in Britain. They would ask questions for a couple of hours, take notes, and then come back the following week. We were also subjected to speeches from the Spanish Commandant of the camp. He used to tell us how wonderful Franco was and how we should mend our ways. Mass was compulsory, whether you were Catholic or not.

Some prisoners were executed, some just disappeared. I shared a cell with the Irish volunteer Frank Ryan, who was later transferred to Germany and was never seen again. Italian and German prisoners were sent back to their own countries where they faced certain death at the hands of Hitler and Mussolini's torturers and executioners. The Spanish prisoners were the most brutally treated of all. The guards showed them no mercy. Very many of them were executed and those that survived had no prospect of release at all, whereas, for us British there was always the hope that diplomatic pressure would eventually mean we would be returned to our own country. After four months I was moved to an Italian P.O.W. camp at Palencia and although life was still hard, it was a vast improvement on San Pedro. We were given a shower, clean clothes and proper food. After seven months there was a prisoner exchange and I was taken to San Sebastian and eventually returned to France. I had been in Spain for nearly two years.

Bob Doyle was also imprisoned in San Pedro. He spent eleven months in the old monastery before his transfer with other International Brigaders to a prison at San Sebastian:

We were forced to march around the main plaza in San Sebastian in front of the local people. Franco wanted to humiliate us but the crowd swarmed around us and gave us chocolates and cigarettes. This really annoyed the guards, who got us into the prison pretty quickly after that. We spent several weeks at San Sebastian before being taken to the International Bridge at Hendaye. We were handed over to the French police and exchanged for Italian prisoners of war.

Lou Kenton made another journey back to Spain. He had one last difficult task. He explained:

Early in the war, the Basque region was the scene of fierce fighting. Towns and cities like Guernica and Bilbao were heavily bombed and there was an appeal from the Basque government, which was still sitting, for the British government to take in children whose parents were either missing in the fighting or dead. The British government wouldn't have anything to do with it, but within days an ad-hoc committee was set up to bring over and house the thousands of Basque children made homeless by Franco. It was a wonderful thing that the British people did to open their doors to four or five thousand Basque children for three years and they looked after them quite magnificently.

After the war, Franco demanded that all the children be

returned to Spain. Some of the committee were prepared to do that but the majority of us demanded that they only be sent back if the International Red Cross supervised it. We decided we would send them back in small groups where we had authorisation from their parents. The committee asked me to take the first group back and I ended up taking 30 back by lorry. It was my job to go around and collect these children from the people who had looked after them for the last three years and they had all been given small presents and clothes and food.

We finally got to Santander on the border and as I looked across the river, I saw the Spanish police in their three-cornered hats for the first time. They sent an officer over who demanded I hand over all the children. I said "I'm not sending any back unless I get a letter from their parents that they are there waiting." After a long negotiation I still wouldn't let them go. It took about two hours all told but finally word came down from the International Red Cross that they were monitoring the situation and the children would be reunited with their parents or next of kin. So then I had the job of saying goodbye to each child in turn as we checked their details and prepared to hand them over. Again, it's something that sticks in my memory, of children clinging onto me and crying. They didn't want to go back because they didn't know what they were going back to. It's one of the saddest memories of my life.

The acts of international solidarity that took place between 1936 and 1939 are a great measure of people's humanity but it did not defeat fascism in Spain. Thousands of anti-fascists from across the world lost their lives. Bernard McKenna argues that these sacrifices played a strategic as well heroic role in the long struggle against fascism:

I feel proud to have served in the International Brigades. I feel that at the very least we delayed the outbreak of World War Two by two years and allowed the Russians time to rebuild their forces before Hitler attacked the Soviet Union. If Hitler had launched his attack on Russia earlier then the whole outcome of the Second World War would have been different. Many of the people who fought against the fascists in Spain also gained invaluable military expertise to form resistance groups when the Nazis occupied their own countries. Most of the Italian and French resistance groups were run by communists who had fought in Spain. In lots of other places there were resistance groups run by International Brigaders. Eighteen of Tito's generals had been Brigaders and they held down twenty German divisions in Yugoslavia. So it wasn't just the fascists who learnt lessons in Spain.

Betty Davis, whose grandfather Ambrose Johnston volunteered to fight in Spain, explains that he felt he had little choice but to volunteer:

I found it strange that he went because he was always against war, but he saw fascism as an evil that had to be stopped. I don't know what battalion he served with, but I know he didn't join up in England, I believe it was in France. I do remember my grandfather telling me stories about how awful Spain was and how he didn't think he was going to get out of it alive. He had a great sense of humour and used to make everything into a joke, but he said many times how he wept with fear while he was over there. He also said how he met some wonderful people, some wonderful comrades that he'd always keep in touch with. Lots of them died. He said what a waste it was because they were mostly people with great ideals and hopes for humanity and they were lying there dead. He never did come to terms with that part of it but he thought it was something that he had to do.

4

On Guard: 1940 –1953

If the period of the Second World War marked a low-point in the fortunes of British fascism, the reverse was true for its principal protagonist, the Communist Party. At the start of the conflict, however, the party was in a state of disarray following the signing of the 1939 Nazi-Soviet Pact, which included a pledge of non-aggression between the two powers. After the pact had been signed, the British Communist Party was ordered by Stalin to reverse its previous position of support for the war effort, and was instead, instructed to start campaigning against it.

After a heated internal debate, the Central Committee of the Communist Party of Great Britain (CPGB or CP) announced to its members that they were no longer supporters of an 'anti-fascist war' but opponents of an imperialist one. With barely a nod towards its previously held position, the party set about propagandising against the war effort. A typical example of communist propaganda of the period is provided by the 1940 by-election leaflet in support of Councillor Charlie Searson, a communist-backed anti-war candidate in Central Southwark, London. The leaflet states 'It is not a war against fascism, it is a war against the standard of living – against the people.' It cites examples of shortages of medical and educational supplies, rising prices, and of local people being evacuated to appalling living conditions and returning to crippling levels of debt. The new line not only alienated many committed anti-fascists within the CP but also singularly failed to attract popular support. Membership of the party went into decline, a process exacerbated by the call-up and evacuation.

The German invasion of the Soviet Union in June 1941 changed everything. Stalin then called for a 'people's war against fascism.' Within days of the invasion, the CP reversed its position again to come full circle and tie itself body and soul to the concept of the anti-fascist war. The change brought almost immediate results, with membership steadily rising to a peak of 56,000 in 1942. Throughout these various twists and turns of party policy, a core of active Party members had remained loyal to the cause of anti-fascism. For many, including former International Brigader, Bernard McKenna, it was a case of keeping your own counsel and waiting for the pendulum to swing your way again:

> I saw the Second World War as a continuation of the fight against fascism. When war broke out, the Communist Party said that it was an anti-fascist war. Then after Stalin negotiated a non-aggression pact with Hitler, they decided it wasn't an anti-fascist war any longer but an imperialist war. I took no notice of them. I thought they were mad. I just carried on as normal. Then when Germany attacked Russia in 1941 it suddenly became an anti-fascist war again.

The change of line from Moscow led the CP to develop a brand of patriotic anti-fascism. Party members were called upon to push for increased productivity in factories to help the fight against Hitler and to discourage strikes in war industries on the basis that it was in the best interests of trade unionists, persecuted under Nazism, to see fascism defeated. This attempt to ride two horses at once risked Communists losing their claim to defend workers' rights. Their 1942 pamphlet, *Trade Union Policy in the War against Fascism*, addressed itself to this contradiction by arguing that increased productivity actually strengthened the hand of the unions in their dealings with employers:

> Backward elements in the trade union movement have pretended that to drive for production is to neglect the

defence of the workers' standards. On the contrary, the unions which show the greatest concern for production have been able not only to defend their standard of life effectively, but to win for the union organisation more rights in the workshop.

Evidence that unions won concessions beyond what could otherwise be expected during a time of great manpower shortages is pretty thin on the ground but the CP continued to peddle the myth regardless. The danger of following this line of reasoning, however, is that anyone who hinders production through industrial action, no matter how genuine their grievance, can be targeted as a 'backward element' or, worse, a supporter of fascism. 'Every trade unionist must be imbued with the understanding that whoever impedes the work of production committees is playing the game of Hitler', or so ran the 1942 CP pamphlet.

Communists went out of their way to quell incipient strikes and issued fierce denunciations of strikers, who, they claimed, had been duped by fascist or Trotskyist agents. The already fractious relationship between communists and Trotskyists following events in Barcelona and Moscow continued to fester as the two camps eyed each other suspiciously. The CP added fuel to the fire with the publication of a scurrilous pamphlet, *Clear out Hitler's Agents! An Exposure of Trotskyist Disruption Being Organised in Britain*, which lambasted Trotskyists for being in league with Hitler:

> There is a group of people in Britain masquerading as socialists in order to cover up their fascist activities... They go among the factories, shipyards and coalfields, in the Labour, Trade Union and Co-operative organisations. They try to mislead the workers with cunning deception and lies... They sow doubt, suspicion and confusion, retard production and try to undermine the people's will to victory... They are called

Trotskyists... Trotsky's men are Hitler's men. They must be cleared out of every working-class organisation in the country.

The Trotskyist Workers' International League (WIL) strongly refuted these claims and in turn accused the CP of being in thrall to Stalin and of placing the needs of Moscow above the interests of the British and international working classes. They also offered a £10 reward:

To any Member of the Communist Party who can prove that the so-called Quotations from Trotskyist Publications in their Pamphlet "Clear Out Hitler's Agents!" are not Forgeries.
- OR -
To any Member of the CP who can show any page of this Pamphlet which does not contain a minimum of five lies.

One positive effect of the CP's renewed interest in combating fascism was a series of articles in the *Daily Worker* highlighting the potential threat posed by small groups of home-grown fascists who had either not been detained during the Regulation 18B round-up or who had subsequently been released from internment. Under the guidance of its news editor, Douglas Hyde, the paper focussed on the activities of the British National Party (BNP), a small but noisy group of fascists. The activities of several other suspect organisations also received coverage, including a number of groups that had been set up, ostensibly, to support 18B detainees and their families. On 8 December 1942, the *Daily Worker* reported on a meeting of the 18B Committee in Central London:

The fascist salute was given by some members of the audience at a meeting organised by a body calling itself the "18B Committee" in Holborn Hall on Sunday. Mosley's name was shouted and there were cries of "Perish Judah" at the end of the meeting.

The article then went on to describe signs of renewed fascist activity in and around the London area:

> swastikas chalked on posters in Central London, fascist slogans crayoned in underground stations, pro-Mosley slogans painted in Staines, Heston and Uxbridge, anti-Semitic slogans chalked or whitewashed in Maida Vale. 'Perish Judah,' 'Jews' War' and 'Watch out for the Blackshirts' all appeared in Hackney Wick and Shoreditch.

When Douglas Hyde's autobiography, *I Believed*, was published in 1951, some three years after he resigned, disillusioned, from the CP, he claimed to have knowingly overstated the fascist threat in war years because it suited the communist agenda. Although the minuscule size and scale of British fascist activity during the early forties suggests that there is some substance to Hyde's retrospective admission, his recollections of this period were undoubtedly coloured by a fall-out with the CP. Exaggerated or otherwise, he might be thanked for highlighting the existence of fascist renegades during a war against fascism.

In April 1943, the BNP formally disbanded. Constant scrutiny of its activities by the *Daily Worker* had finally forced it into voluntary liquidation. Hyde and his small team of reporters had been a thorn in its side from the outset, constantly exposing its pro-Nazi sympathies, its anti-Semitism and its hatred of trade unionism. For anyone who might have been tempted to believe that the disciples of fascism had finally given up the ghost, a report in the *Jewish Chronicle* of 6 August 1943 provided a timely and worrying reminder of the durability of fascist ideology:

> Last weekend, for the first time in three years, fascists tried to break up an open-air meeting in Ridley Road, Dalston... The

trouble began when some disparaging references were made to Mosley. The fascists began to rush the platform. There were some blows exchanged later, and a Jewish lad was arrested. "Although the Blackshirts are illegal," the correspondent was told, "they seem to engage in a lot of local activity; and everyone knows that they are holding private meetings".

A few weeks after this incident, the CP received advance notice from a sympathiser in the Home Office that Oswald Mosley was going to be released from prison on the grounds of ill health. This was confirmed on Thursday 18 November. Mosley and his wife were released two days later. The decision was not warmly received by anti-fascists. Harry Johnson, for instance, remembers feeling a sense of betrayal upon hearing the news:

A lot of people felt let down by Herbert Morrison. He was Labour Home Secretary for the coalition government during the war. He was responsible for Mosley being released from internment on the grounds that he was very ill with phlebitis and was likely to die in prison. In fact Mosley was so poorly that he went on to live for another forty years.

Labour Party supporter, Len Shipton was more circumspect, but even he found the decision difficult to accept:

I suppose I could see the reasoning behind Morrison's decision but my gut reaction was against it. I could see that he didn't want to turn Mosley into a martyr by letting him die in prison. I could also see that it was wrong to keep a man in prison without a proper trial but, on the other hand, Mosley's mates in the Luftwaffe had destroyed half the homes in our street and millions of people were still dying to stop the spread of fascism in Europe.

Sheila Lahr, a young Trotskyist from Muswell Hill in London, took a different view of the situation. Her anarchist, anti-fascist and immigrant father had been interred on the Isle of Man for three months. For her internment itself wasn't the issue:

I went along to a few of the demonstrations when Mosley was released from internment, but I remember thinking to myself, that whether he was released or not wasn't the main concern. It was the ideas he represented that were the problem.

The public mood was less restrained. The overwhelming majority wanted Mosley kept under lock and key. A hastily released CP pamphlet entitled *Keep Mosley in Prison* attempted to voice their concerns:

Yes, this is the Government that will go down in history for deciding, at the moment when it asks the nation to bear great sacrifices in the final stages of the fight against fascism, to set free the first man to import fascism here!

The CP's brand of patriotic anti-fascism found little favour amongst its critics on the Trotskyist left, however. The recently formed Revolutionary Communist Party (RCP) released a special supplement, *Mosley Release – A Challenge to Workers!* with its news sheet *Socialist Appeal*, which criticised what it saw as the Janus strategy of the CP:

the Stalinists cannot have it both ways. They cannot squeal when the National Government releases Mosley and treats the British fascists with kid gloves, and at the same time call upon the workers to support the Government because it is an "anti-fascist" Government fighting an "anti-fascist" war.

Despite these squabbles, the storm of public outrage that greeted news of Mosley's release, triggered protests that went far beyond the normal confines of anti-fascist activism. Two thousand factory workers took time off from work to protest outside the House of Commons on Tuesday 23 November. On the following Sunday, a mass demonstration of 35,000 workers in war industries marched in the pouring rain to Trafalgar Square on Sunday 28 November to register their condemnation of Morrison's decision. A constant stream of trade union delegates representing millions of workers visited Whitehall to demand that Mosley be kept under lock and key. Strikes in war industries were threatened.

Over a million people signed the petition demanding Mosley's continued internment and a total of 51 Labour MP's voted against his release. Even the National Council for Civil Liberties (NCCL) suggested that fascism posed a greater threat to civil liberty than Mosley's imprisonment leading to resignations over wavering on imprisonment without trial. Despite the furore, the decision to release Mosley was not reversed. He was allowed to retire to a house in the country. As a pre-condition of his release, he was obliged to remain politically inactive until the end of the war but there is evidence that he remained in close contact with a number of his former colleagues. As the war drew to a close, a number of different fascist groups and clubs began emerging from the ashes of the BU. Nationally, there were as many as fifty dotted around the country, with a combined membership of several thousand.

One of the largest groups was the British League of Ex-Servicemen and Women, led by Jeffrey Hamm, a former BU member and 18B detainee. The group became notorious for their provocative open-air meetings and anti-Semitic activities. The first British League meeting in Hyde Park on 5 November 1944 met with considerable hostility but Hamm was undeterred. He continued to campaign publicly in the East End and Hampstead areas of London. Following Hamm's lead, several other fascist groups began to step up their public campaigning, leading

Douglas Hyde to declare in the *Daily Worker* on 5 May 1945 that:

> former Fascists are more active in Britain today than they
> have been for the last five years. They play an active part in
> newly-created organisations and old ones that are being
> resurrected.

As an avid reader of the *Daily Worker*, Betty Davis could barely
believe what she was reading:

> A lot of people hoped that at least fascism had been finished
> by the war, but to our horror it came back up again. I thought
> the whole world would be ashamed of fascism and couldn't in
> any way defend it, but they did. It came up strong again, with
> the marches and insults and people being beaten up.

It was around about this time, that Ken Beddoe, a teenager from
Paddington in West London, encountered his first post-war
fascist meeting:

> I stumbled upon an outdoor fascist meeting on a patch of land
> near the Prince of Wales pub on Harrow Road. There was a
> speaker on the platform shouting all the usual stuff about
> Jews. I don't know who he was but I took exception to what
> he was saying and shouted something back at him. The next
> thing I saw was two big blokes heading in my direction and I
> had to make myself scarce.

Mosley had a part in fostering this resurgence of British fascism.
He spent his days covertly directing and encouraging the various
fascist groups, preparing them for the day when they would be
united under his leadership once more. His followers were
ordered to form book clubs and discussion groups in preparation
for his comeback. An important arm of this strategy was the

publication of the *Mosley News Letter*, which was due to go on sale in November 1945. Workers at a firm of wholesale newspaper distributors in London refused to handle the publication, however, and effectively stopped its distribution. One worker told his trade union official that having spent four years fighting fascism during the war he was 'not prepared to handle this stuff now.' Mosley took the union to court but lost the case and had to find another distributor.

On the 15 December 1945, Mosley addressed an audience of 800 ex-18B detainees and fascists at a Reunion Dance at the Royal Hotel in London. There were numerous fascist salutes and chants of 'Hail Mosley' when he appeared on stage. A *Sunday Pictorial* journalist who was present at the meeting, reported seeing:

> a girl dressed in the uniform of a Hitler maiden, several Servicemen in uniform, including a naval officer and a bemedalled RAF officer. And with them there was a generous sprinkling of unsavoury mufflered characters.

The journalist was later kicked and punched from behind as he was ejected from the building for taking notes during Mosley's speech. The fascists were still trying to remain undercover, but as the pace of their activities quickened they inevitably attracted attention. On 4 January 1946, the *Daily Worker* noted that:

> There is a tremendous amount of coming and going in ex-fascist circles today. Former Mosleyites are being contacted and sounded out as to where they stand. The Mosleyites have, it appears, the leading cadres, the framework of a national organisation, the basis of a rank-and-file of some thousands, a number of friendly bookshops in existence with more planned, and the prospect of a flow of new material from the proposed Mosley press. In addition the reappearance of a Mosley organisation would probably be quickly followed by

mergers with a number of kindred organisations.

Meanwhile, the various strands of the anti-fascist movement had not been idle. The NCCL published a list of British fascists who had aided and abetted Germany during the war, so that the issue did not disappear from public view after the hanging of William Joyce for treason on 3 January. At the same time, the Association of Jewish Ex-Servicemen (AJEX) had started to hold rival street meetings on the same pitches as those used by the fascists, resulting in confrontations between the two groups. Henry Morris, a young Jewish ex-serviceman, recalls being invited to participate in the AJEX campaign:

I came out of the Navy in February 1946 and more or less straight away joined the Association of Jewish Ex-Servicemen, principally because I was concerned with fighting fascism and anti-Semitism. By this time, the Board of Deputies had become concerned that Mosley was setting himself up again and they called on AJEX and asked us if we would conduct an outdoor speaking campaign against fascism. As a member of AJEX, I saw that this was an opportunity for me to do something about fascism and I enrolled. I had a short course in public speaking, and from 1947 to 1952 I was continually engaged in either surveillance of fascist meetings or speaking at places like Hyde Park Corner, Ridley Road, Earl's Court, and various other parts of London where the fascists had their pitches. Major Lionel Rose was the director of our outdoor campaign. He was a brilliant orator himself. He was an extremely well educated man. He trained the speakers, often spoke himself, and produced quite a number of pamphlets.

Lionel Rose was responsible for compiling the *Factual Survey* series of pamphlets, which documented the activities and organisational abilities of fascist groups in Britain. Through surveillance of fascist meetings, AJEX managed to piece together a comprehensive picture of the various components of the emerging fascist movement.

The anti-fascist movement was re-mobilising. 5,000 anti-fascists rallied in Hyde Park to protest about Hamm's anti-Semitic campaign in Hampstead. It was in this quiet north London suburb, rather than the traditional battlegrounds of the East End, that one of Britain's fiercest anti-fascist organizations emerged. Its name was the 43 Group, and Morris Beckman was there at its inception:

When I got back from the war, I met up with several other fellows such as Sam Klampf and Gerry Flamberg, who were ex-paratroopers, at Maccabi House, in West Hampstead, which was home to London's Jewish sports organisations. They had returned from the war and were quite bemused to find that Mosley had been released from his internment under regulation 18B and was busy resurrecting his pre-war Blackshirt party. To our consternation and anger, we encountered again the same anti-Semitism that we had encountered before the war. The demobilised and ex-POW's were coming into Maccabi House saying "Look at this leaflet." It would be full of anti-Semitism, going on about "The aliens in our midst" and so forth. Jewish shops and Synagogues in Bethnal Green, Burnt Oak and Edgware were being daubed with Swastikas and the letters PJ, which meant "Perish Judah".

In those days you could go to a Movietone News theatre or Pathe Gazette theatre and see the first documentaries of the concentration camps. I went with a cousin of mine, Harry Rose, who had been a Sergeant in the Chindits, the unit that had fought behind Japanese lines in Burma. He'd had a very tough war out there. Anyway, we watched this film about Belsen. We saw the piles of bodies being pushed by bulldozers into large pits. It made us feel sick seeing these bodies like skeletons covered with skin. Then we came out of the cinema, walked down Edgware Road towards Star Street in Kilburn and we saw a fellow on a platform, a released 18B detainee, talking to an audience and he was saying things like "Not enough Jews were burned at Belsen" and things like that. There were a couple of policemen present but their job was to protect the speaker not run him in for incitement. They were there to protect him from hecklers. Harry said "I can't believe it." He was still in his uniform, wearing his bush hat and medals, and he went up to the policeman and said "What the bloody hell are you doing standing there? Arrest him." The policeman just shrugged his shoulders and walked away. Harry said "Well I'll get the bastard." I grabbed Harry, and another fellow in military uniform said "Look mate, don't cause any trouble or you'll get arrested" and between us we managed to restrain him.

We went back to Maccabi House and met up with other fellows who were also beginning to feel anger at what was going on. We felt that we hadn't come back from the war to put up with this but we didn't know quite what to do about it. We contacted the Houses of Parliament and six of us went up and spoke to a number of MP's, including Tom Driberg, Ian Mikardo, Woodrow Wyatt and Clinton Davis. We also spoke to Manny Shinwell, who was a real feisty old socialist. Manny had been a boxer in Glasgow in his younger days, and when we asked him what we should do, he replied "Kill the bastards." Questions were asked in Parliament but due to the efforts of Chuter Ede, the Labour Home Secretary, they became lost in deep sand and nothing was done. So we went to the Jewish Board of Deputies and saw Professor Brodetsky, Rueben Lieberman and Louis Hydleman. They were academics and legal gentlemen and they were, of course, more than double our age. Of course we didn't see eye to eye with them and they got very nervous about us. They said,

"Look boys, for god's sake, don't cause any more trouble. There's enough anti-Semitism caused by the troubles in Palestine what with the Irgun killing British soldiers." We replied "Yes, but we're not going to stand for this. You've got to do something." They said "Well, we're seeing some Members of Parliament next week. We're having lunch with them, we're going to discuss it with them." One of our fellows, a Pole called Jules Kopinsky who was wounded during the storming of Monte Casino said "Well, you won't stop the fascists by passing bits of paper backwards and forwards and having lunches at the House of Commons. That's no bloody good. You've got to do something more." Their reply was to plead with us not to do anything impulsive but we said "Well, if you're not going to anything about it, we will." Anyway, one Sunday on the last weekend of February 1946 after deciding that we were fed up with the canteen talk and egg and chips on offer at Maccabi House, we decided to go up to Jack Straw's Castle, a famous old pub on top of Hampstead Heath. Four of us jumped into my old Ford Prefect and drove up there. After parking the car, we noticed this meeting on a strip of grass alongside the pond. The meeting was being held by the British League of Ex-Servicemen and on the platform was Jeffrey Hamm, who had been one of Mosley's pre-war inner-circle. He'd been interned for two and a half years during the war under 18B regulations. The government had got rid of him by sending him down to the Falkland Islands to teach. We got out of the car, hung around the edge of the crowd, and listened to Hamm's speech. It was the usual sort of guff. "While our boys were away fighting and dying, Jewish landlords made lots of money and now our boys can't afford a place to rent." "We shouldn't have fought the Germans, they were our kith and kin." All that sort of stuff. In front of the platform were four young fascist thugs selling the first post-war fascist paper, *Britain Awake*. My three fellow 'aliens' and I decided to act.

Len Sherman, an ex-Welsh Guard Sergeant, who was also the Maccabi Judo and wrestling champion, nudged me and said "I'll take those two on the end. They're mine." Gerry Flamberg, the paratrooper who had won the Military Medal at Arnhem, was on my other side. He nudged me and said "The platform's mine." I nodded towards one of the fascists and said "I'll take him" and Alec Carson, who had a more sedentary role as a fighter pilot in the RAF, said rather nervously "Well, I'll take the other one then." We walked into the crowd, which numbered about a hundred, and Len approached the two fascists he'd singled out. Len was one of those Jews like Danny Kaye and Kirk Douglas who were very blond-haired and blue-eyed. He was a very good-looking chap and would have made the perfect model for a Nazi propaganda photograph. Len walked over to his two fascists, and said "Bloody good job boys. I can't stand the bleeding Jews myself." As they stepped forward to talk to him, I saw his hands come up and heard a loud thud as he bashed their heads together. They went down as if they'd been pole-axed. I saw the platform go over. Gerry was kicking hell out of Jeffrey Hamm, lifting him up, knocking him down again. I kicked my target in the balls and he went down in a heap, before hobbling away. Alec's target got away by running down the hill into some bushes and trees.

We got back safely to Maccabi House and told all the fellows there about the fight and they said "Well, if nobody else is going to do anything about it, we'll do it ourselves." We convened a meeting the following week at Maccabi House and 38 ex-servicemen and five ex-servicewomen turned up. At the meeting we decided to launch an all out attack on the post-war fascist movement. We decided that we were going to tackle them by throwing away the Marquis of Queensbury rulebook. We were going to regard them as much an enemy as those we had been fighting during the war. Unfortunately, we couldn't use weapons against them, we couldn't shoot them or bayonet them but we were going to attack them nevertheless. It was at this meeting that the 43 Group was born, named after the number of war veterans in the room.

We started to get organised straightaway, and within two months we had three hundred members, mostly Jews, but with a sprinkling of Gentiles. We were very disciplined. We had to be. Our job was to put as many fascists in hospital as we could.

One of first activities of the 43 Group was an attempt to disrupt a meeting of the short-lived British Vigilantes Action League at the Albert Hall in March 1946. Group commandos had taken their place in the stalls and waited for the right moment to make their presence known, when large numbers of communists invaded the hall and began to shout down the speaker. Faced with a situation beyond their control, the fascist stewards and speakers deserted the meeting. Former International Brigader, Bob Doyle was one of a number of anti-fascists who commandeered the microphone and lectured the fascists in the audience on the error of their ways. 'Very nerve wracking', is how he described it. Several other speakers joined him and turned the fascist rally into an anti-fascist celebration. The meeting was eventually closed down on the orders of the police, and the various anti-fascist groups went their separate ways. The Albert Hall meeting had not turned out exactly as planned for the 43 Group but, as Morris Beckman explains, they soon got into the swing of things:

By early summer, 43 Group commandos were attacking between six and ten fascist street meetings a week with about a third being ended by the speaker's platform being knocked over. Once the platform was knocked over the police would close the meeting and we would make our getaway. Many young fascists and new recruits had been told by their leaders that the Jews were an easy touch but within a few weeks of joining they might have been beaten up two or three times. They then started to realise that what they had been told wasn't true.

Within six months we had nearly a thousand members, all ex-service. We had loads of East End boys. Ten years earlier they had been schoolboys and had suffered under the depredations of Mosley's Blackshirts, but by now they were a different cup of tea. They were tough, they were seasoned. They had been to war and survived. Metaphorically, they spat on their hands and said "Lovely. This is just what I want. Let me get at the bastards." We had between eighty-five to ninety different trades within the group, including doctors, lawyers, journalists, porters, locksmiths, printers and so on. A lot of these trades came in very, very useful at different times. There were about 200 ex-servicewomen in the 43 Group and they were very useful. They were the cement that linked the commandos to all the other activities. They could speak every language, they could look at photos and blow them up and pick out and recognise faces. We also had about fifteen cab drivers who were our eyes and ears on the street. If they spotted any fascist meetings or paper sales they would phone us up immediately.

We had a fellow who joined us called Jeff Bernard. He'd been in the film business and produced and directed films. He was a very austere fellow, very tall and thin with horn-rimmed spectacles, and he demanded discipline. He was Chairman of the National Executive Committee (NEC) of the 43 Group. There were twelve of us on the committee, including Jeff. When we had our meetings, we had no papers or pencils, just an agenda of what we were going to do. At one meeting, Jeff laid down the following ground rules for the group. A: The 43 group was apolitical. There had to be no politics inside the group. Anybody promoting communism or conservatism or whatever or who introduced any Zionist or anti-Zionist politics in the group would be kicked out. Within the group we had just one objective, to knock out Mosley's post-war fascist movement. B: If a 43 Group member pledged to turn up to attack a fascist meeting or raid a fascist bookshop or whatever, then they had to do it. There was no backing out. C: If a group member saw another group member in difficulties during an action, it was mandatory that they went to his assistance.

Phil Kaiserman notes some of the different anti-fascist strategies within the alliances between Jewish ex-service organisations, the 43 Group, communists, civil liberty campaigners and even the Labour Party:

The majority of anti-fascist work I was involved in came after the war. I came home in February 1946 and found to my great surprise that the fascists were starting up again. Jewish ex-servicemen formed organisations all over the country to deal with the problem. We had one here in Manchester, the Union of Jewish Ex-Servicemen and Women and they did a lot of anti-fascist work. Many of the leaders of this group were leading Communist Party members. My brother Leon and me were on the Executive Committee, as were comrades like Martin Bobker, Maxie Druck, Louie Rubens, and Hymie Davis. We set up the group with the idea of fighting fascism and protecting the local Jewish community. The Manchester Union of Jewish Ex-Servicemen and Women organised many public meetings and invited speakers from many different groups, including the 43 Group and the National Council for Civil Liberties. As well as the physical fight to clear the streets of fascism, Manchester UJEX campaigned to get legislation passed making fascist and racist propaganda illegal. D. N. Pritt from the NCCL and local Labour MPs supported our campaign but, despite the fact that a Labour government was in office, this struggle was unsuccessful. We always favoured persuasion over violence. We would try winning people over by political argument rather than force. When there was no other choice we'd end up punching them, of course, but only as a last resort. There were very definite links between the 43 Group in London and UJEX. We invited their speakers up to Manchester on several occasions. Len Johnson came up to Manchester, as did Gerry Flamberg and a number of others.

Monty Goldman, a YCL member from Hackney and one of the 43 Group, recalls how the membership of political groups and anti-fascist organisations overlapped:

I was mentioned briefly in Morris Beckman's book on the 43 Group. He didn't mention me by name but I was the young boy who kept pestering the group to be allowed to go out with them. I was only young at the time really but I attended every anti-fascist meeting in Hackney I possibly could, whether it was the Communist Party, the YCL, AJEX, the 43 Group, the National Anti-Fascist League. You name it I was involved.

The 43 Group were out on the streets every Sunday at either Ridley Road or John Campbell Road trying to shut down fascist meetings by either pushing over the platform or making so much trouble the police had to close them down. They were supported by members of the Communist Party and the YCL. There was very close co-operation between the leadership of the 43 Group and the leadership of the Communist Party. People like Gerry Flamberg and Harry Pollitt met regularly in the Communist Party's headquarters in King Street. Harry Pollitt spoke at a mass meeting in York Hall in Bethnal Green, which was jointly stewarded by the 43 Group and the Communist Party. Bethnal Green was a fascist stronghold and you needed a lot of stewards when you went down there. The Party provided a hundred stewards and the 43 Group provided three hundred. So in addition to the three thousand people inside the hall, there was an array of people outside to prevent any trouble.

There were some real hard-cases in the 43 Group, people like the Goldberg twins, who were hard as nails. Fatty Raines was another. His family supported the group financially and physically. There was also Jackie Myerovitch who had wanted to be a boxer but very sensibly turned it in after he lost his first fight. Someone else I remember was Big Sid Tonga. Big Sid wasn't all that bright, but he was a great fellow. There was a story about Big Sid, which always got retold when people were recounting tales of previous battles. Big Sid had got hold of a fascist down in Hackney and he turned to Jackie Myerovitch and asked "Shall I break his arm or break his leg Jackie?" It wasn't always a case of having a punch-up though. We'd have a punch-up when there was provocation. If the fascists marched through Kingsland Road shouting "The Yids, the Yids. We gotta get rid of the Yids" we'd have a go at them. If they spoke at Hoxton and weren't abusive, we'd oppose them but it would be less aggressive and would usually just take the form of mass heckling.

Morris Beckman confirms the mutually beneficial relationship between the CP and the 43 Group:

There were occasions when the communists would phone us up, or we would phone them up and exchange information on the fascists, because we had a common enemy. On quite a few occasions the communists turned up to attack the same fascist meetings as the 43 Group and we fought alongside them but we kept ourselves separate. The communists were very effective. They were the only people attacking the fascists in the same way we were.

There was also a cell of communists inside the 43 Group based around activists like Len Rolnick, Wolf Wayne and Tony Clayton. This cell attempted to influence the 43 Group from within to take more leftward political direction. Communists who engaged in militant anti-fascist activity, whether inside or outside the 43 Group, were doing so without the official approval of the CP. In the years following the street disorders of the 1930s, the CP was happy to be seen as the champion of the radical anti-fascist tradition but its official anti-fascist strategy in the 1940s was based upon calling for the state to stamp out the fascist menace. This brand of anti-fascism was more or les ignored in places like Dalston, where communists continued to directly and physically confront fascists. Militant communists rallied to Ridley Road where they rubbed shoulders with Jewish anti-fascists, anarchists, activists from Hackney Trades Council and Trotskyists from the Revolutionary Communist Party. Sheila Lahr had only just joined the RCP when news of the fascist revival prompted the group into action:

> I joined the Revolutionary Communist Party, which had a centre in Harrow Road, in about 1946 or 1947. I'd been working for the Independent Labour Party on their newspaper, the *Socialist Leader*, before that but at the time I felt they were a bit too wishy-washy for me and they were more or less on the way out by that time in any case. I hadn't been in the RCP very long before we heard that Jeffrey Hamm and the fascists had begun speaking in Dalston. So of course, Jock Haston and Millie Lee said "We've all got to go and take over the pitches so they can't speak." And that's exactly what we did. We would sometimes go down there on a Saturday evening and take over the pitch in order to prevent the fascists from grabbing it the following morning. I never stayed out

overnight myself, my mother wouldn't have had that but a number of comrades did and on the Sunday morning, we'd all meet up in Ridley Road. The RCP wasn't a large party by any means, but there would be about thirty or forty comrades there. Then of course there would be the 43 Group, a number of Stalinists, mostly YCLers, and lots of other different people. The Stalinists absolutely hated the Trotskyists and even physically attacked people selling *Socialist Appeal*. Jock Haston was attacked several times by communists. They were absolutely shocking, the Stalinists. We used to call them goons. The YCL never attacked us at Ridley Road. That would have been stupid. They viewed attacking the fascists as more important than attacking Trotskyists. There was no question of the two groups working together though. People from Hackney Trades Council were also active, as well as a few left-wing Labour Party people. There were quite a few anarchists at Ridley Road as well. There was a direct action group, which had broken away from the Freedom Group, who also took part in the events. So it was quite a mixture of people. There might have been one or two individual members of Common Wealth who took part, but that's all. Another group that used to go down Ridley Road was Hashomer Hatzair. They were a Jewish youth group, who were connected to the labour movement but I don't know if they were officially affiliated to the Labour Party or not. They were quite a large group and had a few hundred members in London.

Once we'd taken over the pitch, someone like Haston would start making an anti-fascist speech and the fascists would usually move away. We'd all be in our different groups but there were so many of us milling around that I think the fascists knew they would lose if they tried to shift us. They didn't have enough strength to clear us away and would disappear. After a while, the police would come along on their horses and ride into the crowd and try to clear the area. It was a very crowded area and it could quite quickly develop into a terrible mêlée. It could be quite frightening but I suppose when you're young you take it in your stride. The police were very antagonistic. I wouldn't say they were supporting the fascists. I wouldn't go as far as that but I think they saw the anti-fascists, who were all communists in their eyes, as the troublemakers. They didn't like the disorder and decided that it was the anti-fascists who were to blame for the disorder on the streets rather than the fascists. Of course, it was a lot of excitement but most of the time we did actually stop the fascists getting the pitch. On occasions when we didn't get the pitch, everyone would heckle the fascist speakers, or the 43 Group would rush the platform and chase the fascists off.

Jock Haston and Tommy Reilly were arrested on one occasion when they rushed a platform and tried to push the speaker off his soapbox.

Although the actual membership of the RCP was tiny, anti-fascism formed an important part of its activities so it assumed a greater prominence in this field than its numbers perhaps warranted. The RCP took part in numerous street actions against the fascists as well as published and distributed a series of anti-fascist leaflets, pamphlets and supplements. Issue 50 of *Socialist Appeal*, for instance, carried

R.C.P. Banners in the Front

WORKERS DEMONSTRATE AT FASCIST MEETING
The above picture was taken at the Albert Hall "Vigilante Action League" meeting. The banners in the forefront are carried by our comrades. ("News Chronicle" photo.)

'R.C.P. Banners in the Front', *The Menace of Fascism*, 1948, Revolutionary Communist Party, 1948.

reports of RCP activists recapturing pitches taken from the CP by the fascists in Paddington and Ilford and at Kilburn they 'took part in opposing the fascists at a local meeting.' The main focus of the RCP's anti-fascism was still in Hackney, where their message, according to Tommy Reilly in *Socialist Appeal*, was 'meeting with a sympathetic response.' He reported '20,000 – Smash the Fascists – leaflets being distributed at public meetings and pasted on walls. North London comrades whitewashed the Hackney area with our slogans.'

The most well-known RCP publication was *The Menace of Fascism: What It Is and How to Fight It* by Ted Grant, which, in an echo of the CP of the 1930s, called for the formation of 'a working class united front against fascism' and the establishment of a Workers' Defence Corps based upon the 'Trade Union, cultural and political organisations of the working class.' This message was taken onto the streets by RCP members and apparently found favour. *Socialist Appeal* reported one such incident at an anti-fascist meeting at Ridley Road:

> Trotskyist speakers – Comrades T. Reilly and J. Haston – put our point of view from the united anti-fascist platform offered by Common Wealth. Our policy for a united front and the formation of workers' defence guards got a great reception from the crowd, which at one stage reached 2,000.

Whilst it remained critical of the CP's call for a state ban on fascism, the RCP also demanded government legislation against fascist propaganda and activities but argued that such legislation should be 'backed by determined and organised activity on the part of the workers.' This, the RCP suggested, would ensure that the enforcement of such a ban would not work to 'the disadvantage of the working class.' The theory was not without merit at a time when an anti-fascist consensus existed amongst the organised workers but the RCP had negligible influence amongst them and could therefore offer no guarantees that its policy would not backfire on the left. In fact, the Labour government of the day had no intention of banning fascism, arguing that such a ban would be an attack on freedom of speech. Britain was the only country in Europe, apart from Spain and Portugal, where it was still possible to glorify Hitler and preach undiluted fascism whilst enjoying the full protection of the law.

News reports of the situation in Palestine gave British fascism fresh impetus in 1947. A total of 338 British subjects were killed by Jewish paramilitary gangs between 1945 and 1948. Public outrage at these deaths reached a peak in August 1947 when two British military policemen, Mervyn Paice and Clifford Martin, were kidnapped and killed by the Irgun. The incident sparked a wave of anti-Semitic rioting across the country forcing Jewish public speakers like Henry Morris onto the defensive:

The very first AJEX meeting that I addressed was outside Gloucester Road tube station. It was just after the death of the two sergeants in Palestine. I don't know if you're aware of the situation but in reprisal for the execution of two Jewish men for terrorist activities, two British soldiers were taken and hanged. Well, it created, quite understandably, a very unpleasant atmosphere in Britain at the time and Mosley's crowd were quick to take advantage. When I stood up to make my first speech, it just kept going round and round "Why don't you go back to Palestine" and "What about the sergeants?" And it ended up with my platform being smashed. A similar situation occurred at Durdham Downs in Bristol. One of our speakers, a lady, was addressing a meeting, when one of the men in the audience introduced himself as being the father of Sergeant Paice, who was one of the two soldiers. She sympathised with him, explained the situation and then closed the meeting out of respect.

One of the few journalists awake to the resurgence of British fascism was Frederic Mullally, political editor of the *Sunday*

Pictorial, who wrote numerous articles, pamphlets and books on the threat to democracy posed by 'Britain's fascist maggots', including one called *Fascism Inside England*. He challenged Jeffrey Hamm to a public debate at Ridley Road on 17 August, an offer that Hamm gratefully accepted. A large crowd had gathered in anticipation of the meeting but when Mullally arrived he was immediately set upon and eventually dragged to safety by a squad of 43 Group commandos.

Ridley Road in Dalston was home to a thriving street market during the week but on Sundays or on the long summer evenings after the stallholders had packed up their wares and the shopkeepers had pulled down their shutters, it would attract an entirely different crowd. At one end it opened up into a square, which provided an ideal venue for soapbox orators and public speakers. The market was in the centre of a working class Jewish neighbourhood, making it a tempting target for anti-Semites like Hamm and his associates. They were opposed by anti-fascists of all persuasions so the area increasingly found itself at the epicentre of the growing conflict. Pitched battles were fought between fascists and anti-fascists on a regular basis throughout the summer and autumn of 1947. Weekly reports began to appear in the national press detailing the latest clashes and number of arrests. Crowds of excited onlookers were drawn to the street and mounted police were frequently called into action in an attempt to quell the disorder. Despite police intervention, anti-fascists succeeded in severely disrupting or closing almost every single fascist meeting in Ridley Road during this period.

One way of stopping fascists from speaking was to 'jump the pitch' as Sheila Lahr and others have mentioned in their accounts of Ridley Road. Jumping the pitch was such an accepted practice that the police would allow the first arrivals to occupy a speaker's spot regardless of any counter-claim by their opponents. A kind of political musical chairs developed as fascists and anti-fascists vied with each other to be first to occupy the most popular pitches. Members of Hackney Trades Council, the AJEX, the RCP and all used this tactic, although it could involve arriving at the designated spot many hours beforehand or even sleeping out overnight. Henry Morris remembers AJEX speakers jumping the pitch at Ridley Road as well as the more direct tactics of the 43 Group:

Ridley Road was probably the most notorious spot at the time. We stayed up all night there on several occasions, so that we could steal the pitch. There were aspects to Ridley Road, pros and cons. To some extent it was confrontational, because there were fascists in the crowd who would try to heckle and disrupt the meeting but our speakers always managed to come out on top. We made sure we had plenty of security to make sure nothing happened to our pitch but we would try to beat the fascists by defeating their ideas and arguments. When the 43 Group were involved in confrontation with the fascists down at Ridley Road, things were done that I couldn't approve of. Some of the things I saw down there was not the way we would have gone about it.

Morris Beckman saw things differently, of course. For him, physical force was a necessary and successful weapon against the fascists:

By 1947, the 43 Group was well underway. We were attacking fascist meetings all over London by this time. We worked out two methods they couldn't cope with. When they had a big meeting of three to four thousand, say in Ridley Road, we would insert into different parts of the audience three wedges of very hard men. At a given signal they would start moving slowly through the crowd towards the fascist platform. They picked up speed as they approached the platform, shouting "Get out of the way. Move away" at the audience. The crowd, sensing danger, would part before them and the wedges would hit the fascist cordon around the platform at speed. If only one commando got through to push over the platform, the police would close down the meeting and wouldn't allow the fascists to set it up again. At Ridley Road, there was a brick wall adjoining Woolworths where the fascists would have their meetings. The police would line up in front of this wall and in front of them would be the fascist platform and surrounding the platform would be three cordons of fascist stewards whose job it was to protect the speaker. Our aim was to penetrate these cordons and knock over the platform so the police would close the meeting. The other method would be to start arguments and scuffles in half a dozen places in the crowd. These would usually spread like wildfire and the police would get fed up with trying to sort out all the trouble and tell the speakers to pack up the platform.

In his autobiography, *Action Replay*, Jeffrey Hamm claims that the 'Battle of Ridley Road' was fought and won by the British League although he fails to explain how he reaches this conclusion. There was an increase in police numbers, which coupled with an influx of officers with a bias against Jews and communists, contributed to making the job of anti-fascists a lot more difficult but, as Morris Beckman explains, it didn't halt the fighting:

A lot of the police absolutely hated us. When the British quit Palestine, the police in Palestine, who were the equivalent of the Black and Tans in southern Ireland, who were real bastards, came back and joined the British police. Quite a few of them were allotted to G Division where a lot of the fighting was taking place and they were very hostile to us. There was one, Inspector Satterthwaite, who was really anti-Semitic. He used to walk about with his stick, pointing at 43 Group members shouting "Grab him. Arrest him." And if a group member's head came within swinging distance of his stick he would whack them. He was quite notorious with us but, during one fight near Pembury Corner, Len decided to get even with him. He sneaked around behind him, tapped him on the shoulder, and as Satterthwaite turned around Len hit him. He really hit him hard. He knocked him down and broke his nose. From that moment onwards, the Inspector became determined to find the fellow who hit him, and it became a standing joke within Dalston Lane police station. They'd say "Have you found him yet?" It didn't matter how many police they put on duty, or how fascist-minded they were, we still managed to close down 85 per cent of the meetings we targetted.

Monty Goldman also remembers the notorious Satterthwaite and the biased policing at Dalston:

I went down to Ridley Road a lot and there were two Chief Inspectors down there who were very fascist-minded. One was Superintendent Watson and the other was Chief Superintendent Satterthwaite. Satterthwaite was actually mentioned in Parliament by Phil Piratin, Communist Party MP for Mile End, because of the racist ideology that he had.

Satterthwaite was involved in a further violent incident in Ridley Road on 13 July 1947. Two Jewish men were jailed on 18 August following an alleged assault on Satterthwaite during a British League meeting in Dalston. David Goldstein of Bow and Murray Silver of Hackney were both charged with assaulting Satterthwaite, the former accused of kicking and biting, the latter using insulting behaviour at a public meeting.

In fact, it was not fresh reserves of police nor the anti-fascist arrests that finally quelled the fighting at Ridley Road. Fascist meetings in the area tailed off significantly after 1947. Hamm claimed that this was due to the particularly severe winter of '47-'48, but when the warmer weather returned in the spring the fascists were largely absent. Sheila Lahr confirms that the fascists no longer seemed to have the stomach for the increasingly bitter struggle:

These disturbances went on week after week at Ridley Road and eventually, I think, the fascists decided that they weren't getting anywhere with it and called it a day.

Morris Beckman also identifies autumn and winter of '47 as the moment when Ridley Road was ceded to the anti-fascists:

It was towards the end of 1947 that the first fascists started coming over to us. "No more fighting, we've had enough" they would say. "I'm leaving. Can we have a talk?" They were leaving in droves. They would be in a cordon protecting a fascist speaker and when they saw the 43 Group commandos coming towards them they would make their decision to leave. On some occasions they even left the cordon on the spot and come over to us through the crowd and say "I've finished with it all. I'm going." They couldn't deal with it at all.

It was this very moment when fascists had been defeated at street level that Mosley chose to make his comeback. In anticipation of the fresh impetus that the re-appearance of Mosley might give British fascism, anti-fascists also mustered their forces and braced themselves for the expected onslaught. According to Morris Beckman, the 43 Group experienced a considerable expansion during this period:

The 43 Group continued to organise and grow. We divided London into North, Northwest, South, East, and Central London branches. We also developed a branch in Newcastle-

Upon-Tyne. They got rid of the fascists up there. The Geordies hated the fascists. They never did have much time for them. We had a good branch in Leeds and the fascists were snuffed out there. In Manchester we established links with the Manchester Union of Jewish Ex-Servicemen and Women, known as MUJEX, who had roughly a thousand members. They were bigger than we were and we liaised with them on a regular basis. They would come down to London and we would go up there. The fascists were cleared out of there. We also had a branch in Nottingham and a very good branch down in Brighton. We printed a broadsheet newspaper called *On Guard* and we had a lot of top people who wrote articles for us. Dr Hewlett Johnson, the 'Red Dean of Canterbury,' wrote for it. Douglas Hyde, the news editor of the *Daily Worker* wrote for it, as did James Cameron, the top foreign correspondent of the Beaverbrook Press. We printed 5,000 copies of *On Guard* monthly and could have sold many more.

The October 1947 edition of *On Guard* revealed that Mosley was intending to make his political comeback the following month. 43 Group sources got it spot on. On 15 November 1947, Mosley addressed a meeting at the Memorial Hall in Farringdon attended by delegates from more than 50 different fascist organisations. He informed them he would be re-entering politics with a new organisation, the Union Movement (UM). Thanks to its spies in the various fascist organisations, the 43 Group knew the meeting was due to take place but because of the elaborate security arrangements undertaken by the fascists, they were unable to pinpoint its exact location in advance. Monty Goldman was one of those tasked with the job of finding out where the fascists were headed:

I was a scout for the 43 Group when Mosley made his comeback. The 43 Group commandos had all gathered in

Fleet Street by the Express building and it was my job to follow the fascists to where they were holding their meeting and report back. The fascists were assembling at the Salmon and Ball and I followed them on the bus to where Mosley was speaking and then immediately returned to the 43 Group and passed on the details.

As the meeting got underway, 43 Group commandos attempted to storm the building. Truncheon wielding police officers joined forces with fascist stewards to thwart the attack. Missiles were thrown at the doors and windows. When further police reinforcements arrived, the anti-fascists dispersed before wholesale arrests could be made. One demonstrator told reporters 'We are the 43 Group, Jewish ex-servicemen. We are heeding the advice of police and are going away.' A few days later, the 43 Group discovered the location of another 'secret' Mosley meeting at a school in Wilmot Street, Bethnal Green. The police prevented a crowd of 43 Group members from approaching the school allowing the meeting to go ahead without incident. After Mosley had been driven away at high speed, a crowd of fascists swarmed out the meeting to attack the counter-demonstrators. Fighting lasted for twenty minutes.

As the official launch of the Union Movement drew nearer, Mosley announced plans to hold a further public meeting in Hackney on 15 December. During the build-up to this meeting, he wrote to the Home Secretary, the Director of Public Prosecutions and the Lord Chancellor in a vain attempt to persuade them to take legal action against Hackney Trades Council for remarks reported in the *Hackney Gazette* on 8 December. Bob Darke, Secretary of the Trades Council, was reported as saying 'We are trying to get Fascism banned in the Borough by constitutional means, but they seem to be exhausted.' It was also alleged that he said 'Mosley is coming to this Borough and disturbances must take place.'

The Union Movement was formally launched on 8 February 1948 at Wilfred Street School near Victoria Station. Mosley addressed an audience of 300 people drawn from numerous fascist groups, book clubs and literary societies. The *Manchester Guardian* reported that 'the meeting passed off quietly except that Sir Oswald spoke rather loudly.' In its wake, leading UM figures embarked on a speaking tour of the provincial towns and cities in order to establish UM branches. This led to another bout of fights between fascists and anti-fascists. Phil Kaiserman was one of the organisers of the anti-fascist mobilisation when the UM tried to set up shop in Manchester in March 1948:

> Towards the end of the forties, we heard that the fascists were planning to hold a meeting in the city centre and immediately started to organise a counter-demonstration. The fascist meeting was meant to take place on a site bombed by the Luftwaffe during the war but when the fascists turned up in their armoured van they found a huge crowd of anti-fascists waiting for them. The van had been designed so that the speaker could address his audience without having to leave the safety of his vehicle. This was because the fascists were so unpopular that their speakers couldn't address the public without fear of attack. People started throwing bricks and stones at the van but when this didn't make much of an impact the crowd surged forward and began rocking the van from side to side in an attempt to turn it over. The driver of the van panicked and drove off as quickly as he could. That was the last we saw of them for a number of years.

The UM also tried to maintain a regular pitch on Market Street in the city centre selling *The Union*, its weekly paper. This was opposed by Jewish anti-fascists selling *On Guard* nearby. Mutual hostility between the two groups erupted into a pitched battle one weekend with the result that six fascists and three anti-fascists appeared before Manchester magistrates. The UM abandoned their sales pitch thereafter.

On 21 April in Leeds, 100 members of the Jewish Ex-Servicemen's Association joined forces with a similar number of communists to stop an outdoor Union Movement meeting in the city. Their mere presence in the vicinity intimidated the fascists into abandoning their meeting. Communists also broke up UM meetings on three separate occasions in Liverpool. There were regular clashes between anti-fascists and fascists in Derby and Nottingham and when Jeffrey Hamm attempted to speak outside the City Hall in Sheffield, he received exactly the same treatment as he had grown accustomed to in London. He was knocked off his platform. Morris Beckman recalls that an attempt by the UM to gain a foothold in South Wales also met with determined opposition:

> Len Sherman used to go across to Wales to visit his old mates from the Welsh Guards and one day he found out through 43 Group intelligence sources that the fascists were going to have a big meeting in Newport in South Wales. They wanted to try and open up a branch in the town and build up the fascist movement in Wales. So Len went down to Newport and he warned his ex-wartime colleagues that the fascists were planning to come down in force. Len's mates said "Don't worry about that. We'll sort them out."
>
> Len went down the day before the fascists were due in town and stayed overnight with his mates. In the morning the fascists started to assemble on the forecourt in front of Newport station. They were planning to form up there and march through the town with their marching band and all their flags. All was going well, until bodies of very tough Welshmen suddenly appeared on the forecourt. They were slate workers, coal miners, dockers, rugby players and they completely surrounded the fascists. Three of these Welshmen

walked into the middle of the fascist crowd and approached the fascist leaders, Keohane and Raven Thompson, who was one of Mosley's closest associates. These three Welshmen were very tough-looking characters according to Len and for Len to say that really meant something. Anyway, they told Thompson "You're down here but you're not leaving the forecourt and you're going back straight away. Now you've got the option of going back vertically, on your feet, or horizontally. Either way, we're not having you here." One of the Welshman noticed the fascist band, and he said "That big drum, that must have cost a lot of money. We'll see if we can smash that up." The fascists looked around the forecourt and they obviously didn't fancy their chances much. They made the very sensible decision of going back to wherever they had come from. They didn't leave the forecourt and it was a victory for anti-fascism in Wales.

The first opportunity for anti-fascists in the capital to test their mettle against the UM came on May Day 1948. Mosley announced that he intended to address a meeting in Hertford Road in Dalston before marching with his supporters via Highbury Corner to Camden Town. For several weeks prior to the rally, UM supporters flooded Hackney and Dalston with handbills and posters advertising the fact that the 'Leader' was speaking on May Day.

The Home Secretary, acting on police advice that there would be considerable trouble if the fascists marched through the East End, invoked the Public Order Act (POA) banning all political processions in East London for three months. As Dalston fell within the proscribed area, this presented Mosley with a problem. Since the meeting had been widely advertised, a change of venue at such a late stage would result in confusion and loss of prestige. He decided that he would speak at Hertford Road and tell his supporters to make their own way to Highbury

Corner, where they could legally form up and march to Camden.

Although it was raining heavily on the morning of May Day 1948, a large crowd of fascists and anti-fascists had gathered in Dalston. A procession of warm-up speakers attempted to keep an expectant and now bored audience half-interested in the meeting. Scuffles broke out around the edges of the crowd. The police made some arrests. Then a green saloon car pulled up to the platform and, as Mosley alighted, hundreds of fascists in the audience roared "Sieg Heil" in unison. According to many observers, Mosley's comeback appearance was unimpressive. The fire of his oratory had disappeared and he singularly failed to inspire his followers to the heights of rapture of yesteryear. After a rambling, monotone discourse lasting forty minutes, Mosley finally gave the signal for the meeting to end leaving hundreds of fascists and anti-fascists to make their way individually or in small groups to Highbury Corner. It was an explosive mixture. Violent clashes immediately broke out. As numerous small-scale running battles were fought all along the route, the police found themselves hard pressed to keep a lid on the situation. As soon as they stopped one fight, another one would break out somewhere else.

As the Mosleyites finally formed up at Highbury Corner, they looked a sorry bedraggled bunch. It was still raining heavily as the fascists prepared to march behind their standard bearers and drum corps. A large loudspeaker van began blaring out the Horst Wessel Lied as it eased between the lines of foot and mounted police to join the march. Several hundred anti-fascists were pushed into the side streets by mounted police and were kept constantly on the move. This tactic was designed to prevent them from forming into larger groups and launching a full-scale attack on the march. Nevertheless, several small-scale clashes did break out as the march wound its weary way up the Holloway Road. Volleys of missiles were thrown. Stones smashed the windows of the loudspeaker van as it came under repeated attack.

A decision was taken by the police to curtail the march near the junction of Holloway Road and Camden Road, well short of its final destination. Mosley did not contest the decision and the ragged band of marchers turned into line outside Holloway Prison. With a brief inspecting of his troops, Mosley jumped back into his car and was driven away. Shortly after his departure, the most violent incident of the day occurred. Groups of anti-fascists lying in wait for the march at Camden Town had marched up towards the Holloway Road to arrive on the scene just as the police and fascists were dispersing. Running battles ensued. It took the remaining police officers over an hour to contain the fighting.

The Union Movement suffered an even more resounding defeat in Brighton the following month. The town was home to a significant Jewish community, which led to it being dubbed 'a British Tel Aviv' by *The Union*. Never slow to show their faces in places where they weren't wanted, the local organiser of the UM, Captain Derek Lesley-Jones, decided to organise a march and rally in the town on Saturday 5 June 1948. 43 Group learnt that Jeffrey Hamm and Raven Thompson were travelling down to address the rally and were going to be accompanied by a large number of supporters from London and the southeast.

The response to the rally was co-ordinated by local members of the 43 Group and Major David Spector, an AJEX member who had become disillusioned with the response of the Board of Deputies to fascist activities. The call went out to all Jewish ex-servicemen in the area to stop the fascists from meeting. 43 Group members also travelled down from London to join their counterparts on the south coast. As the fascists marched through the town centre towards their final destination on the Level, they began to encounter considerable resistance. Stones were thrown. Fighting erupted. The police struggled to contain the situation.

Len Shipton had met and married a Brighton girl during the war, and moved to the south coast in 1945. He was amongst the many counter-demonstrators on the Level that day:

There was a small group of fascists in Brighton led by a fella called Jones, who, I believe, was a teacher. He used to hold meetings on the Level with a few of his supporters and bang on about the Jews and whatnot. There was the occasional punch up down there, usually with the communists, but this one particular meeting was meant to be special and there was a lot of talk about everyone getting together and shutting it down. I'm not sure of the exact date of the meeting but it must have been sometime in the summer of 1948. I'd arranged to meet up with a few pals in a café but, as I was running late, I ended up walking across to the Level on my own. As I got closer, I could hear the sound of drums in the distance, which, as you can imagine, was a bit nerve wracking. Then I turned the corner and saw this big mass of people approaching the Level. It was quite a sight, because there were all these fascists with flags and drums being attacked and barracked by a big crowd of anti-fascists with only a handful of coppers trying to keep them apart. I'd no sooner taken this in, when another load of blokes rushed out of the park and there was a massive punch-up. There was fighting all over the place with a lot of people charging backwards and forwards across the Level and out onto the streets. I eventually spotted a couple of my pals in the thick of things. They were going at it hammer and tongs with a couple of Mosley's boys, and I ran over to help them out. Not that they needed it because they were both ex-army and tough as old boots.

One incident sticks in my mind because it got a bit nasty. A couple of Mosley's boys got isolated from the main group and ended up being chased onto Lewes Road. The two of them were surrounded and given a really bad beating. I'm not particularly proud of being involved in that but I suppose those bastards would have done a lot worse to us given the chance. Not long afterwards, Jones climbed up on to the back of his lorry and started to make a speech. He'd not said more than a few words when someone slung a brick at him and down he went. He went down like a sack of spuds and never got up again. There was a huge cheer when this happened. After a while, a whole load of police reinforcements arrived and I made myself scarce. I think Jones tried to carry on as normal afterwards but he was a finished man in Brighton. His little fan club didn't seem to have the heart for it anymore and he ended up more or less on his own.

Another casualty of the 'Battle of Brighton' was Jeffrey Hamm, who was hospitalised after being attacked by 43 Group commandos. It was neither the first, nor the last time that he would be forced to sample the delights of hospital food.

The UM did not have to wait long in order to exact revenge. When a unit of 43 Group commandos turned up to attack a fascist meeting in Romford, Essex, they were ambushed by a group of gangsters hired by the UM. The gang, led by Joseph Marguerat, AKA Maltese Joe, a Soho nightclub owner and pimp, forced the 43 Group into a headlong retreat under a hail of razor blade embedded potatoes. Morris Beckman describes this incident as the only time the commandos turned tail and fled. The ante had been upped and it was down to the 43 Group to respond. On 26 August, Jeffrey Hamm was once again taken to hospital, this time huddled on the top of a loudspeaker van after being hit by a missile whilst attempting to address a meeting in Mile End. UM officials couldn't seem to make up their minds as to how he had been injured. One claimed that he had been hit by 'a potato into which razor blades had been inserted' while Organising Secretary, Alf Flockhart claimed that Hamm had been 'hit on the head by a brick and was cut by razors.' Monty Goldman remembers the occasion more for its ironic aftermath than for the confrontation itself:

One incident I remember, in about 1948, was Jeffrey Hamm getting a brick slung at him in Mile End. Nobody knew who slung it but all we knew was that they took him to hospital and in the next bed to him was this Orthodox Jewish fellow. We used to get reports from the hospital and they told us that Jeffrey was very well behaved while he was recuperating and kept himself very quiet.

A further blow to the morale of the UM came when its Birmingham organiser, Michael Maclean, became disillusioned with fascism and left the organisation. Unlike many other former fascists, he did not slip quietly into the background, grumbling and complaining to himself. He set up the National Anti-Fascist League (NAFL) with other disillusioned ex-fascists and vigorously campaigned against his former colleagues. After suffering this series of setbacks, the UM attempted to hit back at the anti-fascists. Over 100 fascists attempted to force their way inside a meeting of the Hackney Trades Council at Stoke Newington Town Hall in November 1948. The 43 Group had been tipped off that an attack was planned and managed to repel several concerted attempts to gain entry. Petrol bombs and broken bottles were used during the fierce fighting.

As 1948 drew to a close, it was clear that the expected upsurge in fascist recruitment and activity following the re-appearance of Mosley had not materialised. In fact, the opposite appeared to be true. The lack-lustre performances of the 'Leader' coupled with the determined anti-fascist onslaught against every aspect of UM activity seemed to sap the vitality out of the movement. In the early months of 1949, the fascists made a determined effort to put things back on track. On 31 January, Mosley addressed an audience of 700 people at Kensington Town Hall in London. He had spoken for no more than 15 minutes when someone let off a tear gas canister. Near panic ensued as Mosley, who was furthest away from the gas, appealed for his audience to stay seated.

Nearly one hundred people left the hall with thirty or so requiring further treatment.

Outside 3,000 anti-fascists paraded and 300 members of the 43 Group attended a torch-lit wreath-laying ceremony at the war memorial dedicated to 'Our comrades who died in the war against fascism.' Attempts were made to force an entry into the hall, thwarted by mounted police riding into the crowd. After Mosley had been escorted to his car and driven away, enraged fascists attacked nearby crowds. Scuffles broke out.

Mosley's attempt to revive the fortunes of British fascism ironically provided the 43 Group with an opportunity to boost its depleted bank account. Morris Beckman explains:

I'll tell you a story that never made it into my book. One day, Jeff Bernard told the NEC that we were about £4,500 in the red with Barclays Bank. The 43 Group relied on goodwill from the Jewish community to keep itself afloat financially but at the time we were short of money because we were dishing out a lot on medical and legal expenses and so forth. Jeff told us how he intended to rectify the situation. He told us that he'd invited twenty of the top Jewish businessmen to a dinner at the King David Suite in Marylebone. We all sat back and said "What? That's going to cost us a fortune." Jeff said "It doesn't matter. I've invited them." We said "Well, they won't come" but on the night they did come. I think they came mainly out of curiosity but also because of the feeling of solidarity amongst Jews. Not only were we fighting the fascists in London but Jews were fighting to create their own national homeland in Palestine and rescuing death-camp survivors who were still incarcerated in camps in Europe. There was a lot of support for the new generation of Jews who were deter-mined to fight their corner. Three group members also went along and we all had a good dinner. We thought "Well, we're paying for it. We might as well enjoy ourselves." We sat at a table on our own but some of the businessmen came across to our table and talked to us, shook us by the hand and patted us on the back saying "Well done boys" and "Good show." When the dinner had finished, Jeff jumped on the stage and said "I want you all to listen now to Mosley making a speech last week. We managed to slip someone inside the hall and tape his speech and we want you to listen to Oswald Mosley speaking." He switched on the machine and Mosley made the vilest of anti-Semitic speeches. It really was the works. He chucked in stuff about the Protocols of the Elders of Zion, everything. The businessmen all sat in silence listening. They were very quiet, very attentive and when it finished, Jeff got on stage and said "Well, now you realise how the 43 Group is protecting the community and what we're protecting it against. We hope you have enjoyed your dinner but remember that we do need money. We can't carry on without money. If you don't give, no hard feelings and we hope you've had a nice dinner." The three of us sat at our table with our fingers crossed, feeling very nervous, wondering what would happen next. Well, one fellow got up and said, "I'll pledge a thousand pounds", which in those days was a lot of money. Somebody else jumped up. "Five hundred". Then, another, "Fifteen hundred". Cyril Stein, who was a great supporter of ours, pledged two and a half thousand pounds. He said "What use is bloody money. Give it to them." They all pledged and not a single one reneged. It all came in and it turned an overdraft into a very healthy balance.

Years later, when I was writing my book, I went down to see Jeff in Walton-on-Thames and I asked him how he managed to get the tape of Mosley speaking. Jeff said "Well, only two people knew about it. Me and Syd Tafler." Now Syd was a commando in the 43 Group but before the war he had been a vaudeville artist. He was a song and dance man, doing impersonations and playing the halls. "Syd Tafler?" I asked.

"Yes" said Jeff. "Syd spent two whole days listening to Mosley speaking, again, and again, and again. I told him to keep at it until he got every inflection." I said "Well, that really did sound like Mosley" and Jeff replied "Yes, Syd did a wonderful job."

Support for fascism continued to fall away during the early months of 1949, despite Mosley's best efforts to rally his troops. Fascist street meetings were sparsely attended and decreasing in number week on week. A dangerous rump of hardcore fanatics remained active, however. These last desperate remnants grew increasingly violent as the possibility of defeat stared them in the face. Fascist speakers at street meetings grew ever more abusive towards the Jewish community, while gangs of fascists roamed the streets of Jewish areas at night looking for easy prey.

The forces of anti-fascism were changing as well. In Manchester, UJEX had undergone a series of political changes, and according to Phil Kaiserman, had lost its sense of direction:

The Union of Jewish Ex-Servicemen was set up by the Communist Party in Manchester to protect the community and fight fascism. We set it up as a left-wing body with links to the Trade Union movement, but after a couple of years the Zionists managed to gain control of the Executive Committee and started to move it away from its original position. It became linked with the Jewish establishment and lost its independence. There was a lot of internal wrangling between the Zionists and the left, but we eventually lost out. I walked out along with Maxie Druck and all the others.

The RCP voluntarily dissolved itself in 1949 with the majority of the remaining members joining a breakaway Trotskyist grouping that had entered the Labour Party some time earlier. Several other members, tired of the splits and recriminations, retired from political activity altogether.

Many of the original members of the 43 Group had also packed it in as family or work commitments took precedence as the fascist threat faded. Some suffered under the strain of the continuous threat of arrest or personal injury and decided to quit. Monty Goldman recalls that these ex-servicemen were replaced by younger elements from the Jewish community, who were keen to test their mettle:

> Towards the end of the Forties, a younger crowd started to come to the fore in the 43 Group. People like Harold Bidney became a section leader and started to take on more responsibility. Harold was a good strategist and was normally very careful but we nearly came unstuck on one of his operations in Wood Green. Normally, there would be a good crowd of maybe two or three hundred anti-fascists whenever we went out on an operation but for some reason, on this occasion, there were a lot fewer of us. Harold led us around the area for a bit when all of a sudden we were surrounded by fascists. "Don't panic" said Harold as the fascists closed in around us "We've got them worried." I looked at him and said, "I don't know about them being worried but I know I am." We got out of there by the skin of our teeth.

On the 20 March, the UM attempted to march from Ridley Road to West Green in Tottenham along a route that would have taken them through the heart of the Jewish community in Stamford Hill. As the day progressed, it became obvious that things were not going well for the UM. Their rally at Ridley Road attracted roughly 150 supporters, who were cordoned off by the police and surrounded by several hundred booing anti-fascists. Around the corner from the UM meeting, a CP rally in Kingsland Road attracted a crowd of more than two thousand anti-fascists. As the UM formed up to start their march, police lines were breached by surges from the anti-fascist protestors. Hand-to-hand fighting broke out in a dozen places. Mounted police charged into the crowd. Fireworks were thrown behind the horses in an attempt to make them unseat their riders.

The UM eventually got their march underway. Any hopes they might have entertained of intimidating the local population of Stoke Newington were dashed by their low turn-out and that the large anti-fascist presence forced the police to re-route the march through a less contentious area. As Monty Goldman recalls:

I was involved in the attempt to stop the Mosley march in 1949. The Union Movement wanted to march from Ridley Road via Stoke Newington, to a rally at West Green in Tottenham. The Communist Party mobilised about ten thousand people to stop Mosley. We managed to immobilise the trolley buses and stopped all the traffic so that instead of turning north up Stamford Hill the fascists had to march all around the houses to get to West Green. I remember very clearly, hundreds of people marching alongside the fascists to make sure they didn't march through Stoke Newington, which, of course, was a Jewish area. The other thing I remember is that the 43 Group in conjunction with the Communist Party took over every seat in the Regent's Cinema in Stoke Newington in case the fascists came there. One reason why people felt particularly strongly about the fascists not marching through Stoke Newington was because in 1941 a German bomb killed more than a hundred people in the Coronation Flats in the area. The thought of hundreds of gloating fascists marching past the scene of the tragedy was too much for many people to bear.

An estimated 5,000 anti-fascists were waiting at West Green for the fascists to arrive. When a rumour swept the crowd that the

UM was being diverted towards Tottenham Town Hall around 2,000 demonstrators broke away from the main body to make their way there. Scores of police on duty at the Town Hall attempted to disperse the crowds only to be met with a hail of bricks and concrete. Steel ball bearings and marbles were rolled into the path of charging mounted police. In the end, the UM were escorted to the rear of the Town Hall, where they dispersed.

It was becoming increasingly clear to anti-fascists that Mosley was losing interest in his dwindling band of British supporters and was more concerned with hob-knobbing it amongst the elite of international fascism. Reports from both AJEX and the 43 Group spies in the Union Movement indicated that Mosley was about to jump ship. One 43 Group spy had particularly good access to the thoughts and movements of Oswald Mosley, as Morris Beckman explains:

Mosley had a lovely mansion house with surrounding gardens and surrounding wall in Ramsbury, near Wilton. It was also his headquarters. Fascists would go there and stay overnight and they'd have meetings and social events there. A fellow joined us called Ben Leviticus. He was, again, one of those Jews who was very Aryan, he was very blond and blue-eyed. He was also a photographer. When he joined, Jeff Bernard grabbed him immediately and said "You're not wasting your time going out fighting. I want you to join the fascists." And, Ben did. He joined the British League of Ex-Servicemen and Women and then moved onto the Union Movement becoming one of Mosley's personal bodyguards. Mosley took a shine to him and invited him down to Wiltshire. Before long, the women who worked in the 43 Group offices started getting letters with measurements of doors, rooms, corridors and windows, all the details of a two-storey mansion house. This was Ben sending secret messages and our budding architects did very well with the information. They produced a blueprint from all the details and a plan was made to raid the house.

On the night, nine commandos met opposite Victoria Station on Vauxhall Bridge Road. They travelled down to Wiltshire on the old A303 and A30 in three cabs and arrived at the house in the early hours of the morning. They drove onto a grass verge underneath some overhanging trees and switched off their lights. They were well concealed. No passing traffic could see them. These nine commandos went over the wall. And they were real commandos, three of them were German lads who'd been with Colonel Popski's private army in the Western Desert. They would put on Afrika Korps uniforms, drive captured German trucks and go behind enemy lines. Two of these German lads took care of Mosley's heavies who were patrolling the grounds and put them to sleep for the evening. Anyway, they went over the wall. They wore plimsolls, football stockings and balaclavas and they each had a blueprint of the house. They entered the house through windows that had been left unlatched by Ben, went up the staircase and into the offices indicated in Ben's letters. They opened up the filing cabinets that Ben had left unlocked and filled four sacks full of letters and documents, then made their escape and got back to the cabs.

One cab drove up towards the Cotswolds, one went straight back to London, while the other went down towards the south coast. When the sacks got back to London, the women in the office went through the all the documents, copied them and sent selected copies out to Trade Union leaders and MPs. The contents of the sacks were very interesting. There were letters from MPs who were in contact with Mosley's party and there was also evidence that two Fleet Street journalists were making a very good living by blackmailing high-up civil servants and MPs who publicly denied having anything to do with the fascists.

Henry Morris of AJEX played a part in gathering information, although much of his work was more everyday and mundane:

> Part of our routine, if we had the bodies to do it, was to attend every outdoor fascist meeting we possibly could and, if we could get in without risking too much, we would also attend indoor meetings. Through this sort of surveillance we could build up an overall picture of the strengths and weaknesses of the fascists. We also found out a lot of very specific information, which we were able to use. Being an official veteran's organisation was very useful for us on these occasions because if we got to hear that the fascists had hired a pub or a hotel for instance, we would step in and inform the owners and nine times out of ten the meeting was stopped. I was also aware that there was some clandestine infiltration of fascist groups but I was never terribly involved in that sort of thing.

It was finally confirmed that Mosley was handing over day-to-day control of the Union Movement to Jeffrey Hamm, Raven Thompson and Victor Burgess. He was to spend most of his time in France and Ireland, visiting Britain only occasionally to oversee the general direction of the UM. He still had the loyalty of a hundred or so supporters in the East End of London. These remnants from the pre-war Blackshirt days were dedicated and unrepentant supporters of fascism and anti-Semitism but without the authoritarian leadership fascism seems to require they were little more than an isolated, violent street gang, who as Monty Goldman testifies, could be easily overwhelmed by the forces of the organised working class:

> The Communist Party organised a protest demonstration against fascism and thousands of people marched from East India Docks, via Mile End and up through Bethnal Green to Dalston. When we got to Kingsland Road, the fascists started

slinging bottles and bricks and everything at us but we had three hundred dockers with us, led by Ted Dickens, and they had a right go at the fascists. We had a victory parade at Amhurst Road, we took over the pitch at John Campbell Road and occupied the whole of Dalston. It was a great sight, to see thousands of people making a stand against fascism in Hackney.

As the new decade dawned, the fascists had been well and truly routed. On 5 April 1950, the 43 Group officially disbanded itself. A number of its members joined AJEX, some went to Israel, a few rejoined the CP, while others retired from political life. According to Morris Beckman, members of the 43 Group considered that eradicating "The obscenity of post-war fascism in Britain" had been successfully completed. Fascism in post-war Britain was always going to struggle to find widespread support amongst the general public. Memories of the war against fascism were too recent. Bomb damage from Nazi warplanes still disfigured British cities. Families still grieved for loved ones lost in battles or the Blitz. Newsreel images of the Nazi atrocities in the concentration camps became deeply ingrained in the public consciousness. The attacks on British soldiers in Palestine had provided new impetus for anti-Semitism but the fascists benefited little from it. As Sheila Lahr points out:

It wasn't the right time for the fascists to re-emerge. The East End was completely different, what with the bombing and people moving out and the Welfare State starting up. Everyone had seen the newsreels in the cinema, so we all knew about the terrible things that had happened in places like Belsen. I think even anti-Semitic people felt a bit guilty about what had happened and kept quiet.

Organised anti-fascist opposition on the other hand enjoyed

considerable public support. Large numbers were mobilised to stop fascist marches. Lesser but determined numbers prevented fascists from meeting regularly and sustaining their organisation. Such physical resistance, without doubt, defeated the followers of Mosley, Hamm et al. As much has been conceded by ex-fascists who spoke to Morris Beckman:

> I interviewed about a dozen ex-Blackshirts and Mosley's post-war Unionists in the early fifties. We used to meet up in Lyon's Tea Houses. They said that what beat them was the fact that they became afraid of us and in a strange kind of way they started to respect us.

In March 1951, Oswald Mosley announced that he was relocating to County Galway in Ireland. Even in this remote outpost, however, there are claims that Mosley was not safe from the attentions of anti-fascists. Just before Christmas 1954, a fire destroyed Mosley's home, Clonfert Palace. The origin of the blaze was officially given as resin in the kitchen chimney catching fire, but rumours persist that it was left-wing Irish Republicans that set the fire.

5

You can't beat fascism with fine carpets on the floor: 1953 – 1967

With Mosley absent abroad, the Union Movement (UM) slipped beneath the radar for most of the 1950s. A number of rallies were held at Trafalgar Square but these were small affairs that attracted little opposition from anti-fascists and no interest from the media.

It was post-war immigration that provided the UM with a new source of hatred and political focus, a phony threat against which they could re-build fascism in Britain. A manpower shortage following the war had prompted the government to invite workers from British colonies to fill the gaps in the labour market. Caribbean peoples took up the invitation only to find themselves trapped in menial, low paid jobs and at the mercy of rack-renting landlords in what were then run-down inner city areas such as Brixton and Notting Hill. The leader of the UM's Brixton branch began a campaign under the slogan 'Keep Brixton White', characterising black people in UM propaganda as work-shy scroungers living off public assistance and the proceeds from dope-peddling, prostitution and street robbery. The campaign spread to other areas. The slogan was adapted to 'Keep Britain White'. The initials 'KBW' were whitewashed on walls all over London. Support for the UM grew in Brixton but also began to pick up again in the East End. New recruits joined the ranks. Candidates in local elections were no longer completely ignored by the electorate. The UM both generated and exploited racism as did other fascist groups.

Elsewhere on the right, Mosley's former right-hand man, A. K. Chesterton, formed the League of Empire Loyalists in 1954. Amongst those who joined the League during this period were

Colin Jordan, John Tyndall and Martin Webster. All were Nazi supporters and all will figure prominently later. The League specialised in high-profile publicity stunts. Members would sneak into functions and meetings disrupting them by shouting slogans, blowing bugles and setting off alarm bells. Conservative Party conferences and state occasions were favoured but anti-racist meetings held by the Movement for Colonial Freedom (MCF) and the Anti-Slavery Society were also disrupted. League members drove a car into a Campaign for Nuclear Disarmament (CND) march from London to Aldermaston led by Pastor Martin Niemöller, author of the famous anti-fascist poem, which begins with the lines 'First they came for communists, and I did not speak out because I was not a communist.' However, the activities of League of Empire Loyalists were hampered by an ageing membership and wracked by a series of political schisms throughout the latter part of the 1950s. In 1957, Colin Jordan left to form the White Defence League (WDL) and John Tyndall helped set up the National Labour Party (NLP).

Both groups had a base in North Kensington from which they were able to stir up racism in the Notting Hill area. A series of inflammatory leaflets, pamphlets and street corner meetings stoked the embers of what was an already volatile situation. In August 1958, a series of riots in Nottingham triggered a week of copycat rioting in Notting Hill. Gangs of 'nigger-hunting' Teddy Boys, sometimes numbering in the hundreds, descended on the area at night looking for victims, their criminality given political legitimacy by fascist orators. George Clarke, a Jamaican carpenter, who moved to Notting Hill some seven years previously, remembers it as a time when communities were literally under siege:

> Black folk were scared to leave their houses at night. They would draw the curtains, lock their doors, and they wouldn't go out after dark. Gangs of Teddy Boys and fascists roamed

the streets attacking any coloureds they came across, shouting things like "Kill the Niggers" and "Keep Britain White." I remember the first time I saw 'KBW' painted on a wall. I didn't even know what it meant at first, but it wasn't very long before I found out.

The first act in a dramatic sequence of events had occurred on the night of Saturday 20 August when a 400-strong crowd of Teddy Boys attacked Majbritt Morrison, a Swedish bride of a Jamaican groom. Incensed by the fact that a white woman would marry a black man, the crowd pelted her with stones, bottles and lumps of wood. She was struck in the back with an iron bar as she tried to get home then her house was besieged by racists. Further attacks on black people resulted in five being left unconscious on the pavements that evening.

Over the next few days, large crowds of white gangs, sometimes numbering over a thousand, roamed the streets of Notting Hill, attacking black people, breaking into their homes and assaulting anyone they could find. In nearby Notting Dale, Seymour Manning, a black student, escaped an attack by three men by running into a greengrocer's shop. The proprietor, a white woman, barred the door to the attackers and faced down what quickly grew into an angry mob until the police arrived.

On the one hand, the police appeared unable, or unwilling in some instances, to stop the assaults. Individual officers attempting to keep the peace were either ignored or, occasionally, attacked by the racist mobs. On the other, black victims of assault also noted instances when police officers deliberately turned a blind eye. Faced with a situation where they knew the police either supported the racists or were powerless to stop them, members of the black community felt they had little choice but to defend themselves. Groups were formed to patrol the streets and guard homes. George Clarke joined one of these groups:

We felt that the police had no interest in protecting black folk, so we formed our own patrol groups. These groups were a defensive thing but only in so far as we wouldn't go to the homes of the Teddy Boys and attack them there. If a white gang came marching into Notting Hill shouting 'Keep Britain White', though, we would attack them on sight. We had machetes, petrol bombs and other weapons, and we would use them if we had to. We were prepared to meet force with force.

Police reports from the time suggest that this was more than mere rhetoric. A police officer reported seeing a 'large group of coloured men' walking along Ladbroke Grove, 'shouting threats and abuse, and openly displaying various most offensive weapons, ranging from iron bars to choppers and open razors.' Shouts included 'Come and fight' and 'What about it now?'

Violent confrontations culminated in a pitched battle at 9 Blenheim Crescent, a Jamaican owned café nicknamed The Fortress. In the 1990s television series, *Forbidden Britain*, Baker Baron, a local community leader, revealed how events unfolded:

When they told us that they were coming to attack that night I went around and told all the people that was living in the area to withdraw that night. The women I told them to keep pots, kettles of hot water boiling, get some caustic soda and if anyone tried to break down the door and come in, to just lash out with them. The men, well we were armed. During the day they went out and got milk bottles, got what they could find and got the ingredients of making the Molotov cocktail bombs. Make no mistake, there were iron bars, there were machetes, there were all kinds of arms, weapons, we had guns.

We made preparations at the headquarters for the attack. We had men on the housetop waiting for them, I was standing on the second floor with the lights out as look-out when I saw a massive lot of people out there. I was observing the behaviour of the crowd outside from behind the curtains upstairs and they say, 'Let's burn the niggers, let's lynch the niggers.' That's the time I gave the order for the gates to open and throw them back to where they were coming from. I was an ex-serviceman, I knew guerrilla warfare, I knew all about their game and it was very, very effective.

I says, 'Start bombing them.' When they saw the Molotov cocktails coming and they start to panic and run. It was a very serious bit of fighting that night, we were determined to use any means, any weapon, anything at our disposal for our freedom. We were not prepared to go down like dying dogs. But it did work, we gave Sir Oswald Mosley and his Teddy boys such a whipping they never come back in Notting Hill. I knew one thing, the following morning we walked the streets free because they knew we were not going to stand for that type of behaviour.

Anti-fascists appear to have been caught flat-footed by the explosion of racist and fascist activity in Notting Hill. A group calling itself the West London Anti-Fascist Youth Committee was formed in 1956 but its impact on the situation appears to have been negligible. One reason for the lack of active participation by anti-fascists may have been that the forces of the left were in a state of flux. The CP was haemorrhaging members at an alarming rate. Stalin's death in 1953 broke the silence about denunciations, torture, purges and mass murder in the Soviet Union. There were revelations about state-sponsored anti-Semitism. Dreams shattered, their utopia in ruins, many communists left in the Party in despair. Then, there was a mass exodus in 1956. Nearly nine thousand members, around a quarter of its membership, resigned when the USSR sent in the Red Army against the workers and students of the Hungarian Revolution.

Former members of the Revolutionary Communist Party were active in encouraging building workers to join a 'workers' defence squad' in Notting Hill but Trotskyists were still small in numbers. It would be a few more years before they would play a leading role in the anti-fascist arena.

The lack of an organised anti-fascist response to the events in Notting Hill meant that it was left to individuals to take the initiative. Robert Doyle, the son of former International Brigader, Bob Doyle, remembers his father's response to the news that black people were being openly attacked on the streets of West London:

We lived quite close to Notting Hill but more down the Harrow Road end. My dad had his first car, a Ford Popular, so we'd drive down to Notting Hill and try and help out however we could. We went out most nights, my dad, my brother Julian, and me. You'd see black guys and girls as well coming home from work and there were so many people just standing around harassing them that it was very easy for someone at some point to just throw a punch or throw something. So we would pull up and invite them into the car and give them a lift home. We did a lot of that. I remember one occasion when we pulled up at a junction on the Harrow Road and there was this big mêlée, a big crowd fighting. When I say fighting, I mean there was a whole load of whites beating up one black guy. Before I'd even had a chance to think about whether I was frightened or not, my dad was in there. He just jumped out the car and was in there. The police arrived and started putting the whole crowd into the Black Maria. That's when I got there, when all the fighting was over. I remember telling a policeman who had grabbed hold of my dad that he was there to help the black guy. So he didn't get picked up on that occasion. Another frightening occasion was when we were down a side street off the Harrow Road. They were all terraced houses there with steps up to the front door. There was a black family living in one of the houses and a huge crowd had gathered outside, shouting and throwing things. A policeman had come along to disperse the crowd but he was on his own and the crowd had started to turn on him. He was actually forced into the house, and the crowd had started to throw petrol bombs at the front door. The door was ablaze. We saw this and ran down the road and found another policeman. We told him what was happening and he got more help there. It was a strange situation because there we were rescuing policemen. I could never have imagined us doing that before. It was very nasty and very disheartening. My dad was especially upset because a lot of people taking part in these race riots were Irish. It was a very heavily Irish area. That very much upset him. He felt they should have known better because they had received the same kind of treatment themselves in the past.

I don't recall any left-wing or anti-fascist group organising down there. There were certainly no big, major interventions. There was a bit afterwards. I was in the Young Communist League and we did organise a few meetings in the area, and I found myself speaking a few times on street corners. We used to take a soapbox around and try to attract a crowd.

There were a small number of Young Communist League (YCL) street meetings, the Communist Party's London District Committee also published a pamphlet by Kay Beauchamp entitled, *Fascism – and How to Defeat It*, which dealt specifically with the situation in Notting Hill but shied away from calling for any kind of direct action against the fascists appealing for 'the united struggle of all workers, white and coloured, against the employers and landlords and their party, the Tories.' As a response to the situation on the ground, it left a lot to be desired. It was not only a case of wrong target and wrong ammunition, but also too little, too late.

Whilst some news reports looked for Union Movement involvement in the Notting Hill riots, their attention probably should have been focused upon the new generation of fascists epitomised by Colin Jordan and John Tyndall. Indeed, Mosley and his followers had been caught on the hop by the speed of events in Notting Hill. They had no idea that the powder keg was about to blow but reacted to it with rather more alacrity than the left. The UM only had a small branch in Kensington prior to the riots, but quickly poured much of its resources into the area. Thousands of racist leaflets and newspapers were issued from the UM's new base on Kensington Park Road, which sent out a continuous stream of speakers to address large crowds of baying Teddy Boys on street corners or in public houses. Glimpsing an opportunity to resurrect his ailing political career, Mosley finally ended his self-imposed exile and announced on 6 April 1959 that he was intending to contest the October parliamentary election in North Kensington.

The following month, Kelso Cochrane, a young Antiguan carpenter, was spotted by a white gang as he was walking past the Earl of Warwick public house, a well-known haunt of UM supporters. He was harangued, chased by six white men, then stabbed to death on a street corner. Although the police knew the identities of those involved in the murder, no one was ever charged. Mosley had thrown himself into the election campaign with renewed vigour, sometimes addressing up to four street meetings an evening. On one occasion, he spoke on the street corner where Cochrane was murdered. According to George Clarke, it was an uncomfortable time for the black community of Notting Hill:

I remember when Mosley stood as an MP for North Kensington. He just seemed to be everywhere. Wherever you went, whatever you did, all you could hear was Mosley, Mosley, Mosley. He held a lot of meetings, and made a lot of speeches, trying to rally his people. He told his followers at one meeting that black folk were so poor they ate cat food. "Lassie for dogs, Kit-E-Kat for wogs," that was the little rhyme he used. Then at the next meeting he said that black folk were living it up at all-night parties. It didn't make any sense to me, but for some reason people believed it. There wasn't the same level of violence as before the riots, but there was still a lot of tension. It was like being swamped in hatred. You just couldn't get away from it.

Even the twin provocations of the murder of Kelso Cochrane and Mosley's return to the fray failed to spark a major anti-fascist response. It was left to individuals to take the lead. William Ash had learnt his anti-fascism in German P.O.W. camps. He was a naturalised Briton who had flown Spitfires for the RAF before the United States entered the war and lost his American citizenship for fighting for the armed forces of another nation. In his autobiography, *A Red Square*, he recalls his own efforts to help the beleaguered black population of Notting Hill:

> When a young West Indian, Kelso Cochrane, was murdered in North Kensington for no other reason than that he was black, I drafted my own leaflet on the shame of it for Britain, had thousands of copies printed and distributed it all around "The Grove" myself, also helping to organise an escort service for West Indian women who were too terrified by yobbos to come out of their houses to shop.

Encouraged by UM canvass returns, Mosley believed that he was on the verge of an electoral breakthrough and would be returning to Parliament. It must have come as something of a shock, therefore, when he polled just 8.5% of the vote and lost his deposit for the first time in his political career. Many UM supporters, men and women alike, openly wept as the result was announced. Mosley left the count in a state of shock but perhaps should not have been surprised by either the power of the two party British parliamentary system or that the battleground of fascism was the streets not the polling station.

Notting Hill's place in the history of physical resistance to fascism cannot be doubted. Communities defended and even armed themselves. Individuals who witnessed racist abuse and fascist violence simply put themselves into the fray. But an organised anti-fascist mobilisation was notable only by its absence. Notting Hill was not a bastion of anti-fascism like the East End, a home to immigrants for centuries that had sedimented relationships between Jewish communities and left-wing organisations, especially the Communist Party. The disillusionment with the communism of the Soviet Union and consequent decline in Party membership effected localities such as Whitechapel and Stepney as well as Cheetham in Manchester but the character of these strongholds of anti-fascism was changing anyway. The ties that bound people and politics were slowly unravelled as working class Jewish communities fragmented. Families were drifting away from urban enclaves to more comfortable suburban surroundings. Party membership cards were discarded or simply left to expire as old loyalties were forsaken or forgotten.

There were other political shifts. Anti-fascism had been a central plank of the internationalism of the left. In the post war period of decolonisation, other international causes took precedence. The Movement for Colonial Freedom (MCF), led by Labour MP, Fenner Brockway, was set up in 1954 to support the anti-imperialist struggles of Asian and African peoples. The parties of the left threw their weight behind the MCF as did many liberals and religious groups. The Anti-Apartheid Movement (AAM) started life in 1959 as boycott of South African goods and attracted a similar spectrum of supporters. Anti-imperialism had replaced anti-fascism as the primary concern of the British left.

That the antics of a handful of Nazis were regarded as being of relative unimportance might seem reasonable enough but the organised left could also be accused of not giving the racism in its own backyard the same level of attention devoted to black liberation struggles in faraway countries. There is certainly evidence to suggest that the upper echelons of the CP, in particular, were unresponsive to the persistence of colonialism and imperialism at home. Claudia Jones, the Trinidadian communist responsible for starting the Notting Hill Carnival, expressed her concerns at the Party's 25th Congress in 1957. She argued that the situation of black people in Britain was ignored:

> Colonial, and particularly coloured peoples in Britain will also want to know what policy the Party Congress advances to meet the special problems facing them in the present economic situation.

The answer to this question appears in the revisions made that year to communist manifesto, *The British Road to Socialism*. It included a statement calling for full social, economic and political equality of colonial people in Britain and for racial discrimination to be made illegal. Two sentences buried deep within a thirty-page document was the sum total of the CP's commitment to anti-racism in the 1950s. There was no plan of action, no call to arms, no urgency to doing anything very much.

By February 1960, Colin Jordan's White Defence League and John Tyndall's National Labour Party had merged to form a British National Party (BNP). The party's name and initials would be used again almost three decades later. This BNP held a couple of rallies at Trafalgar Square, mounted a series of attacks on Anti-Apartheid meetings and demonstrated against the parade of a Jewish Lord Mayor of London. These were poorly attended affairs. Its main activity was putting on noisy demonstrations at railway stations when trains arrived carrying immigrants.

The traditional opponents of fascism were doing their best to ignore the formation of new parties, but these organisations were not about to just go away. As the new decade dawned, fascists stepped up their attacks on the international solidarity networks. Fascists smashed the windows of the *West London Observer*, which covered anti-apartheid events. Racist slogans were painted on the headquarters of Fulham Labour Party where an anti-apartheid exhibition was on display. A gang of fascists attacked a meeting addressed by Ian Mikardo at Porchester Hall in Westminster. An outdoor anti-apartheid meeting in Portobello Road had to be abandoned after fascist hecklers tried to storm the platform. William Ash, a member of the Movement for Colonial Freedom, he recalls how he became part of a fighting force:

My earliest involvement in the rough give and take of this level of political activity was purely spontaneous, tripping up someone who stepped on my toes as he rushed to the platform, helping stewards winkle out a noisy disrupter who was wedged in the middle of the row where I was sitting, or thumping someone who attacked a column in which I was marching along peacefully minding my own business.

But as these occurrences multiplied I found myself being regarded as part of a regular force that could be relied on for protecting meetings or demonstrations. In due course, we had an organised body of stewards, the "heavy gang," adept at removing even the fattest racist from a hall with the minimum of fuss, normally functioning as part of the MCF, but prepared to lend our services to any group of a progressive nature wishing to hold a meeting without interruption.

Physical resistance in its most organised form, a regular group always ready and willing to fight, was developing again. The sense that William Ash is learning the ropes that have been learnt before is pretty unmistakeable. Fending off attacks becomes a regular task that falls to the same people to become part and parcel of their political life. Large scale confrontations that draw in wider circle of activists were also making a comeback. On 28 February 1960, UM members joined forces with BNP activists to attack an anti-apartheid rally in Trafalgar Square. It didn't quite go to plan, as the *News Chronicle* reported:

> Nine people were arrested and several policemen injured yesterday during the ugliest political clashes seen in London since the war. They began when Mosleyites tried to intervene at a Trafalgar Square demonstration where 10,000 pledged to boycott South African goods as a protest against apartheid. A mile-long running battle, involving thousands of people surged from Charing Cross along the Strand down Whitehall and into Victoria Street. Union Movement men headed by Sir Oswald Mosley had gathered in the forecourt of Charing Cross station and they and boycott supporters began shouting at each other. Then members of the Young Communist League, who were selling their official journals moved in to the attack. Within a few moments about 50 people were exchanging blows. I saw a dozen police officers and four men sprawled on the ground. Two other men were knocked down and kicked by the crowd.

The area around Trafalgar Square was the scene of more disorder on 27 March. Fascists attempted to attack a protest about the killing of 69 people in the previous week by trigger-happy South African police in a Transvaal township, known as the Sharpeville Massacre. UM supporters on open backed lorries had heckled the marchers as they made their way through central London. They had waved placards declaring their support for the apartheid regime. Then, as the procession reached the Haymarket, the fascists launched a full-scale attack that was repulsed by determined resistance from the marchers and their stewards.

The fascists finally got their comeuppance when they attempted to disrupt a MCF meeting in Camden. Stewards allowed a group of BNP members to enter the hall, then locked the doors behind them. When Colin Jordan and his supporters stood up to heckle the speakers, they were ambushed by anti-fascists and given a taste of their own medicine. The ambush was another sign that the strategies of organised physical resistance were being adopted once again.

Barely two years after helping set up the BNP, Jordan and Tyndall left to form the National Socialist Movement (NSM). The NSM was mainly composed of former BNP members who belonged to an elite faction within the party known as Spearhead. During 1961 and 1962, Tyndall, Jordan and the Spearhead squad were photographed in full military uniform, including armbands, grey shirts, boots and belts, whilst engaged in mock military exercises in the Kent countryside. The NSM added a virulent anti-Semitism straight back into the mix of British fascism's recent opposition to the rights of immigrants and the freedoms of colonial peoples.

One of the first public activities of the NSM was a 'Free Britain from Jewish Control' rally at Trafalgar Square on 1 July 1962. Jordan's notoriety as a Jew-baiter had preceded him and he arrived to find the square occupied by 2,000 assorted anti-fascists. He tried to speak but he was shouted down, pelted with tomatoes, rotten eggs and coins. The NSM platform was stormed and the rally closed down on the orders of the police after just 20 minutes. Amongst the anti-fascists lined up against the NSM that day were members of the Communist Party, various Trotskyist and anarchist groups, activists from AJEX and the Jewish Defence Committee as well as the MCF. The participants might not have realised it at the time but they were also witnesses to the birth of a new anti-fascist organisation, the Yellow Star Movement (YSM).

One of those present was CP member Ken Beddoe:

> The Yellow Star Movement came about because the Reverend
> Bill Sargent, who was a vicar of the Holy Trinity Church in
> Dalston, demonstrated against a meeting of the National
> Socialist Movement in Trafalgar Square by wearing a yellow
> Star of David badge. Colin Jordan, the leader of the NSM, was
> telling his followers about all the evil deeds of the Jewish
> people and how we shouldn't have gone to war against Hitler
> on behalf of the Jews. Harry Green was a member of the
> Association of Jewish Ex-Servicemen and he joined up with
> Bill Sargent, as did a lot of other anti-fascists. They held a
> peaceful protest at St Martins in the Fields, which attracted a
> lot of support. There was also a big crowd of anti-fascists in
> the square itself and there was a lot of fighting. The fascist
> meeting was eventually closed down by the police.

Oswald Mosley had already pre-booked Trafalgar Square for a
UM rally on 22 July. The UM had held seven such meetings in the
Square since 1959 with little opposition but now his timing could
not have been worse. It became an obvious target for the re-
energised anti-fascist movement. The UM was about to run into
an anti-fascist whirlwind. Once again, Ken Beddoe was a first-
hand witness to events:

> Three weeks later, Oswald Mosley tried to hold a Union
> Movement meeting in Trafalgar Square and there were
> thousands of anti-fascists gathered there to oppose him. Bill
> Sargent and Harry Green handed out hundreds of Yellow Star
> badges to the demonstrators and that was where the Yellow
> Star Movement had its beginnings. Once again, there was a
> lot of trouble in the Square and the police were forced to shut
> down the meeting before Mosley had even had a chance to
> speak.

While the YSM peacefully protested on the steps of St Martins in the Fields, a crowd of seven thousand anti-fascists broke through the police cordon and stormed the UM platform. The police closed down the meeting before Mosley had even arrived, fearing that his presence would further provoke the crowd. Anti-fascists then attempted to reach Mosley's headquarters in Vauxhall Bridge Road but were ridden into by mounted police. Those who attempted to escape by climbing onto buses were thrown down the stairs by the police and viciously assaulted. It took 50 arrests and twelve hours before public order was restored.

There was more trouble brewing for Mosley on the following weekend in Manchester. He and thirty supporters tried to march through the city to Belle Vue. It was, recalls Harry Johnson, a humiliating experience for Mosley:

In 1962, we were told that Mosley was coming to this area of waste ground at Belle Vue to speak. The Union Movement also had a number of candidates standing in Manchester at the elections. The Communist Party organised people to go to Belle Vue and protest because historically we had always been opposed to Mosley. The thing I remember most about Belle Vue was Lily Cole, who was the sister of Maxie Druck, one of the CP's main organisers. She hit Mosley with her handbag before the meeting started. She came to the demonstration by bus and, as luck would have it, just as she stepped off the bus, there was Mosley standing right in front of her. She swung her handbag at him and caught him right on the side of the head. Mosley was knocked to the floor and went down looking stunned. Everybody was really surprised. The thing was, Lily had a brick in her handbag and that was what had floored Mosley. I think there's a photo of it in the papers somewhere. I was stood right there when it happened and everybody was cheering because there was a lot of people mingling around by then. There was a lot of opposition to the fascists that day and

Mosley was knocked down a number of times as the fascists tried to march down the road. The drummers on the march were attacked, the flags were torn down and all along the route of the march people were throwing eggs, cabbages, stones or dropping things off bridges and getting arrested by the police. Eventually they got to this enclosed area near Belle Vue and Mosley spoke to twenty or thirty of his supporters on this piece of waste ground. The police held back everyone else. There were thousands of us surrounding them, shouting at them, singing at them. The thing I remember is that he looked very scared. Well, anybody would be I suppose. I think Mosley only spoke for about ten minutes before the police closed the meeting down and cleared him out of there.

Phil Kaiserman was also present at Belle Vue. His account of events is identical to that of Harry Johnson's in all bar one respect: the identity of the mysterious handbag-wielding assailant. He recalls:

One of our members, Betty Askins, had been working on a market stall and arrived at the counter-demonstration just before Mosley got there. As he was getting out of his car she hit him with her handbag. He ended up on the floor with his head bleeding.

There were a total of 47 arrests in Manchester for Breach of the Peace or similar charges. The police were also kept busy in London, just two days later. Mosley attempted a comeback at Ridley Road. He was waylaid by anti-fascists as soon as he showed his face and knocked to the ground under a flurry of blows. Monty Goldman witnessed the action:

There was one incident at Ridley Road, which I remember very well. Mosley was on his way to a meeting when a few of

213

the boys dragged him to the ground and gave him a good going over. He only escaped being very seriously injured because the police ran in to rescue him. After the meeting he scrambled into his staff car and sped off as quickly as he could. Mosley's son, Max, was arrested at the same meeting and Danny Harmston, the so-called tough guy boxer, was knocked off his feet by a single punch from an anti-fascist.

After his rescue by the police, Mosley climbed onto the back of a lorry to address the crowd, which was several thousand strong by this stage, to be greeted with a chorus of boos and chants of 'Down with Fascism.' Scuffles started, missiles thrown, the plaform rushed. On police advice, Mosley closed the meeting after just three minutes and was escorted from the area. 54 people were charged with public order offences. Tony Hall, a CP member from Stoke Newington, was struck by the reaction of ordinary people to Mosley's attempted comeback:

I remember seeing Mosley at Ridley Road on the back of a tipper truck and everybody was throwing stuff at him. Not just your normal anti-fascist protestors but old mums, shoppers, everybody. I saw one woman take off her shoes and throw them at Mosley because that's all she could find to throw. Other people were throwing eggs, pennies, oranges off the stalls, anything they could lay their hands on. Mosley was trying to duck and dodge the missiles. He had a couple of minders with him from Smithfield Meat Market. Big Danny Harmston and another bloke were trying to protect him but there wasn't much they could do.

The violence was not all one-sided. Amongst those who required medical attention were former Mayor of Hackney Alderman Sherman and his wife, who were both injured after being hit with iron bars. Despite such disorder, or because of it, Bill Sargent pressed ahead with plans to build a non-violent anti-fascist organisation. Ken Beddoe was keen to sign up:

The Yellow Star Movement was launched at a meeting in Battersea. Bill Sargent, Harry Green and the actress Olga Levertoff were the main organisers of the YSM. Because Bill Sargent was a vicar, he wanted the YSM to stage peaceful protests against the fascists and organise petitions against them but a lot of ordinary YSM supporters would just attack the fascists on sight. We would try to oppose the fascists whenever and wherever they held their meetings. Sometimes, we would take over a fascist pitch before they arrived and prevent the fascists from holding their own meetings there. In the main, we would try to disrupt fascist meetings by heckling the speakers, shouting "Down with Mosley" that sort of thing. There were quite a few in the movement who took the view that this wasn't very effective and they decided that they would beat up any fascists they came across. This happened at Union Movement meetings in Ridley Road and Bethnal Green where Mosley was punched and kicked to the ground. I also remember Colin Jordan being attacked at another meeting because there was a photograph in the *Daily Mail* of my mate Larry O'Connell hitting him with a placard. He was really going for him.

One very important thing that occurred was when we managed to convert a fascist who started giving us inside information on what they were doing. There was a record shop on Queenstown Road, which as well as selling second-hand records also sold nazi regalia, old medals, insignia and uniforms. All that sort of thing. Well, I found out that the owner was the Information Officer of the League of Empire Loyalists. They were the group who were responsible for throwing a bag of sheep's entrails at Jomo Kenyatta, the president of the Kenyan African National Union, when he visited London. Well, to cut a long story short, over a period of time, we managed to turn him around completely. I'd go in the shop, buy a few records and have a chat with him. He'd tell me about all the goings-on in the Union Movement, the NSM and the League of Empire Loyalists. He knew what was going on in all these different groups because, of course, they were all linked.

Betty Davis was another communist who was involved with the Yellow Star Movement:

Because I was a member of the Communist Party, I always went on all the marches and was involved in all the campaigns against fascism. One campaign was the Yellow Star Movement, which rose up in the early sixties. In the thirties and forties, we wore the yellow star in solidarity with the Jewish people in the concentration camps and in the ghettos. They were forced to wear it by the Nazis as a mark of shame. We wore it with pride. We adopted it again in the sixties when the fascists reappeared. The Star of David, of course, is blue and white, but the Nazis changed it to yellow because they classed Jews as cowards. The cowards were actually those in power because those with the power were the ones who brutalised people who couldn't hit back. We wore the yellow star to show that we didn't accept the values that had been passed down with it. The Yellow Star Movement also tried to stop Mosley from marching and speaking and there were many demonstrations against the fascists. I remember a meeting where Mosley was inside a building with his organizers and we were lined up on each side outside shouting "Shame" as they walked past us. One of them attacked one of the youngsters on the picket and to my amazement the police arrested the youngster not the guy who was kicking and punching him. The fascists went upstairs to their meeting with Mosley and we were all outside, making sure we had a very visible presence. They were looking out the window taking photographs and we were shouting back at them, asking if we could have some copies.

As Ken Beddoe has pointed out, not all supporters of the YSM strictly adhered to the policy of non-violence advocated by Bill Sargent. Indeed, there was a very violent faction within the organisation that had no interest at all in the peaceful methods advocated by the Dalston vicar. The fact that Levertoff and Green tolerated the violent activities of this group led Sargent to throw his lot in with the London Anti-Fascist Committee, a group that shied away from the confrontational approach increasingly being adopted by elements within the YSM. Harry Green of AJEX and the YSM offered this analysis of Bill Sargent's departure:

Sargent never faced the threat of violence and never made any allowances for it. When it did arise, Sargent abdicated his position as leader by refusing to lead. You can't beat fascism with fine carpets on the floor; you have to get out in the streets and nip it in the bud… You can talk about it all you want, pass bills in Parliament, and offer a better way of life, but it is on the streets where it is beaten, not anywhere else. We're the ones who do all the dirty work; we're the ones who suffer the beatings; and we're the ones who take the blame; but it is us who have beaten the Fascists!

The militant elements within the YSM had begun to coalesce into an identifiable group by August 1962. Officially known as the 1962 Committee, they are commonly referred to as the 62 Group. Monty Goldman was close to a number of its leading members and explained its relationship to previous anti-fascist organisations:

The 62 Group consisted of some of the younger elements of the 43 Group. Harry Bidney was a member of both as was Jules Konopinsky and a number of others. It all got started after the fascists re-emerged in the early 1960s with their "Keep Britain White" and "If they're black, send them back" rubbish. I remember that there were a couple of fascist meetings at Trafalgar Square within a few weeks of each other, which seemed to kick-start everything off again. The 62 Group grew out of that. I think people recognised that the fascists were making a big push and coming out of that there was a need to become better organised. I was never actually in the 62 Group although I was very close to them and worked alongside them. I was friendly with Harold Bidney and a few of the others who had been in the 43 Group. Harold had been quite a high-ranking NCO in the British Army and was very slight. He wouldn't really have a go but he was a strategist and a leader. He did a lot of the intelligence work for the 62 Group. Cyril Paskin was high up in the 62 Group. I knew Cyril quite well. I also knew Leslie Jacobs. He was a real hard case. He liked to have a punch-up. If there was a fight or some trouble with the fascists, Leslie would be there. You could be assured of that. A few other names I remember from that period are Monty Pincus and Bernie Shilling, who were also ex-43 Group.

I'd have to say, though, that overall they were less effective than the 43 Group, because the people that came from the 43 Group were nearly middle-aged by the time the sixties came around. I don't think they were as ideological as the 43 Group either. They didn't have the same links with the Communist Party as the 43 Group did. I certainly don't remember them providing stewards for any CP meetings. The 62 Group did recruit some younger members but they were not of the same calibre as 43 Group people like Gerry Flamberg, Fatty Raines or Harry Tobias. There weren't as many of them either. You have to remember that the 43 Group were active just after the war and many Jewish people had lost relatives in places like Belsen or Austwitzch so they were outraged when the fascists re-appeared and the response from ordinary people was "Let's sort these buggers out." The 62 Group never had the benefit of that. They were like the 43 Group in miniature. They played a part though. There's no doubt about that.

Because of the secrecy surrounding the 62 Group, there remains a deal of confusion over the exact origins and composition of the group. Tony Hall was there at the beginning and has the details:

It became evident in the early Sixties that Mosley and the fascists were starting to hold public meetings again in places like Ridley Road and John Campbell Road. The law at that time was that if you wanted a public meeting you informed the police and they would turn up in force to protect you, which is what happened. You'd get half a dozen scrawny fascists in Ridley Road and 50 or 60 pigs from Dalston Police station would turn up to protect them. Dalston Police Station was famous for providing minders for Mosley's Union Movement. You'd often see them in uniform at Ridley Road, then out of uniform being minders at some other meeting in Finsbury. We determined that we in the CP, and others associated with us, would not put up with this bollocks any more. The neighbourhood was being painted up with anti-black slogans and propaganda. "Blacks bring disease," "Kick the blacks out," "Keep Britain White" and so on and so forth. The local synagogue at Walford Road was always being daubed with anti-Jewish slogans as well.

Gerry Gable was a YCL member at the time, although I don't think he was in it for very long, and he told us that there were car-loads of youths going around picking on young Jews in Stamford Hill. He was involved with some Jewish blokes in the Stoke Newington area, who had got together like us to do something about the problem. We had a number of meetings together, men, women, immigrants, Jews, communists and other left-wingers. We decided that we would organise in the best way we could but we wouldn't have an open, anybody can join as long as they had a party card CP type organisation. Everyone was pissed off with the CP by this time anyway. A few youngsters had gone around the area painting anti-fascist slogans on walls but they had been ordered to scrub them off because it lowered the tone of the struggle or something. We decided that we would organise amongst ourselves to kick the shit out of these local fascists. We weren't going to have endless arguments and discussions. We would just do our best to find them, jump up and down on them and then go home. We didn't bother with a name for the group at this stage, but it was at these meetings that the 62 Group was born.

There were all sorts of people involved in the 62 Group. The background of many of the people involved was CP, people associated with the CP, some people from the left of the Labour Party and a group of young Jews from Stamford Hill. There was I suppose, even at this time, a distinction between what you might call the Marxist faction and the Zionist faction but this only became apparent as time went on. Most of the Jews couldn't really be described as Zionists at this time but some of them turned into Zionists later. Of course there were a few, even then, who were already Zionists and who had served in the Israeli army. They were, again, very handy hard nuts, who were useful to have around when you were kicking shit out of the fascists. We heard of an instance where a West Indian greengrocer kept getting his windows broken and racist slogans painted on his shop. He said that he'd complained to Stoke Newington police and they'd said to him "Some people round here don't like you mate." He never bothered complaining again. We set up a surveillance team and sat about in his place for two or three nights and eventually a car pulled up and a couple of half-wits got out and painted up something on the wall opposite his shop. We followed them and they went back to an address in Howard Road, where a father and two sons lived. Four of us turned up there one night and as soon as the door was opened we burst in. One of the sons escaped over the back wall but his father got a broken leg, the other son was badly hurt and the flat was wrecked. We just said to them "Every time there's an anti-Jewish or anti-black sign painted around here, we're coming back."

Another thing we did was sabotage pubs that wouldn't serve black people or wouldn't let them use the saloon bar. We would turn the water off at the stopcock or turn off the gas or electricity and pour concrete into the hole. Or sometimes we'd go into the pub late in the evening and pour Plaster of Paris into the toilet, and then let them know why we did it. We decided that if you didn't make a serious fuss and nuisance about it, it would just carry on. After a few visits from the 'plumbers', as we called them, things started to change. We also found an address over by Ball's Pond Road, which was a light engineering business. The truck that they used for the business was also used to drag around Mosley's supporters and paraphernalia, all the flags and banners and PA stuff. We emptied the oil sump, took the oil away and cut the oil pressure switch on the night before a meeting, so that it went down the road half a mile and seized up. The information had come from Gerry Gable and his lot, who had got somebody inside the organisation who was passing out information on addresses and meetings and so forth.

London wasn't the only venue for renewed anti-fascist activities. It required the presence of 150 police officers to keep the peace at a UM meeting in Southend on 5 August. Officers with dogs cleared a space in the middle of the crowd to prevent UM supporters and anti-fascists from coming to blows. On 25 August in Leeds, a crowd of 200 communists and Jewish ex-servicemen broke up another of their meetings. That same month, the UM applied for permission to hold a march and rally in Bethnal Green in the following month. The BNP announced that they intended to hold a rally at Ridley Road on the same day, Sunday 2 September. This prompted the Yellow Star Movement (YSM) to announce that they too intended to rally in Dalston. Sir Joseph Simon, the Metropolitan Police Commissioner, invoked the powers of the POA in order to prevent the UM from holding their march but ruled that all three meetings could go ahead.

In order to secure the Ridley Road and John Campbell Road pitches, YSM members camped out overnight and had 136 speakers ready to address the assembled anti-fascist audience throughout the day. The meetings were used to inaugurate a national petition against incitement to racial hatred that went on to attract half a million signatures. The BNP found itself pushed out of Ridley Road by the actions of the YSM. When they tried to reorganise, they were attacked by a contingent of 400 anti-fascists led by members of the 62 Group. The BNP were routed, their speaker system was smashed up, their land rover was wrecked and several fascists hospitalised.

Using whatever transport they could lay their hands on, anti-fascists then made their way over to the UM rally at Victoria Park Square in Bethnal Green. Missiles were thrown as Mosley stepped up to the platform to chants of "Six million Jews" and "Down with Mosley" He lasted two minutes this time. Police closed down the meeting but the UM leader was attacked again before he got to the safety of his car to be driven off at high speed. UM followers who trailed behind the speakers' lorry were later ambushed by stone throwing youths as they passed the junction of Salmon and Ball.

Protected by huge numbers of police, Mosley managed to

finish his speech at Bethnal Green a week later but in the next he was out-manoeuvred at Ridley Road. The Hackney branch of the Young Socialists, the successors to the Labour League of Youth closed down by the Labour Party in 1954 for being too militant, held an all-day meeting at the market. The UM leader was pushed out to Hertford Road where he spoke to a small group of his own supporters for 25 minutes. Some 20 fascists, including Mosley's son Max, then returned to Ridley Road and attacked the Young Socialists. Fights spilled out onto Kingsland Road and nearby side streets, ending with several arrests.

Mosley changed tack after a visit to Manchester on 29 September when it required a total of 250 police officers to protect him from anti-fascists organised by the Northern Council Against Fascism. He announced that he would no longer speak at big pre-advertised open-air rallies. He sought to side-step anti-fascist opposition by addressing meetings without advance publicity and the opposition that it brought. This worked for a while, but as Monty Goldman explains, the 62 Group were quick to adjust their tactics:

> The 62 Group had sympathetic stallholders, taxi-drivers and shop-keepers, who would phone them up when they saw the fascists gathering for a meeting and tell them where they were. Then the 62 Group would get together and attempt to disrupt the meetings by trying to break through the cordon of fascist stewards and attack the speaker or push over the platform. They did this successfully on dozens of occasions over the period of a few years in the sixties.

Tony Hall was one of those on the end of the phone line. In his opinion it was the superior organisation of the 62 Group that the fascists couldn't handle:

> We had a call-out thing arranged with the Jewish crowd from

Stamford Hill. Kosov's in Ridley Road would phone somebody as soon as the fascists showed up for one of their snap meetings and this telephone tree would be set in motion. Everyone would get a phone call saying "The fascists are at Ridley Road," or wherever. We could get between seventy and eighty young hairy yobs down there within half an hour of the start of the meeting. If things were right, which they often were, because the police weren't prepared at the time, we would do this flying wedge thing, get in amongst them, scatter them all and pick them off as they were running away. If it was a Ridley Road meeting we'd all meet on the corner of Shacklewell Lane and Kingsland High Street. We'd get two or three big guys at the front and the rest of us would follow in a wedge shape behind. We'd all jog down the road building up momentum as we went and without any pause or shouting or whatever, we'd go straight in and scatter them. I only saw it a few times but it was very effective. I remember being in a flying wedge when Andrew Fountaine of the British National Party had a meeting in John Campbell Road. Again we heard about it through the telephone tree and got down there as quickly as we could. We formed up in a flying wedge and charged at them. There were only about twenty or thirty of them and we kicked the shit out of them. They took their walking wounded to the Metropolitan Hospital in Kingsland Road, where there was a black doctor in charge in casualty, so they all came limping out again. We were waiting outside for them and helped them on their way again.

Indoor public meetings were a total waste of time for the fascists. For some reason or other they seemed to like Finsbury Town Hall. They would have minders standing about but we managed to infiltrate the meeting and, as soon as someone stood up to speak, we'd shout and throw chairs. The minders would try and throw you out and the police would try and stop the disturbances but as soon as it settled down, it would start off again. Shouting, fighting, throwing chairs through windows so the council wouldn't let them rent the hall again.

The Union Movement used to turn up and try and sell their paper, *Action*, on the corner of Brick Lane on a Sunday morning. There was a period when every Sunday morning they would turn up, get a punch on the side of the ear and have their papers thrown all over the pavement. They stopped trying after a while. Nobody could sustain that. This was all done on the basis that violence worked. They were not going to come back to Hackney if they got a good kicking every time they showed their faces. We'd have rules about not bringing weapons because you'd get a heavier sentence if you got caught with a weapon. The police would try to fit you up with weapons anyway if they arrested you. Some poor bastards got fitted up for carrying dockers' hooks.

We also raided Mosley's headquarters while he was speaking at one of his May Day rallies. We got about fifteen hard people together, including my mate Billy Collins, and went down to the offices, which were on Vauxhall Bridge Road near Victoria Station. We were all wearing Mosley flashes and fascist badges and rosettes as though we were going to the rally. We pushed our way in through the basement entrance and found that there were only about four or five of them left in there, one of which was Robert Row, who was the editor of *Action*. The rest had already gone to the rally. We completely wrecked the place. The printing press was badly damaged, the telephones were ripped off the walls and anyone who resisted was given a nasty kicking. Row was made to kneel on the floor and rip up copies of his paper. We also took away these files full of names, people who had been contributors to Mosley's movement since the thirties and there were all sorts of top people, including bishops and generals, basically the ruling class, the bourgeoisie.

As time went on, Special Branch began to get a lot smarter.

225

At one demonstration I was assigned to get on a toilet roof and take photographs of the fascist supporters. One of our tactics, if there were a lot of police about and not so many of us, was to mingle with the fascists and note who they were and what car they came in. When the meeting dispersed, you'd make your mark, follow them and then have them around the corner. It was easy if you knew what car they came in because you knew where they were going after the meeting. On this particular occasion I noticed that there were these scruffy looking student types who were showing passes to get past the lines of police and then mingling with the crowds. When trouble started they went straight for us. This began to happen more and more frequently. On one occasion, this copper, Barrowclough, got hold of one of our blokes on the corner of Sandringham Road and Kingsland High Street. He got him by the scruff of the neck, got out his warrant card, and said, "I'm a police officer, and I'm arresting you for…" Well, he didn't get any further than that, because he was thrown bodily through the plate glass window of a shop. There were many incidents like that.

In general, we avoided big demonstrations. We preferred little groups who knew exactly what they had to do and went out and did it. We were described as "leftist thugs" by certain people, who should have known better. I was reprimanded by the CP for encouraging youth to go out on these jaunts rather than be doing what they should be doing, which was standing in the rain on Stoke Newington High Street selling the *Daily Worker*.

By 1963, the effects of organised anti-fascism were beginning to show. The UM no longer even bothered to pretend that they could operate publicly and withdrew completely from the street level political activity. After the retreat of the UM, the Yellow Star Movement (YSM) was rather directionless and began to fall apart.

Its secretary, Olga Levertoff, died in the later part of the year. The Movement ran into financial difficulties. The 62 Group remained active, continued to oppose the smaller fascist groups, although their activities took on a more clandestine nature as the number of street confrontations dwindled. Tony Hall was still involved but was beginning to have doubts about some of his allies:

> The Zionists always seemed to have a lot of money. They were getting money from somewhere, probably from sympathisers in Jewish industry. This was useful to us because they could provide things like transport, which we didn't have or had very little of. Gerry Gable and his crowd also did a lot of the intelligence work, putting spies inside the Union Movement and so forth. It was off the back of this that the *Searchlight* newspaper was first set up. We felt that where we could still co-operate together on actions we would because we had a common enemy but, as things moved on in time and Israel increasingly became more of a client state of the United States, it became harder and harder. When I was young, Israel was all Kibbutzim and farmland and socialism but that didn't last very long, and pretty soon it was in the hands of American imperialists and could best be described as the bastion of American imperialism in the Middle East. The final nail in the coffin came when we raided the headquarters of a bloke called Eddie Martell, who ran the Freedom Group. This was a group of newspapers and political groups, which were all very anti-socialist. They ran a fleet of buses during the London bus strike and took part in a lot of anti-Trade Union activity. Someone found out that he had an office over a pub in Soho and a plan was devised to break in one night. The Zionists provided the transport again and we provided the muscle. Someone managed to get themselves locked into the building when it was shut up for the evening and came downstairs and unlocked it for us. We went in at about one

o'clock in the morning and removed all the files. We had an agreement that we would remove them to a safe-house, where we would all get together after the dust had settled and go through it and see what information would be good for us all. We humped all this stuff over to a rented basement in West London and dumped it there with an agreement that we would all get together a couple of weeks later and go through it. One of our blokes smelt a rat. I'm not quite sure why but we went back to this place about five days later and it had all gone. The Zionists had taken it all and we never saw it again. I don't know if it was given to Special Branch or added to their own intelligence files but we were excluded. From then on, the relationship more or less broke down completely.

The 62 Group carried on for some years afterwards and there were all sorts of other incidents and actions against the fascists but the useful part of the group had really come to an end by this time in any case. The success of the 62 Group was evidenced by the fact that the fascists were scared to show themselves on the streets any more. They stopped having meetings in Ridley Road, they stopped having marches in East London and they stopped trying to sell their shit material on Brick Lane. We had our own little projects by this time and operated more or less independently, which worked very well indeed. People like Billy Collins and the other villains involved were very practical, pragmatic people. "No publicity," they'd say "just go and do the job." We had a kind of almost Mafia-like code of silence at the time. You didn't speak to anybody about what you did. It worked very well. And it wasn't long before the fascists were looking over their shoulders, which was our intention.

There wasn't any sudden end to the 62 Group. It just petered out as people moved on and times changed. You'd occasionally get a phone call saying "They've got Finsbury Town Hall again. Let's get down there" but somehow it wasn't as urgent and organised as it had been because the threat had faded away. Don't let anybody kid you that the 62 Group was an exclusively Jewish organisation because it wasn't. There were all sorts in it. The backbone of our part of it was the Stoke Newington branch of the Communist Party. They weren't all members of the CP but people associated with it, sympathisers, friends, villains, all sorts of people. I wouldn't want in any way to denigrate Gable and the Zionists for their efforts, it's just that it was not just an exclusively Jewish organisation.

While the Marxist wing of the 62 Group faded from existence, what Tony Hall refers to as the 'Zionist wing' remained operative well into the early 1970s. The Intelligence Department of this wing of the 62 Group that had recruited informers and placed moles inside all the far-right groups from the very start formalised this role in 1963 by creating the Searchlight Association. The Searchlight Association had the twin aim of gathering intelligence and disseminating the information through its various contacts in the media. A *Searchlight* newspaper was published sporadically from 1965 to 1967, edited by two Labour MPs, first Reginald Freeson, then Joan Lestor.

The underground nature of 62 Group activities in the period after 1963 or thereabouts means that we'll probably never know the full details of their escapades but John Tyndall accused the 62 Group of numerous alleged incidents in the April 1965 edition of *Spearhead*. These allegations include the raid on the Union Movement's headquarters described by Tony Hall but also the breaking and entering of revisionist historian David Irving's flat as well as continuing attacks on the BNP, the NSM, and Tyndall's breakaway Greater Britain Movement (GBM).

In February 1965, the inaugural meeting of the Campaign Against Racial Discrimination (CARD), a liberal, law-abiding organisation set up in the wake of Dr. Martin Luther King's visit to Britain was mobbed by 35 Nazis. CARD was concerned with campaigning to make racial discrimination illegal and opposing racist immigration laws. A spate of fascist violence followed. There were arson attacks on synagogues, desecration of Jewish cemeteries and the vandalism of Jewish properties in London, Liverpool, Birmingham, Cardiff, Manchester and Bournemouth. Individual Jews, Africans, Caribbeans and Asians were assaulted and fiery crosses placed outside the homes of immigrants. A type of guerrilla warfare took place in which one side targetted innocent unaffiliated people for their religion, 'race' or colour while the other sought out fascists and active racists. The small-scale nature of the conflict signalled the relative weakness of fascist forces, however. The tiny rump of organised fascists, many of whom were outright Nazi sympathisers who constituted the membership of the various far-right organisations, still represented an intermittent physical threat, but they were politically insignificant. It would take a major realignment before they would once again trouble the headline writers of national newspapers. And, the era saw the end of Mosley at long last. His 60s comeback ended in ignominious defeat and he retreated from political life for the final time.

6

One, two, three and a bit, the National Front is a load of shit: 1966 – 1979

The formation of the National Front (NF) at Caxton Hall, London, on 15 December 1966 was resisted with force. Anti-fascist opposition was large-scale and militant. There were riots outside the hall as well as attempts by the 62 Group and others to disrupt the proceedings. Only about one third of those due to attend the meeting actually made it inside, but those present pressed ahead with plans to launch the new party.

The NF was an attempt by various far-right parties such as the BNP, the Racial Preservation Society and the League of Empire Loyalists to shed the Nazi image that had plagued their chances of electoral success. Accordingly, neither Colin Jordan nor John Tyndall were present at the Caxton Hall meeting. Jordan was absent because he wanted no part of the new organisation while Tyndall was missing because he was in jail for firearms offences. Within a year, however, Tyndall had disbanded the GBM and ordered its 138 members to follow him into the NF. It would not be very long before he forced his way into a leadership position alongside Martin Webster.

There were protests outside the NF's first annual conference in October 1967 but most anti-fascist activity followed the pattern established earlier in the decade of small numbers of militants engaged in underground actions. 62 Group activists disrupted Colin Jordan's re-launch of the NSM as the British Movement (BM) at Caxton Hall in the summer of 1968 making off with membership cards. Other paperwork was also removed from the scene. NF documents were taken from their Croydon office in May 1969 and in the following month a stolen lorry was reversed into the NF's headquarters in Tulse Hill. In October the

NF's annual conference at Caxton Hall had to be moved after two men smashed up the electrical equipment with axes.

While the NF failed to attract much media attention during the early years of its existence, the racist analysis of immigration made headline news after Tory MP Enoch Powell gave his infamous 'Rivers of Blood' speech on 20 April 1968. The scale of working-class support for Powell shocked many on the left. Thousands of workers downed tools after he was sacked from his post in the Shadow Cabinet. London dockers and Smithfield meat porters marched on Westminster under the slogans 'Don't Knock Enoch' and 'Back Britain not Black Britain.' Left-wing docker, Terry Barrett, claimed that a small group of fascists, who normally had no political influence on the docks, had exploited workers' fears over job losses. Rather than a spontaneous outburst of racist anger, fascists had a hand in its organisation. Nor was support for Powell amongst dockers as widespread as reports suggested. Only 1,000 of the 23,000 employed across London joined the protest and these were mostly from the small St. Katherine Docks. Just 300 voted to strike in support of Powell the following day. However, communist dockers Mickey Fenn and Eddie Prevost regarded the show of fascist organisation and racist politics as a serious setback. Many years later, Prevost remarked that the pro-Powell demonstration was the worst day of his political life. These dockers vowed to step up their work to curtail fascist influence and racist attitudes on the docks, so it never happened again.

The situation at Smithfield Meat Market was worse than on the docks. Support for Powell at Smithfield was widespread and there was an entrenched culture of racism in the market. Mosley's old minder, Danny Harmston, worked there and was an influential figure amongst the porters. Monty Goldman suggests that hard work by CP trade unionists successfully challenged racism at the docks and Smithfield:

Things stayed pretty quiet until Tory MP Enoch Powell came along. For a short period during the late sixties, there was a lot of support for Powell amongst some sections of the workers following his anti-immigration "Rivers of Blood" speech. 800 dockers actually marched in support of Powell after he was sacked by Tory leader Edward Heath. This was eventually turned around, despite the problems the Communist Party had at that time, by the dedicated work of two CP leaders, namely Jackie Dash and Bernie Steers, who were both respected trade unionists and shop stewards on the docks. Erik Rechnitz did a similar thing at Smithfield Meat Market. 400 porters handed in a petition in Downing Street in support of Powell but because Erik was a respected trade unionist at the market, he was able to turn the situation on its head.

These claims might be the subject of some dispute certainly with regard to Smithfield Meat Market, which remained fertile ground for racists for many years to come, but the long hard struggle to turn around racist attitudes in the workplace takes time, requires plenty of patience and determination. In the immediate aftermath of Powell's speech, the groups that defined themselves as 'revolutionary' in opposition to the 'reformism' of both Communist and Labour Parties displayed none of these qualities and behaved as a collection of petty, squabbling sects. A counter-demonstration on 28 April attracted only 1,500 marchers chanting 'Arrest Enoch Powell' and carrying placards depicting him in the peaked cap of an SS officer. As the demonstration reached Parliament, there was some fighting with Powell supporters but the various groups were disorganised and divided. The International Socialists (IS) had a contingent on the march. In an editorial in their publication, *International Socialism*, they attempted to repair the fragmentation of anti-racist and anti-fascist forces by proposing that 'urgent reorganisation of these socialist forces is necessary if the onward march of racialism is to be checked and any long-term fascist development fought against.' *International Socialism* also called for the formation of a single organisation 'to fight these new and urgent battles.' The plea for unity fell on stony ground, a landscape formed by splits and mergers of Trotskyist groups in which the IS had established itself as the main player.

Those already engaged in anti-fascist politics and those for whom it had become a priority did not wait for a new organisation. 62 Group activists and others fought pitched battles in Fleet Street with supporters of the Immigration Control Association. The Association contained a mix of hard-line Tories and NF supporters but their march consisted almost entirely of known fascists. It started from Smithfield Meat Market. Anti-fascists were hard pressed to defend themselves that day.

While they were struggling to cope with the revitalised fascist threat, it was people identified as immigrants that had to withstand the repercussions of Powell's speech. A Jamaican man was shot and killed in Smethwick. A black youth was almost killed after being attacked by a white gang wielding iron bars, bottles and axes in North Kensington. KKK-style burning crosses were placed outside homes in Leamington Spa, Rugby, Coventry, Ilford, Plaistow and Cricklewood. In Wolverhampton, a series of racist attacks culminated in the death of Hiralan Gandabhai Patel. He was killed when he and his friends were attacked by a gang of white youths.

In July 1969, the Burley area of Leeds was beset by riots following the stabbing of a white youth by a young Indian man. Over two consecutive nights huge crowds descended on Burley, smashed windows and vandalised the homes of Asian families. Fascists from the NF, BNP and the British Movement were known to be active in the area and involved in the riots. Leeds and Bradford International Socialists issued a leaflet in their wake that revealed their bewilderment and, with some honesty, recognised the weaknesses of left groups:

> Although we have had members on the spot, we have been
> appalled by our inability to do anything other than arrange
> accommodation for vulnerable families. No single organi-
> sation seems capable of doing anything more. We have called
> a meeting in Leeds on Sunday to give a background to the
> race riot and to discuss the powerlessness at present of organ-
> isations like our own and immigrant organisations, to cope
> with the situation.

In a period when 'race' was turned into a problem, support for
the NF soared. But the green shoots of anti-fascist resurgence
were becoming visible. In 1969, a small group of anonymous
activists known as the Anti-Fascist Research Group began
publishing the *Anti-Fascist Bulletin*. The bulletin, 'an information
service on the revival of fascism in Britain', ran for five issues
between 1969 and 1971 and encouraged its readers to:

> learn, reproduce and distribute this information through
> contacts with potential allies in anti-fascist work in their areas
> – local immigrant organisations; Jewish and other minority
> organisations; left-wing and trades union organisations and
> youth groups.

As well as reporting on fascist comings and goings, the *Bulletin*
also contained reports on the various ad hoc anti-fascist
committees that had sprung up in response to the increased
fascist threat. There were complaints in Issue 4 that 'an
ineffective counter-demonstration was mounted by some 200
anti-fascists' in response to a 300 strong NF march through
Wolverhampton on 28 November 1970 and some displeasure
over the failure of a 'Socialist Alliance' of left-wing groups to
prevent the NF from taking over the 'South-East London Model

Parliament' debating forum in August of that same year, from which it was claimed that the NF was receiving considerable prestige.

Things seem to have improved by 1971 and Issue 5 of the *Bulletin* was happy to report that a contingent of NFers had been successfully routed after attempting to disrupt an anti-racist meeting at Hornsey Town Hall on 19 March. In the ensuing fracas, Terry Applin, the NF Field Organiser was hit over the head by a chair. One fascist complained to the *Wood Green Weekly Herald* that 'A trap was laid and we walked into it.' The same issue carried an account of a counter-demonstration a week later against an NF march in Hitchin. 2,000 anti-fascists organised by the North Hertfordshire Campaign for Racial Equality opposed the NF:

> When the march reached the town centre, the opposition really started. Smoke-bombs and rotten fruit were thrown from among the assembled anti-fascists, who were lining both sides of the road behind a police cordon. For some 10 minutes the road was blanketed by swirling clouds of smoke. The police, taking prompt action, diverted the fascists' march to a small park where for the remainder of the afternoon, the NF speakers were able to address their own members, encircled by 2 rows of policemen.

As 1971 drew to a close, the national press reported details of a 62 Group operation in Brighton. They broke up a meeting of the secretive Northern League, a small, hard-line international Nazi group on 28 November at the Royal Pavilion Hotel. The Northern League had been infiltrated by a Searchlight mole and details of the meeting handed on. Several fascists, including former SS men and NF members, were ambushed in the restaurant and hospitalised. 62 Group members let off smoke bombs to cover their escape.

By now, the left-wing press had woken up to the threat posed by the NF. The pages of the IS's paper *Socialist Worker* and the International Marxist Group (IMG)'s *Black Dwarf* and *Red Mole* alerted readers to the rise of fascism and the state of its opposition. In *Red Mole* Vol. 2 No. 7, R. Neubauer lamented:

> The only forces within the socialist movement with recent histories of active anti-fascist experience are diverse and ill co-ordinated. This is natural in view of the relatively new nature of the reborn Right. A minority of Left organisations and of individual branches inside such organisations have been effective here. To these can be added small bands of militant anti-fascists from the immigrant and Jewish communities, with often confused concepts of who the enemy are and what strategy can defeat them…Proposals for active co-operation should be advanced and debated now. Information and analysis of developments on the fascist fringe of politics should be extended and militants made aware of the potential dangers. A simple system of liaison between separate socialist groups can neutralise fascist interventions and should be erected with care.

To the IMG's call for cooperation and the IS's earlier appeal for a single unifying organisation should be added a trade union initiative. In December 1972, a group calling itself Trade Unionists Against Fascism published *Against Fascism*, a pamphlet identifying fascist activities of concern to its movement, including two marches by Smithfield meat porters in August and September 1972, opposing any support for Asians expelled from Uganda. Once again, Danny Harmston was prominent in these protests alongside NF members. *Against Fascism* also documented the failure of the trade union movement to respond when the NF intimidated striking Asian workers at the Mansfield Hosiery Mills in Loughborough and illustrated the problem of temporary anti-fascist organisations. Trade Unionists Against Immigration (TRUAIM), a fascist trade union front, had tried to hold a major anti-immigration march in Oldham on 18 March 1972. It was opposed by the Manchester Anti-Fascist Co-ordinating Committee, which had brought together 'local activists in union branches, trades councils, socialist and political organisations, student unions and immigrant groups.' When the march was cancelled, the Co-ordinating Committee was 'allowed to disintegrate by anti-fascists in the area' much to the chagrin of the authors of *Against Fascism* who argued for a permanent national anti-fascist organisation.

The development of an anti-fascist strategy in the early 1970s did not follow some preconceived blueprint. There were a series of local reactions to particular fascist activities. Despite calls by left-wing groups for co-ordinated action or even a dedicated organisation, neither strategy was advanced with the vigour necessary to become a reality. This may well have been due to the left's preoccupation with talking shop but it was also true that the NF was not widely perceived as a serious threat at this time. Nick Mullen, a young Irishman living and working in London, explains how he become aware of the NF presence through his involvement in student politics:

I worked on the 'lump' on building sites in London throughout the sixties, so there was always an awareness of the political situation mainly through the unions but it wasn't really until I became a student in 1973 that I got heavily involved. Student politics seemed important in those days and there was quite a bit going on. At the time, there was a growing awareness of the National Front and what they represented. I was at college in Enfield, at Middlesex Polytechnic as it was then known, and one of the NF's heavies, a guy called Roy Painter had stood in a by-election around there. The NF had been very active in the area and we were hearing from other colleges that the fascists were making their presence felt in other parts of the country as well. Of course the NF didn't like students very much either and there was quite a bit of trouble. You see, not only were the NF anti-black, they also hated the left. One of their marching songs was "The Reds, the Reds, we've gotta get of the Reds." The most successful anti-fascist action I took part in was a local one in Enfield. We discovered the Front were having a private meeting in a local school. We turned up totally unexpectedly and physically stopped them going into their meeting. It really shocked them that we were able to do that. They had complete contempt for us longhaired 'red' students but we were willing and able to stand up against them.

The patchy and uncoordinated nature of the anti-fascist opposition enabled the NF to experience considerable growth in the early 1970s. They began a 'Stop the Asian Invasion' campaign, instigating fear and opposition to refugees from Uganda. The centrepiece of the campaign was to be a 'Send Them Back' march set to culminate in a rally at Conway Hall in Red Lion Square on 15 June 1974. Opposition to the NF march was organised by Liberation (formerly the Movement for Colonial Freedom), which announced plans to hold an open-air rally in the square outside the hall to allow vocal opposition to the NF, but no physical contact. It was agreed to by the police.

On the day itself, over 1,500 counter-demonstrators marched from Victoria Embankment to Red Lion Square. The middle section of the march was a militant section comprised of several hundred members of the International Marxist Group (IMG), the Communist Party of England (Marxist-Leninist) and International Socialists (IS) along with assorted anti-fascists of various hues. As the march neared its destination, this section broke away from the main body of the march heading towards the police cordon outside Conway Hall in an attempt to blockade the main entrance and deny the NF entrance. Foot and mounted police reacted by attempting to clear Red Lion Square. They pushed back at the militant anti-fascists and the law-abiding supporters of Liberation. Nick Mullen was to play a central role in the events of the day and in the public inquiry that followed:

I was one of the people who moved a motion at the National Union of Students annual conference in 1974 calling for no platform for racists on campus. Our argument was that the respectability of speaking on a student union platform should not be afforded to fascists and racists and this is quite important because we argued that both fascists and racists should be banned. It seemed to me that this was the correct line to take. The then Broad Left leadership of the NUS didn't like the "No Platform" policy so we had a recall conference at Imperial College in London on 15 June. I went there as a delegate from Middlesex. I spoke in the morning and actually moved the "No Platform" policy in the afternoon. I then promptly left to go down to Red Lion Square to oppose the National Front holding a meeting in, of all places, Conway Hall. The NF were intending to march through Central London to their meeting in the Hall and the anti-fascists were gearing up to stop them. The NF meeting had been organised to protest over the Labour government granting a retrospective amnesty to illegal immigrants and their slogan was "Send Them Back." All sorts of left-wing groups had come together to demonstrate against the fascists and a large breakaway group had decided to occupy the area in front of the hall in an attempt to try and stop the fascists from getting in. It was regarded as almost sacrilegious that the NF were being allowed to use Conway Hall as it had historically been a meeting place of the left.

My girlfriend had gone to the demonstration with a group

from Middlesex Poly and I was hoping to meet up with them at some point in the afternoon. I didn't know if there was going to be any trouble or not but I suppose there's always a good chance that a demonstration against fascism will result in some form of confrontation. Obviously, I hoped that we could stop the Front by peaceful means but I was prepared to use violence if it proved necessary.

I got down there just as the counter-demonstration had got into the Square. As I pushed my way to the front, I realised we'd been stopped and the police weren't allowing us to approach the hall. One section of the march had decided to make a push and try and break through the police lines. That was stopped and there was a lull of about ten minutes during which nothing much happened. People were just standing, chanting slogans, and there was a young black copper right in the front lines and he was generally getting a hard time and I remember saying to people "Be careful how you say this to him" but then saying to the guy "Aren't you embarrassed?" You could tell he was uncomfortable with what he was doing, and he kept saying that he was only doing his job. We reminded him where that line had been used before.

There were two or three rows of police who were pressed up against the crowd and they had their truncheons drawn, although as I said, this was when things had quietened down a bit. Behind these rows of coppers were a number of police on horseback. There was one particular copper there, he was in the second row, and he was frothing at the mouth trying to get at people. He was hurling all sorts of abuse and urging the other coppers to attack us. I then felt a push behind me, and I turned around and saw that someone had fallen over. I didn't have a clue who it was at the time but I now know of course that it was Kevin Gately. I heard afterwards that he had fainted due to the crush of the crowd. There was a shout that somebody had fallen and I shouted "Ease back, ease back.

Give him room." This evil little copper then started shouting "One of the bastards is down. Quick let's rush them. Trample him." I looked at him and said quite calmly "You vicious bastard. I've got your number." I could see he wanted to get at me, but the coppers in the front row were inadvertently blocking his way.

Then all of a sudden there was a charge from the police, who started hitting out with their truncheons. As the mounted police charged in, the crowd gave way and people started running in panic. I didn't see what happened to the lad who had fallen over but lots of people were being trampled and stamped on. One copper got hold of me, grabbed me by the hair and pulled my head back, while the copper who had tried to get me earlier, hit me over the head with his truncheon. I was punched and kneed by several other coppers before they eventually let me go. The wound to the top of my head was quite bad and there was a lot of blood pouring down my face and into my eyes. In fact, at one stage, I thought I was going blind. I didn't realise there was so much blood. I spent the next few minutes wandering around totally dazed and the coppers came up to me and said "We're taking you in" but luckily a couple of St John's Ambulance people said "No, he's injured, we'll take him." They took me to an ambulance and cleaned up my face a little bit. The guy who had fallen over earlier was also in there. I asked how he was and they said "He seems to be in a bad way, but he'll be alright."

After they cleaned me up, I stepped outside the ambulance and there were scenes of absolute mayhem. The police were running riot. I saw one guy, I don't know whether he was a press photographer or not but he had a decent camera. He was sitting on the railings above the road and as this copper ran past he gave him gave him a massive forearm smash right in the face and sent him tumbling over the railings. It was actually quite frightening. Everybody was scattering. I hadn't been able to find my girlfriend or the rest of the people from my college, so I went and got back in the union van hoping to make my way back to the conference because I thought that delegates from the conference should know what was happening. When I got back to the conference, I said to people there "While you lot are talking about opposing fascism, there's people down at Red Lion Square actually doing it, and I can see some of them dying as a result." I didn't know then of course that Kevin Gately had died. I only heard about that later.

In the aftermath of Red Lion Square, there was a public inquiry into the death of Kevin Gately. The Scarman Inquiry was basically a whitewash and cleared the police of all wrongdoing. I wasn't very impressed with it, although the press thought it was the best thing since sliced bread. It was meant to be an inquiry into the actions of the police but Scarman turned it into an inquiry into the tactics of the anti-fascists and how much our actions had contributed to the events. The copper who actually hit me admitted in the inquiry that he'd drawn his truncheon, something which he'd never put in his report, which is against police disciplinary procedures. He also didn't report he'd used it and then admitted he had. He then said he'd used it exactly where I said he had but said that he'd hit a short fat man, whereas I'm a tall thin man. Scarman just skated over all these discrepancies. I think it was all too awkward for him. I've been asked many times if I think the police killed Kevin Gately. I can't say for certain that they did but if someone is charging into a packed crowd, waving around a truncheon and saying "Let's trample the bastard" then, well, I'll leave it for you to judge.

Not everyone on the anti-fascist side shared Nick Mullen's analysis of events. Monty Goldman was also there and took a completely different view:

Hackney Communist Party had a fund-raising jumble sale the same day as Red Lion Square but because my name was down as a speaker at the rally outside Conway Hall, I went down to the Embankment with a group of Party members and joined the march to the Square. Tony Gilbert was there. He wrote a book about Red Lion Square called *Only One Died*. Unfortunately, it soon became clear that there were a number of divisions between the anti-racists on the march and I got the feeling that certain groups of ultra-leftists wanted to take charge of things and steer events in a direction where there would be a confrontation with the police. Unfortunately, they succeeded and there was a police charge on a section of the demonstration and a student from Warwick University, Kevin Gately, was killed. But nobody is going to stand up and take responsibility for provoking the police charge are they? Nobody is going to say we were responsible, are they?

Red Lion Square, followed by the public inquiry into the death of Kevin Gately, put the issue of fascism back at the top of the agenda. It was a wakeup call for anti-fascist movement. In the immediate aftermath of Red Lion Square, 8,000 people joined an NUS sponsored silent march through Central London in memory of Kevin Gately. There was a spate of anti-fascist publications, including important pamphlets by both the IS and the IMG urging anti-fascists to put the 'No Platform for Fascists' policy into practice wherever possible.

Several local anti-fascist committees were launched, re-launched or reinvigorated, around the country. In Oxford, two NF election meetings were disrupted in quick succession by members of the Oxford Anti-Fascist Committee. The first meeting on 22 October ended in ignominious defeat for the NF candidate, Ian Anderson, when a group of anti-fascists forced their way into Headington Middle School, tore down the Union flags and overturned the speaker's table. The assembled audience of five

Get off your backsides...

The I.S. is calling on all its members and sympathisers, on all socialists, trade unionists and students to join what must be a massive demonstration in London this Saturday. If we do not take action now at the first brutal killing of one of our comrades there is nothing ABSOLUTELY NOTHING that will stand in the way of increased fascist and police violence against the workers and student movement. With the economic and political crisis growing more intense every day we must defend tenaciously every basic right that has been won in the past and must move onto the offensive. If through passivity and apathy we are pushed onto the slope, we will find it a very slippery one with a fascist state at the end of it.

and DEMONSTRATE!

« In rememberance of Kevin Gately, the first student to be murdered in the fight against the growing fascist threat.

« For a full and genuinely independent enquiry into Gately's death and the police action.

« For the immediate disbandment of the Special Patrol Group.

« For the banning of the massive joint National Front/U.D.A. march called for 13th July. No freedom of organisation for those who would systematically destroy the hard won rights of the working class and student movement.

STOP THE SPREAD of POLICE & FASCIST VIOLENCE

Demonstration Sat. 22nd June

COACHES from
hall of memory
b'ham univ. union   11am

'Get off your backsides' International Socialists, 1974.

people watched in disbelief as Anderson was physically thrown out of his own meeting. This fiasco was followed a few days later by a much bigger NF meeting at Oxford Town Hall that was invaded by around 100 anti-fascists, who once more succeeded in forcing Anderson off the stage before occupying it themselves then regaling the audience with anti-fascist speeches. In the northwest, the Manchester Anti-Fascist Committee (MAFC) was also busy. The Committee grew out of the North

Fascism: How to Smash It, International Marxist Group, 1974.

245

Manchester Campaign Against Racism (NORMANCAR) centred around Blackley, a large working class area in the north of the city. The NF presence in the area was potentially very problematic, according to local anti-fascist Mike Luft:

> Blackley was adjacent to two Jewish areas, Prestwich and Crumpsall, and the NF were trying to stir up trouble between the two communities. They also threatened Paul Rose, the Labour MP for the area, because he was Jewish. It was quite a struggle getting rid of them. We used to go out regularly, leafleting against them and harassing them when they were out campaigning. The campaign against the NF in Manchester involved local activists from the CP and the Labour left. I don't remember the IS being involved at that stage. After a while, the NF moved into the city centre and we followed them. One group of fascists booked Houldsworth Hall on Deansgate for a meeting in 1974. We approached the owners of the hall, I think they were Christians, and tried to get the meeting cancelled but they said "We've taken the booking and we're honouring it." After that, we campaigned to get people mobilised to oppose the fascists and it was a victory because, although the meeting went ahead, it was held under virtual siege conditions and lots of fascists couldn't get through. After Houldsworth Hall, I think they realised that they weren't going to get anywhere in the city centre and moved out to Rochdale and Stockport for a number of years.

A report in issue 28 of *Mole Express*, a local anarchist newssheet, confirms Mike's view of events at Houldsworth Hall:

> Jim Merrick, leader of the British Campaign to Stop Immigration, and his racist associates have failed in their first attempt to gain a foothold in Manchester. A rally at the Houldsworth Hall, Deansgate, which they expected to attract

900 people, started an hour late with barely fifty, mainly because of a determined attempt by nearly five hundred trade unionists, students and members of a number of left groups, to blockade the entrance to the hall. Police and anti-fascist demonstrators were in confrontation for almost two hours outside and approximately 21 arrests were made.

John Severn was arrested outside the Hall:

I was sort of involved in the left wing scene at Manchester University and one Saturday we got dragged over to the Houldsworth Hall on Deansgate where an NF meeting was due to be held during the day. We tried to block the entrance... Yeah, I got pulled along with a lot of other people. We got into a scuffle with the cops and that was my first arrest and my first taste of anti-fascism.

John only recalls a small number, 'twenty, thirty of us', actually barring the entrance. But numbers were certainly on the increase as the year drew on. On 24 August, 6,000 anti-fascists marched in opposition to a Front demonstration in Leicester where Asian workers at Imperial Typewriters had struck in protest over racism at work and in their union. The Inter Racial Solidarity Campaign Committee followed an agreed route while groups of anti-fascist militants ignored the counter-demonstration and subjected the Front marchers to continuous heckling and abuse. Martin Webster, NF organiser, was attacked. The Communist Party of England (Marxist-Leninist) claimed it as a victory stating that 'Our policy is to be active against fascism'. On the march itself, there were tensions between the local organisers and the IS simmering below the surface. The IS had mobilised more than 1,000 of its members from as far away as Dundee and Southampton. They set up their own platform and loudspeakers at the march starting point drowning out attempts by the local organisers to make themselves heard. The IS then formed up in a separate section with its own stewards and loudspeaker van but made no attempt this time to break away from the official route.

On 7 September 1974, 7,000 anti-fascists occupied Hyde Park in London forcing the police to re-route a Front demonstration in support of the Ulster Loyalists. Other anti-fascists were at the start of the march itself and clashed with Front members only to be rewarded with arrest. *Anti-Fascist* by Martin Lux explains that an informal network of anti-fascist militants existed in London composed of anarchists, Zionists, dissident socialists and communists as well as trade union militants who would all coalesce around the fringes of an NF mobilisation in the hope of physically deterring their march. The numbers were so small that almost everyone involved was on nodding terms but they were growing month by month.

There were more calls to create a single anti-fascist organisation, including one truly hopeless one. Under the auspices of the Provisional Anti-Fascist Committee, the Appeal Group, a dissident CPGB faction based in Bexleyheath and comprised of no more than 30 active members, published the *Anti-Fascist Manifesto*

In Britain at the moment we have three openly fascist outfits and unquestionably there will be one or two within the machinery of the state itself. These are having the anti-Communist ground prepared for them by a network of Trotskyite and other anarchist "organisations". And racialists in Britain and certain religious leaders in Northern Ireland, if they are not grinding their own fascist hatchets are grinding them for others... There must be an anti-fascist committee in every factory, mine, mill and depot to develop the anti-fascist potential and to counter the fifth column and diversionary activities by fascists, Maoists and Trotskyites. These committees must help to build, educate and lead urban and rural area committees comprising dispersed workers (including farm labourers) and democrats from every stratum of society.

Unsurprisingly, neither the great mass of British workers, nor the existing informal network of anti-fascist committees rallied to the clarion call of this tiny Stalinist sect. The anti-fascist movement had not expressed a desire for such leadership but it was in desperate need of information on the fascists. This was met by the publication of *A Well-Oiled Nazi Machine* by former CP member Maurice Ludmer and Gerry Gable of Searchlight Associates. It documented the Nazi pedigree of the NF leaders like Webster and Tyndall and quickly sold out. Its success persuaded Gable and Ludmer to re-launch *Searchlight* as a regular monthly magazine in February 1975.

In March, there were scenes of disorder outside Islington Town Hall as the police struggled to stop sections of a 6,000 anti-fascist counter-demonstration from confronting 400 Front members. This was followed by disturbances in Oxford on 12 May. Oxford Anti-Fascist Committee had organised a protest outside the Town Hall where John Tyndall and Martin Webster were due to speak. A cordon of 250 police officers faced some difficulty holding back 600 anti-fascists, who repeatedly charged at police lines, waylaid fascists as they tried to gain entrance and took on the NF's Honour Guard.

Anti-fascists were also out in force in Glasgow on 24 May, attempting to stop the Front from holding a meeting at Kingston Hall. A largely peaceful picket of 300 people was attacked by truncheon-wielding police officers singing "Flower of Scotland" as they waded into the crowd. 65 people were arrested, including IMG and IS members, trade union officials, members of the local Trades Council, and the secretary of the Scottish CP. The trouble started when the police attempted to clear a path for Mr. J. Kingsley Read, Chairman of the National Front, who, it was claimed, had raised his arm in a Nazi salute as the police pushed the crowd aside. Many of those arrested were subsequently acquitted when their cases came to court. In the immediate aftermath of the riot, the police claimed that 18 officers had been treated for injuries, although a subsequent check of every hospital in the Glasgow area revealed that not one officer had been admitted. There were calls for a public inquiry into what James Milne, secretary of the Scottish TUC, claimed the 'Gestapo-tactics' of the police but the government refused, claiming that the police were capable of investigating themselves.

With the forces of anti-fascism able to field larger numbers at set-piece events, far-right foot soldiers stepped up their violence against their smaller left wing and international solidarity meetings, street paper sales, bookshops and people's homes. Amongst the many reported incidents was an attack on a communist bookshop in Brighton by a gang of 'patriots', a shotgun attack on a left-wing squat in Camden High Street and a concerted attempt to drive Irish Republicans and their supporters off the streets of Manchester. NF members, who always swung along behind the British Empire and British troops in Ireland, carried on their own war against Irish cultural events, civil rights campaigns and Republican commemorations. The Manchester Martyrs annual commemoration of three executed Fenians, which, with some notable exceptions, took place every November with a march that wound its way to Moston's Cemetery would become the fascists preferred target but this November in 1975, the NF also joined forces with Ulster loyalists to attack an NCCL meeting on civil rights in the north of Ireland at the University of Manchester's Institute of Science and Technology (UMIST) Students' Union. They caused £3,000 worth of damage and left six people badly injured. A 60-year old woman was also hit over the head with a bottle, a man required 19 stitches after one was smashed in his face and another had his arm broken. Such levels of violence did not occur everyday but were not rare. In February

1976, 30 stewards fought hard to keep a 40-strong gang of fascists out of a 'Right to Work' meeting at the Spinners Hall in nearby Bolton while in Edinburgh a meeting in support of the South-West African People's Organisation (SWAPO) was broken up by a gang of fascists.

While fascist gangs were busy attacking communities and leftist meetings, the leadership of the NF split. The so-called moderate faction under the leadership of Kingsley Read broke away to form the National Party (NP) to leave a depleted NF firmly in the hands of Tyndall and Webster. As the NF licked it wounds, it was handed a lifeline by the right-wing press hysterical over the admission of Asian refugees from Malawi. Headlines from the spring and summer of 1976 warning of 'floods' of immigrants given 'four star hotel' treatment at the taxpayer's expense were a boon to the NF who held widely reported demonstrations outside London airports. One at Gatwick held by Brighton and Crawley NF members ended in farce when the group mistook black American and West Indian holidaymakers for refugees. The bemused tourists were met with a barrage of insults, including 'Don't unpack, you have to go back,' 'This is our country,' 'You don't belong here,' and 'This is England, not Pakistan.'

The stupidity of racism notwithstanding, the fortunes of the Front were suddenly on an upward spiral. The NF gained 3,000 new members in 1976 and had some significant showings at the polls: an alarming 43,733 votes in Leicester (18.5%), a further 9,399 votes in Bradford (10%), and (when combined with the NP vote) a total of 44% of the vote in the Deptford by-election in south London in July. But they were never un-opposed. A pattern of physical resistance emerged as in Coventry in February when 1,500 anti-fascists held a counter protest to a Front march while smaller numbers of militants sought to directly intervene to stop them from reaching their destination. But the predetermined anti-fascist strategies of counter protest on the one hand or direct

confrontation on the other did not always take different directions on the day. Where there was very large-scale and determined resistance, and this was especially the case in areas where
immigrant groups who were the focus of fascist hatred had been
trying to build communities, anti-fascist opposition ended in full-
scale street battles.

On Saturday 24 April, a 700 strong NF contingent calling for
the repatriation of immigrants marched through Lumb Lane,
Bradford. Opposition, organised by the Manningham Defence
Committee (MDC), numbered 3,000 and included local Asian
youth, left-wing activists, anarchists and trade unionists. The NF
had a police escort into the area that was subject to a sustained
onslaught by sections of the counter protest. Two police vehicles
were overturned. Officers were stoned and pulled off their
horses. Anti-fascists fought with the police. Thirty were arrested.
Mounted officers rode headlong into the human wall that
blocked NF's route to their rally at a local school. Eventually, the
police got them through.

The MDC mobilisation and its aftermath started a campaign
of civil disobedience aimed at curbing the growth of the Front in
Bradford. The following Saturday, they staged a symbolic sit-
down protest in a busy main road in protest over a planned NF
motor cavalcade. It was cancelled after police had refused to
guarantee safety of the NF in their cars but the protest went
ahead anyway.

Then, there was Southall. On the evening of Friday 4 June,
Gurdip Singh Chaggar was stabbed to death on his way home.
Widely believed to have been racially motivated, the exact details
of the attack remain the source of some dispute. But the local
community had little doubt about the causes of Chaggar's
murder. 200 Asian youth marched on the police station to
demand better police protection from racist attacks. The police
initially arrested two of the demonstrators, releasing them after
the station was surrounded. The next day's newspapers were full

of reports of 'rioting Asians' but the winner in the sprint to the sewers was NP leader Kingsley Read, who declared that Chaggar's death was a case of 'one down, one million to go.' This sequence of events, a racist murder, wilful police indifference and press hostility, provided the catalyst for the formation of the Southall Youth Movement and the spread of the Asian Youth Movement (AYM) to most cities in the Midlands and the North. The AYM demanded the right of Asian people to defend themselves against racist and fascist attacks, police harassment and state racism. Defensive action against racist attacks formed the main plank of AYM activity but it also made a crucial contribution, often overlooked, to the politics of anti-racism as it developed in the anti-imperialist, left and labour trade union movements. Bradford AYM, for example, became known for the leading role it played in numerous anti-deportation campaigns. Activists could boast, with justification, that they never lost a case.

Alliances across communities and the left political spectrum had been mobilised around the case of Robert Relf. Former Ku Klux Klan, NSM activist and Colin Jordan's bodyguard, Relf was prosecuted under the Race Relations Act for putting a sign outside his Leamington Spa home that declared it was for sale to an English family. He defied the order to remove the sign, was sentenced for contempt of court and instantly adopted as a race martyr by right-wing media commentators and fascist groups alike. Relf ended up in Winson Green prison close to Handsworth, Birmingham. Local NF members mounted a picket outside the prison and planned a demonstration for May. The British Movement, who also wished to claim Relf as one of their own, threw their weight behind the demonstration. Calls to counter it were quick. The Bangladeshi Workers Association, the Indian Workers Association, the Labour Party, Birmingham Anti-fascist Committee, the Afro-Caribbean Self-Help Organisation, the IS, the IMG and other left-wing groups worked together handing out leaflets to the local community and lobbying local groups. On the day, 1500 assembled at Lozells to march to Winson Green. Fighting between fascists, anti-fascists and police broke out when the demonstration reached the prison. 28 were arrested. Inside the prison, Relf undertook a hunger strike that secured his release on medical grounds. The NF, proud that he had now also joined them, announced that they would march through London behind his original 'For Sale' sign. Unfortunately for them, it was stolen by IS members the day before the march and taken to an anti-fascist demonstration in Southall where it was publicly burnt.

Blackburn was next. A march of 4,500 people, called to take 'the fight into one of the strongholds of the enemy', took place on 11 September. It was organised by Action Against Racism, supported by the IS, the CP, Manchester Anti-Fascist Committee and numerous trades councils. It was part of a longer campaign aimed at turning the tide against the National Party in Blackburn. Two NP councillors, Kingsley Read and John Frankham, had won seats in April 1976. The town was rapidly gaining a reputation as a fascist base. Previous anti-racist marches had been subjected to hostile abuse and volleys of missiles by locals, while the fascists were cheered to the rafters. This march would be different. It easily outnumbered a fascist counter-demonstration of less than a hundred combined NP and NF supporters that was confined to the outskirts of town. As anti-fascists took over the town centre in a show of strength and staying power, local people were markedly less hostile. Blackburn's fascist base was on shaky ground. Frankham lost his seat once it was discovered that he had stood under an assumed name. Action Against Racism, however, continued to keep up the pressure on the fascists over the coming years and was still in business when the NP faded into political obscurity.

Over the summer of 1976, smaller scale skirmishes helped fill the column inches of the national and local press. This is just a snapshot. There were 25 arrests after anti-fascists clashed with the BM at a British Campaign to Stop Immigration rally in Trafalgar Square in April. NF members in Luton broke up two left-wing meetings in quick succession during June and July. The following month, in Gravesend, the sale of National Party propaganda *Britain First* provoked a huge fight. Around 50 locals beset NP members, some used tear gas and others Kung Fu flails.

As the summer drew to a close, anti-fascists began to look again at ways of co-ordinating their activities. The task wasn't helped by the pick and mix nature of local anti-fascist committees. Many were based around trades councils, of which some were dominated by left-wing groups such as the IS and the IMG, whilst others were led by local Labour Party branches, the CP, or the Race Equality Council. These latter groups were described by Colin Sparks in *International Socialism* 94 as 'class-collaborationist anti-racialist committees stuffed full of reformist trade union bureaucrats, jolly liberal clergymen and other such riff-raff.' The participation of Labour Party members on local committees had marked a change of policy by the Party, which, for the first time ever, openly encouraged its members to become involved in grass roots anti-fascist campaigning. Self-interest drove the change. Labour leaders were worried that the electoral successes of the NF might cause a split in the working class vote and allow the Tories to gain power. Local branches were therefore urged to assist in the development and growth of anti-fascist and anti-racist committees at the Party's 1976 annual conference. Then Home Secretary, Roy Jenkins, got cold feet. He reiterated the old official line on fascism that the best way to defeat the National Front was to ignore them.

By the autumn a series of important developments had taken place in the anti-fascist camp. Anti-fascist committees in the northwest and Midlands, in conjunction with Searchlight, began organising on a regional basis. They set themselves the task of producing joint anti-fascist propaganda, co-ordinating responses to fascist activities, exchanging information and intelligence. Some months later, over 20 anti-fascist groups from different parts of London, city-wide organisations, such as the All-London Gay Groups Against Sexism, Racism and Fascism (renamed the London Gay Activist Alliance), came together, again with Searchlight, to form the All London Anti-Racist Anti-Fascist Co-ordinating Committee (ARAFACC). ARAFACC adopted *CARF*, the paper of the Kingston Campaign Against Racism and Fascism, as its bi-monthly paper. The London Gay Activist Alliance outlined the political perspective of these regional initiatives in its publication, *An Anti-Fascist Handbook*:

ARAFACC, the Midlands and North-West groupings shared the conviction that it was not sufficient simply to see the National Front as the enemy; it was necessary to struggle against racism specifically, both because of its intrinsic importance and because the roots of fascism would only be chopped away by the challenging of racism.

Whether anti-fascism addressed or failed to address the problem of racism became the subject of much discussion within and between leftist organisations. But more divisive than the matter of anti-fascist analysis was the question of its strategy. As the London Gay Activist Alliance's *Handbook* summarised:

There has been a debate throughout various sections of the anti-fascist movement as to the tactics to be used against the fascists, centring on the interpretation and the implementation of the slogan "No Platform for Fascists". One of the most important differences which has arisen is over the matter of violent confrontation.

Some of the participants in the 1970s anti-fascist struggle, such as the Labour Party or the Communist Party, the latter of which added to the confusing tapestry of groups and acronyms by launching its own anti-fascist grouping, the All-London Campaign Against Racism and Fascism (ALCARF), were completely opposed to all forms of physical force, argued for state bans on fascist activity and preferred peaceful pickets and protest marches. Searchlight was more ambivalent about the necessity of force but forthright in calling for state and police bans. Even when groups accepted that a No Platform policy inevitably required physical resistance to be enforced there was no consensus about precisely how physical it should be. The IS, for instance, argued that physical confrontation, that is to say, actually fighting fascists, was a vital anti-fascist strategy whilst the IMG called for mass pickets or occupations of buildings as a first strike resorting to fighting only if these actions proved unsuccessful and the balance of forces was 'favourable.'

Sometimes, real events, rather than party policy, have a greater effect. Towards the end of August 1976, around 200 workers, mostly Asian women, went on strike at the Grunwick film processing labs in Willesden, London, in protest over appalling pay, poor conditions, bullying and the right to be represented by a union. The strike became the focus of a national campaign, which lasted nearly two years. Mass pickets, sometimes numbering thousands, attempted to shut down the plant, but a combination of organised right-wing scab labour, aggressive police tactics, unfavourable court rulings and prevarication by high-ranking trade union officials eventually resulted in the collapse of the strike. The Grunwick dispute is not only a turning point in labour history but also that of anti-fascism. It brought together hitherto isolated groups of anti-fascist militants. through an anti-racist struggle. Mickey O'Farrell from Hatfield was one of an emerging generation of anti-fascists who were politicised by the events at Grunwick:

Going down to Grunwicks was the first real political thing I did in my life. My life up until then had revolved around my peer group in Hatfield and being part of the hooligan culture around Manchester United. In fact I'd just come out of jail for some pointless brawl outside a pub. In retrospect I think I was probably looking for a new direction in life. I lived just around the corner from the main campus of Hatfield Polytechnic and knew some SWP students who were going down to support a mass day of action and I decided to go with them. The whole experience was overwhelming. All these thousands of working class people. Miners from Yorkshire and Kent, dockers from Merseyside and Glasgow, print workers, postal workers, builders from here and there and everywhere. With their wonderfully evocative banners. What really impressed me was the amazing level of militancy. I'd been used to the football terraces where a few dozen people would normally be able to push around crowds numbering hundreds and even thousands. Now I was seeing working class people openly challenging hundreds of police for control of the streets and sometimes getting the better of them and all in support of a small group of Asian women. And this was the other eye opener for me. Growing up as I had in a home counties New Town during the sixties and seventies, I can't recall having then ever personally known an Asian person in my life. There were just none in Hatfield in those days and whilst I'd like to think that I could never have been described as an active or malicious racist, I'm sure that being a typical working class *Sun* reader, and to my eternal shame that's exactly what I was in those days, I would have taken on at least some of the crap I was being fed. Things like immigration being linked to unemployment and homelessness. But now here I was experiencing something so exhilarating. It was basically lifting me up and shaking all the crap right out of me. I can recall one occasion on a later date when one of the strikers was being introduced to the crowd. She looked so small and vulnerable and I came over all emotional. I wanted to hug her and tell her how proud I was to be fighting alongside her. I know it sounds corny and naïve now but that's exactly what I was experiencing at the time. It was Saul on the road to Damascus.

On that first day I ended up getting arrested for obstruction. When the scab bus came there was a big surge through the police lines and I was one of those pulled in, I was bailed out quite quickly and made my way back to the Poly bar in Hatfield. As I walked in some of the students started applauding. Well, getting arrested was nothing new but getting applauded for it certainly was. There was talk in the bar about going over for an anti-NF demo that evening. I thought "Yeah, why not." If what I had seen so far was anything to go by I was certainly up for a bit more political activity. And so my first ever picket and first ever anti-fascist activity both happened on the same day

1976 was a busy year for anti-fascists. Rock Against Racism (RAR) was launched in the autumn. The story is a well-known one, but bears repeating. In August, Eric Clapton interrupted his set at the Birmingham Odeon to advise his fans to 'Vote for Enoch Powell' and 'stop Britain becoming a black colony.' In case his audience didn't get the full implications of his message, Clapton expanded: 'Get the foreigners out. Get the wogs out. Get the coons out' and repeated the phrase 'Keep Britain White'. His outburst prompted the photographer, Red Saunders, to write to the *New Musical Express, Sounds, Melody Maker* and the *Socialist Worker* to remind the guitarist 'Half your music is black. You're rock music's biggest colonist.' Saunders concluded his letter with the declaration: 'We want to organise a rank and file movement against the racist poison music. We urge support for Rock Against Racism.'

Clapton was unrepentant. He told *Melody Maker* the following week that Powell 'was the only bloke telling the truth, for the good of the country.' Maybe he was hoping that being a rock star would immunise him from public opprobrium. After all, Rod Stewart had made similar remarks without provoking too much in the way of public disapproval and David Bowie, whilst in a drug-induced haze, had declared that that Britain was ready for a fascist leader and had ridden around Victoria Station in an open top Mercedes giving a Nazi salute. The Bowie incidents did create a brief furore in the press but the anti-racist and anti-fascist movement had failed to muster any meaningful response. Clapton's outburst was the tipping point. The growing anti-racist sentiment of a younger generation challenged both the casual and the politicised racism of their elders. Hundreds of letters supporting Saunders flooded into the papers. Within months, Rock Against Racism (RAR) was born.

Blues singer Carol Grimes topped the bill at the first RAR gig at the Princess Alice pub, East London, on 10 December 1976. On the door were a group of dockers organised by Mickey Fenn, Eddie Prevost and Bob Light from the Royal Group of Docks Shop Stewards Committee. Fenn and Prevost had left the Communist Party in 1972 and later joined Light in the IS. Stewarding RAR events was to become an important activity for anti-fascists. Hundreds of gigs followed the one at the Princess Alice. The RAR movement was sustained by the energy and effervescence of the punk rock explosion. Punks loudly rejected the self-indulgent musings of the earlier generation of ageing rock stars. Their opposition to the musical establishment was part of a wholesale political rejection of an old order. RAR platforms reflected the anti-racism of punk and brought together bands that wrote songs about disenchantment of a white working class with reggae musicians whose lyrics expressed the desire for freedom of African peoples. The manifesto set out in the first issue of RAR's magazine, *Temporary Hoarding*, demonstrated the optimism of the movement's founders, including Ruth Gregory, Roger Huddle, Red Saunders, Syd Shelton and Dave Widgery. It expressed their belief in the power of music to create political change.

'Rock Against Racism', *Temporary Hoarding*, 1976.

Thousands of people got involved in RAR. One who threw his hat into the ring was John Baine, now better known as Attila the Stockbroker:

> I went to Kent University in the mid Seventies, just at the beginning of punk. I got involved in Rock Against Racism. RAR had been formed to counter a shift to the right in the music scene, which was epitomised by some rather crass and reactionary comments made by David Bowie and Eric Clapton. Coupled with this was the worrying rise of the

National Front, which by the mid to late Seventies was beginning to look really dangerous. I was also involved in the music itself as a punk bass player before I became Attila the Stockbroker in 1980. A group of us got together at Kent University and started up a local RAR group. We organised gigs, we sold badges and stickers and ordered loads of copies of the RAR fanzine *Temporary Hoarding*.

It would be difficult to underestimate the importance of RAR. It did more than swell the ranks of anti-fascists. A few key RAR organisers were International Socialists, soon to re-name themselves the Socialist Workers Party. The relationship between RAR and SWP helped the Trotskyist movement to become an increasingly important force in the battle against the NF.

Local anti-fascist committees were also growing in number and membership throughout 1976. The launch of one in Brighton was attended by 70 people. Tony Greenstein describes its political composition:

> It was chaired by Rod Fitch, a Prospective Parliamentary Candidate in Brighton Kemptown for Militant and the Labour Party and it used to meet at the Labour Club, 179 Lewes Road, in the basement. I was one of those who were in the far left, direct action, part of the opposition in the anti-fascist committee, along with the SWP/IS and students and IMG as it was then. There were trade union delegates and a couple of people from AJEX, who we didn't get on with. The Anti-Fascist Committee leafleted the whole of Brighton.

Differences and divisions in the anti-fascist movement over the acceptable forms of resistance, peacefully opposing the NF or physically stopping them, did not disappear with the optimism of RAR or the growth of the local committees. Both strategies were pursued as the movement continued to expand. Fascist violence, such as the involvement of NF supporters in racist attacks in East London towards the end of 1976, increased the militancy of anti-fascists.

On Saturday 23 April 1977, the NF tried their hand at intimidating the North Londoners that lived in and around Green Lanes. They assembled at Ducketts Common to march to Palmers Green. The pattern of opposition will be familiar. Religious leaders, local dignitaries, supported by members of the CP held a counter-protest while the IS/SWP, the IMG, Labour left-wingers, anarchists, members of the Indian Workers Association and local youth from the West Indian, Turkish and Greek communities assembled away from the official rally. In numbers equal to those that listened to the speeches, they lay in wait for the NF. When the NF reached the junction of Westbury Avenue and Wood Green's High Road, the march came under sustained attack. It was subjected to a barrage of missiles, including marine flares, paint bombs, flour, eggs, rotten fruit and every single shoe from the racks outside Freeman Hardy and Willis. Fights broke out. The march, protected by a large-scale police operation including the Special Patrol Group (SPG), buckled but did not break. Eventually, those fighting to stop the NF were cordoned off. The shaken NFers regrouped and continued with their march to be harried the rest of the way by the remnants of the militant opposition. There were 81 arrests, of which 74 were anti-fascists.

In South London, the NF courted the local electorate winning over significant numbers of white voters in Lewisham with a campaign that included an assault on two communist canvassers and the Liberal candidate, Laurence Spicer, as he delivered his leaflets. 'They called me the usual things', he told reporters, '"Liberal bastard, wog-lover, traitor," then I was knocked down and kicked.' In retrospect, it was easy to see that Lewisham was a tinderbox. It was sparked off in May 1977 by police dawn raids on the homes of 60 black youths. These internment style swoops were the opening play in a police campaign to tackle street robbery called 'Operation PNH,' an acronym widely believed to stand for Police Nigger Hunt. 21 youngsters were eventually charged with conspiracy to steal. The racism of the police contributed, as Mickey O'Farrell recalls, to the volatile mix of Lewisham:

> You have to remember that during the Seventies the police could pick you up on 'suspicion of loitering with intent' and, with police attitudes being what they were in those days, a lot of young black kids were being picked up. I've met blokes inside for it, so this isn't some whinging lefty making something up. There was such an offence, and people did get done for it. A defence campaign was started up for the kids who got arrested and the SWP, who at the time did have some roots in working class communities, were there to push it along.

The arrests were accompanied by newspaper headlines proclaiming a black crime wave. Such stories were gifts to the NF, which increased its presence in Lewisham with a campaign against 'black muggers' and promises to 'drive the muggers off the streets.' Violence accompanied the NF campaign. A Lewisham 21 Defence Campaign stall set up at the clock tower in central Lewisham was attacked by the NF and SWP members fought back. One anti-racist teacher from Deptford was left unconscious. The SWP Central Committee then took the steps to organise physical opposition. This is how Mickey O'Farrell, who had joined the SWP not long after they changed their name from the International Socialists, remembers it:

> I wasn't involved personally but later I got to know Mickey Fenn very well who told me how a fella called John Deason who was on the Central Committee of the SWP went down to

see him and asked him to get some people together to defend the stall. There must have been 6 or 8 dockers who were like Mickey in the SWP at the time and there were other people in the East End, a few working class characters, who said "Look, we can't put up with this. We've got to do something about it." So they got together and waited up the road for the NF and when they turned up the following Saturday to turn over the stall they battered them. And that was the first appearance of the Squads, as they were called. The Squads took the streets back for the anti-fascists and the whole thing escalated from there.

The activities of the Squads would prove to be the source of some controversy over the next few years. The term Squadist had positive connotations in 1977 but would in a few short years, become a term of abuse.

On Saturday 2 July, nearly 200 fascists attacked a rally organised by the Lewisham 21 Defence Committee. Over 60 people were arrested and almost that number appeared in court on the following Monday and Tuesday. A few were discharged but 35 NF supporters and 17 anti-fascists were remanded on bail. Then, the NF announced they were to hold an 'anti-mugging' march from New Cross to Lewisham on 13 August. This had the immediate effect of intensifying the tension and violence. Left-wing paper sales were rushed by fascists, local people experienced higher levels of harassment, a Sikh temple in Woolwich was vandalised and, in the immediate run up to the march, the offices of the Trotskyist group, Militant, were fire-bombed.

As the day of the NF demonstration neared, the anti-fascist movement was once again divided along the predictable lines. The local anti-fascist committee, the All-Lewisham Campaign against Racism and Fascism (ALCARAF), stated that it intended to hold a peaceful protest on the morning of the NF march while the SWP were determined to stop the Front in Lewisham.

ALCARAF had the backing of the Council, the mainstream political parties as well as the Communist Party, several churches and trade unions. The SWP knew it could count on the support of members of the Lewisham 21 Defence Committee, anti-fascists and left-wing militants and a fair percentage of the local population. Lewisham has become one of the most well known battles but it is not always remembered that before the fight with the fascists began, the two sides of anti-fascists reached an agreement. The ALCARAF march and rally was timed to finish early enough for those who wanted to join the SWP mobilisation to reach their assembly point at Clifton Rise, on the proposed route of the NF march.

Differences over strategies of opposition to fascism and attempts to resolve them were played out beyond Lewisham. Tony Greenstein recalls divisions within Brighton and Hove Anti-Fascist Committee:

I think the first major conflict we had with Militant was over the August 1977 Lewisham demonstration. The argument was over supporting the morning march, led by Mervyn Stockwood, the Bishop of Southwark, or the one in the afternoon. I can remember I had long letter, which I've long since lost, from Rod Fitch, Militant chair of the Anti-Fascist Committee, quoting Trotsky as to adventurism and so on. I should say that Rod did a very good job at building and keeping the Committee together and he died tragically, young and too early, some years later. In retrospect I think that Militant came to accept that the afternoon march confronting the NF was the most important. At the time there was no resolution but we booked a coach between Sussex University and Brighton Polytechnic, where I was based.

The first incident of the day itself occurred at 3am. Two bricks were thrown through the bedroom window of Mike Power, chief steward of ALCARAF, and a member of the CPGB National Executive. The next occurred 180 miles north of Lewisham. A coach parked up in Manchester city centre carrying NFers to the march and awaiting late arrivals was ambushed by anti-fascists, some wearing motorcycle helmets and carrying baseball bats. Windows were smashed and some fascists injured. Members of the SWP, Manchester Anti-Fascist Committee and the CP, alongside several Moss Side youths, had participated in the ambush. The vicious assaults carried out at UMIST in 1975 and subsequent continuing disruption of left wing events by the NF had convinced anti-fascists to combine their resources and go on the offensive.

By 11 am, a crowd of 4,000 assembled at Ladywell Fields. The ALCARAF march, led off by Martin Savitt of the Jewish Defence Committee, the Labour Mayor of Lewisham Roger Godsiff, Bishop Mervyn Stockwood and Mike Power, arrived at Railway Grove without serious incident and listened to speeches denouncing the evils of fascism. Members of the SWP handed out leaflets calling on all counter-protestors to oppose the NF march itself in the afternoon. The Communist Party also produced a leaflet, a spoiler, denouncing those who 'insist on the ritual enactment of vanguardist violence' and demanding a boycott of the afternoon action. The finer points of whether direct action developed or deterred mass action would have to be left for the SWP and the CP to debate another day as hundreds of anti-fascists from the morning march voted with their feet and joined the afternoon mobilisation. The number of anti-fascists waiting for the NF at Clifton Rise has been estimated at 3,000 to 6,000. One of them was John Baine:

I went to the Battle of Lewisham in 1977. I travelled up on a coach from Brighton with my band, the Brighton Riot Squad, another punk band called Joby and the Hooligans and some Brighton and Hove Albion supporters. We were at Clifton

Rise when the NF march got split in two by a wedge of anti-fascists. We charged through and threw things at the retreating fascists. It was absolute chaos but incredibly, incredibly exhilarating. The feeling I had going back to home that evening was unbelievable. We saw that the fascists weren't invincible. We saw that they could be stopped. It wasn't just your normal hippies and students. It was loads of black kids from the estates, and loads of white people coming out saying "We don't want the NF here either."

Suzy Harding, an unemployed school leaver from Chiswick in West London,was also there:

Lewisham was my first political demonstration. The National Front were starting to look like a serious threat at the time, and it felt like we'd reached a point in history where you had to stand up and be counted. Four of us travelled across from Chiswick. There was Spud, Ruth, Wilko and me. We were all punks off the local estate, a bunch of know-it-all kids whose hearts were in the right place, I suppose. When we got to Lewisham, we made our way to the anti-racist rally, where a big crowd of people were listening to speeches. I really didn't know what to expect but I remember being surprised at the number of black people in the crowd. I suppose I'd fallen for all the media lies about these things being dominated by white, middle-class do-gooders.

This is her account of the afternoon's events:

The anti-racist crowd seemed to double in size within a short space of time and this seemed to unnerve the cops, who started trying to push people about. I remember being surprised when the anti-racists refused to give way in the face of these really angry cops hitting them with truncheons. A few of the cops started to lose it and were lashing out at anyone they could reach but the anti-racists refused to budge. Then I heard people shout that the Front were on the move. Looking down the road I could see lines of Union Jacks heading our way and that encouraged everyone to start pushing against the police lines. I was about two or three rows from the front and it was difficult to stay on your feet with the crowd surging backwards and forwards. I'd lost Ruth and the others in all the commotion but I didn't really want to go looking for them in case I missed anything. Loads of people were throwing bricks and bottles and smoke bombs at the Front as they drew nearer. I saw a couple of NF guys knocked down by missiles but the march just kept going. It was just starting to look like the Front were going to get through when, all of a sudden, there was a huge surge and before we knew it, we had broken through the police lines and were in amongst the Front. There was a bit of fighting but most of the NF guys were so terrified that they just ran away. I have to confess that I didn't have a clue what to do in the middle of all this. I caught the eye of this one particular NF guy, a big, scary-looking middle-aged bloke. He just turned and ran off down the road. Most of his mates did the same. Those that hung around got beaten up. The march was completely smashed and the NF were scattered in all directions.

The next thing I remember was a load of mounted cops heading our way. I decided to leave. No point in hanging around to get arrested like some of the other silly sods. I read in the papers that there was a lot of trouble later in the day and the police brought out riot shields for the first time ever, but I can't tell you about any of that, because I was on my way home by then.

Despite the disapproval of the CP leadership, there were CP members at Clifton Rise, Monty Goldman among them:

269

I was arrested at the Battle of Lewisham. I'd just come back from holiday in the GDR with my wife and family and I went down to Lewisham with a few comrades from the party. We went there to cut the fascists off because they were marching from New Cross to Lewisham and we wanted to stop them getting to Lewisham High Street. The police had blocked off all the roads to the NF march, but as I was standing there beside the police lines, the anti-fascists charged from behind me and I got pushed over. I ended up at the bottom of a pile of blokes. There must have been twelve of them on top of me. I could hardly breathe. As they started getting up, the police came along and because I was stuck at the bottom I ended up being arrested for obstruction. I was chucked into the back of this Black Maria and on the floor was this bloody great big knife. I thought it was a plan to fit me up, so I said to the driver "What's this big knife doing here?" And he said "Oh somebody must have dropped it earlier." I said "Well, would you mind taking it away?" And he did. The fascists were stopped at Lewisham though. They couldn't get through and it was a big defeat for them.

Almost hidden amongst the hysterical denunciations dished out by leading media commentators and mainstream politicians in the wake of Lewisham was a statement by Mike Power, who told the *Kentish Mercury*:

We totally condemn the approach of the Socialist Workers Party. It's counter-productive - because the NF thrives on violence - and undermines the work done day-in, day-out for community relations in the borough.

For SWP member, Jim Kelly, Lewisham delivered a completely different lesson. In his 1995 pamphlet, *The Anti-Nazi League: A Critical Examination*, he wrote:

This victory changed the momentum of the struggle at both local and national level and it produced a tremendous feeling of elation on the part of the anti-fascists involved. The NF strategy was to win control of the streets, this was to be their first major setback. The next day at Brick Lane we took the initiative and moved our paper sellers up into the market, meeting only verbal resistance from the Nazis who turned up. Many could not comprehend how a group that they had held in total contempt had stopped them so emphatically.

Hot on the heels of Lewisham came the Ladywood by-election in Birmingham. The NF had put up a candidate, Anthony Reed Herbert, and planned a public meeting at Boulton Road School in Handsworth. Local anti-racist and left-wing groups began to rally their forces. On the day of the meeting, the SWP, Socialist Unity (an IMG front group) and the Labour Party Young Socialists mounted a picket of around a 100 outside the school. Then, 2000 Handsworth youths, mobilised by a loudspeaker van touring the area and by activists visiting local cafes, clubs and billiard halls, joined them. The police helped the NF avoid the now sizable protest by smuggling them through the school's back door. Angry anti-fascist pickets tried to storm the building. Police lines just about held firm while police vehicles were overturned and set on fire. And, this wasn't the last shot in the Ladywood by-election. On the night of the count, the Socialist Unity candidate Raghib Ahsan punched Reed Herbert in the face. The NF candidate was only saved from complete humiliation by beating the Liberals into third place.

Ahsan's loss of temper was understandable. A petrol soaked cross had been put in his front garden. Fascists failed to ignite it but tried to glorify their ineptitude with threatening letters and stickers that warned: 'We failed to burn the cross, but we won't fail to burn YOU.' The physical intimidation of political opposition was typical NF fare in the second half of 1977.

Incendiary devices were thrown at left-wing bookshops in London and bookshop workers were assaulted in Liverpool, Leeds, Bradford and Tyneside. There were arson attacks on the SWP's offices and the headquarters of the Community Relations Council. A Labour Party meeting in South London was attacked by a group of forty men dressed in black shirts and wearing black leather gloves.

On 8 October, the Chief Constable of Greater Manchester, James Anderton, handed the NF a momentary regional win by helping them march, in secret, through the Longsight area of the city to a rally at Belle Vue. Anderton had informed the media that he was banning all marches in Manchester for a limited period. He seemed to be invoking the Public Order Act (POA). Martin Webster, insisting on the right to be racist, declared he would march alone if necessary. Accompanied by 2,000 police officers, a phalanx of journalists and TV crews, and a large group of anti-fascist hecklers, he walked through Hyde in East Manchester.

Meanwhile, several thousand anti-fascists were gathering five miles away in Stockport where they believed the main NF contingent was about to march. The police had pulled off a double bluff. Anderton had misled the media about a ban and counter-protestors about the location where a march would be permitted. Several hundred NF were bussed to Crowcroft Park on the edge of Longsight. They marched through the area to Belle Vue. They were harassed all along the route by forty Manchester Squad members. Squadists had suspected the Stockport rumours were a red herring. A network of spotters positioned on the motorways and main roads had tracked the NF coaches to Crowcroft Park. Joined by several dozen Asian youths keen to stop the NF in their area, they ransacked a milk float for weapons and threw missiles at the march. Some individual anti-racists and anti-fascists also made it to Longsight and heckled the NF but there were nowhere near sufficient numbers to prevent the NF from reaching their destination. The policing bill for the whole fiasco was a cool quarter of a million pounds.

Towards the end of 1977, the process of unifying anti-fascist groups into a single organisation mooted at the beginning of the decade began in earnest. Paul Holborrow of the SWP put out feelers to left leaning and establishment figures including Peter Hain, anti-apartheid campaigner and Labour Party member, Ernie Roberts, a leader of the Engineering Union and another Labour Party member, Maurice Ludmer, a committed anti-racist, communist and founder of Searchlight, and Fenner Brockway, veteran peace, anti-colonial and anti-fascist campaigner with a life peerage. Labour MPs Syd Bidwell, Dennis Skinner and Neil Kinnock also became involved in talks about mounting a broad-based anti-fascist movement culminating in the launch of the Anti-Nazi League (ANL) at the House of Commons on 9 November 1977. Their founding statement was sent to the press:

> For the first time since Mosley in the thirties, there is the worrying prospect of a Nazi party gaining significant support in Britain... They must not go unopposed. Ordinary voters must be made aware of the threat that lies behind the National Front. In every town, in every factory, in every school, on every housing estate, wherever the Nazis attempt to organise they must be countered. Millions of leaflets and posters will have to be distributed. To have the necessary impact this demands a campaign on a national and massive scale.

The Communist Party initially refused to participate in the ANL while other organisations and individuals queued up. Political activists of various left hues, including Tariq Ali of the IMG and Arthur Scargill, President of the National Union of Mineworkers, pledged support with a host of cultural figures adding their names and influence: actors Alfie Bass, Warren Mitchell, Prunella Scales and Miriam Karlin, comedians Dave Allen and Derek

Griffiths, playwrights Arnold Wesker and David Edgar, authors Melvyn Bragg and Iris Murdoch, and football managers Brian Clough, Jack Charlton and Terry Venables.

An ANL national steering committee was elected with many of those involved in kick starting the organisation taking up positions. There was a seat reserved for the CP should they change their minds, which, in due course, they did. They swallowed their pride but some groups with a long-standing interest in anti-racism and anti-fascism stubbornly stayed away. Amongst the refuseniks were the Jewish Board of Deputies, Militant and the Workers Revolutionary Party (WRP). This made little or no difference to the rapid and massive growth of the ANL. Certainly, Tony Greenstein's experience was of a fairly narrow political opposition to truly popular force:

> Well, the Brighton and Hove Anti-Fascist Committee opposed the ANL setting up. But in a sense the Committee was starting to become less active anyway. I was actually at the first, very big ANL meeting. I was nominated because I was then Vice-President of the Student Union of Brighton Polytechnic. I can remember David Spector, he was from AJEX, was equally vehemently opposed and he was heckled and shouted down for his pains. The main period of our activity in Brighton began in 1977-8 when the ANL was formed. We had every month meetings at the Resource Centre (which was burnt down, we suspected, by the NF) of between 300 and 500 people. It was a mass movement. No doubt.

The grassroots appeal of the ANL exceeded the expectations of its establishment founders. The movement mushroomed. Over 250 local branches were established. Mickey O'Farrell, active and militant anti-fascist for over a year, welcomed the launch of the new organisation:

It was a move to the right by the SWP, but it was a very necessary move to the right. It enabled the party to draw thousands of people into the fight against the NF who might not have got involved otherwise.

After initial doubts, Nick Mullen also began to see the possibilities opened up by the ANL:

I was very sceptical when the ANL first started. It seemed to me that it wasn't a serious movement. It just seemed to be a way for the SWP to cash in on the enormous amount of anti-fascist feeling that there was in the country at the time. I did go along to a few of their events, which were very well attended and it was very strange, and quite pleasing, to see groups of youngsters with bovver boots, braces and very short hair shouting anti-fascist slogans. It was quite a nice reminder to those of us who were a bit older that the way people dress isn't the way in which you judge them. It was good to see so many young people expressing their opposition to the fascists. I'm not so sure too many of them took part in direct action to stop the Front because Brick Lane was happening at the same time and you didn't get so many of the ANL people down there actually opposing the NF but I was wrong to be so critical of it in retrospect. It certainly raised awareness of the dangers of fascism.

As the ANL grew, it spawned a number of sub-sections such as Football Fans Against the Nazis (FFAN), Gays Against the Nazis (GAN), Teachers Against the Nazis (TAN). In response to the NF recruitment outside schools, School Kids Against the Nazis (SKAN) was launched. John West from St. Albans was a somewhat reluctant member of this group:

I got into the Anti-Nazi League through being a punk really.

A group of about ten of us used to hang around together. We were bored of football and running around on a Saturday afternoon and we wanted something with a little bit more to it than fighting for the colours of a football team. There was a lot of stuff going on at the time about the National Front and the Anti-Nazi League and it was almost like the words of that old Tom Robinson song, "Better decide which side you're on." There were decisions to be made. Some people I knew went with the Front and we still knew them within the community, but they believed in all that stuff, while we went red.

We went up to a guy in town selling Anti-Nazi League and Rock Against Racism badges. We had a chat with him and went along to a meeting in a local pub. Before long we were selling the badges and going along to all the meetings. We were told that because of our age we should join School Kids Against the Nazis, which we thought was a pretty demeaning and patronising title. We tried to get the title changed, because we thought it was pretty poxy, but we were trapped with SKAN.

Over five million leaflets were distributed by the ANL during the first year of its existence, carrying the messages 'The National Front is a Nazi Front' and 'Never Again.' The 1962 photographs of Tyndall in Nazi garb and his and Webster's writings in praise of Nazism made the case. The simple equation of 'NF = Nazis' was a political success. Hundreds of public meetings, marches and rallies were held. This was not the whole story, however. Militant anti-fascism also developed through the ANL. Jim Kelly explains:

The image of aggressive, confrontational street politics, which the SWP leadership encouraged, led to a massive influx of young working class people. Other SWP initiatives, such as The Right to Work campaign and Rock Against Racism were also drawing many young people towards the Party. Some of the new recruits gravitated to the more experienced working class militants and began to develop a more aggressive anti-fascist agenda. This meant clearing the fascists off the streets of East London, attacking NF paper sales and meetings. Stratford, Brick Lane and Chapel Market were the main focus. Hoxton Market, which had a long history of fascist activity, was a much tougher nut that was never really cracked. Attempts to sell socialist papers there often ended with violence. Unfortunately the left was on the receiving end more often than not. The launch of the ANL signaled a move to the right by the SWP leadership. A new strategy meant working with pop stars, actors and mainstream politicians, especially those Labour politicians who were under electoral pressure from the NF. At the same time anti-fascist militants were moving in a different direction, organising independently of the SWP and developing links with other anti-fascist groups similar to our own.

This was Mickey O'Farrell's experience:

The Squads began to develop in parallel with the official movement. There would be regular initiatives and demonstrations and instead of taking part in them we'd meet up in a pub nearby on the basis that if you're with the official demonstration you couldn't get stuck into the Front. I first got involved in that side of things during an SWP march in Clapton in East London. That was the start of it. There was a regular group of us, including Malcolm, Scots Pete, Moonface, a bloke called John Walker, who was a bit of an organiser from East London and several others. It was pretty much all SWP at that time. There was also a link made with a similar group from Manchester. I got to know people like Steve Tilzey, John Penney, and Ian MacIntosh, who unfortunately is dead now, and there was a good rapport between the groups. There was a social element to the whole thing too. At the time Rock Against Racism was up and running, so there might be a demo on the Saturday and then a do in the evening. So a social circle developed in tandem with the political side. It was heady days. I was spending nearly every weekend in London meeting people of a like mind and I have to say that it was enjoyable and very fulfilling experience. In retrospect, I can see that by organising separately from the official mobilisation you do open up the danger of elitist attitudes developing. But by the same token if you are always going to be bound by the limitations the authorities inevitably place upon the official demo then you run the risk of having them run the demo for you and achieving little or nothing. Now I think the answer is to be aware of the drawbacks to both approaches and see neither as a fixed strategic approach but employing either tactically as and when the situation requires.

RAR gigs were not only important alternative social spaces for anti-fascists, they were where the cultural movement and militant activity crossed over. RAR played its part in the physical resistance to fascism. Some gigs were put on with the sole purpose of confronting the physical threat posed by the NF and the BM. RAR worked with Sham 69 and lead singer Jimmy Pursey to disown their unwanted Nazi following. One of Sham's gigs at the Rainbow, London, had been disrupted by a 70-strong mob of BM Leader Guard and at two subsequent appearances Nazi skinheads had vandalised the venues and assaulted members of their audience.

On 24 February at Central London Polytechnic under the banner *Smash Race Hate in '78*, Sham 69 played a RAR gig with reggae outfit Misty in Roots. It was a tense affair. Stewards from North London, Southall and the docks managed to keep the lid on a highly volatile situation. The BM was present in numbers, but decided that discretion was the better part of valour and did nothing. Jimmy Pursey helped wrap up the night and hammer home its political message by joining Misty on stage for a version of the old skinhead reggae classic, the Israelites.

RAR's most famous event, the Carnival in Bethnal Green's Victoria Park on 30 April 1978 is remembered for its punk and reggae line up. X-Ray Spex and Steel Pulse, the Ruts and Misty in Roots shared the stage. The Tom Robinson Band made the Carnival their own and Jimmy Pursey appeared with the Clash for a rendition of White Riot. Now part of music history, the Carnival began as an initiative to deal with a persistent fascist threat. RAR collaborated with the ANL and local anti-racist groups to organise a big event that would challenge the NF and BM in the East End area that was supposed to be their stronghold.

An ANL *Sponsors' Newsletter* estimated that 'there may be as many as 20,000 people participating' but over 80,000 turned up to march the five miles from Trafalgar Square to the Carnival in Bethnal Green. They came from all over the country. 80 coaches were booked from Manchester, 25 from Leeds, 12 from Sheffield, a train was chartered from Glasgow and, according to Mickey O'Farrell, two coaches were booked from the Hilltop pub in Hatfield alone. Like most of the Carnival-goers, Suzy Harding, had a great time:

The first Carnival was a fantastic experience. I remember walking up to Trafalgar Square from Charing Cross with Spud and Ruth and our little gang, and being astounded by the size of the crowd. There were thousands of people milling around the place. Most of the day passed me by in a bit of a daze to be honest, but I do remember the pathetic group of fat racists outside their pub near Brick Lane. They were trying to intimidate the marchers, but ended up looking pretty pathetic as thousands and thousands of anti-racists marched past them laughing. I went to the Carnival mainly to support the anti-racist cause but also to see the Clash. It was very important that the Clash came out against the NF and I think it was absolutely vital that they played at the Carnival. It was also great to see Jimmy Pursey of Sham 69 join them on stage for White Riot but, if I'm being honest, Tom Robinson stole the show. He just seemed to fit the bill perfectly and got the whole crowd going.

Nick Mullen had less happy reasons to remember the day:

I was arrested on my way to the big Rock Against Racism festival in Victoria Park in the East End. I was on a tube and this fascist said something to me so I said something back and we ended up fighting. He had a Stanley knife on him but the police never charged him with carrying an offensive weapon because he was a painter, although why he was carrying a knife on a Sunday afternoon was never explained. We both ended up getting fined when we went to court, but what was really nice was that my fine was paid by a pensioner who was sat in the public gallery. He said he remembered the fight against the fascists in the old days and gave me the money.

Despite the enormous success of the RAR Carnival, some anti-fascists still considered it a missed opportunity. The NF was to march through the East End the following day but there had been no attempt to mobilise the Carnival-goers to oppose it. There had been no call to arms from the ANL leadership on the day, no announcement from the stage, no mass leafleting of the crowd. This omission, if indeed that was what it was, raised the first niggling doubts that the formation of the ANL was actually a move away from the confrontational tactics of previous years. It was a case, as one activist put it, of 'off the streets and into the parks.' It was far too soon to make this criticism stick, however.

During 1978, anti-fascists, including the ANL, took the fight to the NF. The SWP leadership were no more able to influence ANL than the passengers on a runaway train and some, no doubt, enjoyed the ride. The growth of the ANL turned it into a grassroots movement with a membership that was not beholden to obey any party line and beyond the control of party functionaries. In Birmingham, for instance, a Young National Front (YNF) meeting at Digbeth Civic Hall on 18 February was opposed by 2,000 counter-demonstrators, including ANL members, assorted left-wingers, local punks and Handsworth's youth. When the police smuggled the fascists through the back door, as they were wont to do, sections of the demonstration began stoning police lines. Running battles between anti-fascists and the forces of law and order continued for several hours.

There were similar scenes outside Bolton Town Hall a week earlier. John Severn, unaffiliated anti-fascist who had already chalked up his first arrest at blocking a fascist meeting at Houldsworth Hall was busy again:

I didn't come back to any kind of activity until the late seventies when the NF were developing their campaign in Bolton where I lived. It was simply a matter of trying to stop meetings taking place at the two Town Halls in Fairnworth and Bolton, surrounding the entrances and making sure that people were intimidated enough not to walk in so presumably there were a lot people who would have gone in that didn't. There wasn't, as far as I know, any activity within the meeting because there wasn't any need. The numbers were far bigger at that point in terms of anti-fascists and the actual NF meetings that took place numerically were tiny. Hardly anyone went in, certainly in Bolton Town Hall. I think only one person actually walked in to the meeting they were going to hold there and so that was a good result.

An estimated 1,000 ANL supporters barracked and jostled NF members as they entered a meeting in Leeds in April and tackled them again as they left. Martin Webster had to be taken to Leeds Infirmary for treatment. NF election meetings were opposed wherever they were held. On 8 July, an outdoor NF by-election meeting in Moss Side, Manchester, was attacked by a group of 60 to 70 anti-fascists, made up of Squadists and locals. Fighting escalated as more locals arrived to help the anti-fascists. The police were forced to escort the NF out of town. An ambush of John Tyndall was attempted as he was driven away in a minibus and a Rochdale NF member was rumoured to have been run over by a car driven by an ANL supporter.

The range of ANL activities, from physical confrontation to symbolic marches or just the distribution of badges, was the strength of the organisation in the late 70s. It provided a way for people to get involved in the anti-fascist struggle. A teenager from Manchester's working class Irish community, Sean Gaughan, tells his journey into anti-fascist activism:

My first demo was an ANL march in Manchester in 78 or 79, I was 17 or 18 and had been thinking about going for a few weeks previously but I'm not sure if I would have if it hadn't been for a chance encounter on a bus. I had been up to my mam's to collect my giro and on the bus back to my mates house some fella approached me and said that I see we are going to the same place and nodded towards an ANL badge that I was wearing, I was too embarrassed to tell him that was not where I was going and ended up on the march. I was glad that I did attend and found it really stimulating. A few weeks later I went along to a WRP march in Hulme but when I got there I was too embarrassed to go on it, because of how small it was and for some reason because of the look of those attending.

Playing a part in large-scale events enabled the ANL to sustain the anti-fascist movement. RAR's second national Carnival took place at Brockwell Park, Brixton on 24 September 1978. It was another punk and reggae mix with acts including Elvis Costello and the Attractions and Aswad. Sham 69, still trying to shake off their BM skinhead following, had agreed to play but pulled out after a series of death threats. Belfast punk band Stiff Little Fingers (SLF) took Sham's place and Jimmy Pursey bravely took to the stage to explain his band's absence. The second Carnival exceeded the first one in terms of size, an estimated 100,000 marched from Hyde Park to Brixton. Suzy Harding was amongst the revellers:

> I was the only one of our little crew to go to the Brixton Carnival. Spud was in Borstal and the rest didn't really fancy it for one reason or another so I went along on my own. Despite not knowing anyone and despite the really long march through South London I really enjoyed the whole day. We were entertained on the march by bands playing from flat bed trucks, which was brilliant. I got into the park in time to see SLF start their set and had a look around until Elvis Costello came on. It was while I was wandering around the park that I became aware that something was happening in the East End. I overheard people talking about the NF marching through Brick Lane, but nobody really seemed sure what was happening. Some people decided to go down there but others decided to stay at the Carnival. I half thought about going but because I was on my own and didn't know anyone I stayed put.

John Baine made the journey up from the south coast to enjoy the music and occasion of his second RAR Carnival but he, too, recalls finding out too late that the NF were on the streets in the East End:

The one blot on my memory of the Brockwell Park Carnival was finding out later that the NF had marched through Brick Lane on the very same day and that the organisers of the Carnival had known about it in advance and decided not to tell us.

Indeed. Almost as soon as the date for the second Carnival had been advertised, the NF countered it by declaring that they intended to march through the heart of the East End's Bangladeshi community in Brick Lane on the very same day. Their move, which was an acknowledgment of the opposition generated by RAR events, sought to disrupt the Carnival and divide the anti-fascist movement. Prevarication followed by political expediency on the part of leading SWP members almost allowed them to achieve their goal.

It was announced from the Carnival stage that the situation in the East End was under control so people should stay and enjoy themselves. In fact, local ANL activists had telephoned their ANL national steering committee and begged them to send more people down to help the anti-fascists at Brick Lane. Alongside the local ANL, members of various Trotskyist groups, anarchists and local anti-racists from the Hackney and Tower Hamlets Defence Committee tried to harass a 700 strong NF march but their numbers were too small to create any more effective action against the marchers and their police escorts. Local Bengali youth were kept away from the Front invaders by large numbers of antagonistic police. A rally at Church Road concluded the march and opened another fascist offensive. Groups broke away to threaten and cause damage to the area and its people. One gang of 50 to 60 skinheads smashed up shops on Brick Lane before being driven off by locals. Those anti-fascists who left the Carnival under their own initiative, and a few thousand did this, arrived too late. They were stopped by police as they exited the tube stations and cordoned off.

For its critics, partying in Brixton while the NF marched in Brick Lane provided all too obvious proof that the ANL had decidedly moved away from militant anti-fascism. In fact, the formation of the ANL meant that the SWP leadership would always be torn and compromised on this question. The ANL's success, its grassroots growth, had derived from its broad front approach, at least initially. But local ANL activists, working alongside other anti-fascists with black and Asian communities threatened by fascist organisation and violence, inevitably found themselves involved in some physical confrontations. Such direct action threatened to scare off the moderate elements that made up the ANL's broad front. Anti-fascist activists, especially those from within the Trotskyist movement, wanted to know which side of the fence the SWP were on.

'We collectively bungled it' admitted Paul Holborow shortly after the Carnival and SWP leader Tony Cliff took up full page of *Socialist Worker* to apologise for his party's mishandling of events. An 'Open Letter to Tony Cliff' by James Ryan published in an October edition of *Worker's Action* responded:

> You say quite plainly: "We have to organise demonstrations against the Nazis, and smash them on the streets." But how does that square with your remark that calling for the mobilisation to take on the fascists in the East End would have disintegrated the ANL? Won't that always be true of a campaign which refuses to define its attitude to the issue of direct confrontation with the fascists? Aren't many of the ANL's sponsors and leading lights resolutely opposed to smashing the fascists on the streets?

Other critics on the left also took the opportunity to join in the bun-fight but most people were prepared to give the SWP the benefit of the doubt over the Brick Lane debacle. Although it is difficult to explain how the leaders of the SWP/ANL did their best to ignore the NF's East End march unless they were, at least at this point, distancing their organisations from confrontational politics. The Brick Lane area had long been notorious as a focal point for fascist and racist activity in East London and the NF had recently ratcheted up the tension in the area. Clashes between fascists and anti-fascists were commonplace. The NF sold papers at two or three pitches in the area, including the symbolically important one at Bethnal Green Road, and had moved into new headquarters at nearby Great Eastern Street. Gangs of fascists, or fascist-inspired racists, routinely attacked representatives of local Asian communities, vandalised Asian owned or run properties and harassed people on a day-to-day basis. Two racist murders took place in East London in the time between the first and second RAR Carnivals. Both sparked widespread community resistance. On 4 May 1978, Altab Ali, a 25-year-old Bengali clothing worker, was murdered by three teenage boys as he walked home from work.

Ten days later, over 7,000 people, mostly Bengalis, marched behind Altab Ali's coffin to Hyde Park to demand an end to racist violence. The killing of another Bengali youth, Ishaque Ali, in nearby Hackney, on 25 June, sparked two successive days of angry protests in July. A mass sit-down protest at Bethnal Green Road on 16 July was followed by the first ever strike against racism. Brick Lane was shut for business as people struck in protest over the intolerable situation in the East End.

'Who Killed Altab Ali?,' *CARF*, Number 6, 1978.

Left-wing paper-sellers and local anti-racist activists were also routinely assaulted and physically intimidated. Anti-fascist activists from the local area, including, of course, many SWP members and ANL activists, defended themselves but required reinforcements. To their credit, SWP and the ANL responded to criticism of their conduct over the Brixton Carnival by sending them in. John West and his friends from St Albans became regular attendees at Brick Lane on Sunday mornings:

> We started getting coaches from St Albans down to Brick Lane in the East End, where the NF used to sell their *Bulldog* magazine. The idea was to cause as much trouble as possible and basically disrupt the selling of the newspaper. This was quite appealing to our little group because we'd just left football hooliganism and things were very quiet in St Albans. This kind of thing seemed much more up our street. One funny thing about going down to London all the time was that I had to tell my mum that I was going ice-skating in Queensway. That's how I explained all the bumps and bruises I used to come home with. Brick Lane at the time was a really shit market because of all the trouble down there. A lot of the market traders blamed the Anti-Nazi League for that. They said that when it was just the NF down there, things weren't bad. It was only when the ANL showed up that it started deteriorating. Some of the pitches were just piles of clothes. They didn't even have a stall, it was just piles of mouldy clothes on the floor. So we ended up getting the blame for the state of the market at the time. The area was pretty well policed and it was hard to get away with too much down there because the police were on top of it. We had little covert operations. We used to walk miles all around Brick Lane just to get at the NF. There was one day when we went on this really long bloody walk to get in front of the National Front. The main ANL group was at one end of the street, the NF at the other with the police in between. Because there was a lot

of police we couldn't really do anything, so we all walked past them doing the Monty Python goose-step. It was quite funny at the time, but the National Front were going bloody nuts.

There was a guy down at Brick Lane who we used to call the General. He got his head kicked in outside a pub one day by the NF. There's a picture of him lying in the gutter, which appeared in the *Daily Mirror* the next day. It was a story about how bad the situation was getting down at Brick Lane. The picture was of somebody sweeping the road, while this body was lying in the gutter with blood around his head. That was the General I believe. He used to wear one of those Palestinian scarves and had really coiffured hair. He was bang up for it and was one of the main instigators. I never knew his real name. I remember the day he got his head kicked in because for once we'd got together in a big mob and I thought we'd really be able to have a real go at the NF. It started off as usual with little groups of people wandering around the area while the main demonstration was taking place. We were in one of those little off-shoot groups looking for the odd Nazi to bash when we met up with this really large group of Gays Against the Nazis, which was another one of those little ANL sections like SKAN. They insisted that they wanted to bash up some Nazis and did we know where they were. Well, we always knew where they were, we just didn't have the manpower to do anything about it. Now all of a sudden our ranks were swelled with this large group and there was enough of us to take on the NF in this pub. So off we marched with our new brothers and sisters to this pub, which was one of those big London pubs on the corner of the street. The General was leading the way and when we got to the pub, he threw a brick through the window, which is a good way to start a fight. The pub immediately emptied onto the pavement and the whole road started filling up with them. Well we braced ourselves for the onslaught. Luckily the NF decided that me and my mates were unworthy of a decent kicking, but the General was big enough for a kicking and he got splattered all over the pavement.

Mickey O'Farrell was also active at Brick Lane:

Brick Lane was a contested area between the National Front and the SWP and there was a lot of trouble over who sells papers down there. It was a similar situation to Lewisham. And, fair play to the SWP, they took up the challenge because obviously the Front considered it their patch. I went down there several Sunday mornings. If there was a Rock Against Racism do on a Saturday night, I'd crash over at someone's house and then Sunday morning off to Brick Lane and then have a curry afterwards. There were loads of brilliant curry houses down there. I couldn't say I was there every Sunday by any means, but I'd go over when a big mobilisation was called or when I knew a group who were going over. The SWP managed to keep a regular paper sale going, but in fairness it wasn't all that difficult because there was always police presence there. We used to sniff about on the edge of things looking for a chance to have a fight with the Front. It was all little groups running around. You'd go off walking and there would be rumours that a few of them were drinking in such and such a pub and we'd all rush off over there and sometimes it would be true and there'd be a fight. I personally don't remember any big confrontations, just skirmishes.

Elsewhere in the country, a similar pattern was emerging. Manchester ANL members disrupted NF paper sales in the city centre by deploying mass pickets that completely surrounded the sellers and prevented them from distributing their wares to the public. Members of the Manchester Squad also ambushed NFers prior to the sale. After several months on the case, this combination of tactics proved successful. The NF conceded the pitch. The NF Sunday League football team, the Lillywhites, were subject to a similar array of strategies. Mass picketing and smaller scale but more physical actions, such as turning over the NF team's van as players were getting changed, were mixed with political pressure on local councils to prevent the hire of facilities to racists to bring an early end to their season.

The phenomenal rise of the ANL had a detrimental effect on local anti-fascist and anti-racist committees, depleted by SWP members and other activists drifting away to form ANL branches. Potential new local recruits were drawn to the ANL's more dynamic organisation with high profile events, colourful propaganda and opportunities for direct action. The situation wasn't helped by the by the failure of the national *CARF*/Anti-Racist Anti-Fascist (ARAFACC) Conference on 3-4 June. It attracted only 152 delegates when 500 were anticipated and ended in acrimony. Issue 7 of *CARF* claimed that inability to build a national organisation of local anti-fascist and anti-racist committees was:

> a reflection of a movement fragmented by all the year's events. Black people felt excluded from the discussion, labour movement members were alienated by debates which tended to focus upon the ideological aspects of fascism, and there was no common programme or recognised set of tactics which could unite the many 'sects' which had been drawn to the movement during the year.

Searchlight was in a more accusative mode. The issue 37 editorial placed the blame squarely on the shoulders of 'certain women, gay and Left groups.' It claimed that Women Against Racism and Fascism (WARF), the Gay Activist Alliance, Lesbian Left, Gay Left, and North London Gay Socialists brought an alternative agenda to the conference and:

sought continuously to confuse issues and saw the question of "sexism" as one of the dominant themes of the conference. The trade unionists, Black and Asian organisations present were clearly upset and disconcerted by these tactics and withdrew their support.

WARF and the Oxford Anti-Fascist Committee replied to *Searchlight*. WARF's letter pointed out 'a grossly unjust simplification' and that while the relationship between fascism and sexism was an issue requiring discussion rather than 'an over-riding theme to displace all others in the anti-fascist struggle.' ARAFACC disbanded itself in September 1978 but many local anti-fascist and anti-racist committees ignored its collapse in the wake of the conference and continued to work within in their own localities.

The slickly organised, well-attended ANL conference at the Porchester Hotel, London, on 8 July provided a contrasting scene. 810 delegates heard speeches from Tariq Ali, Arthur Scargill, Peter Hain, Maurice Ludmer and Ernie Roberts. Contributions were allowed from the floor but as *Forewarned Against Fascism*, which was otherwise enthusiastic about the conference noted, 'it was not convened to decide any major issues.' Anti-Fascist Democratic Action (AFDA), a strange little Stalinist grouplet based in Birmingham and Charlton, published *Forewarned Against Fascism*. The leading light in AFDA was Dave Roberts. A former member of both the CP and the Appeal Group, he attained a degree of notoriety after he received a prison sentence for attempting to firebomb a Communist bookshop whilst working undercover in the NF. Although its membership was tiny, AFDA itself became infamous after *Forewarned Against Fascism* began publishing the names and addresses of hundreds of fascists. Reprisals came from fascist publications, including *Bulldog* and *South London News*, who put out anti-fascist hit lists.

1979 was the year of the General Election, when the NF would announce that they were standing candidates in 303 constituencies, but for the first month at least, it was business as usual. On 25 January, a gang of fascists in black uniforms with 'Anti-Communist League' badges broke into a film show held by the Brighton Campaign for Homosexual Equality and the Sussex University Gay Group at the Wagner Hall. The fascists started to attack people at the back of the hall, but were forced to back off in disarray when the audience started fighting back. An assault on a teacher on his way home from work in Bow by a Front supporter was reported in January's *Searchlight*. The name of the teacher, a SWP member, an ANL supporter and President of the East London Teaching Association, was Blair Peach. He received 'black eyes, bruising, cuts, and a badly bitten finger'. It was the second time in six months that fascists had attacked him.

The NF predicted their political breakthrough at the General Election. Their number of candidates was greater than any fielded previously and guaranteed them free broadcasting time on national television. Pre-election meetings and rallies were booked up and down the country throughout April, concluding with a national election rally at Caxton Hall in London on 1 May. As the ANL geared up to oppose the NF, the tension between keeping big name sponsors while grassroots supporters got stuck in to street battles persisted. Both the dignitaries and the activists had concerns about the dominance of the SWP and the lack of internal democracy. The problem for John West, for example, was that 'in order to be regarded as a proper member of the Anti-Nazi League, you had to be a member of the Socialist Workers Party, and my allegiance didn't really lie with them.' But in this election year, as in every other important battle in the past, anti-fascists just got on with the task ahead. 'Any differences were temporarily ignored' wrote Jim Kelly. For many anti-fascists, the election was an opportunity to show their opposition to the NF. 'It was really the beginning of our fight with the fascists,' recalls Tony Greenstein:

There was a by-election meeting in Fairlight School in Brighton. We held a very big counter-mobilisation. The whole road, off Lewes Road, was swimming with people… but it all catalysed around the 1979 General Election.

RAR, still alive and kicking, announced a 23-date 'Militant Entertainment' tour. Billed as 'a show of anti-racist enthusiasm aimed at racialist candidates of whatever party,' they put together a pool of thirty acts including John Cooper Clarke, Stiff Little Fingers, the Specials, the Ruts, the Leighton Buzzards and the Angelic Upstarts. In the final show at the Alexandra Palace on Easter Sunday, fourteen bands played for over six hours.

The opening salvo in the election campaign, however, had already been fired by Margaret Thatcher, Tory Party leader, back in January 1978. In a Granada TV interview she claimed 'I think people are really rather afraid that this country might be rather swamped by people of a different culture.' This trapped the NF between a rock and a hard place. Thatcher was poaching the NF's soft-core voters, while militant anti-fascists sought to stop, actually and physically stop, the hard-core in their tracks. It was an ironic, unarranged and unhappy marriage of convenience given the mutual loathing that existed between Tories and ANL supporters. Thatcher had her own agenda, which involved 'wiping socialism off the face of the earth' whilst the SWP, including those in the ANL, urged its supporters to 'Vote Labour Without Illusions.' Surely one of the least inspiring political slogans ever coined.

The NF election campaign was preceded by two defeats, one in the heart of rural England, in sleepy Hampshire, the other in the East End. Robert Relf had been sent to Winchester prison after indulging in a fresh bout of illegal racist activity. He vowed to 'fast to the death.' Placing Relf in a quiet cathedral city jail, the Home Office was surely wishing to avoid the scenes that took place outside Winson Green in Handsworth some four years

previously. It was a vain hope. On 10 March, an NF demonstration of 800 was prevented from getting to the jail by 2,000
ANL supporters. Fights between fascists and anti-fascists left
several NFers with sore heads to accompany their dented pride.
They threatened to return in greater numbers but only 200
bothered to turn up the following weekend. It was around this
time that one of the NF's Sunday paper sales was effectively
closed down in Brick Lane. Hoxton NF leader, Derrick Day, had
to make a retreat. He hid under a parked lorry to escape kicking
from anti-fascists. His group of notorious Hoxton thugs fared no
better than their glorious leader. Those that weren't knocked over
ended up being chased down Bethnal Green Road.

The first headline-grabbing incident of the election campaign
proper occurred in Leicester. The NF had planned to march
through the city centre on 21 April. A large and determined anti-
fascist presence of somewhere between 2,000 and 5,000 people
meant that the police had to redirect it. The march was then
harassed all the way along its a shorter route. In one incident,
recorded by Martin Lux in *Anti-Fascist*, stone-throwing counter-
demonstrators in the grounds of Leicester University dispersed
only after police dogs and riot cops were unleashed on them. In
another, the NF's Colour Party was waylaid by anti-fascists from
Manchester, who had waited behind a large advertising hoarding
for the march to pass. Under normal circumstances, April 21 in
Leicester, with its total of 82 arrests, would have passed into anti-
fascist folklore, but the day was soon to be overshadowed by
protests outside an NF election meeting at Southall Town Hall.

Such a meeting can only be described as an act of provocation.
The NF member, John Fairhurst, who would appear on the ballot
paper, was at best just that, a paper candidate. The NF branch
structure in the area was practically non-existent. The fascists had
no real base of support in Southall and there were very few places
in the whole country where their presence would be less
welcome. They would be opposed, and knew they would be, by

the well-established Southall Youth Movement, the Indian Workers Association (IWA) with its large membership and an active local ANL branch. One NFer, in terms that were both racist and imperialist, stated that the meeting at Southall Town Hall would be 'like the battle of Khyber Pass.'

The Indian Workers Association (IWA), the more moderate organisation in Southall, initially considered ignoring the NF meeting but agreed to organise a sit-down protest outside the Town Hall. That the sit-down would be an entirely peaceful affair was emphasised time and time again. The IWA's non-violent message was also printed and distributed on 25,000 leaflets. Nevertheless, from the early morning of Monday 23 April, the area around Southall Town Hall was turned into a mini police state. Thousands of police were drafted in to seal off roads, stop traffic and search pedestrians. At about 1pm, 200 or so members of the Southall Youth Movement endeavoured to congregate on the road opposite the Town Hall. They had heard rumours that NF members would enter their meeting hours ahead of its scheduled time. Police officers made a bid to disperse the impromptu picket by making arrests, which had little effect as more protestors kept on arriving. Their next tactic was clearing the area by splitting the protestors into smaller groups and pushing them away from the Town Hall in different directions. People resented being forcibly removed from the site where the fascists were due to meet. Those gathered to picket the Town Hall fought with the police who repeatedly charged into them with truncheons, shields and horses. While all attention seemed focussed on the picket, anti-fascist militants broke into the Hall via a rear building to occupy it before the NF arrived. The police intervened, swiftly and brutally.

As the day wore on, more and more people collected outside the Town Hall. The police drove vehicles into the packed crowds. Flares, smoke bombs and petrol bombs were thrown at them. The hyped-up Special Patrol Group (SPG) units waded into the crowd with truncheons. Some used unauthorised weapons. The recollections of those present are dominated by the actions of the police and their awful effect. For Suzy Harding, it was like walking into a nightmare:

> I really don't remember all that much about Southall, except that it was really, really scary. I remember joining up with a group of anti-racists near the town centre and then running for my life as we were chased back down the road by these lunatic cops on horseback. My sole memory of the evening is running and hiding from these horrible bastards. They were lashing out at anyone within reach, men, women, pensioners, even religious people who were appealing for calm. I really wasn't surprised to learn the next day that they had killed someone. The way they were hitting out at people's heads meant they could have killed ten or twenty people easily. They had completely lost control. It certainly made me think twice about going on any more demonstrations.

Betty Davies, still active at 62, was also at Southall. She, too, recalls the behaviour of the police and the death of an anti-fascist:

> I also remember the march where Blair Peach was killed. I was on that, and I still can't believe to this day that they brought in the Special Patrol Group to attack the anti-fascists. Look at the forces they bring in against you, like you're the ones who are in the wrong. You're not in the wrong at all. You're standing up for your beliefs. The behaviour of the police at Southall was shocking. They were really nasty. Lashing out at anyone they could reach, pregnant women, young boys, even people who were trying to stop the violence. It was quite shocking and I believe to this day that it was all planned in advance in order to smash the anti-fascist movement.

Even a *Daily Telegraph* reporter, not a likely friend of protestors, reported that:

As we watched, several dozen crying, screaming, coloured demonstrators were dragged bodily to the police station. Nearly every demonstrator had blood flowing from some sort of injury.

These are the bare facts of Southall: over 700 protestors were arrested of whom 342 were charged, 97 police officers were reported injured as were 64 members of the public. One member of the public died of his injuries. The facts, however, hardly contain what actually happened. They do not tell the story of the 80 mainly elderly people taking refuge in Holy Trinity Churchyard who were surrounded and beaten by foot and mounted police. They do not convey the full brutality of the police raid on the Peoples Unite building in Park View Road, a distribution point for leaflets, placards, information which doubled as a first aid post. Doctors, first aid volunteers and those already being treated for injuries were beaten about the head with truncheons. Amongst the most seriously hurt was Clarence Baker of Misty in Roots. He was hit so hard his skull fractured, he suffered a blood clot on the brain and went into a coma. Nor do the facts reveal the sense of anger and betrayal felt by local communities who witnessed seig heiling fascists being bussed into Southall under heavy police protection for an inflammatory and pointless meeting. An audience of fewer than 50 people heard NF candidate John Fairhurst speak of his desire to 'bulldoze Southall to the ground and replace it with an English hamlet.'

The facts only just begin to account for the death of an anti-fascist activist. Blair Peach, an ANL member who had recently been suspended by the SWP, was with a group leaving the area around the Town Hall when they were caught up in a police charge on Beechcroft Avenue. Witnesses at an Unofficial Committee of Enquiry held by the NCCL described seeing the Met's riot police hitting out indiscriminately with their truncheons and systematically beating protestors lying on the ground. Peach's 'skull was crushed by a single blow.' He was hit by an SPG officer wielding what forensic experts later concluded was either 'a lead weighted rubber "cosh" or a hosepipe filled with lead shot, or some like weapon.' Taken to hospital with a

'...Southall: Murder of Blair Peach', *Merseyside Anti-Nazi League Bulletin*, 1979.

suspected fractured skull, he died that evening. 'Cosh' type weapons, and in one case Nazi regalia, were found in the lockers of the SPG unit deployed in the area of Beechcroft Avenue. The Cass Report into his death, released after thirty years, admits that Blair Peach was 'almost certainly' killed by a police officer. No one has ever been charged with his murder.

It took almost two months for the Coroner to release Blair Peach's body. 10,000 or more joined his funeral procession. 8,000, most of whom were Sikhs, attended his open coffin in Southall theatre the night before. Rock Against Racism organised concerts at the Rainbow Theatre featuring Pete Townsend, the Clash, the Members, the Ruts, Aswad, the Pop Group, and a defiant Misty in Roots. £5,000 was raised for those arrested at Southall and a Dance and Defend tour made donations to those charged following other election meeting protests.

In the final week of the election campaign, vast numbers of police were deployed at NF meetings. Some 4,000 officers were sent in to Newham in East London on 25 April. Over 1,000 were present in West Bromwich on 28 April, although were unable to stop anti-fascists heckling and fighting NF stewards inside their meeting hall. Another 1,000 attended the NF in Bradford two days later. An incredible 5,000 protected the Front's final election rally at Caxton Hall. Notwithstanding the military scale of the police operation, all sixteen NF election rallies were opposed by anti-fascists, who still managed to score the occasional success. At Plymouth on 24 April, 200 ANL supporters led by local anarchist Graham Short, occupied Coburg Street School hall prior to the arrival of Front leader John Tyndall and his followers. A picket was set up outside while those inside resisted removal by the police by staging a sit-down protest. The NF no sooner arrived than they turned tail and left. Tyndall's car was damaged as he sped off. Jubilant anti-fascists took over the school hall, celebrated with beer, political discussion and a piano player. On the same night in Binas Powys, South Wales, another

NF meeting was cancelled when the venue was surrounded by a 200-strong anti-fascist picket. Six foolhardy fascists showed up to be bundled into a car by the police and escorted out of town.

When the votes were cast on 3 May, the Front averaged barely more than 1% in the constituencies where they stood candidates and lost every single deposit. Humiliated and bankrupt, the NF turned in on itself, split into factions and rekindled old rivalries. So what exactly caused the disintegration of the NF? Many put it down to the siren call of Thatcher, tempting disillusioned Tory voters back into the fold by playing the race card. Others argue that the ANL played the largest part by challenging the Front wherever they raised their heads, exposing their Nazi origins, and mobilising tens of thousands of people in anti-fascist shows of unity and strength. The Front, for all their macho posturing appeared puny and small. Suzy Harding suggests that two years of unrelenting anti-fascist pressure finally paid off:

I don't think Thatcher had a lot to do with the NF going down the pan. She played a small part, but I think it was a lot more to do with the ANL opposing them on the streets, exposing them as bullies and cowards who only wanted to fight when the odds were in their favour. The other aspect was a cultural thing, because you had Rock Against Racism making fascism look really old and boring. I mean, who wants to live in a country run by fat old farts like Tyndall and Webster? We'd all be listening to Wagner and Nazi marching songs if it was down to them. I think that the slogan NF = No Fun was absolutely correct. It was uncool to be in the Front. None of the girls I knew were interested in NF blokes. We just thought they were ignorant bullies with their brains in their boots.

Even those who expressed a degree of scepticism towards the ANL, like John West, believe it was a success:

I'd have to say that the Anti-Nazi League did its job though. It was pretty successful because the National Front was more or less finished by the 80s. It was quite a big turnaround from the situation in the 1970s.

7

No Retreat: 1979-1990

Watching while fascists fall out with each other is heartening, even entertaining, although doesn't quite count as a form of physical resistance. But, it is important to keep abreast of the new groups spawned from the swamp. Internal feuding followed the NF's pitiful electoral performance. The Front spilt. A rump of several thousand members, led by Martin Webster until he was hounded out for his homosexual affairs, remained loyal to the NF. The leadership was taken up by a new generation of fascists, including Nick Griffin, Ian Anderson, Patrick Harrington and Martin Wingfield. The NF did not find an alternative to its failed electoral strategy but in the late '70s and early '80s still comprised the most significant body on the extreme right. About 750 old Fronters joined John Tyndall to form the New National Front, renamed the British National Party (BNP) in 1982. There was only token opposition at the BNP's press launch and the party had little effect in its early years but has since become the group that has upheld and adapted the prejudices of the British fascist tradition. The immediate beneficiary of the NF splits was the British Movement. Its ranks were swollen by disillusioned Fronters, boosting both their membership and potential for violence. The openly Nazi BM boasted a notorious hardcore of street fighters who had never held any interest in electoral politics and simply continued their campaign of intimidation.

Realignments in the fascist camp did not halt fascist violence. Far from it. Just a small sample of reported attacks on black and Asian peoples as well as anti-fascists can quickly turn into quite a long list. An Asian man on his way home from a night club in Burnley was badly beaten by two NFers. Two Asian men were attacked by a group of Liverpool NF members at Keele service

station. In Rochdale, three of
the Front stabbed a man
wearing an ANL badge. There
was a gang attack on a 16-year-
old anti-fascist in Norwich and
an assault on two members of
the SWP in the same city. In
London, an ANL stallholder in
Finchley Road was assailed by
fascists. A follower of the ska
band, The Beat, was stabbed
outside their gig in Camden as
60 BM skinheads rioted. 15
members of the BM, armed
with bricks and bottles, broke
into an Ealing flat, the home of
an Asian ANL supporter. An

British Movement: Nazis on Our Streets, Anti-Nazi League.

SWP meeting in Lambeth was stormed by NF supporters
carrying coshes and bottles. Five people required hospital
treatment, one needed 120 stitches. The NF members also tried to
blow up a left-wing printing press in Brixton, prevented only by
a combination of luck and the bravery of the occupants of the
building. Just outside London, in Welling, which was to become
a notorious venue for battles with fascists, a black railway
worker, Lloyd Chambers, was nearly blinded after a gang of
jumped him after a BM rally. In addition to fairly continuous
street level violence, several fascists were convicted for
possession of firearms and ammunition. In one case, NF member
Harold Simcox was found with a sub-machine gun, semi-
automatic pistols, revolvers, rifles, a double-barrelled shotgun,
CS gas, 5,000 rounds of ammunition and bullet making
equipment.

All this might be sufficient to make the point that despite its
factionalism, fascism did not disappear with the dawn of

Thatcherism. In fact, one of the most important arenas of struggle against fascism was the cultural scene of punks and squatters that grew in opposition to the authoritarianism of her right-wing conservative government. Squatters were a target for fascists. Issue 58 of *Searchlight*, for instance, reported on a horrendous case:

> Four skinheads, all supporters of the British Movement, were jailed for a total of twenty years for offences that included an attack on punks living in a squat in Camden. The four subjected the punks to a two hour ordeal of violence – they hit them over the head with bottles, beat them with broomsticks, slashed them with a razor, stubbed out cigarettes on their bare skin, and one of them had a broom handle forced up his anus. As they were doing it they told their victims how they did not like Jews, anti-Nazis or punk rockers and that they had knives and petrol bombs.

Suzy Harding was living in a squat off the Caledonian Road in north London at the time. She recalls an atmosphere of fear and trepidation amongst the squatting community:

> There was a very heavy atmosphere around the squatting scene in London at that time. You'd hear all these rumours that such and such a place had been broken into by fascists, that women had been raped and blokes stabbed and slashed with broken bottles. It was a very scary situation and sometimes you'd jump out of your skin at the slightest noise outside. We were very careful not to tell strangers where we lived or invite anyone in that we didn't know. Nothing happened to our squat but a place around the corner was firebombed by skinheads. A neighbour called the police but it was a week before they came around to take witness statements.

Gangs of skinheads claiming affiliation to the British Movement were a regular hazard for punters at punk gigs, as John Baine explains:

> While a lot of the bigger RAR gigs were well stewarded, some of the smaller gigs were targeted by fascists. In the early days it was quite possible for ten fascists to come in and completely disrupt a gig with two hundred people in it, purely because people weren't prepared to stand up to them. I'm not a violent person but I'll stand up for myself and for what I believe in. If it has to be done, it has to be done. That's one of the things that started to annoy me, because first and foremost if you're an anti-fascist you have to be able to defend your activities from fascist attack. There were a number of times in the beginning when there would be a lot of trouble. The fascists would turn up at a gig and because they were big and intimidating, I'd fight back, a few others would fight back, but there would be maybe only ten of us against twenty of them with a roomful of so-called 'anti-fascists' watching from the sidelines.
>
> In 1980 I started gigging as Attila the Stockbroker and it wasn't long before I started to get quite a lot of publicity, becoming known for my politics as much as for my performances. I used to perform at all kinds of venues and play alongside all kinds of different bands and performers. On the one hand I'd support left-wing bands like the Newtown Neurotics and on the other hand I'd also support Oi bands, who while they might not have been racist or fascist themselves, had found themselves saddled with a fascist bonehead following. I'd always regarded preaching to the converted as a bloody pointless exercise. I wanted to get through to those people who were swallowing fascist ideas and try to make them think about what they were doing. The NF had suffered a heavy defeat at the 1979 General Election.

This was in part due to the sterling efforts of RAR and the ANL but also because the Tories had stolen a lot of their policies on race and immigration. The immediate threat of fascism seemed to diminish in many people's eyes. The fascists were certainly less high profile but from my point of view, out doing gigs most evenings, I could see that they were no less dangerous. It became very clear to me very quickly that not only were the fascists actively recruiting at gigs but that they were attempting to take over the whole scene. I received a number of death threats from the British Movement as did the Newtown Neurotics and a number of other bands. I remember a small gig in Milton Keynes that ended in absolute carnage when fifty boneheads turned up. It was a free-for-all and because they were better organised than us and had more numbers, they came out on the winning side.

SWP and ANL activist Mickey O'Farrell describes how the balance of forces began to be readdressed. He, and the Hatfield Squad, took matters into their own hands, literally. The fight back started in earnest at a Crass and Poison Girls gig at Conway Hall, 8 September 1979:

To be honest it all started pretty much by accident. About half a dozen of us from Hatfield had been on the 1979 Right to Work march and had got friendly with some punks from Scotland and a few other lads and girls from London and the home counties. A short time later we arranged to meet up with some of these to go to a gig at Conway Hall, which was a Persons Unknown benefit for some anarchists who had been charged with some very serious conspiracy offences. We started out at a pub nearby and then just started drifting up to the hall and when I got outside the hall I can remember, Vim, a mate of mine who's now dead, coming out saying "Fucking hell, its full of Fronters." So we gathered up and went in, and

I think it was Vim who just launched into the first one we saw. It was all over pretty quickly and we chased them all out. To be honest, I never considered skinheads much of a threat. Sure, there'd be one or two who were genuinely tough but in my experience the majority were posers. A similar scenario to many football fans at the time. There was some controversy afterwards because one of the defendants got hit, presumably by one of ours. I actually got to know this man quite well later and he certainly never bore any grudge. Obviously, this was not something to be celebrated. It did go a bit wild but we were young and bold and it does go wrong sometimes. But when it goes wrong with people beating up fascists, it's still better than nobody taking a stand. What I am pretty sure of is that even if we hadn't turned up that night I don't think there is anyway it would have finished peacefully. Those skinheads would have kicked off, stormed the stage and smashed up the gig.

Not long after that we went to a gig in West Kensington. At that time we'd met up with a gang of Finchley kids who had a squat around the corner from the Torch at Wembley. It was a massive house, god knows what it would be worth these days, probably a million plus, maybe two or three million. We used to use it as base when we went to gigs. On this one particular occasion, we went to watch a band called the Angelic Upstarts. There were about a dozen from Hatfield and three or four from Finchley. We weren't expecting any trouble. It was just a night out and a drink. We were in the public bar and the gig was in the hall at the back. Someone said that there was a load of skinheads in the gig and before long a gang of them came bouncing through the door with their chests puffed out, going "Ooh, ooh, ooh." In amongst this crowd was a Cockney Red, who I used to see at United matches and as soon as he saw me he stopped and slinked back. He just sort of melted away. I don't remember exactly what happened because I had a bit of a blank out, but apparently one of us launched into them and then everyone else who had been scattered around the bar piled in from all sides. The three things I remember seeing are firstly, the last few skinheads all trying to get through the door at the same time, secondly the white ball sitting in the middle of the pool table somehow covered in blood and lastly one skinhead crawling across the floor wailing "Patrick, Patrick. Look what the commies have done to me."

So on the first two occasions at least, the trouble was pretty much accidental, but the next time we went to a gig we were very much up for the possibility. This was because it was a Madness gig at the Electric Ballroom in Camden. And it was they who, at the time, probably had the worst reputation of all for having a fascist presence at their gigs. This time it was very much more than a Hatfield initiative. There were also a good few others from London, Clapton, Kilburn and Finchley. Probably about 20 odd in all and basically our aim was just to go down wearing our ANL badges to show that we weren't scared and just see what happened. In the event, nothing did.

By this time talk about the Hatfield anti-fascist squad was very much doing the rounds. But so often with urban myths much of it was exaggerated. In truth there were never more than a handful of us who could have been described as committed political activists. For the rest there were a variety of reasons. Some were very much influenced by the punk scene and the fact that so many punk stars had come out with such a strong anti-fascist stance made an impression on them. Some others were maybe just looking for a bit of excitement and adventure, most had come up on the wrong side of the tracks and had seen the inside of borstals and prisons. So there was a strong anti-establishment feeling within the group and being for the most part decent and intelligent lads it wasn't difficult for them to equate racism with evil and fascism with oppression. And above all there was an overriding esprit de corps. We were all together and my brother's enemy was my enemy.

The next month, on 27 October, the Hatfield squad took the fight to the fascists at the town's Polytechnic, a Two Tone Music Tour venue. The Specials and Selector had anti-racist credentials but Madness were on the bill and they attracted a hardcore BM and NF following:

Given the background with Madness and their following immediately there was talk about the possibility of trouble. It spread round the town like wildfire. In the weeks leading up to the gig people kept coming up to me all the time wanting to know what was going on, people who you would never normally associate with political activity. But this had now become a parochial as much as political thing. There was talk of outsiders coming down to their town and the townies weren't having it. On the day itself, we were out from early in the morning. Down in the town centre we had banners out. We were down the station checking out who was coming in and patrolling around the town centre. We saw hardly any suspicious characters. Those we did we checked out for fascist insignia. A few of us had been over to Belfast with Troops Out by then and saw how working class communities policed themselves. As the day turned to evening, a crowd of us were parked in a pub in the town centre along with a few political contacts who had turned up from Liverpool and London. Reports started coming in of small groups of skinheads being chased all over the place. There were people showing up who I didn't even know. Eventually, several dozen of us moved off toward the Poly. The design of the Poly was that the music hall was upstairs with a large bar area at ground level. When we arrived outside we could see that the bar area was packed with skinheads. Immediately, a few of the lads started breaking the windows, climbing through the broken panes and launching into the skinheads. I had a ticket but I can't remember if I used it or went through the newly established tradesman's entrance. By the time I got in, the skinheads were all fleeing upstairs towards the music hall. They were run everywhere. As we got up there, the last few disappeared into the hall and the doors slammed shut and were bolted up. I sat down on a table by the doors. About five minutes later, the police arrived and one immediately grabbed me. I was taken to Hatfield nick and as I arrived I saw written on a cell door "O'Farrell GBH + Affray". In the end, they fitted me up on a charge of criminal damage. A copper swore he saw me throw a table through a window even though a porter testified he only phoned the police when he saw that table being thrown. I later heard how, at the end of the evening, the police rounded up the remaining skinheads and escorted about 200 of them back to Hatfield station. As they neared the station, a group of the lads were waiting on top of some garages. They had a big spiked chain that they'd liberated from outside a garden and the police and skinheads went past them they swung it round and ploughed it into them before disappearing into the night.

University venues, especially the more radical Polytechnics, were important venues for punk, ska and reggae. Promoted by student unions but open to all comers, these gigs, whether or not they were officially under the Rock Against Racism banner, were a scene of anti-fascists struggle. Tony Greenstein recalls:

We put on a number of gigs, which were primarily at Brighton Polytechnic. The far-left controlled the student union at that time and I was Vice-President. We held a number of gigs both in the Sallis Benney Hall, part of the Art College, and at

Cockcroft, which is two miles out of Brighton at Moulsecoomb. A number of well-known groups played, Misty in Roots, The Piranhas. I can remember squaring up at one gig at the Art College to a member of Madness. [There was this question about whether] one of two of their members had close relations at one time with the BM. But then they denied that and said they were anti-fascist.

Whilst fascists and anti-fascists fought it out either to the rhythm of ska beats or to crashing guitars, some street activity continued. Fascists were still selling their papers at Brick Lane and Chapel Market in Islington. Recruiting football supporters at club grounds was commonplace as Tony describes:

They certainly did a lot of work round the [Brighton and Hove Albion] football club. At first it was pretty hostile and we had to take 20-30 people for our own protection. After some time, however, we turned the tide there. They used to sell their paper in Air Street, in the centre of Brighton, on a Saturday, and again we would have mobilisations to stop them. By and large they were successful. [There were] a number of punch-ups with them in Queens Road.

The NF also attempted to march in Brighton. Differences between the anti-fascist strategy of the trade union committees and that of the ANL, which had been fiercely debated through the organisation of large counter-protests like Lewisham, persisted at a local level. Tony takes up the story, again:

Between 1980 and 1982 there were three NF marches. The first one and the biggest started in Hove and we did have a major disagreement with the Anti-Fascist Committee [AFC] over this. They mobilised about a thousand people at the Level, which is in the centre of Brighton about 3 miles away from

Hove and has been used traditionally as a place for the Labour movement to rally at the end or start of demonstrations. But the NF mobilised in Hove and the AFC didn't think of trying to stop them marching. They waited for them to come to the hallowed labour movement turf. A lot of us went up to greet them and there were heavy arrests that day. I was arrested. We gave them a pasting where we found them but they mobilised quite a number themselves and [one of the squares] on the border between Brighton and Hove was a sea of young NF faces. They certainly had got themselves a base, if not locally then regionally.

It was about a year later when they decided to hold another march from Norfolk Square, which is just over the border into Hove. And the AFC again, although it was meeting much less frequently then as it had fallen essentially into abeyance, put out the call to meet at The Level again. The ANL, which had been particularly active, decided to meet where they met, which is what we did, but one hour earlier. We basically flooded Norfolk Square and there was no way they were going to get in there. I had a small green Honda 70 bike. It was very nippy and I went round all the area. Eventually I spotted them assembling on the beach. We had the police surrounding people in Norfolk Square, so we quietly got people to leave there, dribbling down to the south and the beach, where we caught them. No police around then and we gave them a hammering before the police managed to get there. I think we put two of them in hospital, including [Steve] Brady. Although they eventually managed to assemble for a march, which was then bricked and had a bottle thrown at it, which put another fascist in hospital. That was an extremely successful counter-mobilisation. I remember when coming back to the Level being applauded by all 50 people who were there, including Dave Lepper who [was] the Labour MP for Brighton Pavilion. Again we lost quite a lot of people to arrests and one of them

was subsequently jailed for 3 months for assault on a particularly obnoxious police inspector on the beach.

Then they held a third march. They had decided to become
animal lovers! Against Jewish Ritual Slaughter. It was
through the Jewish area of Hove. We weren't totally together
then because they had initially decided to march from Hove
Town Hall and then switched to Norfolk Square. I remember
there were about 30-40 of them, totally surrounded first by 3
concentric rings of police and then by us! And the police by
that time had had enough, they were understandably nervous
that we would break through and they just stopped the
meeting and pushed them onto the coaches. That was the last
march of any significance that they held.

From 1980, when the NF first tried to march from Hove into
Brighton until their phoney animal rights debacle of 1982, there
were numerous battles between fascists and anti-fascists at
political meetings, constituting, according to Tony Greenstein, a
state of 'constant warfare':

Troops Out meetings were attacked and the first Unemployed
Centre in Brighton at Coalbrook Road hosted a meeting with
a member of the IRSP [Irish Republican Socialist Party] and
got a plank through its window. We picketed and tried to
close down their meetings. The NF was pretty active.

Throughout this period, it was the ANL that held fascists of
whatever faction at bay. The ANL was still the main body of
militant opposition. But while activists kept on working
together, their organisation was only being intermittently
sustained by the SWP leadership. Tony remembers that the ANL
had to be re-started after the 1979 election:

The ANL reformed about 1980 and I was the Secretary and the

key SWP guy was Roger Barton who was on the buses until he got victimised and sacked. He was the other main person involved. The SWP then was into physical force anti-fascism. Of course, later on it was different.

The revival of ANL activity was widespread. Ambitious campaigns to counter the presence of fascists on the terraces of First Division clubs like West Ham United, Manchester United, Manchester City, Tottenham Hotspur were launched. 600 anti-fascists were mobilised against a planned BM march in Oxford in July 1981 and 200 of them, a mixture of Squadists and locals from the Blackbird Leys estate, rumbled a pub full of BM members, leaving a trail of destruction and wounded Nazis in their wake. 4,000 anti-fascists gathered in Paddington in November to counter a BM march. And, a variety of actions were taken to prevent Andrew Brons, an NF organiser and former National Socialist Movement member, from teaching at Harrogate College of Further Education in Yorkshire.

It would not be long, however, before this mass, militant movement was shut down. With the demise of the NF as any kind of electoral force and establishment of a right-wing Tory government, leading SWP members began winding down the ANL. Believing that the movement had achieved its goals, the urgent task was now opposing Margaret Thatcher. On the face of it, it was a sensible enough political decision, but one that failed to take into account that for NF members, if not their leadership, and to a greater extent the BM as a whole, fascism was never about winning elections. The SWP leadership were also, to varying degrees, apprehensive about the ANL's commitment to physical resistance and that of the Squads to physical confrontation. They were, especially after Lewisham, very wary of their names and that of the party being always associated with mass public disorder and were increasingly keen on steering the ANL away from fighting with either the fascists or the police.

Their fears about the movement as a whole were directed at the Squads. A schism had developed between anti-fascist militants and party devotees. The Squads were increasingly autonomous. Squadists were usually members of the SWP but determined for themselves when and what kind of anti-fascist action it was necessary to take. And as they did so, they built up local allegiances with numerous non-aligned individuals, anarchists and members of rival left-wing groups.

Squadists were expelled from the SWP. Several militants from Manchester received their marching orders whilst they were in prison serving sentences for anti-fascist activities. As so often is the case when people are ousted from political parties, spurious cases of individual misconduct mask fundamental political differences. Those that emerged between the SWP leadership and the Squads in the early 1980s are all too familiar in anti-fascist history. As activists took practical steps to deal with fascism in the places where it arose, they developed autonomy from party structures and a strategy that included the use of force. Party officials, however initially supportive, ended up disapproving. Active Squadist and dedicated anti-fascist fighter, Mickey O'Farrell, was expelled after the Rock Against Racism Carnival at Roundhay Park, Leeds in July 1981, which ought also to be remembered for its lineup: the Specials, Misty in Roots, Aswad, the Au Pairs as well as local Chapeltown reggae band Wolfrace. Mickey had been asked by the Carnival's chief steward, London based SWPer Paul Baker, to help steward the event and had agreed to put together a group to secure the stage. The night before they were due to set off, Paul Baker called to say he had been 'relieved of his job as chief steward because the SWP didn't like the people he was planning to use. The message arrived too late in the day to undo all his plans, as O'Farrell explains:

Now because we'd already booked the minibus and because

people had taken time off work, we decided that we'd just go up for the gig anyway. There were 17 of us in the van. It didn't have any seats, and we all just squeezed in the back. Georgie, my girlfriend at the time, who was a social worker was the driver, and Claire, a workmate of hers, was with us, so it wasn't a nasty mob by any means. Well, we got up there, found the park and the stage, parked up the van and had a look around. We all had our sleeping bags with us because the original arrangement was that as we were all going to be stewards we were going to sleep on the stage. We found a pub nearby and settled in for a drink.

Here, Mickey recalls a party worker warning him: '"The thing is Mick. You know we've changed the arrangements, and you won't be stewarding anymore... you won't be going into the staging area ... We've got an elaborate security operation."' He replied that he understood that he and those with him had been stood down as stewards but had come for the gig and needed somewhere to stay overnight: '"Woah. Hang on. I've been arranging all week for people to come up here on the basis that we're sleeping on the stage. There won't be a problem."' Anti-fascists have slept out at open-air venues since Ridley Road, if not before, keeping up a tradition of vigilance against attempts to jump the pitch. While the 17 who had travelled from London and Hatfield waited in the van for a place to sleep, if not steward, Mickey walked over to the stage and appealed to the SWP members leaning against the fence:

"Look, all we want to do is get our heads down for a sleep. There won't be any problems. We won't cause any trouble." And they've gone "No, it can't be done." It's gone on and on and on until finally I said "Is that really your last word?" They said "Yes." So I replied "OK, I tried." I went back over to the van, went bang, bang, bang on the side and told everyone to get on the stage. They've all got out with their sleeping bags, threw them over the fence, pulled each other over and started climbing on the stage. One of the ANL leaders went berserk. He started shouting "Right. It's come to my attention that some of you are drunk. I intend to see to it that any of you who are in the SWP are expelled." There was a brief pause before he screamed "So which of you are in SWP? Come on, hands up now." We rolled about laughing and in the end they all walked off and left us to it. We stayed on the stage that night, left it in the morning in perfect order for the Carnival and slept on it again the next night. After the Carnival, when we woke up on the Sunday the local SWP were down the bottom of the field looking at us as if we were an alien life form. We swept up the stage and went home. Within days a leaflet was doing the rounds saying how we stormed the stage drunk, threatened people with knives, blah, blah, blah. It was basically a load of bullshit. But perhaps the most significant thing about it was how after listing the litany of our supposed crimes it suddenly asserted "Cleary a minority of SWP members believe that the building of the Squads is a preferable way of taking on the fascists than mass workers' action." Now where the hell did that come from?

Mick O'Farrell reflects:

In my opinion what scared the SWP leadership most, and I'm not privy to the inner machinations of the central committee so I can only go on my own political analysis, was that the Squads had developed a certain autonomy which they could not directly control. In my experience the concept of working class autonomy or spontaneity is something they celebrate when they talk in the abstract but not when it occurs within their own organisation.

The fight with fascists has never politely waited in the wings while left wing parties realign themselves. In 1981, there was an important battle by anti-racist activists and one of the very few active ANL branches to stop the NF selling their papers at Chapel Market in Islington, North London. The NF had a strong presence in the area, backed by a notorious criminal family with fascist connections that stretched back to the days of the Blackshirts. Mickey O'Farrell's response to being expelled from the SWP was to devote himself to defending the Chapel Market pitch:

All the stuff with the expulsions more or less overlapped with the campaign at Chapel Market, where we were keeping it all together. It was a disputed paper sale. A local anti-racist called Anna Sullivan used to sell papers there and the Front used to turn up there as well. Eventually we said "Right. We're having this." This wasn't like Brick Lane, where I'd only go along on a Sunday if I happened to be staying over in London on a Saturday night. We were obsessive about it. I'd go up to London especially to sell papers at Chapel Market on a Sunday morning. We were there every week, and there were regular clashes with the Front. After the expulsions it almost became our reason for existence. The SWP were pulling out of any sort of confrontation with the Front and along with a few local anti-racists, we were the only ones prepared to do anything about the situation.

I had got arrested during the riots of 1981, remanded for six months and while I was still inside, the Front turned up at Chapel Market with a big mob and kicked some people around a bit, so the very next week our crowd turned up at a National Front paper sale at Kingsbury and kicked the living daylights out of them. How they never got nicked I'll never know because there were pictures in the local paper showing some of our lot as clear as anything. It shows that the police at that time weren't taking too much notice of it. After Kingsbury, there were a number of clashes between our crowd and the Front but the campaign at Chapel Market eventually started to pay off. We began to notice that the Front weren't turning up as often as they used to and after a while they stopped altogether. Whether or not it was purely our efforts that brought this about is difficult to say but all our hard work seemed to pay off.

Squadists, now former Squadists, maintained their commitment to anti-fascism and began to consider creating their own organisation. O'Farrell describes the formation of Red Action:

After the expulsions, there was a brief period when I suppose we were all a bit uncertain about what we should do next, but bubbling under the surface was the idea that we've got to set up our own thing. I was very much in favour of this and while I was on remand I was smuggling out statements to meetings that were taking place, urging people to take this course. Eventually I got out after the charges against me were dropped. There were a couple more meetings and finally the idea to set up a new independent group prevailed and that's how Red Action came about. It is perhaps worth recalling that whilst Red Action was later to become known primarily as a white male anti-fascist group, at the beginning this was not specifically the case. At the meeting where the organisation was established nearly a third of those present were women and over half had a trade union as much as an anti-fascist background.

One of Red Action's first moves was to renew efforts to curtail the BM presence on the punk circuit. John Baine, aka Attila the Stockbroker, had been facing down fascist skinheads from the stage but the threat they posed and the performer's isolation was not simply fading away. After an anti-fascist gig at Skunx in Islington was mobbed by fascists in May 1982, the punk poet persuaded the promoter to announce a 'No Pub Is A Nazi Pub' gig. The bands Newtown Neurotics and Sub-Active joined Attila but precious few of the organised left. This gig fared no better than the last. John Baine paints the scene:

> There were twenty or thirty little punks against forty BM boneheads and Chelsea Headhunters. These were blokes with serious reputations for violence and I knew we wouldn't have a cat's chance in hell against them. Chris Dean, lead singer of Redskins was there with his mate, Dagenham Pete, a big and very hard, anti-racist skinhead. From his vantage point under a table, Chris was able to watch as Pete saved my arse that night. A lone bonehead invaded the stage as I was performing and smashed my mandolin over my head. This was the signal for the whole mob of them to join in the attack. Pete waded into the BM mob and it was only his intervention that rallied the opposition and saved me from a serious kicking.

He remembers the moment when anti-fascist reinforcements arrived:

> The turning point as far as the fascist presence at gigs came when a number of anti-fascists from outside the punk scene realised what was going on and started to do something about it. They weren't people who would normally go to gigs all the time but they were anti-fascists who recognised what the BM were trying to do and decided to stop them. Many of them were ex-SWP members like me, people who had either left or were expelled from the party when the ANL was wound up. A lot of these people went on to become core members of Red Action and Anti-Fascist Action. I'd first met the Hatfield mob on May Day 1981. We had organised a May Day festival at

Harlow Playhouse. It was the normal sort of Trots and hippies and punks thing, when all of a sudden these thirty lads turned up, pissed out of their heads, singing republican songs and "If I die on a Welwyn Street" and "H I L L T O P, Hilltop, Hilltop!!' We were most impressed.

From my point of view, events reached their climax at the Brixton Ace in 1983 when I did a gig with the Addicts and the Newtown Neurotics. A big group of fascists turned up, and I remember Chris Henderson coming over and asking me if I knew who he was. At the time I didn't and he said "I'm Chubby Chris from Combat 84." It was like he was announcing who he was and then standing there and saying "Well, what are you going to do about it?" I thought we were going to get beaten up but they just hung around intimidating people. They started seig heiling intermittently and it was quite a nasty, oppressive atmosphere. Then right in the middle of the Addicts set, there was a big commotion at the door and, again, a load of the Hatfield mob, charged in. All of a sudden an awful lot of fascists decided to leave the venue very quickly, some of them nursing a number of wounds and injuries. After that I had very little trouble at gigs.

It would be wrong to assume that the SWP entirely abandoned the anti-fascist cause. Their student activists sustained one of the largest and longest protests of the mid-80s. Protests against enrollment and attendance of NF organiser Patrick Harrington at North London Polytechnic had been initiated by philosophy students in February 1984. Mass pickets, supported by the Socialist Worker's Student Society, lecturers' trade unions, hundreds of students and assorted anti-fascists were mounted outside the Poly from March onwards. A High Court ruling and heavy police protection enabled Harrington to enter the building to find every seat in the library occupied. Picketing continued into the new academic year. Two students, John Leatham and

Steven Tisane, were jailed for flouting the injunctions against the protest.

While national organisations folded and formed, anti-fascists continued to work in their local areas. Since participating in blockading fascist meetings in Manchester and Bolton in the late 70s, John Severn maintained his interest. 'I don't know. Something inside me said I wanted to keep an eye on what were going on, just individually.' The British National Party (BNP) contested seats in the 1983 General Election. Anti-fascists might be forgiven for not taking much notice of changing fascist party acronyms since almost half the BNP's 54 candidates had previously stood for the NF and, at this point, elections were an excuse for building the BNP as a 'racial nationalist party' with its ideology of white superiority rather than as an end in themselves. It was in response to the BNP's presence in the former industrial towns of the northwest that John became a regular anti-fascist:

I wasn't part of any group but I did join an anarchist group in Bolton and it was there really that we started attending anti-fascist events particularly in Rochdale and Oldham. It was a mixed anarchist group. Some were more committed to the anarcho-syndicalist line and more interested in the work place struggle, some were general anarchists, one or two were animal rights activists. A good mixed band. But having said that despite those differences in the 80s we pulled out most of the anarchist group into anti-fascist events regardless of whether they were a particular tendency or another. They were able just to get on practically.

Rochdale tended to be the centre of our activity at that point and that was simply going along with other people. We were a political grouping but we were alongside all sorts of different political tendencies. We would turn out as a group when there were various call outs. Usually, call outs were posted quite publicly. I don't think at that point we had any real network going that wasn't more than simply a poster on the wall. The links were very informal. My recollection of Rochdale was a lot of waiting around at a local community centre for the BNP to turn up. Walking around the town, keeping an eye on things and the occasional, very occasional, bit of activity. Most of all it was just establishing a presence in the town and protecting the immigration centre that existed in Rochdale. I think the most important things we attended were the election counts, trying to pick of fascists who were coming to the counts and the little bit of a rally that they would try and hold in the Town Hall. In the early days the activity was quite passive really. It was simply a matter of keeping a presence in the town and warding off the opposition. It wasn't until later that we took a more pro-active stance towards fascists and that was a very different ball game. In the early days, it was simply a matter of mass presence on the streets and very little else.

For Sean Gaughan, the Manchester-Irish young man, who attended an ANL march back in the late 70s, it was the aggressive alliance between loyalists and fascists against left campaigns to end the British occupation of Ireland that made him renew his commitment to anti-fascism:

While becoming more politically conscious I did not get involved in politics until I stopped to sign a petition at Longsight market calling for the troops to be removed from Ireland and a public meeting a couple of days later, both were organised by the RCG [Revolutionary Communist Group]. This was the summer of 84. After that I attended a lot of stuff organised by them and while I have nothing but admiration for them and the hard work and dedication they put into political work, I was getting more and more frustrated by the harassment, attacks and intimidation from loyalists and fascists, particularly on any Irish demo that I attended and desperately wanted to hit back, but felt completely isolated.

The Manchester Martyrs Commemoration march, a target for fascists throughout the 1980s, continued to be attacked. For fascists, it was a wholly anti-British affair, the height of unpatriotic behaviour. They were not far wrong. They would not, however, have recognised the different motives of those who participated in the commemoration. Some marched for recognition of the experience of being Irish in Britain, their age-old contribution to the British economy as manual labourers and their equally entrenched discrimination by the British justice system. Some were left activists who wanted to expose the myth of Britain as peacekeeper in Ireland and oppose British imperialism. They valued internationalism far higher than sectional interests of the country where they lived. Marching together, they pitted themselves against the power of the British state. The Manchester Martyrs Commemoration was always tense and often violent, as Sean recalls:

> The first time I attended that march was 84. We started from outside Strangeways prison and ended up in some side street somewhere and were boxed in by the Police, I think it is called kettling today. We were harassed and followed non-stop by a large crowd of loyalists and fascists and the march was attacked at least once which was repelled by marchers themselves not the police who did nothing until we started to defend ourselves and then they arrested some of the marchers. It was a horrible experience.

The following year, he helped in the organisation of the march but was also searching for support to deal with those who threatened it:

I joined the Manchester Martyrs Commemoration Committee for the 85 march and attended as a steward. It was my first time being involved in organising anything at all and, looking back, despite the fascist presence the year before at no time at all did we ever discuss security or how we would defend the marchers. Through the lefty grapevine I heard about an organisation called Red Action that had built a reputation for physically confronting both [fascists and loyalists], I can't remember how but I met a few people in Manchester who had links to them and was involved in a number of minor run ins, mostly around Irish marches. At this time all the street confrontations seemed to be in London and after being introduced to a couple of Red Action members from London who were up visiting Manchester and hearing first hand what was happening, I became determined to move down there and get involved.

Back in London, the mission to free the punk scene from fascists developed into something akin to gang warfare. Mickey O'Farrell relates:

There was a pub just up the road from Chapel Market called the White Horse. A band used to play there every Saturday night called the Connolly Folk, an Irish band who played all the rebel songs. The pub was run by Ronnie Parrish, an old time Tottenham Hotspur football hooligan, and he used to do lock-ins until four or five in the morning. The pub became our base but just down the road was another pub called The Agricultural and a load of fascist skinheads started drinking in there. The thing about The Agricultural was that the skinheads were using it as an international base. The rumour was that they were bringing over fascist skinheads from all over Europe and it was obviously going to end in tears at some stage. Small raids escalated into a couple of big confrontations. I remember on one occasion after a meeting in London we parked ourselves in another pub between the Angel tube and The Agricultural and I think it was on that occasion that we ended up chasing a group of skinheads off and smashing windows in the pub. I remember we all scattered from the scene and me and one other lad were walking off trying to look non-descript when a police transit started tailing us slowly down the road. They must have known that we were involved but we never got pulled.

A couple of weeks later, we were at a Jobs for Change festival at Jubilee Gardens. Early in the day we noticed a few skinheads one of whom even had a Screwdriver T shirt. I argued that it wasn't worth getting involved with anything as they didn't seem to be any threat and, who knows, having come along to an unemployed movement benefit one or two of them might even learn something. Well, so much for my liberal approach because later on in the day about 40 of them got together and invaded the stage while the Redskins were playing and for a while disrupted the whole event. We were raging at being caught with our pants down and none more than me. We caught up with a couple of groups on the fringes of the Festival and after that we went to The Agricultural hoping to find the main group. As I remember it, there was hardly anyone in there so we just took it out on the pub and trashed it. Shortly after that the pub changed hands.

The Festival, a Greater London Council (GLC) event in June 1984, was a turning point. Members of Red Action recognised that their fight with fascists was in danger of becoming depoliticised and dependent upon too small a body of activists. A new national anti-fascist organisation was proposed and a leaflet produced inviting groups to an opening discussion. Mickey O'Farrell remembers the very first moves in the making of Anti-Fascist Action:

Anti-Fascist Action was formed after the trouble at Jubilee Gardens. We felt that militant anti-fascism needed a wider base of support than just the usual suspects gathered around Red Action. You know, white working class males between the ages of 20 and 35, which we had become by that time. At the very first meeting I had jotted down a few notes for a founding statement which stressed the need to oppose fascism physically and ideologically and it was from this that Gosh came up with the line about the constitution being written on the back of a beer mat. This was at a meeting at The Cock in Euston in 1985. It was an open meeting and we didn't really know who was going to turn up but in the end it was very successful because ten or twelve different groups turned up. Groups like Class War, the Jewish Socialist Group and the Newham Monitoring Project turned up as well as various local anti-racist groups, few of which were funded by local government and, I think, Workers' Power sent some people down on the day as well.

Anti-Fascist Action (AFA) was officially launched at Conway Hall in London on 28 July 1985. A total of 300 people attended. Alongside Red Action, Class War, the Jewish Socialist Group, Newham Monitoring Project and Workers Power from the Euston meeting were representatives from Searchlight, the Refugee Forum, and local anti-racist bodies from places some distance from the capital, including Bradford and Tyneside. Red Action and the East London Direct Action Movement (ELDAM), acting on information that AFA's founding conference would be targeted by fascists, spent the entire time outside stewarding it. Inside and in their absence, the organisation took on a distinctly less militant flavour than its original sponsors would have liked. Notwithstanding the different agendas of AFA's composite bodies, according to Mickey O'Farrell, it got off to a good start:

One of the first things AFA did was to organise opposition to the Front's annual march to the Cenotaph on Remembrance Sunday. They had called for their supporters to meet in Bressenden Place near Victoria. So what we did was meet up in Kings Cross a couple of hours earlier and then went down and took over their assembly point before any of them arrived. A good 200 people turned up and there was a wide variety of people. There was black and Asian groups, different socialist groups and plenty of women as well. We used the same tactic to very great effect on another occasion when they were due to rally near Tottenham Hale tube. We got there very early and packed out this pub right near the tube and as the fascists turned up they quickly saw they had no chance of establishing themselves. As I remember it, their rally never even started that day.

The week after the Remembrance Sunday mobilisation, the NF tried to march in Stockport. Activists from the newly formed Greater Manchester Anti-Fascist Action responded. An *AFA Bulletin*, dated January 1986, reported:

> Some 40 fascists held a short meeting at the back of the Town Hall and were then literally 'run out of town' under police escort. Despite the fact that fascists were heavily armed and looking for trouble, only 2 NF supporters were arrested. 12 anti-fascists now face a variety of charges.

In the book *No Retreat*, Steven Tilzey provides some more details. A group of Fronters were chased onto the railway station where they barricaded themselves in the ticket office and hid behind a police dog handler and his Alsatian. Stockport's NF organiser and two of his henchmen were knocked unconscious. Traffic lights held up the escape of four fascists in a nice new Saab, giving members of Greater Manchester AFA time to smash its windows and throw in flares and smoke bombs. It looked for all the world like, Tilzey wrote, 'a poor man's version of the Red Arrows.'

The trust and cooperation AFA required for successful street activity did not translate into its own political arenas. During its very first national conference, held in Manchester on 22 February 1986, its federation of different political forces was almost completely undone and was certainly badly damaged. Searchlight claimed that the leadership of Class War had been infiltrated by fascists. Tony Greenstein, elected to the AFA's national committee at the conference, recollects that 'a whole group of us went from Brighton to Manchester.' Searchlight, he states, 'made a quite bogus allegation, without providing any proof' but Class War was suspended. All anarchist groups and Red Action walked out in solidarity. Red Action returned to AFA. Class War, and those anarchists it mobilised, did not.

The problems and priorities of national anti-fascist organisations can have little effect on local struggles. Just as the ANL's leadership and its grassroots groups were not the same kind of beast, AFA as national body would never be simply reflected in its local branches. Activists who identified with AFA, just got on with the job of mobilising in their area. For example, Tony outlines how:

Brighton is and always was a different place. It was always a radical place and the gay community was represented [as far back as] the Anti-Fascist Committee. AFA down here was unaligned left, anarchist. It was really an alliance of students and anarchists and unattached. It was based on both student unions, Sussex and Brighton. We built our own mailing lists.

Nor did the false start at the national conference appear to hold up AFA's ability to mobilise outside their areas. In July 1986, three minibuses set off from London to Bury St Edmonds to oppose a march by an NF faction, the Political Soldiers. Led by Nick Griffin, now be-suited leader of the BNP, and Patrick Harrington, infamous student infiltrator at North London Polytechnic, the Political Soldiers was a bid to radicalise what was left of a divided Front through aligning themselves with Arab nationalists, Ayatollah Khomeini and Colonel Gaddafi. Their march was against a United States nuclear base in the Suffolk countryside. In *Bash the Fash*, K.Bullstreet of anarcho-syndicalist Direct Action Movement (DAM), catalogues the day's events:

> as the NF march proceeded through the town the main group of anti-fascists started to attack. Half a dozen of us went into a building site just as the march was passing and lobbed loads of bricks over at them. Some hit cops too. The fascists started to pick up some of the bricks that we had thrown and hurled them back at us. So the sky was filled with bricks and other building materials going in all directions. It was pande-monium. At this point a contingent of anti-fascists attacked the back of the march and managed to get one of their banners. The mayhem went on a bit longer, but the police started to get a wee bit upset, so all the anti-fascists went back to the town to regroup.

There was a fight outside a chip shop and one in the market place. Once AFA activists headed off in one of their minibuses, a foolish skinhead who thought he was safe on the pavement jeered at them. He received the final blow of the day through the van window. The Political Soldiers did not march again. Nick Griffin, who had participated in this failed NF demonstration in Suffolk, later claimed that his fascist base in Bury St Edmonds did not waver but nor did they welcome the disruption marches caused them. Whatever his supporters may have thought, party members were not impressed. The Political Soldiers were eventually ousted by NF traditionalists, Ian Anderson and Martin Wingfield, who favoured electoralism which Griffin himself would also later advocate. But, the Anderson-Wingfield faction, The Flag Group, did not fare much better than the Political Soliders. A pre-election NF meeting in Greenwich a year or so after the Bury St. Edmonds demonstration was disrupted when AFA activists, using the Representation of the Peoples Act, got inside. With chairs as weapons, they made it impossible for the meeting to go ahead until the police arrived to restore order.

On Remembrance Sunday 1986, 2,000 anti-fascists marched up Whitehall and Celia Stubbs, the partner of Blair Peach, laid a wreath at the Cenotaph to all those, past and present, who lost their lives in struggle against fascism. For the next two years attending the anti-fascist Remembrance Sunday march was a regular feature in AFA's calendar and was always followed by regrouping in Trafalgar Square to defend the non-stop picket outside South Africa House calling for Nelson Mandela's freedom. Sean Gaughan had moved to London by this time:

At the end of our march we got into the habit of heading back into Trafalgar Square as the fash had taken to attacking the picket at the South African embassy at the end of their own march. The first year that I remember doing this was 87. As we approached the steps of St Martin's all the picketers, who had organised their own mass mobilisation in order to defend themselves, assumed we were fascists and shouted abuse at us. This happened the next year, too. On the third year as we passed by the side of the embassy, there was an eerie silence as for a minute or two the picketers just stared at us trying to suss out who we were. After a while some of them started to climb over the fence and then it was like a floodgate opening as hundreds of them climbed over, ran across the road and joined us.

Shortly after the picketers joining us, we heard lots of

shouting on the far side of Trafalgar Square, it was the [Chelsea] Headhunters. As they went through the motions of trying to get to us, the police lined themselves up forming a human barrier between them and us. The Headhunters then disappeared for a while so it was decided to stay where we were for the time being. A short time later they appeared again on the opposite side of the road to us, having given the police the slip. They started to come along their side towards us but without any of them actually coming over the road to where we were. So we started to climb over the barriers on our side of the road and then as usual there was a shout from someone on our side, I have never found out if it was the same person or different people taking the initiative, but as usual it was like a cavalry charge as we all stormed towards the fash. They did what they always do, started running. And, we chased them down through Leicester Square and passed many of the theatregoers who must have wondered what the hell was going on.

Later on, we were still wondering around the Leicester Square and the West End area picking off groups and lone fascists. We jumped some bones and I had a rush of blood to the head and started to chase one. As he turned down a laneway, I kicked his back leg and he went down. I was just about to break a bottle over his head when a copper jumped on my back, I had not realised that as I was chasing the bone a copper was chasing me.

Confrontations also occurred prior to the Remembrance Sunday marches, as Sean explains:

A favourite tactic of AFA was to find out where the fascists were meeting up and take over their meeting point. One year we decided to take over some pub near Victoria that they had been using to meet. This always provided for some funny moments for us and nasty ones for fascists. This Scottish bloke approached us as we were standing in the pub doorway and started saying "I always used to march with you boys back in Glasgow." Then he asked us "What time are the Paki army arriving?" So I shouted over to an Asian AFA member and said "Unmesh, there is a fella here who wants to know what time the Paki army is arriving." The look on the fella's face was pure gold. He just bolted away from us and over beside the police who had turned up in force when they realised who we were and asked for an escort out of the area.

Despite some success in reclaiming war commemoration from the right-wing, the role of anti-fascists on Remembrance Sunday become the subject of a well-rehearsed and divisive debate: symbolic march versus direct action. Some AFA members argued that the anti-fascist march had dwindled in numbers and did not effectively oppose the fascist one. In 1989, 500 people committed to physical confrontation, occupied the NF's Victoria assembly point, disrupting and delaying their march while around half that number, other AFA members alongside trade unionists, took the message of anti-fascism to the Cenotaph.

It is a little too simplistic to claim that the anti-fascist movement fell out along lines of marchers and fighters. Another event in AFA's calendar was the Anti-Internment demonstration held in early August to mark the date when Northern Ireland's Stormont government authorised swoops on catholic-nationalist communities and the detention without trial of so-called 'suspects.' The most serious attack, an NF charge to the front of the march, occurred in 1988. Sean remembers numerous confrontations on the Holloway Road and its tube station, as well as around Euston and Kings Cross, between AFA members and fascists who had tried to harass the Anti-Internment marchers. He recalls an incident on the march itself:

As the march made its way along Holloway Road there were a lot of fascists following as we passed a side street, a member of DAM charged out from the march to attack them on his own, a few of us chased after. I had more intention of bringing him back before he got nicked than doing anything else, but he attacked a fascist before anyone could catch him. As he got into one of them, another attacked him from the side just as I managed to catch up. I punched the fash and then threw him on the floor. At this moment they all turned and ran, so I knew that the police were right on top of us. Instead of grabbing me or the DAM member they chased after the fascists who had all run off allowing us and those who had followed us to just casually walk back and rejoin the march.

Some AFA members attended Irish solidarity marches to defend that community as they would another subject to fascist attacks. Other members had much common ground with the marchers, shared the belief that all peoples have the right to self-determination and its expression through armed struggle. Sean's involvement in anti-fascism was part and parcel of his Irish republicanism. He and two other activists travelled to a Birmingham event:

Three of us travelled up to Brum to attend a Republican march, which I think was a hunger strikers commemoration. After the march we were sitting on some steps outside the building that the rally was being held in, I think it might have been a library, there were us three and a large crowd of bandsmen and their followers from Scotland. We were approached by about 10 to 15 fascists that we recognised, who had been following the march shouting abuse and threats. As they neared, I turned to the band and their mates and said "Get ready. Here's the fash." We were stunned by what happened next as they all got up and ran inside the building leaving us three to face the fascists. We all stood up and just stared down at them as they came to a stop before getting to the steps, the only thing we had that could be used as a weapon was a tin of coke that I held behind my back. They knew I was holding something but not what it was. After a moment or so a couple of them seemed to lose their nerve and said something about the police to what appeared to be the main one. He was game enough to have a go. Luckily enough for us, he agreed with his mates and they all turned and walked off again. I think that it was only our collective embarrassment at the way the bandsmen had all run away that caused us to stand our ground. Later the three of us headed off to some police station where we heard that some marchers were being held. We did not know them but thought that they might need some help if the fash were hanging around. Shortly after we got there the first of the marchers were released. There were four or five. Then the police let a fascist out, we gave him a few digs outside the station before he was let go. A bit later a second one came out he seemed more game for a fight so I hit him over the head with the tin of coke I had. It knocked him on his arse. He was not hurt but it did put the fight out of him as he ran off when he stood back up.

Whilst the use of physical force was once again dividing the anti-fascist movement, it was not the only string to AFA's bow. In the last year of the 80s, AFA initiated what would become one of anti-fascism's longest running battles. Blood and Honour, a neo-Nazi music enterprise still in operation, promotes bonehead bands who blast out a message of race hate generating funds for fascism through gigs, recordings and merchandise. AFA activists, using pressure group style lobbying such as petitions and the influence of friendly politicians, stopped the sale of Blood and Honour's Nazi commodities in two central London outlets. One shop was forced to close.

335

CUTDOWN SHUTDOWN

After four months of campaigning, picketing and leafletting against Cutdown selling nazi propaganda, the shop has finally closedown

Since March Cutdown's premises in Riding House Street, central London, has been acting as the base for the neo-nazi organisation, Blood & Honour, distributing fascist regalia, records and propaganda thus becoming a focal point for fascists world wide. Regular pickets were held outside the shop, organised by AFA and the Polytechnic of Central London Student Union. Approximately 200 people attended the pickets, as was the case in Carnaby Street, Cutdown removed most of the offensive material on display replacing them with Rock Against Racism t-shirts, which , ironically enough, were actually produced by Cutdown. Some of the pickets were spontanous and, although consisting of considerably fewer numbers, were of equal importance to the larger pickets and just as effective. Ian Stewart certainly looked a worried man when all of PCLSU converged in the entrance to the shop. The sight of RAR t-shirts, northern soul badges and a Red Wedge video (placed along side a Blood & Honour video) promoted such questions like 'Ian does this mean that you're not a racist anymore ' and 'Ian, have you got any Upstarts or Blaggers records' but the man showed no signs of amusement. The police soon arrived to move the protesters on, obviously annoyed at having to indulge in such a time-wasting proceedure. The shop was a nuisance to the police due to the disturbance it's prescence created. This, plus illegality of the shop distributing material which might incite racial hatred, culminated in a raid on the shop in June. At the same time, the shops manager was due to appear in court on an eviction order served by the property owner of Cutdowns premises, James Coigley. Coigly had been trying to evict the fascists on the grounds that they had changed the trade of the shop (it used to be a launderette) without his permission, and also because of the disturbances it generated as well as pickets highlighting the public annoyance, anti-fascists smashed the shop window on several occasions which resulted in the insurence company eventually refusing to pay out any money. He won his case under a section of the Property Act which states that if the leaseholder causes a public disturbance liable to be a nuisance to the property owner then that lease may be withdrawn. It would have been more satisfying to see the shop forced to close on the simple basis of what it represented, but the important matter at the moment is that Cutdown no longer exists. The importance of campaigning against the shops distributing Blood & Honour propaganda can never be under estimated. Sucess was achieved over the issue of the shops in Carnaby Street and Riding House Street. Constant pressure on the pubs and the breweries in the vicinity of the shops has resulted in the fascists being banned from the pubs in these areas. A press conference ensured extensive media coverage to the degree of articles in Time Out, City Limits, an interview on local radio, and a feature on televisions Reportage programme. The issue has also been discussed in the House of Commons having been brought up by a Labour MP. Although Blood & Honour have no visible outlet at the moment they are still potential danger. There can be no room for apathy or complacency, and CSB urges all those who participated in the fight against Cutdown to keep on fighting the fascists in what ever form they appear in.

'Cutdown Shutdown', *Cable Street Beat Review*.

But this style of campaigning was always accompanied by direct confrontation with neo-Nazi bands and band members, the most notorious of which was Screwdriver and its lead singer Ian Stuart. Sean pitched in:

One Saturday afternoon me and a mate were coming out of Kings Cross station by Caledonian Road exit when Ian Stuart walked past us. My mate was on the run at the time for an armed robbery but told me to go ahead and he would keep a look out for the police, so I walked back in and called Stuart by his name. As he stopped I hit him over the head with a Lucozade bottle that I had been drinking, causing quite a bloody cut to his head.

Another night we got word that Skrewdriver were playing over near Swiss Cottage, so a small group of us decided to have a look around the area, we found Stuart along with other fascists including Ken McClelland who was in another fascist band called Brutal Attack. Because of the area we were in and the particular pub, which was a tourist attraction, we knew that we would have to be in and out again quickly or we would all be nicked. The idea was to just walk in, do them and walk out again, but Stuart saw us coming and tried to run behind McClelland. It kicked off for a little while and one of the lads hit Stuart over the head with a glass ashtray that he picked up from a table. Later at the gig we heard that Stuart had gone on stage still covered in his own blood and given it the big'un about fighting off a load of reds but the truth was he had hidden behind one of his mates or the gig would not have been able go ahead that night.

There was also a meeting in a Quakers' meeting house near Euston that was featuring an ex-fash who Searchlight had bought and at the time it was known that Stuart was living in a B&B nearby at Kings Cross. A couple of us decided to have a look around the area on the off chance and as we came around a corner there was Stuart out jogging and coming right towards us. As he came closer it was obvious that he recognised us and tried to bolt past. I managed to pull a bit of an iron bar that I had in my jacket but could only get one swipe at him, which he blocked with his arm.

Kings Cross B&B became well known as a haunt not only for British fascists but for their international contacts. It was a site for what Sean Gaughan calls 'sniping'. Instead of 'waiting around and reacting to what the fascists were doing we would take the fight to them, whenever we heard of a racist attack or that they were starting to hang around certain areas or pubs we

would get together in small groups and go looking for them.'
This is an example:

> One Sunday evening I was sitting at home when a radio report
> said that two Africans had been attacked and stabbed in a
> racist attack, not too far away from where I was living at the
> time. So I got three other activists together and we headed
> down around the Kings Cross area as we knew of a B&B that
> was owned and used by fascists. At a pub a few minutes' walk
> away we saw that there were two big bones who turned out to
> be German Nazis along with a third English man. We hung
> around outside until closing time and followed them when
> they left. Sure enough, they headed straight to the B&B along
> with some women that they had picked up in the pub. As they
> got to the door we attacked them with hammers and iron bars.
> All three of them were severely beaten and left lying where
> they had fell. We found out later that the English one was a
> member of Screwdriver and the band had to cancel a gig due
> to him having a broken arm. A short time later again we heard
> that a group calling themselves the Gay Liberation Army had
> claimed the attack.

The effectiveness of physical versus symbolic action had already
divided AFA's broad front over the Remembrance Sunday mobilisation. But a bigger problem, according to Mickey O'Farrell, was
not the now well-rehearsed debates about physical force versus
symbolic action but that AFA's parent organisation, Red Action,
began to be caught up in left factionalism:

> There were two main problems as far as I was concerned.
> There's always a danger, and I'm certainly as guilty as anyone
> with regards to this, of the violence becoming gratuitous. And
> it's dangerous once you start doing that. So I've started to get
> a bit worried about that but I also became concerned about the

tendency to turn inwards rather than outwards. Red Action had originally been thrown together almost by accident when we found ourselves out in the cold and forced to either go it alone or go home. Consequently and beyond a generally accepted commitment to militant anti-fascism and support for the Republican position in Ireland we had no real political identity. It was in 1982 that we made our first tentative attempts to establish a broader political programme and point number two of this was quite unambiguous calling for "United action between socialist groups. For the class and not the party." This was a direct response to so many left groups seeing themselves as the sole bearers of the political truth and shunning positive engagement with others. Towards the latter part of the 1980s there were signs that such tendencies were now emerging in Red Action itself. At a national meeting in 1988 a motion was adopted, by a large majority, which in describing "the representative groups of the left" as being "neither worker nor revolutionary" called upon Red Action to "break links" with such groups. For me there was a clear sign that Red Action was now exhibiting signs of the sort of elitist left sectarianism that we had originally set out to oppose. A year of increasingly strained debate followed, but when the motion was reaffirmed with a still significant, if slightly reduced majority, I felt that our positions on this crucial issue were now too far apart and along with a handful of others, I left. I think that if you look at the editions of the Red Action newspaper in the period after we left with its reams of text devoted to slagging off every other left group and the omnipotent sanctity of Red Action then I think we can say that our position was borne out. But if mistakes were made, and no doubt I also made my share of them, then a lot that was positive was also achieved. And one thing is for sure, when the chips were down you would search a long time before you would find a finer group to have standing alongside you.

8

Getting out of bed: 1990-2011

Broad front anti-fascism was not abandoned by all AFA activists. In 1991, Manchester AFA was re-launched at a meeting attended by groups from across the left spectrum. It was an important turning point in the struggle against fascism in the northwest, recognised as such by activists at the time. John Severn relates:

> We went down as a group to the initial meeting. It was a very positive, happy occasion almost, because represented there was every shade of lefty opinion. There seemed to be a strong commitment that we buried our differences and simply got on with the job of physical opposition to fascism.

Teresa Marr also recalls the re-launch of Anti-Fascist Action in Manchester. Her route to anti-fascism had been via anarchism and its friendships, as she relates:

> I fell into it through the Bolton Anarchist Group. Bolton Anarchist Group had been up and running for quite a long time, a long time before I was involved in it and I got involved in it through Gary Fletcher and I remember we were doing a zine called the Bolton Evening Noose and doing it on the cheap just putting it around Bolton freely. It was in the mode of Class War at that time. It had an anti-fascist bias that was quite obvious. Around that time I remember AFA reforming in Manchester. It must have been the early 90s. I didn't know any of these people but some of the older people from Bolton knew the old crew from Manchester. We were invited down for the inaugural meeting, which was in a pub that is still there actually, the Hare and Hounds on Shudehill. I just

remember it sort of really taking off from there. Initially feeling quite cautious and a bit suspicious of everybody as everyone is, especially when you've got anarchists meeting Trotskyites meeting Stalinists. Everyone altogether, just all leftist, but everyone thinking "Who is this lot here?" But fairly soon it sort of fell into place and those who weren't comfortable with working like that in what I think was a fairly open and inclusive group very soon fell away and I think what happened then was those people who were of that mind very soon become the core of Manchester AFA and everyone else was kind of a little bit peripheral and came along to things as and when but there was always that hard core and that hard core was quite a strong social group as well and that was always important.

Manchester AFA countered two different types of fascist activity. Firstly, it gathered its forces to oppose the reforming of British fascism under the banner of BNP, which had started to exploit elections to gain footholds in the northwest former cotton towns without, at this point, serious expectations of winning seats but using the opportunity as a platform for their racist nationalism. Secondly, it mobilised against the alliance between British fascists and Ulster loyalists that continued to threaten republican marches and organisations such as Irish in Britain Representation Group or the Troops Out Movement which campaigned against anti-Irish racism and injustices of Britain's war in Ireland. As Teresa pointed out, Manchester AFA sustained its broad front through friendships that cut across party lines. It also involved all activists in the act of physical resistance, albeit in different ways. A new generation of people, such as Mike Garcia, were encouraged to join the struggle against fascism:

> I got to hear about it from my brother who went to the launch meeting. What I heard I liked and when I went on my first

AFA Action I realised straight away that that I was with the right people with a similar frame of mind as my own. What I initially found intriguing about AFA was why were all these 'white' people willing to risk getting beaten up or arrested for their beliefs. I soon learned that AFA was part of a long line of militant anti-fascist groups who at certain times during the past had formed in order to oppose fascism.

Mike had been searching for what he calls a 'political home':

I myself am not a 'white' person but more Hispanic/white never the less growing up in Wigan during the 70s was not a good place to be especially as the town at the time had no ethnic groups whatsoever. The town until the early 90s was considered to be one of the 'whitest' towns in the country and as a consequence there was little tolerance towards people like myself. From a young age I had to learn how to fight in order to stand up to the daily abuse I encountered. My brother tells a story of when he was a child waiting at a bus stop and a man in a car pulled up to the bus stop only to open his door and shout at him "You nigger. You fucking black nigger." Being the only dark face within a working class community with the National Front at their peak and programmes like *Love Thy Neighbour*, a blatantly racist comedy from the 1970s, being the flavour of the day made me politically and socially aware of my colour from a young age. I would get racist comments off everyone including teachers, friends, neighbours etc. and unlike many ethnic groups I had no ethnic group to at least be part of. I was in fact on my own. Because of this and the blatant racism that I faced everywhere it was not long before I encountered organised racism in the form of the NF on a daily basis with people I knew openly trying to convince me of their NF viewpoint. Before I joined Anti-Fascist Action I was looking for a political home to belong to with ideas about what should be done about organised racism. The first organised action I remember being part of was when the NF decided to hold a national meeting in town. I noticed that the people present opposing the fash were vocal but harmless. I needed an organisation that was not harmless but meant business.

John describes the business of anti-fascism, which at this point consisted of the regular opposition to the BNP meetings in Lancashire towns:

I don't know how many call outs we went through but it must have reached a hundred over the years, during the time that Manchester AFA was still functioning. Most of them were around Rochdale and Burnley. We used to visit those towns quite regularly. There were little towns to the east of Burnley where they quite often had to meet because they thought that Burnley was insecure. Most of it was fairly mundane really, a matter of a phone network relaying to everybody where we would meet at a certain place, usually the train station, pick people up in this battered animal rights van. We'd probably head off to a meeting point usually in Rochdale or Burnley or wherever, meet up sometime in a pub outside of the town waiting for orders, waiting for the spotters to relay information back. It usually lasted all day. We tended to have to hang on and hang on until the bitter end. They absorbed a lot of time those particular days, usually a Saturday but it could well be another day. We'd try snatch a bite to eat. But we sort of lived on thin air really, I think, because most of us were on the dole. How we managed to maintain this dilapidated van and ourselves escapes my belief at times. Sometimes we'd just be outside behind the lollipop brigade, the ones that wave the Socialist Workers' placards, waiting for an opportunity to strike, to see where or when we could physically intervene on a particular meeting in a pub, which it usually ended up as, a pub meeting that the BNP were holding somewhere. [Where there was no-one protesting] we could enter a pub and maybe wave a union jack at them. We tended to have short haircuts and look and dress quite similar to the opposition. Wave the flag. They'd greet us to be met with a hail of fists and kicks. Several pubs I could mention that suffered this treatment.

There tended to be two groupings within AFA. I suppose you'd call them the hit men and the foot soldiers. I was one of the foot soldiers. The hit men probably numbered no more than five, six or seven and they went in mob handed, did the business and we, if required, would steam in after them and protect them against any real fight back then beat a hasty retreat. I tended to drive a van around full of people. And quite often we'd be just waiting for people to come out of a particular pub after having, hopefully, done the business on one or two of the opposition or several of them. There was a bit, I suppose, some slight elitism amongst people who were hit men, they tended to stick together and the foot soldiers tended to stick together. There was a bit of a divide in that sense but that was natural enough because of the intimacy and secrecy that they really had to observe, you know.

Quite often action wasn't available. It was a mixture of 5 per cent action and 95 per cent boredom so a lot of it was spent chewing the fat with people and waiting and waiting and waiting for some little gem of information that you could act on. A lot of it also was being chased around by cops around the town, evading and getting out of town as fast as you could after certain activities. It was a mixture of intense excitement at some points and intense, I can't phrase it very well, just waiting.

Teresa Marr also recalls playing a waiting game in Lancashire towns like Nelson and Colne. 'It was always kind of little places, where there was nothing going on' and 'was really grim, grimmer than Bolton, God forbid', she remarks. She cut her teeth in Rochdale, however:

> That was my first experience of not just AFA but anti-fascist counter demonstrations where it wasn't so much a counter demonstration as a you sit in the pub. You wait, you wait. You move to another pub. You wait, you wait. Nine times out of ten that's what happened and inevitably some people got really pissed and you went home. And then other times it was really quick the way word would come round and it would be straight out. You would run like fuck to wherever it was supposed to be or jump in the old sab van and suddenly you would descend on a small group of skinheads, which they usually were, or you go into a pub and there would be a group of them all meeting in there planning to go onto somewhere else and all hell would break loose. I have to say it was all about numbers, I think. So us weedy girls who are not used to punching people or kicking people just stood there and made sure no one got in the way.

Occasionally, the manoeuvres of Manchester AFA made the local newspapers. The *Lancashire Telegraph*'s coverage of the 1992 local elections in Rochdale contained an account of twelve arrests from a group of 120 people that had rushed the Lord Nelson public house where 25 BNP members were meeting. The fascists were escorted away by police. 'BNP had not revealed the venue for its meetings, to be addressed by election candidate Ken Henderson,' ran the report, 'but demonstrators somehow got word of the location.' The *Rochdale Observer* stated that police were investigating damage to the van belonging to another BNP candidate, David Taylor. Its four tyres were slashed and every one of its windows broken. The distribution of 10,000 leaflets by AFA members did not make the news while confrontations in

SMASH THE B.N.P IN ROCHDALE

SATURDAY 2nd May 1992.

Rochdale British Nationalist Party(Open Fascis`;`) are planning to hold a pre-council election rally in Rochdale this Saturday(May 2nd)for their 2 candidates.

So far anti-fascists have successfully disrupted and stopped their dubious activities on the past three occasions that the B.N.P. have tried to carry them out.

They gained a worrying 620 votes in the general election,

we need to prevent them from gaining on ⁺his!

we need to ensure that the fascists have no platform this or any other saturday!

Coach leaves10.30 Saturday2nd May outside the MPSU(Oxford rd.) building

Rn There !

'Smash the BNP in Rochdale', Anti-Fascist Action.

other towns continued to be considered noteworthy. 'About 20 men burst into the Hare and Hounds in Burnley Road, Todmorden, smashing windows and overturning tables.' BNP members had arranged to meet in the pub before election canvassing in Burnley. One newspaper stated that 'the attackers wrecked their Ford van before making their own getaway' and another that 'the troublemakers disappeared before the police arrived.' In 1993, the BNP election campaign in Colne included its members accepting 'police advice' to be again 'escorted out' of the area after their rally in a local recreation hall had been disrupted. 'Shortly before their meeting was due about 75 members of AFA, many with scarves covering their faces, stormed down the hill from Keighley Road.' The Anti-Nazi League had been leafleting in the town centre and marched near to the BNP rally. An ANL spokesperson stated, 'The AFA does tend to take more direct action. AFA were not invited by us – it acts on its own and has its own plans – its own way of working.' Presumably, no AFA member was available for comment.

The AFA call out, the mobilisation in order to find and fight fascists, was its reason for existence but it was part of a round of everyday political activity, as Teresa describes:

We put on benefit gigs. We put fliers up, actually created them because we had come out of that zine culture. Creating those posters that was something that was quite easy. Making them was pen and ink, photocopying. Collage was used a lot because that Class War and green anarchist, that sort of aesthetic was really strong then. Crass, of course, had that look, all their albums had that look. So it was just a cut and paste sort of thing and then we bought a second hand photo-copier from somewhere and I swear that thing was the size of this room and it was in the flat. Flyposting [was] bucket and wallpaper paste and late at night and someone on the lookout on the corner. [We went] leafleting in town when we could get away with that because very often the police would come and chase you out.

Involvement in a Do-It Yourself music scene contributed to AFA as a broad front movement and helped create the social bonds that can sustain activists committed to physical resistance. John Severn tells how Manchester AFA developed as a social collective that could work together to deter fascists whenever necessary:

We tended to get on very well, we used to go to gigs and stuff, hold our own gigs as well. The Ex came over from Holland, a

347

very strong anarchist anti-fascist band that we were pleased to see arrive at a gig in the middle of Manchester. There was some social life involved. Some people overdid the steroids, which ended up in tears. We had several gigs at the Swinging Sporan. That come under attack once, but that wasn't particularly threatening because we were able to drive people away.

D. & D. Promotions

presents

AHNREFN
+ Raging Kipper

at THE SWINGING SPORAN
Sackville Street, Manchester

on

SATURDAY, 28th. AUGUST, 1993
at 9 pm till 2 pm

Admission £3.00

Anhrefn, Dance and Defend Promotions, Saturday 28th August 1993.

Anhrefn, the pioneering Welsh language punk band that had toured with Joe Strummer on his Rock Against the Rich tour, played for AFA in Manchester as did Citizen Fish. Teresa recollects that Oi Polloi came down from Edinburgh and her job was to feed them. 'I do remember they weren't a small band there were about six of them, all in the front room. Ate a lot. But they were really nice, nice boys.'

AFA activists based in other cities had similar experiences to that of Manchester activists. They went on call outs that required as much patience as courage and participated in the anarcho-punk music scene. The crossover between anarchism and anti-fascism was commonplace. The direct action of the animal rights movement provided a pathway. Stephen Rider's anti-fascist activism began in this way:

I first came across anti-fascism and Anti-Fascist Action in the day in Birmingham in the early 1990s. At the time I was actively involved in animal rights and hunt sabotage. Almost everyone who was involved in hunt sabbing at that time, which was an anarchist expression, by and large, was into Anti-Fascist Action. So there would be benefit gigs and so on. We were very much foot soldiers, we would occasionally go out, sit in a van wait for something to happen with lots of other people, hard looking people from other parts of the country. Nothing would happen. I must admit for the whole of that time the fascist remained to me to be virtually mythological. I never laid eyes on one, an actual fascist. That was my experience of anti-fascism in the early 90s. There was never any questions of being involved with the ANL simply because I entered any form of politics through hunt sabbing with the emphasis on direct action and illegal activity.

Ciarán Lynch's journey into anti-fascism began in the same way. Located in London, he caught a few more fascists in his sights:

My own involvement with AFA came about in the early 90s. I had been an active hunt sab with the Brixton group and was squatting with mates at the time. I had been on a few big demos but my first taste of action was a trip to Gravesend with the Brixton mob. A dodgy band called Squadron was supposed to be playing at a pub in the town. We arrived about thirty handed only to find the band did a no-show. While we were drinking in the pub, a group of hard-looking fellas about ten strong and all dressed causally in leather jackets bowled into the pub. This was my first encounter with Red Action who were none too pleased to discover they had had a wasted trip from London. I guess being out sabbing had whetted my appetite for the direct approach AFA certainly had. I think a few friends of friends were involved and that's how I met people. I remember being visited at my mum's home by two burly blokes to check me out before I was invited to a meeting. I suppose I must have been in my early to mid twenties. South London AFA at that time consisted of anarchists, Red Action and some socialists from the old Militant lot. My first action with AFA was at Charlton Football Club. I'd been asked to go alone to a certain pub near the ground and look out for a certain bloke who was known to be an active fascist by the local AFA boys. I think one of ours did a left-wing football fanzine that he sold at home matches. I spotted the bloke in question but one of ours in the main group at the ground was nicked for carrying an offensive weapon, which put pay to whatever action was planned. Another action was in New Cross where we got info that Nazi skins would be attending a Bad Manners gig. We had a good thirty in a pub nearby while several of us went into the gig to spot the skins. After clocking them we followed them outside. Time was running out as they were nearing the train station. Two of us got in front of the group of skins and turned to face them. Out came a chain with a bunch of keys and a CS cannister. Just as we steamed into them we saw the rest of our group running toward the scene. The skins ran in all directions. I remember having to get out of the area as the sounds of approaching sirens filled the air with the CS stinging my face! One funny early memory is from Brick Lane. We were in a group over a hundred strong when the chief steward, a socialist lad, got a call. He gathered us all around saying that a large group of fash had been spotted in the area and it was no shame if anyone wanted to back down or leave. A few nervous glances were exchanged but no one wanted to lose face so we all agreed to face whatever was coming our way. Five minutes later the phone goes again only to inform the same steward that the group that had been spotted was us. Cue relieved faces all round.

The local work of AFA branches is less noticed than its national actions. AFA's most well-known victory, the Battle of Waterloo, began as a takeover of re-direction point for a Blood and Honour gig. Mid-afternoon on 12 September 1992, hundreds of anti-fascists mobilised by AFA branches up and down the country converged at the south London railway station to prevent neo-Nazi skinheads from reaching a Screwdriver concert. Fights between anti-fascists and fascists started in the station bar and continued on station concourse, forecourt, under the bridges and, in the end, along the South Bank. By 5pm four rail stations, including Waterloo and Charing Cross were closed. The scale of opposition to the Blood and Honour organisation was a high point in its campaign to curtail the culture and economy of European fascism: the spread of racism through music, recruitment to fascist parties and providing funds for them. John Severn recounts his Waterloo:

We came down from Manchester by van. I think there were several vans. Numerically, maybe there were about forty people from Manchester came down, stayed overnight. I can't remember the exact point in north London where we massed. We all caught the tube and basically took over the whole tube train with a load of more local groups, which was a good feeling. Hit Waterloo station and immediately we knew there were fascists meeting upstairs in the café. But Waterloo for me was a bit of a nonsense. I remember backing up people going into the café. We were keeping watch for any problems that might arise from coppers or whatever. Judging by the noise, all hell broke loose up there. Quite a few injuries were inflicted on people. Finally, the coppers arrived in large numbers and gave us all a weapons search at which I had to surrender a knife, which I shouldn't have been carrying anyway. But unfortunately, I was pulled for a little lump of cannabis in my pocket. So I was hauled off and I missed the main action on the street afterwards, rejoined it when people were wondering what to do next. They wanted to go to north London were they knew there were different fascist elements meeting. We realised that the tube trains had been cancelled by that time so we had to go across by bridge and the bridge we chose was Westminster Bridge and something like thirty of us decided to go across. It looked suspiciously quiet because the police had blocked the bridge off at some point but we didn't see any police. We ran across the bridge and suddenly from the dark depths emerged these huge Specials, they looked like they were from some sort of commando unit. A few of us got some bad head injuries from it but we were driven back across the river at which point we decided to call it a day.

Teresa, also at the Battle of Waterloo, considered the number of people AFA could count was crucial. There was a large body of anti-fascists making their way through the underground network to the station, 'everyone just cramming into trains'. She registered the surprise of the other passengers faced with such 'a rag bag of dreadlocked anarchists and skinheads.' Teresa testifies that 'If ever there was a national call out people made the effort to go, made a huge effort to get to wherever there was anything going on.'

Gathering in large enough numbers to head off fascists claiming any kind national victories is a long-standing anti-fascist strategy but the ability of anti-fascists to sustain a local presence in areas other than their own is a different matter. In September 1993, BNP candidate Derek Beackon, won a local Millwall by-election. The BNP's electoral performance in the General Election of the previous year had been considered to be poor with 7,000 votes for 14 candidates but a third of these votes were cast in Tower Hamlets. The election of Beackon should not have been a surprise. The BNP had been busy going local with a doorstep campaign that claimed immigration endangered 'Rights for Whites.'

The Anti-Nazi League (ANL), which had reformed again in January 1992, called a demonstration against the BNP's national headquarters in Welling on 6 October 1993. In the month following the first fascist electoral success since 1976, older anti-fascist organisations, including AJEX, CARF and Searchlight, came together with newer bodies such as Youth Against Racism in Europe, made up of Labour Party Militants, and Tyne and Wear Anti-Fascist Action. The AFA leadership regarded the march, like other marches, as a merely symbolic affair or worse a distraction from the real business of opposing the BNP where they were able to organise. Welling is eight miles southeast of Millwall and the other side of the Thames. The Anti-Racist Alliance, an initiative not more than a year old that had attracted high profile left political support for the principle of black self-organisation in the struggle against racism and fascism, held an alternative rally in Trafalgar Square. However, it was the ANL march that brought out numbers on the day, 60,000 according to the highest estimates, a brief return to the scale of anti-fascist mobilisations of the 1970s. Police tactics had not changed since then. They reneged on the agreed route past the BNP headquarters, a bookshop. When the march reached the diversion away from the bookshop, it halted. Police on horses charged. Baton charges followed into a crowd of people that could not retreat or disperse even if they had wanted to because police had closed all small suburban roads out of the area. A cemetery wall collapsed under the weight of compressed people and anti-fascists used its bricks to throw at the police. Colin West, in his reflections on Welling, entitled *Ready, Welling and Able,* stated that a 'furious battle was fought on the streets and in the cemetery' but 'the only real surprise in policing on the day, was that the paramilitary approach was so overt.' That injuries far outnumbered arrests suggests that the police picked a fight rather than imposed public order. It was the right-wing press, *The Sun* and *Evening Standard*, who took up the task of rounding up the usual suspects, identifying and vilifying anti-fascists.

The BNP's councillor lasted 6 months. Beackon failed to keep his seat in the local elections of May 1994. His failure is not attributed to the work of any anti-fascist group but a faith-based initiative from local churches that encouraged Isle of Dogs Bangladeshi communities to participate in the electoral process. Legal observers prevented intimidation at the polling stations. But when Beackon lost, he did so with more votes. The BNP had retained its base of support by avoiding the fascist rhetoric of white superiority used by all its predecessors from Mosley's BUF onwards, which even right wing voters post '45 have found difficult to publicly endorse. The BNP's 'Rights for Whites' line expediently swapped white supremacy for white victimhood and argued that a beleaguered British culture was threatened by cultural differences of any kind. British fascism was re-branded. In public BNP members were seen in suits. They did not wear their collar and ties at the White Pride and Blood and Honour performances that helped fund their election appearances.

The BNP's message that white rights are being eroded as other communities are allowed access to housing, education or social care is a reworking of older fascist ideology that reduces economic hardship and political disenfranchisement into an issue of 'race'. Any lack of resources, locally, regionally or nationally is blamed on immigrant communities while it is assumed that the indigenous population, which fascists rather foolishly and erroneously believe it is possible to define, have natural rights to better treatment than others. But packaged up as discrimination against white British people, the BNP has sought the semblance of political respectability necessary to gain votes in elections with its fascist message. This same old story encourages violence against people who are not white or not obviously British, regardless of where they might be from or who they chose to be.

The notion that white British rights have been taken away supplies the justification for a racist backlash, the brunt of which has been borne by young black and Asian men. In 1993, Stephen Lawrence was stabbed as he waited for a bus on Well Hall Road in Eltham. It would be almost 20 years before two of the gang of five that killed him would be convicted and, in that time, racist violence would be the cause of 89 more deaths.

The numbers mobilised for anti-fascism in the early 1990s, the hundreds of AFA activists at Waterloo or the thousands of ANLers at Welling, left the BNP with little option other than to keep tunnelling their divisive way into communities via local elections. Street confrontations still occurred at Irish solidarity marches. In fact, the threat to Irish activists escalated at this point. Talks, or least talks about talks, between John Major's Tory government and Sinn Féin meant that destabilising violence suited loyalists. They declared an open season on catholics living in Northern Ireland and forged links with fascists who had swallowed whole the mantra of defending the Union and the remains of the British empire against the left and the supporters of Irish Republicanism in Britain. The Manchester Martyrs Commemoration continued to be the focus of combined fascist and loyalist aggression. Manchester AFA become involved in stewarding and defending the Martyrs march, which remembered the oppression of Irish people in the nineteenth century and the continuing injustices of a war in Ireland not yet at its end. John Severn relates:

> In terms of AFA activity, it was mainly defensive. We would attend the rally, being aware that there were a lot of loyalist groups arriving from outside of town that would try and prevent the march from carrying on. So basically it was simply a matter of maintaining a presence along the whole march if we could do and possibly picking off people that were likely to be hostile afterwards. I remember a few chases,

a few incidents in pubs usually after the event. I remember driving the van madly around Manchester looking for people we thought were hiding in a certain place. Invariably, I'd be waiting in the van with a few mates while other people went in. The main point of our presence on the Martyrs march was to defend it from any kind of attack whatsoever, you know. There were individual incidents but very little sustained combined attacks on the marches even though there was a lot of hostility from within the loyalist community towards the republican movement, which was strong in Manchester.

In January 1995, another annual commemorative march came to Manchester. The Bloody Sunday March, which called for truth and justice for the relatives of 14 people killed by British paratroopers in Derry in 1972, had been held in London for many years. It was a regular target for fascists. Manchester activists had no doubt that the march would attract unwanted attention, not least because travel and broadcasting restrictions had just been lifted from Sinn Féin's Martin McGuinness who was to address the rally outside Manchester Town Hall. As Mike Garcia, who became AFA's chief steward in his own town, a main steward in Manchester, delegate to the Northern Network and 'for a time at least' member of Red Action, put it, 'as usual the fascists had said they were going to attack it.' AFA's Northern Network mobilised:

We ourselves shadowed the march with a contingent at the front and a contingent at the back. While proceeding up Oxford Road we came across a group of fascists who were outside a pub on the route of the march. As they came out shouting abuse and threats both of our groups came together. Thinking that we must be the soft lefty types who would turn the other cheek they continued their abuse until our chief steward for the day gave us the nod. The scene was set. A Republican Flute Band played their music throughout the events that transpired. We rushed them and entered the pub and hammered them smashing windows and overturning tables in our pursuit of the fascists. One fascist rushed out the back and my brother chased him, the fash jumped over a fence and my brother was about to do likewise but then we noticed some very mean looking guard dogs. My brother was pulled back from the brink before jumping this fence. The fascist had no such luck. I saw a dog clamped onto the arse of this fascist tearing lumps out of him all to the sound of the flute band.

AFA's affinity with Irish Republicanism, which ranged from fielding anti-fascists to defend Irish solidarity groups to outright political support, was not welcomed by all activists. Stephen Rider states:

[A]s I become more involved I do remember finding the imagery and a lot of the associations of Anti-Fascist Action being quite hard to deal with politically. They had a very macho reputation and at the core of it there seemed to be a need to support the IRA in their struggle. It was never actually explained why you had to do that, it was just something that you had to do. Now I understand a bit more about that struggle but at the time I baulked at that. It was never actually explained to me and any questioning of that would lead to you being denounced as a time wasting liberal so that was the end of that. So you weren't able to ask that question. I remember people really gloating about using weapons and myself being very dubious about whether that kind of attitude was really valid. I suppose I wasn't politically hardened at that time and the way it was presented made me reluctant about getting involved anymore.

The last AFA call out that John Severn answered was also to

357

counter a loyalist parade in Bolton:

I'm not sure of the exact loyalist groups that were meeting in Bolton. There was one, a Salford loyalist group. The names I'm not too sure of. But there was obviously a call out from AFA. This must have been toward the end of AFA as a large working network of anti-fascists in the Manchester area. We were able to gather something around about seventy people together. Met in a pub outside Bolton knowing that the loyalists were having a rally in the centre of Bolton, near a pub called The Swan. So eventually we decided to do a head on attack on the loyalist demonstration. We reached the bottom of, I think it is called, Bank Street and ran up the hill towards the fascists. The fascists didn't understand that we were the opposition, they considered us friends. It was just the dress. It was a normal tactic to wear the green combat jacket, the short cropped hair and all this. The naivety of fascists was legendary. They thought we were battling to join them and the police were stopping us. So in fact what happened was that the police were under attack from both sides because the loyalists were trying to break through to create a gap for us to get through to them, not knowing that we were wishing to attack them head on. Dogs were used. Police dogs came out in force. One of our number decided to attack a police dog but basically we were driven back down the hill quite strongly. We had to flee over the river and make some strange climbing manoeuvres to get away from arrest. Meeting up in the pub later we learnt that a few of our number had been attacked. The scouts, particularly, had been attacked. They had been looking to see what they were up to. So it was not a good result at the end. We also learned that, which was a better result, the Combat 18 factions, North London and Oldham, had decided to try and beat each other up which led to a lot of ambulances being called at the venue that they had that night for a social.

By the mid-1990s the neo-Nazi Combat 18 was more or less all that remained of a fighting fascist force. There is no doubt that AFA had beaten the BNP off the streets. The impressive displays of large numbers of anti-fascists at high profile national set piece events served a warning that was fulfilled by the direct action taken against all and any fascist meetings at a local level. But the BNP had not simply retreated; they had regrouped as an electoral force. The response of AFA's founding group and its leading faction at a national level, Red Action, was to overturn more or less everything in the militant anti-fascist bible: the broad front organisation united by a single aim and physical strategy of confronting fascism was abandoned for a political party with a range of alternative policies that would be able stand up to the BNP at elections. AFA was to be funnelled into Independent Working Class Association (IWCA). John Severn outlines the end of AFA:

> Red Action went down the electoral road. They seemed less and less concerned about physical opposition. They considered the only important strategy was to undermine the working class vote of the BNP in areas where they stood. We considered that secondary and as anarchists we consider the electoral system as something not worth wasting our time on. So really it was that split that emerged in the late 90s where we'd attend meetings that Red Action would try and host and quite often would end up with us walking out or just simply saying we can't agree to carry things on.

When AFA folded, many of its activists were reluctant to stand down. Ciarán Lynch was one of them:

> We existed as a group called No Platform [NP] for several years and although largely anarchist based we worked with Socialist Party members on a regular basis. The groups or

areas involved in this were from London, Leeds, Essex, Brighton, Nottingham, Bristol and Bradford with some individuals from other towns and cities. Tactics were more on a small scale due to numbers and a more hit and run policy was used but always on intelligence information. The women in NP at the time were very good spotters and we had good access to intel, photos etc. on the fash. We always seemed to be one step ahead. Perhaps the group being relatively small, around sixty core members countrywide, made information sharing and organising the group pretty simple and more effective. We also put out a fair bit of propaganda with leaflets and stickers and put on various fundraising benefits. We did security work for some large squat parties and donations for that went into the pot.

No Platform opposed the fascist presence on the Remembrance Day parade and undertook some successful direct actions against the BNP canvassers at election time. The group also took up the responsibility, which had fallen to preceding anti-fascist organisations, for defending Irish solidarity events from fascist attack. Ciarán recalls his part in deterring a National Front demonstration outside a Republican meeting at the Cock Tavern, the Euston pub where Anti-Fascist Action had been formed:

About twenty of us found a little alley that ran through to the main road where the NF was demonstrating. The idea was that us twenty would casually stroll up to the demo as we all looked fairly nondescript and steam into them. The main mob protecting the pub were then meant to break through from the other side so we could totally smash them as the police lost control in the confusion. Well, let's say our group kept to the plan. We walked right up to them past the police and went straight into them. Unfortunately the cavalry never arrived and we were all arrested. It was all over in minutes and a good few of us got bound over in the courts.

Old school British fascists, the National Front, had been polishing their marching boots for a series of outings along Kent's immigration frontline. Stephen Rider, who had some experience with AFA of waiting, even hoping, for a confrontation, now found the fascists:

The first time I saw a Nazi was in Margate in summer of 1999. I could date it by a photograph of me wearing baseball cap, shades, mask and a balaclava top on Red Watch under Margate Reds, which is inaccurate on so many levels it's not true. I had moved to Brighton. We had a very strong hunt sab group. We became a bit of a rent-a-mob. There was no organised anti-fascist group in Brighton that I knew of. There was a call out to oppose the National Front's rally in Margate. We went down there. We didn't know what to expect. We knew that this was a national demonstration by the NF. A lot of people were out on the streets supporting it but the main march of the NF, their national turn out was about 85. I remember gloating because we'd just had the Carnival Against Capitalism on June 18. I remember walking alongside in amongst their demo shouting "There is fuck all of you. There is nobody here." We just took the city of London to pieces a month ago. "You are nothing". Giving it all of that.

My memory of the day is like a Crass album cover. There were 300 or 400 anti-fascists out to halt the National Front from marching down the road met by a phalanx of riot vans, police dogs with their short shield handlers, using the riot vans to move forward and behind them skinheads with union jacks and the whole bit: bomber jacket, oxblood DMs, Hitler saluting, proper full blown Nazis. On that day we effectively stopped them, a few of us were bitten by dogs but there was no actual hand-to-hand fighting with the NF, it was very much a police operation. But on that day we stopped them and went home very pleased with ourselves. We went back for a return match the year later and that didn't go quite so well. Same brief. Similar group of people, once again based around the hunt sabs just going over to have a crack. I'm guessing this would probably have been outside the hunting season. There was a really horrible incident. One of ours, a girl who we all called Reiki Anna. She had originally been called Iraqi Anna because her father was Iraqi and her mum was English and then we realised that as a sab group to identify somebody by their ethnicity probably wasn't all that acceptable. She was a complete hippy and a reiki healer. So she became known as Reiki Anna. She was arrested on the second time when we were in Margate. Anna is picked up by two riot police. A small girl. Held up in front of National Front supporters. She's on Red Watch as Paki Bitch and this is what all of them were screaming. The police held her up to be jeered at. That stuck with me. The day ended up with us being chased by fash through an amusement arcade, which wasn't very amusing, through a hall of mirrors with weird shapes and stuff being thrown by all and sundry before we escaped to our trusty Sherpa van and fled the area.

It was anarchists that sustained anti-fascism in this period working in local groups and informal regional networks as well as in national structures. John Severn describes how Bolton Anarchists fared:

In terms of the anarchist group, it maintained its existence and maintained our relationships. We lost two of our number, one to drugs and one to diabetes complications. Both of whom were very important people within our group. One Gary, Gary the Axe we nicknamed him, who was dedicated to violent opposition. It was probably his death that reduced our appetite for physical confrontation. That it not so say that we haven't involved ourselves since in that, it just that he was our main hit man and without him we were playing second fiddle. Manchester AFA having disappeared nevertheless retained some people that were able to keep the network going on an individual basis. For example, we went down to Leicester for an anti-gay march or rather a gay march that was faced with attack. We were able to score some hits on the fascists around the train station and get out without any incident. We no longer maintained any relationship with any group in Manchester. It was more people in Sheffield that we were involved with. There was a network but a very loose network.

Ciarán Lynch was in Leicester with No Platform:

We travelled to help steward the gay and lesbian march in Leicester. It was tense. We stewarded the back of the march but the fash never attacked even though there were pockets of them about. I remember thinking we had a tidy number out that day and with smaller roaming groups of ours about. Although we did get reports of a few running battles that day our own group didn't meet any of the master race head on.

From the last years of the twentieth century to the opening ones of the twenty-first, anti-fascists kept up the fight without the coordination and support of any sizable organisation. A continuing commitment to physical force anti-fascism led to the formation of a group, 'largely anarchist based with most members coming from a direct action background' that adopted the name Antifa. It became part of an international autonomous militant anti-fascist movement, strongest in Germany and Poland, which has successfully mounted blockades of neo-Nazi demonstrations. People from No Platform 'came on board' with

Antifa, Ciarán Lynch explains. 'At its height, it could probably call in several hundred activists' and he notes 'autonomous groups aligning themselves to Antifa were popping up.' The pamphlet *Antifa England: What We Think* recognised, with some realism, its small size but stuck to its guns: 'We cannot accept that militancy against the fascists is not an effective strategy as we know it can and does work.' Antifa not only steadfastly refused to be seduced by the BNP's bid for acceptability by retreating from the streets to the polling booths, it did not restrict its attention to one fascist party:

> First off, we'd like to point out from the outset that while the BNP are without doubt the main threat in electoral terms, Antifa, as a militant antifascist organization, target the far right in any shape or form they take. Whether that is the organized parties or the small groups of sad nutters that would like to be organized parties, down to the boneheads of 'Blood and Honour'... To us a fascist is a fascist... it is true that the BNP would have us all believe that they are a 'whiter than white' (pun intended) reincarnation of their former selves, but we did not buy this for a moment. What is respectable about a party that cannot accept that we live in a multi-cultural society and at heart would enforce a fascist state if they ever seized power ... The fight against fascism and organized fascists is an ongoing battle. There will always be extreme right wing groups and we believe that we are at the forefront in the fight against them. Though we would dearly love to see any far right group consigned to the dustbin of history we are convinced that the battle will rage on ... These people sow the politics of hate and division. They are our natural collective enemy.

Assorted anti-fascists, comprising Antifa activists, anarchists and non-aligned lefties would gather together at any whisper of a fascist event, such as a talk by a Holocaust denier David Irving in a quaint tourist location in West Sussex. Stephen Rider experienced an ad hoc anti-fascism:

> People have always rallied together on an ad hoc basis. We found out David Irving was giving a talk in Arundel. In fact we found through the gossip column in *The Independent* randomly enough. This columnist called Pandora said Irving was going to do a talk in Horsham. So we went and were redirected to Arundel. We got a good group to Arundel. A lot of people came down from London, a lot of people went over from Brighton. We found the hotel, White Hart, I think, where it was going to be. We rushed in and occupied the room of the hotel. The hotel owners were informed about what the talk would be about. At this point we didn't know who was going to turn up to a David Irving talk. He had been a big deal in Germany. His revisionist views had gone down quite well with the German far right. We stopped that going ahead. It ended up in a surreal slanging match in the car park about Palestine. David Irving's supporters looked more like a bunch of crop circle enthusiasts than out and out boneheads. They assumed that we'd been sent by the Jews to interrupt his meeting, that Elders of Zion had dispatched us. They were shouting "Don't you know what's going on in Palestine?" Some of us had just come back from there after working with the International Solidarity Movement. That was weird: a far right and far left slanging match about Palestine in a pub car park in rural Sussex. They tried to reschedule the meeting to go ahead in a pub, the meeting was invaded, broken up and loads of David Irving's books ended up in the river. There was a scuffle. Two of ours were arrested and then were released, bizarrely. Apparently, a police officer went off and googled who David Irving was and then didn't want to know. He came back and said they didn't want Irving in Arundel.

Bursts of activity, like the descent of Brighton and London activists upon an unsuspecting Arundel, were typical of a pattern of anti-fascism in the opening years of the century when the BNP was only chasing votes. Stephen reflects:

> The BNP had broken through at an electoral level but nothing else was regularly going on. They were taking advantage of the bigotry behind closed doors that enabled people to go and vote for them and that was happening. The BNP didn't need to do any campaigning a lot of time because the papers were doing it for them. That's when anti-fascists became involved in a much broader struggle because you are against the latent or blatant racism of the tabloid press, which was giving the BNP their sucour. They were not trying to put boots on the streets. In fact, they had abandoned it by 1994 with the "No more marches. No more punch ups". I think there was a realisation that the BNP were dangerous electorally but no-body had really come up with a strategy for combating that because we don't get involved in elections because we are anarchists. There was a barrier, a mental barrier to getting involved in all of that. Whenever anything dangled itself in front of our noses, people would get together. This was all very ad hoc, not based around an anti-fascist group but around a general sense of anti-fascism and knowing who our enemy was.

At this time, anti-fascists were 'on guard' to borrow the title of the 43 Group's publication but still committed to physical resistance. As Antifa had identified, the electoral manoeuvres of the BNP did not mean that other fascist groups had bowed gracefully from the scene. Antifa fought the British People's Party (BPP) and held off their development as serious contenders for the streets abandoned by the BNP. Ciarán states:

> One of the early successes of Antifa was practically closing

down the British People's Party in Leeds after attacking their redirection point outside the rugby ground. Our female spotter on the day did a grand job of talking the team into and right up to the point of the hit, which was no mean feat as there were thousands going to the rugby that day. As well as being battered that day Eddie Morrison was relieved of his briefcase, which led to some interesting intel. A few years later they tried to hold a meeting in London, only to have their meeting place sussed and their number taking a few casualties to boot.

Stephen Rider also recalls Antifa's success against the BPP and an encounter with another group, the British Freedom Fighters, which shared their right-wing conspiracy theories:

We would always keep an eye on what I would call the old fascism, the anti-Semitic, anti-New World Order, conspiracy theory fascists that produced tiny splinter groups: the British Freedom Fighters, Vanguard News Network, Stormfront. They would organise around these websites, which ultimately were anti-Semitic. "The Jews were behind everything." That would be their mythos. So, for example, there was a guy in Saltdean, Sid Williamson, together with an Eddie Morrison who tried to cobble together another to the right of the BNP type party, the British People's Party. It was very much in the old school of fascist organising. They were turned over one day, near Victoria station. They were trying to have their national meeting. Antifa counter mobilised and the whole thing ended up in a punch up that the fascists lost. No arrests. Police arrived on the scene later. That, and the Antifa attack on the Eddie character in Leeds, pretty much spelled the end for them at that point. It was a good example of a small group being successfully pushed out of existence by the use of physical force. Job done. Physical force fascism worked there.

The British Freedom Fighters were another similar grouping. There was a character in Brighton calling himself Buster who, like Sid Williamson, has been involved in all these groups. They came to the Cowley Club, the anarchist social centre. Yeah, I suppose they tried to attack the place. Made racial insults to all and sundry. A number of us were called, a number of us went down there and found the pub they were drinking in, The King and Queen. They were gloating that they had gone in the reds club and "Done the business." Whereas in fact they had bought some coffee and made some racist remarks before leaving. Whether that was doing the business or not I don't know but the business was then done, not in the pub but round the corner. A punch up went on outside Infinity Foods on a sunny Sunday afternoon in front of the pavement café drinking denizens of Brighton. I think they thought the whole thing was put on as an example of street theatre for their entertainment. I remember one of their characters, their big guy, unwisely as it turns out, giving it the "Come on then, you red scum," then after being punched a couple of times by some skinny punk lad, running away and someone who was with us shouted "Run, you fat fucker run" and he turned round saying "I am running, I am running". So it was a bit of a humiliation for them. This was what we were dealing with then, tiny groups with a weird ideology that did not resonate with people anyway, at least then.

It would be years before the British People's Party warranted any further notice. They became beneficiaries of a new fascism that had caught up with a changed world politics. The European far right learnt to ride on the back of the so-called 'war on terror' and its attendant vilification of Islamic culture. A stereotype of the Muslim extremist was widely and arbitrarily applied to all Muslim communities. An anti-jihadist wing of European fascism grew and traditional anti-Semitic parties, such as BNP, adopted an Islamophobic stance.

In 2003 Unite Against Fascism (UAF) was launched. The year before Love Music Hate Racism formed. Taking its name from a line in Rock Against Racism's 1976 manifesto, it is the child of that movement in the same way that UAF is the successor of the Anti-Nazi League (ANL). The UAF followed the ANL's formula of securing endorsements from a mix of politicians and artists and establishing local branches but, in the years between the heyday of the ANL and UAF, its Socialist Worker Party (SWP) activists had established a larger presence in the public sector unions and stronger links with organisations representing ethnic minorities and faith-based groups. UAF began its work by building coalitions between left activists and local communities in order to halt the electoral rise of the BNP, which was, they pointed out, 'polling the highest votes ever for a fascist organisation in British history.' The fascist vote at local elections had increased from 3,022 in 2000 to 238,000 in 2006. The BNP held around 50 seats. Local elections were, for the UAF, the most important arena of anti-fascist struggle. They geared up for political campaigning to challenge the racism of the BNP where they saw it was most evident. Under Nick Griffin's leadership and the turn to local politics, the BNP had made inroads into communities, trying to divide a white British working class from almost everyone else, those defined by skin of a different colour, refugees from persecution in the world's war zones and young European migrants. Local elections were also, the UAF argued, a means for fascist party 'apparatus' to grow sufficiently to support a national political breakthrough. '[T]he priority is to stop such an advance in the first place', they stated. Door-to-door leafleting, community meetings, Love Music Hate Racism carnivals combined to build a 'broad coalition to mobilise the anti-fascist vote'. By the May 2010 elections, the UAF's strategy showed results. The BNP lost every single one of its 12 council seats in Barking. The following May, it lost all five in Stoke-on-Trent. Meanwhile, another fascist party marched onto the scene.

Stephen Rider recollects how he learnt of the new English fascists:

There's a Brighton newsletter called *Schnews* that followed up on a story from Luton. Some Muslims from Luton, just some, maybe they weren't even from Luton but were in Luton, had greeted a home coming parade of the Royal Anglian Regiment back from Iraq with 'Butchers of Basra' posters. There had been a kick off and that kick off had ended up with Asian shops getting smashed. Luton is one of the most divided towns I've ever seen in the south. There is clearly a Muslim quarter in the way that medieval cities used to be divided and have a Muslim quarter. I could see how that dynamic happened. Groups like Muslims Against Crusades were seized on, used, and the English Defence League was born. There were predecessors such as Stop the Islamification of Europe, Casuals United. But the EDL caught everyone by surprise. Anti-fascism had rested on its laurels. I think it is difficult not to do that in an era when not much is happening on the streets and ad hoc responses are enough, when the fascists are marginalised and the ones that aren't are concentrating on electoral politics leaving us floundering a bit. All of a sudden we were dealing with this quite weird phenomenon of the English Defence League. At the time, we thought that the EDL were to be the street wing of the BNP. We put two and two together and made five. Nick Griffin had concentrated his own rhetoric on Islamophobia and pointed out that would be a more profitable direction than anti-Semitism, which is now very much a conspiracy theorist's racism because Jewish people are so assimilated. It is Muslims that look funny and dress funny and behave differently and are an easy target for bigotry. As soon as I heard about the stuff in Luton, I thought

"This is a fascist movement." This is a nationalist, flag waving, pro-war, anti- Muslim movement. The mask may not have completely slipped and they were able to pose as simply anti-radical Islam but really they were there for all to see as old-fashioned Paki bashers in new clothes.

Birmingham was their first outing as the English Defence League. A hundred fifty showed up. The first time the EDL gathered they were opposed. There was a big punch up and they got run. Now what I thought was interesting about that at the time was how it got portrayed by them. The image from Birmingham they chose for their next outing in Manchester was of an older white guy having the Union Jack pulled out of his hands by Asian youth. It was a very powerful image that conjures a race war into being and plays straight into right-wing hands. This was the brains behind the EDL. Obviously, there were a lot of anti-jihadist intellectuals out there. In the post 9/11 environment a lot of people, such a Samuel Huntington of *The Clash of Civilizations*, put out the idea that the banging heads between Islam and essentially Christendom, but misnamed the West, was an inevitability. They made out there was a Muslim fifth column inside the West. In Britain we had had the 7/7 bombings and the whole country was saturated with the kind of propaganda necessary to sustain a war effort in Afghanistan and in Iraq.

Brighton's ad-hoc anti-fascists began travelling to oppose the EDL. They headed up the M6 to join a protest on 10 October 2009:

My initial thought was we need to go to Manchester, to the next one, to oppose them. This is a new thing. Just 150 of them is quite worrying. Given that at one time the National Front had a turnout of 85 on their national demo, a regional event pulling 150 is an alarming development. We pulled a group together to head up to Manchester in the October. We pretty much took anybody who wanted to go, a minibus load. Stayed over in Manchester. Unfortunately, the day exposed the extent to which the anarchist movement can be a theoretical thing, very theoretically based, which had been nice, had been safe up until then. We didn't have an oppositional culture to what we were doing. We had the authorities behaving in rule bound ways, being oppressive but in rule bound ways to do that. So, in the mix of people we took with us, most weren't accustomed to any form of confrontation. It was the first time I saw the EDL, a small knot of football casual looking, Stone Island gear, working class with money look, with England flags and, I think, a Union Jack. Then, there was quite a large crowd of people summoned by Unite Against Fascism. Really, they had called the counter demonstration. That's the case. Initially it looked like quite an easy victory, a number of us hemming them in. But as the day wore on, the EDL had boxed quite clever and there were groups of them scattered in pubs all round town slowly turning up and mobbing up far quicker than the UAF did, or we did. The police had decided that both groups were going to be able to have a rally in the same place. Piccadilly Gardens. By the end of the day, the numbers were pretty even at six or seven hundred on each side. The EDL was almost entirely male, I don't think there was a single woman with them that day, and quite up for it. The UAF were fairly feisty. Our side mixed, more fluffy, a lot of students, not up for it in the same way and, I think, it was indicative of the break down on the day that when there was some scuffling the police kettled me with the EDL, just on the basis of my size. Then I had to take a gamble. What do I do now? Do I try bluff my way with the EDL or do I tell the police that I shouldn't be kettled with this lot, that I'm left-wing. In the end I was allowed out into my own kettle.

The emergence of the EDL had brought John Severn and the Bolton Anarchists back into the fray. They, too, were in Piccadilly Gardens amongst new and old faces:

> You had the feeling that people had arrived to oppose the event that weren't really connected with each other. Really, it was like coming to anti-fascism for the first time in a way because you were thinking who is your enemy who is your friend, who could I talk to or who could I not, because of the danger of grasses and your own paranoia about the event. One of our number was pulled for a hit on a particular EDL supporter who was mouthing it. And although it was a first time and people were obviously awkward and a bit disconnected from each other there was a good sense of camaraderie and coming together again. It was almost like a reunion for some of us. In terms of physical opposition, it was more maintaining a presence than it was physically opposing their numbers because their numbers were superior to ours, unfortunately, partly because of the factionalism involved. There was a group of Trotskyists who maintained a little kind of island in the middle of Piccadilly Gardens and the rest of us were more pro-active in terms of attempting cut the demonstration in half or disrupt their physical presence on the street by the Gardens. The rally itself was quite worrying, to see the numbers that were gathered towards the end by Victoria station. Some people said thousands. I'm not too sure about thousands. But the EDL was able to pull, at that point, a lot of people. The cops did our jobs for us by bussing them out. It ended up like a damp squib.

The BBC's online news stated that the protests had started early with 100 or so UAF supporters arriving at Piccadilly ahead of the EDL. Using an old style jump the pitch move, they ensured that the EDL were kept at the edge of the Gardens. The *Manchester*

Evening News reported that the police imposed a lock-down and made 44 arrests. The paper gave the numbers of UAF as greater than EDL. Numbers are often contested, in part because anti-fascist opposition has not always gathered in one place. The policing of fascists has divided anti-fascists, physically and polit-ically. Large gatherings of anti-fascists to oppose the EDL immediately attracts police lines and cordons often called kettles. Anti-fascists working outside the kettle have then found themselves in numbers too small to take collective action and not near enough to the fascists for direct confrontation. But there are always exceptions. In March 2010, 2,000 EDL bussed in to Bolton. 1,500 anti-fascists mobilised by the UAF opposed them, some of whom kicked off the day by occupying the EDL's designated protest zone. The UAF jumped the pitch again only to be driven off by police. Hemmed in, they later toppled over barriers separating the protests. Police forced anti-fascists back. They returned in kind and pushed at their lines. The EDL had to be escorted away. Over the daylong confrontation, there were 70 arrests. 55 were from the UAF side, including UAF organisers Weyman Bennett and Rhetta Moran. They faced conspiracy to violent disorder charges, which were later dropped.

Something akin to a fascist bandwagon toured various cities. At each stop, the EDL offered some Islamophobic posturing as justification, such as fears of a new or established Mosque, accusations that all Muslim men practice paedophilia or that racist violence against white people is rife and ignored. Stephen Rider comments:

2010 was the EDL at their most alarming, growing rapidly across the country, unopposed except by the UAF. The EDL weren't so active in the south or southeast. They never really pulled anything together for London. We weren't dealing with them coming to us, at that time. They were going to towns with a large Muslim population and taking over the town centre. We should ask, so what's it's like for your average EDLer on a day out? If there are a thousand of you, you've been able to drink in your muster pubs, get pissed up, walk down the street feeling big. It's like an Orange march effectively. You feel big, you feel intimidating. These things have been understood by fascists in the past, the demo, the march, the parade. This is how you build followers. And, if you get to break out and run rampage and smash up a kebab shop then tell all your mates about it when you go home so much the better. There is the intoxicating power of mob violence, which is why it is that people turn up for the next demo when the last one was successful and not when it isn't which is why it is important to develop the strength to confront them, disrupt their demos, to make it so that their demos are crap. Through 2010 the EDL were doing a major demo once a month and really the opposition was coming entirely from the UAF, who were coming under a lot of pressure.

John Severn reflects:

They play this game, which is rather an empty game, walking around the town yelling anti-Muslim slogans. I'm not sure I want to say this but I know they will go into immigrant areas and commit large-scale violence on local people, because without that incentive they won't be able to survive as a group. It is the physical aspects of what they are doing which cements them. Ideologically, they have nothing. The whole basis of the EDL is fear, fear of people that they don't know, fear of religion that they don't know, fear of immigrants that they never talk to or have not met. There is a whole galaxy of the fears that they are pandering to and insecurities as a result. The current economic crisis ain't going help one bit. It is going to make things worse in that sense. There are going to be a whole lot more disaffected people who will put their energies into something entirely negative and entirely reactionary and that is where the EDL merges into fascism.

The EDL announced a demonstration in Bradford for 28th August 2010. By this time anti-fascists whose political allegiances lay beyond the mainstream left and who worked independently of the party-type structures of the UAF had started to create their own, albeit rather informal, organisations. Regional alliances were pulled together. John and the Bolton Anarchists travelled to Bradford with one:

It was a grouping of us with Manchester Anti-Fascist Alliance. I think they formed specifically in relation to the Manchester EDL event. And that was a brilliant thing to happen. I'm not too sure now about whether it is going to be able to be sustained because people have been sidetracked into various other activities. At Bradford, initially it seemed that the coppers were trying to do our jobs for us in a sense. They had bottled a lot of them up at Halifax and prevented them from reaching Bradford at all. So a lot of them were just kicking off in Halifax against the coppers, which we noticed afterwards when we came back through there. The Bradford event was again was a matter of establishing a presence in the town. We very nearly got a hit on one of the EDL supremos arriving at Bradford station, which was shame that we missed that. It wasn't appropriate. It was too public. There was a good local presence in Bradford, verging thousands or a thousand, I would think, outside the rally that the EDL were holding in the compound that the police had pushed them into. It was only at the point at which some of them decided to leave the compound that something like four hundred people decided to run along the road and round to the other side. They were quite secure had they stayed in their particular area but once they left it we were able to double round to this shopping centre area that a few hits were made on them before they decided they'd enough and ran off. We left with a good feeling even more when we saw the EDL were stuck in their coaches back in Halifax feeling sorry for themselves.

Stephen Rider was also in Bradford with a handful of other Brighton activists:

The next big thing I went on was Bradford. We went to a festival called Shambala, which is a lovely, friendly, fluffy, family, hippy festival where it is not unusual to see a whole family dressed up as teapots all different sizes. That's pretty normal behaviour at Shambala. We went there to do an anarchist information stall and talk about anti-fascism, which, it has to be said, nobody wanted to know about. Four of us went up to Bradford in a Ford Fiesta from the festival. Got up at four in the morning then went up to Bradford. We chose to oppose this one because the EDL had said "This is the big one. Burn, baby burn." They had done a *YouTube* video that suggested they were going to get to Bradford and get out and they were going to burn down a Mosque. That was their plan. It was out and out obvious race hate. We thought this is an important one even if it involves doing it from Shambala. Went up to Bradford, which has this peculiar geography, like a bowl. All the estates look down onto the centre of town. We get there. First of all there is a UAF Festival of Peace, something like that, further up one of the hills in Bradford. Went there and there were more police than anyone else. Nobody chose to go to that. The local population didn't stay in the Mosques and didn't then go to this alternative event to prevent conflict.

The EDL were bussed in. Because of the geography of Bradford there wasn't really any other way of getting in. Turn up on a coach or turn up on the train. The police shepherded them all into the dip. The EDL weren't really penned in at all. There was a building site. I think it was going to be a shopping centre before the credit crunch. The first thing we saw when we got there, were these two guys, one Asian and one white, being interviewed by the press. A lot of us stood there for a bit and thought it was some political debate between the EDL and some representative of the Muslim community. It wasn't at all. It was Guramit Singh, the EDL's tame Sikh, who has since been booted out or left. There was a lot of police around. They were then hustled back into their pen by anti-fascists. A lot of the UAF broke out of their pen and there was this big tense stand off with police lines facing in either direction. Bottles, fireworks, coins were flying backwards and forwards between the two sides. This is a four, five hour carry on. What was strange about it was the sheer amount of booze that the EDL had managed to take in there with them. The EDL went into their pens through a police cordon and metal detectors and yet blatantly carried in what they liked. Then they figured out "Hey, we don't have to fight our way out. We can just climb out." A load of them poured over the back of this plywood hoarding around the building site. By then, there was a sizable crowd, there were Asian youth, us lot, the non-aligned for want of a better word. I remember seeing some old faces from hunt sabbing years ago in Birmingham and I mean old faces. We all ran. This mob started running. Then, in front of PC World, probably should be re-named un-PC World, was one of those classic crowd stand offs where you're there, they're there, everyone is eyeing each other up and the tension is live in the air and then this guy threw an almighty punch. There was an Asian bloke who stepped through, right hand, beautiful crack, and knocked this EDL character over. He stumbled into a hedge and somebody managed to run over and get a few digs in while he was in there. Then the rest of them legged it. I know in those situations, it might have been us who broke and ran but in the end it was them that broke and ran. They left Bradford with their tail between their legs. We left Bradford ourselves about 7 o'clock by which time the Asian youth were driving around in cars looking for stray EDLers. The important thing about that scrap is how the tide can be turned by one punch in the right place and also that it was a really mixed crowd who opposed the EDL. The majority of the muscle was provided by the Asian youth but they were not standing alone, which, ironically, does as much to counter the rise of radical Islam as anything else.

We got back quite pleased with ourselves. On Sunday I did my best to enjoy myself at the festival but there were too many mental gear changes. Those of us from Brighton packed up on Sunday night and came back home because three weeks earlier the English Nationalist Alliance say they are going to march in Brighton.

Bank Holiday Sunday, 30 August, the ENA, a small but virulently racist and right-wing group of former EDL bedfellows, mounted a revenge match demonstration against the 'anti-English activities' in Brighton, its 'militant students', 'Palestinian militants' and 'socialist extremists.' Earlier that year, around St George's day, a March for England event, supported by the ENA, was ridiculed and opposed by anti-fascists. Stephen Rider provides the background details:

We knew that the March for England had been going on in Brighton for two years without any opposition. We'd heard about it and this is how much things have changed. In April 2009, the idea that anyone marching would be fascist did not seem plausible. We weren't aware that behind the scenes people were trying to organise a trans-European counter-jihad movement. That was going on, but we didn't know that at the time. I didn't know anything about that at all. Someone went and watched March for England and that was about the extent of the opposition because it was so far away from what we were doing or we didn't know or really care. That person reported that racist comments were shouted from the March for England. That started the first inkling. "What's this about?" It might have been that year they were led by the Ghurkhas and this was not the racism we were used to because the BNP are white supremacists at heart. Now, the BNP is a British movement or they would like it to be. This development of English nationalism left the BNP floundering. It makes more sense, it's more rational in a post-colonial Britain with everybody going for devolution, left, right and centre, and Cornish independence and whatever else. The mood was ripe for an English nationalism.

We had a big meeting at the Cowley Club but we weren't sure about the March for England, we weren't sure about them at all, what they were. We knew they were presenting a very parochial affair, but we didn't want to misstep. We decided, and this was a decision made in a mass meeting, we should all attend the March for England as participants, to attend the march for our England, march for a different England, march for equality and take the piss out of their thing, cause some ideological issues for them, cause a confrontation and not set up a dynamic whereby the police were going to control the whole day by forcing us into one pen and them into another. This is what is interesting about these new movements they have to pretend not to be racist, not to be sectarian. A mass meeting made the decision but actually only some of the individuals in that meeting want to go through with it. On the day, our cover was blown by the UAF. They said these guys are Nazis. The UAF got stuck in its rhetoric.

A reasonable number of people from the mass meeting Stephen mentioned trailed along just behind the March for England and argued for a radically free country rather than a racist one. They looked like a cross between contemporary travellers and medieval minstrels, an alternative England that the new fascists despise. The combination of this anarchist opposition and the more traditional left stance of the UAF undermined the right-wing politics of the march and upset the organisers sufficiently that they announced the re-march. Stephen picks up the story as people prepared to oppose the second try by the fascists to march in Brighton in four months:

There was a big attempt to stop the English Nationalist Alliance from trying to march in the August. This was a group of forty or fifty that were trying to be like the EDL and some were EDL in their branded clothing, their uniform. We had a good counter mobilisation, about seventy or eighty anarchists. Our plan was to get to the station, give the signal of a horn, get everyone to block the route of their march and pen them in the station ourselves. It looked very promising to start with. We'd encouraged people to meet in the same street as the UAF and they had a good turnout. The ENA are behind police lines and people are giving them some grief. The police were a bit flummoxed but in the end persuaded the UAF crowd to march through town to a prepared pen opposite The King and Queen pub, which was the ENA's ultimate desti-nation. Brighton police had taken the political decision to force the ENA march through. Police re-routed the march down Trafalgar Street rather than along Queens Road and used horses and dogs to clear the way. A few people were arrested during that initial confrontation. The horn never got blown and people didn't really take advantage of the situation. Maybe we are more comfortable making trouble on other people demos than having our own. The ENA were marched past The Albert pub and people fought them all the way. People were dragging wheelie bins into the road, pub tables were dragged into the road. All sorts of obstacles and barricades were created by 70 or 80 people fighting with 250 police and fascists who seemed determined to march through the North Lanes, the hippy, liberal part of Brighton. It was the whole bit. It was homophobic. It was racist. They really went to town. They certainly didn't restrict themselves to be anti-radical Islam. I think they started off with "Allah is a Paedo" and ended with "You lot all take it up the arse." I got nicked. We took a lot of arrests. They were able to get to their march destination and, unfortunately, one of them, Stephen Sands, was able to come out from a pub and knock one of the anti-fascists out, from behind, and the anti-fascist was then arrested and charged with assault police. Sands was never charged with anything despite a clear police statement saying who he was and what he did. That's what we contend with. Anarchists have a legacy with Sussex Police. We have probably pissed them off. There have been huge fights over the right to march in Brighton, specifically over Smash EDO, and I think the police were making a point. They had a huge presence.

Six weeks later, the fascists tried again. The next outing by the ENA and EDL members that had gathered around the March for England was on 13 October. Smash EDO, a long running campaign by local anti-war activists to shut down a local Brighton-based weapons factory, was mounting a mass blockade on that day. A statement issued by the ENA revealed that the new English fascists adhered to conspiracy theories no less than the old ones: Smash EDO was funded by 'Palestinian Exiles and Islamic groups to generate socialist political activities' that 'weaken our capabilities in carrying out military activities in the Middle East conflict and Afghanistan.' The mass blockade, explains Stephen Rider, was taken as a 'personal affront.' He continues:

It is an interesting example of how the new fascists are pro-Zionists and see Israel as a bulwark against radical Islam. They set Brighton in their sights because of our anti-militarist track record. Full of reds and pro-Palestinian militants, that's what they say. Despite an absolutely dismal showing in August, when the fascists would have got nowhere had it not been for Sussex Police's massive presence, they decided that they would counter mobilise against the Smash EDO demonstration, called Hammertime after the tools used to decommission the factory by activists during the bombing of Gaza. It saw a huge mobilisation by Sussex Police, 350 officers, horse units from as far away as Wales and a relatively small turn out by peace activists, 200 or so. The police took control of the day, had made about 60 arrests by 1 o'clock in the afternoon. The crowd broke up and dispersed. Then the word started spreading. The ENA posted on the *The Argus* forum, the local paper was running a live blog for the day, to say they'd be in town and would pick off a few soap dodgers. I'd be surprised if that's not a direct quote from them. This was an interesting political development. Suddenly the fascists were showing an interest in the left. I felt that in Manchester they didn't even know who the left were. So, we caught up with a group of EDL, shouting E, E, EDL, waiting at Brighton train station for people. A fight ensued that they lost spectacularly. They got a sound thrashing. It had to be done. But it marked the way things were going to go. We realise we are dealing with something quite serious now, a street fighting right. We're not just going into areas, even if we ever were, to show solidarity with a beleaguered population, they are coming for us.

This was a wake up call. Many anarchists had become accustomed to leaving work of anti-fascism to Antifa whose ability to meet, plan and act had been effectively curtailed by the arrest of

23 activists following a fight with neo-Nazis at Welling train station. They were charged and awaiting trial. With a new variety of fascists on the move, something needed to be done. Back to Stephen:

A lot of people had been in favour of physical force anti-fascism theoretically, might have read books about it but nobody on the anarchist left had organised in any way nationally against the EDL or the threat they represented. The core of Antifa as it was had been immobilised by a large conspiracy trial to do with a confrontation with Blood and Honour skinheads, the old fascists, in early 2009 before the EDL were on the scene at all. So far various anarchists were going to EDL events but really to stand there and observe. That was about all that did happen. We were out-gunned. It was frightening and anarchists were in an absolute state of denial about it. They didn't want to know. It became obvious that we needed a proper anti-fascist group. And that's where Brighton Anti-Fascists came from. For me, the initial thing it was a recognition that we were on the back foot. If they were going to start gunning for us, we didn't have anything to oppose them with. By turning a blind eye as a movement to their development we had followed the Niemöller formula. We hadn't done anything when they come for the Muslims and then they came for us. We needed to start pulling our finger out and getting on with it. It's too arrogant to say because we haven't achieved enough yet but we should not repeat some of the weaknesses of previous anti-fascist groups. You can't just be a street fighting organisation. In this era of CCTV, of phone monitoring, the state has much more ammunition to clamp down on this. You've got to rely upon people not blab on facebook. Things that were prosecuted as punch up are now prosecuted as a big conspiracy case with all that entails, the house raids, the seizures of servers. The case for anti-fascism has to be re-stated. One of the weaknesses with anti-fascism is the idea that all we need to do is to point out that the EDL are secretly Nazis, which they aren't. Some might be. Most are not anti-Semitic Hitler worshippers. But they are fascists.

On 5 February 2011, the largest EDL demonstration to date took place in Luton, the home town of their leader Stephen Lennon, who had dumped his Irish immigrant name for the resoundingly English Tommy Robinson. The day before, Prime Minister David Cameron gave his failure of multi-culturalism speech, which was directed almost entirely at what he called the 'extremist ideology' of young male Muslims. Singing the same tune as anti-jihadist European fascist movement, Cameron gave the green light to EDL violence. In April, thirty chanting and flag waving EDLers attempted to invade a Brighton UAF discussion about defending multiculturalism. Two Brighton Anti-Fascists and several UAF stewards fought them off in gardens in front of the Quaker Meeting house where the discussion was held. The following month, Liverpool EDL followed in the footsteps of the NF as they sought to intimidate workers in the radical bookshop News from Nowhere. In the next, Bradford EDLers tried to barge their way into an anti-fascist benefit in Leeds. When they were chased away, they threw bricks. The Occupy movement has been a regular target for EDL and their Infidel splinter groups. The most serious attack took place in Newcastle in October. Supporters of the peaceful global movement against staggering inequalities of capitalism were punched, kicked, stamped on. Pitting itself against collective or working class self-organisation and left challenges to political authority, the EDL's fascism was now impossible to mistake for naïve nationalism. Their religious hatred and their racism were always obvious. In the twelve months between the summer of 2010 and that of 2011, the desecration of Mosques was widespread and regular. The windows of Muslim places of worship have been smashed, walls sprayed with the letters EDL, BNP and, in some cases, swastikas. Attackers have also urinated on or in the buildings, thrown beer and bacon. A pig's head was stuck on a pole on a development site in Nottingham in June 2011 with the words 'No Mosque Here.' EDL Notts was scrawled on the pavement. There have been arson attacks on Mosques in Accrington, Birmingham, Ipswich, London, Stoke-on-Trent and Sussex. A social club that was to house an Islamic Cultural Centre in Shotton was destroyed by deliberate fire, set after an EDL march in the North Wales town in February 2011. Violence follows EDL events. Two Muslim brothers were beaten up after an EDL protest in Chingford, Essex, in August 2011. One sustained serious injuries. Muslim takeaway workers, or workers that are mistaken for Muslim because of their appearance or the type of food they serve, have been threatened and assaulted in places as disparate as Somerset and Leicester by those claiming to be members of the EDL.

That fascism had entered a new phase as serious as any other post-1945 was now impossible to ignore. The importance of physical resistance in the opposition to fascism, past and present, was recognised by those who mobilised against the EDL's attempt to march through Tower Hamlets on September 2011. Anti-fascists followed, with great respect and some humility, in the footsteps of those who fought the Battle of Cable Street. Hundreds occupied the junction of Whitechapel High Street, Commercial Street and Leman Street close to the very place where thousands had gathered 75 years before. Stephen Rider was there:

The EDL had been building for this all year, in fact there had been a lull in big EDL demos for three months because Tower Hamlets was so significant. They had accused the Mosques there of inciting radical Islam and so on. Once again, a huge police presence. The police have a blanket policy that they roll out for the EDL. They don't take any risks. They corral them. What was interesting about Tower Hamlets was the extent to which the coalition against the EDL had been built up by then. In many ways, the real stars of the day were the RMT [Rail, Maritime and Transport workers union]. They caused them problems from the word go by refusing a police request to put on special trains to take them into Tower Hamlets or even to work at all if their members were placed at risk by assembling racists. The EDL had to change their muster points for the day several times, met up near Kings Cross in the end. I'm not sure exactly how it was done but the EDL got on a tube train. Apparently, the police let them through the gates drinking, smoking and shouting racist abuse. In the event they were cordoned just off Tower Hamlets. The Asian population turned out en masse. There were a lot of anti-fascists. The UAF, in a more proactive stance, were there with their Unity demo blocking the road and they were ready when the moment came. That demonstration did come down to the front line. You could honestly say this time round, the police were protecting the EDL. The police turn out was immense. Breaking through their lines ended up as token efforts. There were attempts by us lot to get at the EDL and I was shoved against a wall and told "You're hard left. You're not going anywhere in that direction." There were various crowd surges. There were rumours. It looked like a nil-nil draw until the main action of the day, the coach. We heard something and sprinted up the road, hundreds of us all running up the road, out-distancing the traffic, typical London traffic, to get to where the police had just got control of the situation. An EDL coach had somewhat foolishly decided to go past East London Mosque and then give it a bit of verbal. They then found themselves sitting in a coach full of barney rubble and no windows and got arrested for violent disorder.

He reflects upon the last two years:

> The EDL started with single issue fascism, anti-radical Islam, and they very rapidly went through the trajectory and ended up being a full blown patriotic, right wing, authoritarian, fascist movement who saw the left as their natural enemies. Factional ideological disputes undermine anti-fascism, the idea that we don't work with some groups, can't work with others. Well, it's nonsensical because we risk being outnumbered. We haven't got the luxury of these kind of schisms. It is all very well and good for armchair anti-fascists to sit there and say don't work with that lot or this lot, but it's no use, it undermines active anti-fascism. You know, lets build up our numbers until we can comfortably have a split rather than have a split now and ensure we never have any numbers. Ultimately, it may be decided on the streets by numbers. Whoever stands there is with me and whoever doesn't isn't.

Postscript

The words of Stephen Rider echo those of past activists. 'The most important thing with anti-fascism is to show up' wrote Direct Action Movement's K. Bullstreet. 'There are a thousand excuses we could give to other people and ourselves, so I believe that the hardest part of anti-fascism is getting out of bed.' This direct, and rather literal, appeal to anti-fascists to make the effort to be there has always seemed histori-cally significant, at least to me. I think I can hear in the call to get out of bed another to overcome political differences in the fight against fascism. Bringing this book to a conclusion has been a process of listening to echoes from the past. My editing has been guided by remembering conversations with its author. Discussions with Dave circled around the existence of a collective anti-fascist struggle and the importance of a continuous one. But tracking between past and present in the completion of his book has not been a merely personal affair. One of the leaflets I found among the piles of papers that accumulated on our floor was written by E. P. Thompson some time after 1947 and published by the Communist Party under the title Fascist Threat to Britain. For the most part, it makes the case for sedate lobbying against a post-war fascist presence but ends with an entreaty for continuous physical resistance much like the call to get out of bed, except it is rather more grandly phrased. 'We must never drop our guard. We must place our bodies between the fascists and our freedom.' In fact, in the completion of Dave's book, the present more often intruded upon the past rather than the other way around. As I was scanning over the account of the Battle of Cable Street on the computer screen one last time, I received a letter from an anti-fascist prisoner then serving a 21 month sentence following a confrontation with neo-Nazis at Welling train station. The words in the letter I held in my hand collided with those I was reading on the screen. For a moment, the years between 1936, when crowds ran down Leman to Cable Street and 2009, when a group of Antifa activists had gathered around a railway platform,

389

collapsed into a single frame. This was nothing as trite as history repeating itself. The past is not simply re-played in the present and nor is it ever completely dispelled. In the collective history of anti-fascism, past and present run into each other. For almost a hundred years, anti-fascists have committed themselves to continuing a struggle begun by those who came before them.

Louise Purbrick

Bibliography

Alexander, Bill. *British Volunteers for Liberty: Spain 1936-39*. London: Lawrence and Wishart, 1982.

Anderson, Gerald D. *Fascists, Communists and the National Government: Civil Liberties in Great Britain, 1931-1937*. Columbia and London: University of Missouri Press, 1983.

Anti-Fascist Action. "Fighting Talk." Nos. 1-25 (September 1991-May 2001).

Anti-Fascist Action, London. *Anti-Fascist Action: An Introduction to London AFA*. London: AFA, 1991.

Anti-Fascist Action, Manchester. *They Shall Not Pass: An Introduction to Manchester Anti-Fascist Action*. AFA, 1992.

Anti-Fascist Forum. *The Militant Tradition: Commemorating Canadian Volunteers of the International Brigades*. Toronto: Insurgence Publishing, n.d.

Anti-Nazi League. *The Liars of the National Front*. London: Anti-Nazi League, n.d.

—. *The National Front is a Nazi Front*: Anti-Nazi League, c1976.

—. *The NF Nazis: No Fun, No Freedom, No Future*. London: Anti-Nazi League, n.d.

Anti-Nazi League/Friends of Blair Peach Committee. *Remember Blair Peach*. London: Anti-Nazi League/Friends of Blair Peach Committee, 1979.

Arnison, Jim. *Hilda's War*. Preston: Lancashire Community Press, 1996.

Ash, William. *A Red Square: the Autobiography of an Unconventional Revolutionary*. London: Howard Baker, 1978.

Atholl, Duchess of. *Searchlight on Spain*. Harmondsworth: Penguin 1938.

Auty, David. *The Trophy is Democracy: Merseyside, Anti-Fascism and the Spanish Civil War*. Liverpool: Hegemon Press, 2000.

Barrett, Neil. "A Bright Shinning Star: The CPGB and Anti-Fascist

Activism in the 1930s." *Science and Society* Vol. 61, No. 1 (Spring 1997).

Baxell, Richard. *British Volunteers in the Spanish Civil War.* Pontypool: Warren and Pell, 2007.

Beckett, Francis. *Enemy Within: the Rise and Fall of the British Communist Party.* London: Merlin Press, 1998.

—. *The Rebel Who Lost His Cause: The Tragedy of John Beckett, MP.* London: London House, 1999.

Beckman, Morris. *The 43 Group: the Untold Story of Their Fight Against Fascism.* London: Centreprise Publications, 1992.

Beevor, Antony. *The Spanish Civil War.* London: Cassell, 2003.

Bell, Ray Hill with Andrew. *The Other Face of Terror: Inside Europe's Neo-Nazi Network.* London: Grafton Books, 1988.

Benewick, Robert. *The Fascist Movement in Britain.* London: Allen Lane, 1972.

Berg, Leila. *Flickerbook.* London: Granta, 1977.

Bermondsey Trades Council. *Bermondsey Says 'No' to Fascism.* London: Bermondsey Trades Council, 1936.

Birch, Lionel. *Why They Join the Fascists.* London: People's Press, c1935.

Booth, Syd, Maurice Levine, Edmund and Ruth Frow,. *Greater Manchester Men Who Fought in Spain.* Manchester: Greater Manchester International Brigade Memorial Committee, n.d.

Bowes, Stuart. *The Police and Civil Liberties.* London: Lawrence and Wishart, 1966.

Bradshaw, Ross. *Germany Calling: A Short History of British Fascism.* Nottingham: Mushroom Bookshop, 1993.

Branson, Noreen. *History of the Community Party of Great Britain 1927-1941.* London: Lawrence and Wishart, 1985.

—. *The History of the Communist Party in Britain 1941-1951.* London: Lawrence and Wishart, 1997.

Branson, Noreen and Margot Heinemann. *Britain in the Nineteen Thirties.* St Albans: Panther, 1973.

British Board of Deputies. *Speakers' Notes No.2: Anti-Semitic Lies*

Exposed. British Board of Deputies, 1936.

—. *Speakers' Notes No.3: Fascist Lies Exposed*. British Board of Deputies, 1936.

British Youth Peace Assembly. *"The World we Mean to Make': A Report of the World Youth Congress*. London: British Youth Peace Assembly, 1936.

Brome, Vincent. *The International Brigades: Spain 1939-1939*. London: Mayflower-Dell, 1965.

Burke, Barry. *Rebel With a Cause: the History of Hackney Trades Council*. London: Centreprise Publishing Project, 1975.

Cable Street Beat. "Cable Street Beat Review." (c1989-1990).

Campaign Against Racism and Fascism. *CARF: Campaign Against Racism and Fascism*. No. 3, 6, 7, 9 (c1977-1979).

Ceplair, Larry. *Under the Shadow of War: Fascism, Anti-Fascism and Marxists, 1918-1939*. New York: Columbia University Press, 1987.

Christie, Stuart et al. *Commemorative Booklet on the Spanish Civil War: North West Trade Unionists*. Manchester: Greater Manchester 70th Anniversary Spanish Civil War Remembrance Group, 2006.

Clarke, John. "Football Hooliganism and the Skinheads." Department of Cultural Studies, University of Birmingham, Birmingham, B15 2TT, January 1973.

Cockburn, Patricia. *The Years of the Week*. Harmondsworth: Penguin Books, 1971.

Cohen, Hilda. *Bagels with Babushka*. Manchester: Gatehouse Project and North West Shape, 1989.

Cole, J.A. *Lord Haw-Haw: the Full Story of William Joyce*. London: Faber and Faber, 1964.

Coleman, Jud. *Memories of Spain*. Manchester: Link-Age, n.d.

Column, An "Uncontrollable" from the Iron. *A Day Mournful and Overcast*. London: Kate Sharpley Library, 2003.

Communist Party. *"Drowned in a Sea of Working Class Activity": September 9th*. London: Communist Party, 1934.

Cook, A.J. *The Workers Under Fascist Terror*. London: International Class War Prisoners' Aid, c1926.

Cook, Judith. *Apprentices of Freedom*. London: Quartet Books, 1979.

Copsey, Nigel. *Anti-Fascism in Britain*. Basingstoke: Macmillan, 2000.

Copsey, Nigel and David Renton, eds. *British Fascism, the Labour Movement and the State*. London: Palgrave Macmillan, 2005.

Corkhill, David and Stuart Rawnsley. *The Road to Spain*. Fife: Borderline Press, 1981.

Coward, Jack. *Back From the Dead*. Liverpool: Merseyside Writers, n.d.

Crick, Bernard. *George Orwell: A Life*. Harmondsworth: Penguin Books, 1980.

Cronin, J. *The Workers' Next Step Against Fascism*. London: Printing and Allied Trades Anti-Fascist Movemen, 1934.

Cross, Colin. *The Fascists in Britain*. London: Barrie and Rockcliff, 1961.

Croucher, Richard. *We Refuse to Starve in Silence: a History of the National Unemployed Workers' Movement, 1920-46*. London: Lawrence and Wishart, 1987.

Cullen, Stephen. "Four Women for Mosley: Women in the British Union of Fascists, 1932-1940." *Oral History* 24, no. 1 (1996): 49-59.

Cullinen, George. *Wild Grape and Rattlesnakes: Memoirs of a Premature Anti-Fascist*. Ist Books Library, 2004.

Dalley, Jan. *Diana Mosley: A Life*. London: Faber and Faber, 1999.

de Courcy, Anne. *Diana Mosley*. London: Chatto & Windus, 2003.

Deegan, Frank. *There's No Other Way*. Liverpool: Toulouse Press, 1980.

Dorril, Stephen. *Black Shirt: Sir Oswald Mosley and British Fascism*. London: Viking, 2006.

Doyle, Bob. *Brigadista: An Irishman's Fight Against Fascism*. Dublin: Currach Press, 2006.

Driberg, Tom. *Ruling Passions*. London: Quartet Books, 1978.

Dutt, R. Palme. *Fascism and Social Revolution*. London: Martin Lawrence, 1934.

Farndale, Nigel. *Haw-Haw: the Tragedy of William and Margaret Joyce*. London: Macmillan, 2005.

Finlay, J.L. "John Hargrave, the Green Shirts and Social Credit." *Journal of Contemporary History* 5, no. 1 (1970): 53-71.

Francis, Hywel. *Miners Against Fascism: Wales and the Spanish Civil War*. London: Lawrence and Wishart, 1984.

Fraser, Ronald. *The Blood of Spain*. Harmondsworth: Penguin Books, 1981.

Frederic, Mullally. *Fascism Inside England*. London: Claud Morris, 1946.

Frow, Edmund and Ruth. *Radical Salford: Episodes in Labour History*. Manchester: Neil Richardson, 1984.

Fyrth, Jim. *The Signal was Spain: The Aid Spain Movement in Britain 1936-1939*. London: Lawrence and Wishart, 1986.

—, ed. *Britain, Fascism and the Popular Front*. London: Lawrence and Wishart, 1985.

Fyrth, Jim with Sally Alexander. *Women's Voices from the Spanish Civil War*. London: Lawrence and Wishart, 1991.

Gerwitz, Sharon. "Anti-Fascist Activity in Manchester's Jewish Community in the 1930s." *Manchester Region History Review* IV. No.1 (Spring/Summer 1990).

Getty, Thomas. *Long Live Death: International Volunteers for Franco in the Spanish Civil War 1936-39*. Charles Martel Comms, 2005.

Gilbert, Tony. *Only One Died*. London: Kay Beauchamp, 1974.

Gilroy, Paul. *There Ain't No Black in the Union Jack*. London: Hutchinson, 1987.

Goldberg, Alf. *World's End for Sir Oswald: Portraits of Working-Class Life in Pre-War London*. Lewes: The Book Guild, 1999.

Goldman, Leonard. *Brighton Beach to Bengal Bay: the Adventures of a Young Man in Thirties London and Wartime India*. Brighton: Leonard Goldman, 1999.

Goldring, Douglas. *Marching with the Times 1931-1946*. London: Nicholson and Watson, 1947.

Gollan, John. *30 Years of Struggle: The Record of the British Communist Party*. London: Communist Party, 1950.

Graham, Frank. *Battles of Brunete and the Aragon*. Newcastle: Frank Graham, 1999.

—. *The Battle of Jarama: The Story of the British Battalion of the International Brigade's Baptism by Fire in the Spanish Civil War*. Newcastle: Frank Graham, 1987.

Gray, Daniel. *Homage to Caledonia: Scotland and the Spanish Civil War*. Edinburgh: Luath, 2009.

Green, Nan. *A Chronicle of Small Beer: The Memoirs of Nan Green*. Nottingham: Trent Editions, 2004.

Green, Nan and A.M. Elliot. *Spain Against Fascism 1936-39*. London: The History Group of the Communist Party, 1976.

Gregory, Walter. *The Shallow Grave: A Memoir of the Spanish Civil War*. London: Victor Gollancz, 1986.

Groves, Liane. *The Life and Times of Alf Salisbury*. London: Cities of London and Westminster Trades Council, c1993.

Grundy, Trevor. *Memoir of a Fascist Childhood*. London: Arrow Books and Random House, 1998.

Gurney, Jason. *Crusade in Spain*. Newton Abott: Readers Union Linited, 1976.

Hall, Christopher. *"Disciplina Camaradas": Four English Volunteers in Spain 1936-39*. Pontefract: Gosling Press, 1996.

Hamerquist, Dom, Sakai, J. , Anti-Racist Action Chicago, Salotte Mark. *Confronting Fascism*. Chicago: Anti-Racism Action Chicago, Arsenal and Kersplebedeb, 2002.

Hamm, Jeffrey. *Action Replay*. London: Howard Barker Press, 1983.

Hann, Dave and Steve Tilzey *No Retreat*. Lytham: Milo Books, 2003.

Hannington, Wal. *Fascist Danger and the Unemployed*. London: National Unemployed Workers' Movement, 1939.

—. *Unemployed Struggles 1919-1936: My Life and Struggles Amongst the Unemployed.* London: Lawrence and Wishart, n.d.

Hartog, Alexander. *Born to Sing.* London: Denis Dobson, 1978.

Hernon, Ian. *Riot! Civil Insurrection from Peterloo to the Present Day.* London: Pluto Press, 2006.

Hill, May. *Red Roses for Isobel.* Preston: Preston Community Press, 1982.

Hillman, Nicolas. "'Tell me chum, in case I got it wrong. What was it we were fighting during the war?' The Re-emergence of British Fascism 1945-58." *Contemporary British History* Vol. 15, No. 4 (Winter 2001).

Hodgart, Rhona M. *Ethel MacDonald: Glasgow Woman Anarchist.* London: Kate Sharpley Library, 2003.

Hopkins, James K. *Into the Heart of Fire: The British and the Spanish Civil War.* Stanford: Stanford University Press, 1998.

"How We Stopped the Nazis in the 1970s." *Socialist Worker* 22 October 2005.

Humpheries, Steve and Pamela Gordon. *Forbidden Britain: Our Secret Past 1900-1960.* London: BBC Books, 1994.

Hyde, Douglas. *I Believed: the Autobiography of a Former British Communist.* London: Pan Books, 1951.

Independent Labour Party. *They Did Not Pass: 300, 000 Workers Say No to Mosley.* London: Independent Labour Party, 1936.

Ingleton, I et al *Volunteers for Spain: The Spanish Civil War in Britain.* Crowle: North Axholme School, 2004.

Jacobs, Joe. *Out of the Ghetto: My Youth in the East End, Communism and Fascism 1913-1939.* London: Phoenix Press, 1978.

Jenkins, Mick. "Fighting Fascism in the 30s." *Comment: A Communist Fortnightly Review*, Part 18 (1972).

—. *George Brown: Portrait of a Communist Leader.* Manchester: North West Communist Party History Group, 1973.

Jewish People's Council Against Fascism and Anti-Semitism. *Conference Report: 15th November 1936*, 1936.

—. *Jewish People's Council Against Fascism and Anti-Semitism and the Board of Deputies*. London: Jewish People's Council Against Fascism and Anti-Semitism, n.d.

—. *Report of the All London Jewish Organisations Against Fascism and Anti-Semitism*. London: Jewish Labour Council, 1936.

—. *To the Citizens of East London*. London: Jewish People's Council Against Fascism and Anti-Semitism, n.d.

Joannou, Maroula. *'Ladies, Please Don't Smash These Windows: Women's Writing, Feminist Consciousness and Social Change 1918-1938*. Oxford: Berg, 1995.

Jones, Jack. *Me and Mine: Further Chapters in the Autobiography of Jack Jones*. London: Hamish Hamilton, 1946.

—. *Unfinished Journey*. New York: Oxford University Press, 1937.

—. *Union Man: the Autobiography of Jack Jones*. London: Collins, 1986.

Jones, Nigel. *Mosley*. London: Haus Publishing, 2004.

Jump, Jim (ed). *Poems from Spain*. London: Lawrence & Wishart, 2006.

Siegbert Kahn, *German Anti-Fascists in Britain and Canada. The Rise and Fall of Hitler Fascism*. Toronto: The Ryerson Press, 1944.

Kenny, Mary. *Germany Calling: A Biography of William Joyce Lord Haw-Haw*. Dublin: New Island, 2003.

Kerr, David. "Fascism in Ulster 1926-40." *Belfast Magazine*, no. 44 (Summer 2004).

Key, Anna. *Beating Fascism: Anarchist Anti-Fascism in Theory and Practice*. London: Kate Sharpley Library, 2006.

Kibblewhite, Liz and Andy Rigby. *Fascism in Aberdeen: Street Politics in the 1930's*. Aberdeen: Aberdeen People's Press, 1978.

Kirk, Tim and Anthony McElligott. *Opposing Fascism: Community, Authority and Resistance in Europe*. Cambridge: Cambridge University Press, 1999.

Klugman, James. *History of the Communist Party of Great Britain: Volume 2: 1925-1926: The General Strike*. London: Lawrence and

Wishart, 1969.

Kusher, Tony and Valman, Nadia, eds. *Remembering Cable Street: Fascism and Anti-Fascism in British Society*. London and Portland: Vallentine Mitchell, 2000.

Labour Research Department. *Who Backs Mosley? Fascist Promise and Fascist Performance*. London: Labour Research Department, 1934.

Levine, Maurice. *Cheetham to Cordova*. Manchester: Neil Richardson, 1984.

Lewis, D.S. *Illusions of Grandeur: Mosley, Fascism and British Society, 1931-81*. Manchester: Manchester University Press, 1987.

Lewis, Joel A. *Youth Against Fascism: Young Communists in Britain and the United States, 1919-1939*: VDM Verlag, 2007.

Linehan, Thomas. *British Fascism 1918: Parties, Ideology and Culture*. Manchester: Manchester University Press, 2000.

—. *East London for Mosley: the British Union of Facists in East London and South-West Essex 1933-40*. London: Frank Cass, 1996.

Lister, John, ed. *Ending the Nightmare: Socialists Against Racism and Fascism*. Nottingham: Socialist Outlook 1995.

Litvinoff, Emanuel. *Journey Through a Small Planet*. London: Robin Clark, 1996.

Lowles, Nick. *White Riot: the Violent Story of Combat 18*. Bury: Milo Books, 2001.

Lowles, Nick ed. *From Cable Street to Oldham: 70 Years of Community Resistance*. Iford: Searchlight, 2007.

Lowles, Nick and Steve Silver eds. *White Noise: Inside the International Nazi Skinhead Scene*. London: Searchlight, 1998.

Lux, Martin. *Anti-Fascist*. London: Phoenix Press, 2006.

Macklin, Graham. *Very Deeply Dyed in Black: Sir Oswald Mosley and Resurrection of British Fascism after 1945*. London: I.B. Tauris, 2007.

Mandle, W.F. *Anti-Semitism and the British Union of Fascists*.

Longmans, 1968.

—. *Fascism*. Hong Kong: Heinemann Educational Books, 1968.

Manchester United Anti-Fascists. "Newsletter." No.1, 2 (Winter 1995, Summer 1996).

Manning, Maurice. *The Blueshirts*. Dublin: Gill and Macmillan, 1970.

Manning, Toby. "Fighters for the Cause." *Red Pepper* (November 1994).

Max, Arthur. *The Real Band of Brothers: First-Hand Accounts of the Last British Survivors of the Spanish Civil War*. London: Collins, 2009.

McCall, J.J. "Are We Being Fair to the Jews? Let Us Laugh Again at Goebbels." *Glasgow Daily Record* (28 May 1943).

Members of Merseyside Socialist Research Group (Sam Davies, Pete Gill, Linda Grant, Martyn Nightingale, Ron Noon, Andy Shallice. *Genuinely Seeking Work: Mass Unemployment on Merseyside in the 1930s*. Birkenhead: Liver Press, 1992.

Michael, O'Riordan. *Connolly Column: The Story of the Irishmen who fought for the Spanish Republic 1936-1939*. Pontypool: Warren and Pell, 2005.

Montagu, Ivor. *Blackshirt Brutality: The Story of Olympia*. London Workers' Bookshop Limited, 1934.

—. *The Traitor Class*. London: Lawrence and Wishart, 1940.

Mosley, Nicholas. *Rules of the Game: Beyond the Pale*. Elmwood Park: Dalkey Archive Press, 1991.

Mosley, Sir Oswald. *My Life*. London: Nelson, 1968.

Murphy, J.T. *Fascism! The Socialist Answer*. London: The Socialist League, c1934.

National Council of Labour. *What is this Fascism?* London: The Labour Publications Department, c1934.

National Unemployed Workers' Movement. *Who Prevents the United Front Against Unemployment and Fascism*. London: National Unemployed Workers Movement, 1933.

National Youth Congress Against War and Fascism. *'Hit Back- &*

Win'. London: Youth Anti-War Movement.

New World Fellowship. "Green Band: Official Organ of the New World Fellowship." Nos. 19, 20, 31, 22, 23, 46, 49,52, 53 (1933-1934).

Norman, O'Neill. *Fascism and the Working Class*. Southall: Shakti Publications, 1982.

Orwell, George. *Homage to Catalonia*. London: Penguin Books, 1988 [1938].

Pankhurst, Richard. *Sylvia Pankhurst: Artist and Crusader: An Intimate Portrait*. London: Paddington Press, 1979.

Pelling, Henry. *The British Communist Party: A Historical Profile*. London: Adam and Charles Black, 1958.

Perrin, Jim. *Yes, to Dance*. Yeovil: Oxford Illustrated Press, 1990.

Peoples Democracy. *Fascism and the Six Counties*. Belfast: A Peoples Democracy Publication, n.d.

Piratin, Phil. *Our Flag Stays Red*. London: Lawrence and Wishart, 1948.

Pollitt, Harry. *The Nazis Shall Not Pass*. London: Communist Party, c1952.

Pollitt, Majorie. *Defeat of Trotskyism*. London: Communist Party, c1938.

Preston, Paul. *Comrades: Portraits from the Spanish Civil War*. London: Fontana Press, 2000.

—. *Doves of War: Four Women of Spain*. London: Harper Collins, 2003.

—. *The Spanish Civil War*. London: Fontana Press, 1999.

Pugh, Martin. *'Hurrah for the Blackshirts!': Fascists and Fascism Between the Wars*. London: Pimlico, 2006.

Purcell, Hugh. *Fascism*. London: Hamish Hamilton, 1977.

Quail, John. *The Slow Burning Fuse: the Lost History of British Anarchists*. London: Granada Publishing, 1978.

Ransom, David. *Remember Blair Peach: Fight On*. London: Friends of Blair Peach Committee, 1980.

"Red All Over: The Manchester Socialist Paper." No.1 (May 1989).

Renton, Dave. "Anti-Fascism in the North West: 1976-1982." *North West Labour History Journal*, No. 27.

—. *Fascism, Anti-Fascism and Britain in the 1940s*. Basingstoke: Macmillan Press, 2000.

—. *Fascism: Theory and Practice*. London: Pluto, 1999.

—. *Red Shirts and Black: Fascists and Anti-Fascists in Oxford in the 1930s*. Oxford: Ruskin College Library Occasional Publication No.5, 1996.

—. "The police and fascist/anti-fascist conflict 1945-51." *Lobster* 35 (Summer 1998).

—. *This Rough Game: Fascism and Anti-Fascism*. Stroud: Sutton Publishing, 2001.

—. *When We Touched the Sky: the Anti-Nazi League 1977-1981*. Cheltenham: New Clarion Press, 2006.

Revolutionary Communist Group. *The Anti-Nazi League and the Struggle Against Racism*. London: RCG Publications, 1978.

Rose, Lionel. *Survey of Open-Air Meetings held by Pro-Fascist Organisations April-October 1947, Factual Survey No.2*, 1947.

Rosenberg, Chanie. "Labour and the Fight Against Fascism." *International Socialism*, No. 39 (Summer 1988).

Rothman, Bernard. "The Mosley Rally, King's Hall Belle Vue, February 1933." *North West Labour History Journal*, No. 18 (1994).

Rust, William. *15 Years of Anti-Fascist Struggle* London: Daily Worker, c1943.

—. *Britons in Spain: The History of the British Battalion of the XVth International Brigade*. London: Lawrence and Wishart, 1939.

—. *Mosley and Lancashire*. London: Labour Monthly, 1935.

Ryan, Nick. *Homeland: Into a World of Hate*. Edinburgh and London: Mainstream Publishing, 2003.

Scaffardi, Sylvia. *Fire Under the Carpet: Working for Civil Liberties in the Thirties*. London: Lawrence and Wishart, 1986.

Scott, Neil. *People of Hulme*. Manchester: Neil Richardson, 2003.

Searchlight Association. "Searchlight." No. 1-2, 6-58 (Spring 1965,

May 1975-October 1975, January 1976-April 1980).

Searchlight Information Services. "Skinhead Subculture" In *Project 1991-1993 Interim Report No 2*, August 1992.

Shermer, David. *Blackshirts: Fascism in Britain*. New York: Ballantine Books, 1971.

Sherwood, Marika. *Claudia Jones: A Life in Exile*. London: Lawrence and Wishart, 1999.

Silver, Steve. "The Fighting Sixties." *Searchlight*, no. 62 Group Special Feature (July 2002).

Skidelsky, Robert. *Oswald Mosley*. London and Basingstoke: Macmillan, 1975.

Smalley, Robert. "Ethel Carnie Holdsworth: Her Place in the Lancashire Protest Tradition and Her Distinctive Propaganda Style." *North West Labour History Journal*, No. 32.

Snook, D.C.M. *To Hell with War*. London: Labour League of Ex-Servicemen, 1928.

Somerset Clarion Dec 86/Jan 87, August 1990, September 1991, December 1991.

Sparks, Colin. *Fascism and the National Front*. London: Socialist Worker Pamphlet, c1977.

—. "Fighting the Beast. Fascism: The Lesson of Cable Street." *International Socialism*, No. 94 (1977).

—. *Never Again: the Hows and Whys of Stopping Fascism*. London: Bookmarks, 1980.

Squires, Mike. *The Aid Spain Movement in Battersea 1936-1939*. London: Elmfield Publications, 1994.

Strachey, John. *The Menace of Fascism*. London: Victor Gollancz, 1933.

Stradling, Rob. *Cardiff and the Spanish Civil War*. Cardiff: Butetown History and Arts Centre, 1996.

Stradling, Robert. *Wales and the Spanish Civil War: The Dragon's Dearest Cause?* Cardiff: University of Wales Press, 2004.

Stratton, Harry. *To Anti-Fascism by Taxi*. Port Talbot: Alun Books, 1984.

Strawbridge, W.A. *Trade Unionism and the Menace of Fascism*. London: London Caledonian Press, n.d.

Student's Anti-War Council. *Student Front Against War and Fascism*. London: Student's Anti-War Council, November 1934.

Sussex Daily News June 1948.

Thayer, George. *The British Political Fringe: A Profile*. London: Anthony Blond, 1965.

The Cable Street Group,. *The Battle of Cable Street*. London: The Cable Street Group, 1995.

The Guardian 26 April 1976, 3 May 1976, 21 June 1976, 25 June 1976, 26 July 1976, November 25 1994.

The Manchester Guardian 1 March 1934, 2 March 1934, 15 March 1934, 27 March 1934, 4 May 1934, 5 May 1934, 9 May 1934, 4 June 1934, 2 July 1934, 9 July 1934, 13 July 1934, 1 September 1934, 3 September 1934, 4 September 1934, 5 September 1934, 8 September 1934, 10 September 1934, 10 October 1934, 26 November 1934, 9 March 1936, 16 March 1936, 23 March 1936, 31 March 1936, 13 April 1936, 29 April 1936, 18 May 1936, 8 July 1936, 11 July 1936, 17 July 1936, 18 July 1936, 20 July 1936, 1 September 1947, 6 September 1947, 19 September 1947, 8 September 1947, 15 September 1947, 29 September 1947, 4 October 1937, 11 October 1947, 13 October 1947, 20 October 1947, 27 October 1947, 9 February 1948, 3 May 1948, 26 August 1948, 1 February 1949, 21 March 1949, .

The Union of Democratic Control. *Eye Winesses at Olympia*. London: The Union of Democratic Control, 1934.

Thomas, Hugh. *The Spanish Civil War*. London: Penguin Books, 2003 [1961].

Thompson, E.P. *Fascist Threat to Britain*. London: The Communist Party, c 1947.

Thurlow, Richard. *Fascism*. Cambridge: Cambridge University Press, 1999.

—. *Fascism in Britain: From Mosley's Blackshirts to the National*

Front. London: I.B. Tauris, 2006.

—. *Fascism in Modern Britain*. Stroud: Sutton Publishing, 2000.

Thurlow, Richard "The Guardian of the 'Sacred Flame': The Failed Political Resurrection of Sir Oswald Mosley after 1945." *Journal of Contemporary History* Vol. 33, no. 2 (1998).

Todd, Gray. *Blackshirts in Devon*. Exeter: The Mint Press, 2006.

Todd, Nigel. *In Excited Times*. Whitley Bay and Newcastle-Upon-Tyne: Bewick Press and Tyne & Wear Anti-Fascist Association, 1995.

Tomlinson, John. *Left-Right: The March of Political Extremism in Britain*. London and New York: John Calder and Riverrun, 1981.

Toynbee, Philip. *The Distant Drum: Reflections on the Spanish Civil War*. Abingdon: Book Club Edition Purnell Services Limited, 1976.

Trory, Ernie. *War of Liberation: Recollections of a Communist Activist*. London: People's Publications, 1987.

Turner, David. *Fascism and Ant-Fascism in the Medway Towns 1927-1940*. Rochester: Kent Anti-Fascist Action Committee, 1993.

Unofficial Committee of Enquiry, Michael Dummett (Chairman). *Southall 23 April 1979: the Report of the Unofficial Committee of Enquiry*: National Council of Civil Liberties, 1980.

Vulliamy, Ed. "Blood and Glory." *The Observer Magazine* (2 March 2007).

Walker, Martin. *The National Front*. Glasgow: Fontana/Collins, 1977.

Watson, Don and John Corcoran. *An Inspiring Example: The North East and the Spanish Civil War 1936-1939*. The McGuffn Press, 1996.

Weale, Adrian. *Renegades: Hitler's Englishmen*. London: Warner Books, 1995.

Webster, Jason. *Guerra! Living in the Shadows of the Spanish Civil War*. London: Black Swan, 2007.

Wells, H. G. *The Mosley Outrage*. London: Daily Worker League, n.d.

West, Colin R. *Ready, Welling and Able: Reflections on the Events at Welling*. Pentagon b Publisher, 1994.

West, Rebecca. *The Meaning of Reason*. Harmonsworth: Penguin Books, 1965.

Wheeler, George. *To Make the People Smile Again: A Memoir of the Spanish Civil War* Newcastle-Upon-Tyne: Zymurgy Publishing, 2003.

Who Was Harry Cowley? Brighton: QueensPark Books, 2006.

Widgery, David. *Beating Time: Riot 'n' Race 'n' Rock 'n' Roll*. London: Chatto and Windus, 1986.

—. *Preserving Disorder: Selected Essays 1968-1988*. London: Pluto Press, 1989.

—. *The Left in Britain 1956-1968*. Harmonsworth: Peregrine Books/Penguin Books, 1976.

Wilkinson, Ellen and Edward Conze. *Why Fascism? A fearless, provocative study*. London: Selwyn & Blount, 1936?

William, Alun Menai. *From the Rhonda to the Ebro*. Pontypool: Warren and Pell, 2004.

Wolveridge, Jim. *They Shall Not Pass: A Poetry Anthology to Celebrate the East Enders Victory over Fascism October 1936*. London: Reality Press for the Tower Hamlets Movement Against Racism and Fascism, n.d.

World Youth Congress Against Fascism and War. *"You Are The Pioneers"*. London: Youth Anti-War Movement, 1933.

Worley, Matthew. "Who Makes the Nazis? North West Experiences of the New Party 1931-32." *North West Labour History Journal*, No. 32.

Yates, James. *Mississippi to Madrid: Memoir of a Black American in the Abraham Lincoln Brigade*. Greensboro, North Carolina: Open Hand, 1989.

Young Communist League. *10 Points Against Fascism*. London: Young Communist League, 1934.

Youth Fight Back/Socialist Organiser. "How to Beat the Racists."
c1991.

Youth Front Against Fascism and War. *Organisational Bulletin,*
c1935.

—. *Organisational Bulletin,* 1934.

zero
books

Contemporary culture has eliminated both the concept of the public and the figure of the intellectual. Former public spaces – both physical and cultural – are now either derelict or colonized by advertising. A cretinous anti-intellectualism presides, cheerled by expensively educated hacks in the pay of multinational corporations who reassure their bored readers that there is no need to rouse themselves from their interpassive stupor. The informal censorship internalized and propagated by the cultural workers of late capitalism generates a banal conformity that the propaganda chiefs of Stalinism could only ever have dreamt of imposing. Zer0 Books knows that another kind of discourse – intellectual without being academic, popular without being populist – is not only possible: it is already flourishing, in the regions beyond the striplit malls of so-called mass media and the neurotically bureaucratic halls of the academy. Zer0 is committed to the idea of publishing as a making public of the intellectual. It is convinced that in the unthinking, blandly consensual culture in which we live, critical and engaged theoretical reflection is more important than ever before.